HOLMAN
Old Testament Commentary

HOLMAN *Old* Testament Commentary

Jeremiah, Lamentations

GENERAL EDITOR

Max Anders

AUTHORS

Fred M. Wood
and Ross McLaren

HOLMAN REFERENCE

Nashville, Tennessee

Holman Old Testament Commentary
© 2006 Broadman & Holman Publishers
Nashville, Tennessee
All rights reserved

ISBN 13: 978-0-8054-9474-7
ISBN 10: 0-8054-9474-X
Dewey Decimal Classification: 224
Subject Heading: BIBLE. O.T. JEREMIAH/BIBLE. O.T. LAMENTATIONS

Jeremiah, Lamentations / Fred M. Wood and Ross H. McLaren
p.   cm. — (Holman Old Testament commentary)
Includes bibliographical references. (p.).
ISBN
  1. Bible. Jeremiah—Commentaries.   2. Bible. Lamentations—Commentaries I. Title.
II. Series.

—dc21

1 2 3 4 5 6 09 08 07 06
L

To

Eudora Baptist Church,
Memphis, Tennessee
(including the thousands of people,
living and dead,
who have been and still are a blessing
to my family and me),
where I had the privilege of serving as
pastor for thirty-one years,
and who designated me as pastor
emeritus on retirement.
May God bless you!
Fred M. Wood

To

Hsu Shaolu
(with apologies to the Tang Dynasty
poet Li Bai)
"Taohua Tanshui shen qian chi,
Bu ji Xiaolu ai wo qing."
"However deep the Lake of Peach
Blossoms may be,
It's not so deep, O Shaolu, as your
love for me."
Ross H. McLaren

Contents

Editorial Preface ix
Holman Old Testament Commentary Contributors xi
Holman New Testament Commentary Contributors. . . . xii

Introduction to Jeremiah 1

Jeremiah 1:1–19
    Jeremiah's Calling to a Twofold Task 11

Jeremiah 2:1–4:4
    Can a Bride Forget? 29

Jeremiah 4:5–6:30
    God's Chastising Punishment 53

Jeremiah 7:1–10:25
    The Decay of Proper Worship 75

Jeremiah 11:1–12:17
    Covenant: Our Relationship with God 105

Jeremiah 13:1–27
    Pride: Vice of Fools and Ruin of Nations 127

Jeremiah 14:1–17:27
    Past the Point of No Return? 149

Jeremiah 18:1–20:18
    A Visit to the Potter's House 175

Jeremiah 21:1–23:40
    Leadership's Accountability 199

Jeremiah 24:1–29:32
    Who Speaks for God? 225

Jeremiah 30:1–33:26
    The New Covenant 251

Contents

Jeremiah 34:1–39:18
    Truth That Endures 275

Jeremiah 40:1–45:5
    Rebels to the End 299

Jeremiah 46:1–52:34
    God and the Nations 323

           Introduction to Lamentations 353

Lamentations 1:1–5:22
    From Sin to Suffering 357

    Glossary....................................... 377
    Bibliography 381

Editorial Preface

Today's church hungers for Bible teaching, and Bible teachers hunger for resources to guide them in teaching God's Word. The Holman Old Testament Commentary provides the church with the food to feed the spiritually hungry in an easily digestible format. The result: new spiritual vitality that the church can readily use.

Bible teaching should result in new interest in the Scriptures, expanded Bible knowledge, discovery of specific scriptural principles, relevant applications, and exciting living. The unique format of the Holman Old Testament Commentary includes sections to achieve these results for every Old Testament book.

Opening quotations stimulate thinking and lead to an introductory illustration and discussion that draw individuals and study groups into the Word of God. Verse-by-verse commentary interprets the passage with the aim of equipping them to understand and live God's Word in a contemporary setting. A conclusion draws together the themes identified in the passage under discussion and suggests application for it. A "Life Application" section provides additional illustrative material. "Deeper Discoveries" gives the reader a closer look at some of the words, phrases, and background material that illuminate the passage. "Issues for Discussion" is a tool to enhance learning within the group. Finally, a closing prayer is suggested. Bible teachers and pastors will find the teaching outline helpful as they develop lessons and sermons.

It is the editors' prayer that this new resource for local church Bible teaching will enrich the ministry of group, as well as individual, Bible study and that it will lead God's people truly to be people of the Book, living out what God calls us to be.

Holman Old Testament Commentary Contributors

Vol. 1, Genesis
ISBN 0-8054-9461-8
Kenneth O. Gangel and
Stephen J. Bramer

Vol. 2, Exodus, Leviticus, Numbers
ISBN 0-8054-9462-6
Glen Martin

Vol. 3, Deuteronomy
ISBN 0-8054-9463-4
Doug McIntosh

Vol. 4, Joshua
ISBN 0-8054-9464-2
Kenneth O. Gangel

Vol. 5, Judges, Ruth
ISBN 0-8054-9465-0
W. Gary Phillips

Vol. 6, 1 & 2 Samuel
ISBN 0-8054-9466-9
Stephen Andrews

Vol. 7, 1 & 2 Kings
ISBN 0-8054-9467-7
Gary Inrig

Vol. 8, 1 & 2 Chronicles
ISBN 0-8054-9468-5
Winfried Corduan

Vol. 9, Ezra, Nehemiah, Esther
ISBN 0-8054-9469-3
Knute Larson and Kathy Dahlen

Vol. 10, Job
ISBN 0-8054-9470-7
Steven J. Lawson

Vol. 11, Psalms 1–75
ISBN 0-8054-9471-5
Steven J. Lawson

Vol. 12, Psalms 76–150
ISBN 0-8054-9481-2
Steven J. Lawson

Vol. 13, Proverbs
ISBN 0-8054-9472-3
Max Anders

Vol. 14, Ecclesiastes, Song of Songs
ISBN 0-8054-9482-0
David George Moore and Daniel L. Akin

Vol. 15, Isaiah
ISBN 0-8054-9473-1
Trent C. Butler

Vol. 16, Jeremiah, Lamentations
ISBN 0-8054-9474-X
Fred M. Wood and Ross McLaren

Vol. 17, Ezekiel
ISBN 0-8054-9475-8
Mark F. Rooker

Vol. 18, Daniel
ISBN 0-8054-9476-6
Kenneth O. Gangel

Vol. 19, Hosea, Joel, Amos, Obadiah, Jonah, Micah
ISBN 0-8054-9477-4
Trent C. Butler

Vol. 20, Nahum, Habakkuk, Zephaniah, Haggai, Zechariah, Malachi
ISBN 0-8054-9478-2
Stephen R. Miller

Holman New Testament Commentary Contributors

Vol. 1, Matthew
ISBN 0-8054-0201-2
Stuart K. Weber

Vol. 2, Mark
ISBN 0-8054-0202-0
Rodney L. Cooper

Vol. 3, Luke
ISBN 0-8054-0203-9
Trent C. Butler

Vol. 4, John
ISBN 0-8054-0204-7
Kenneth O. Gangel

Vol. 5, Acts
ISBN 0-8054-0205-5
Kenneth O. Gangel

Vol. 6, Romans
ISBN 0-8054-0206-3
Kenneth Boa and William Kruidenier

Vol. 7, 1 & 2 Corinthians
ISBN 0-8054-0207-1
Richard L. Pratt Jr.

Vol. 8, Galatians, Ephesians, Philippians, Colossians
ISBN 0-8054-0208-X
Max Anders

Vol. 9, 1 & 2 Thessalonians, 1 & 2 Timothy, Titus, Philemon
ISBN 0-8054-0209-8
Knute Larson

Vol. 10, Hebrews, James
ISBN 0-8054-0211-X
Thomas D. Lea

Vol. 11, 1 & 2 Peter, 1, 2, 3 John, Jude
ISBN 0-8054-0210-1
David Walls and Max Anders

Vol. 12, Revelation
ISBN 0-8054-0212-8
Kendell H. Easley

Holman Old Testament Commentary

Twenty volumes designed for Bible study and teaching to enrich the local church and God's people.

Series Editor	Max Anders
Managing Editor	Steve Bond
Project Editor	Dean Richardson
Product Development Manager	Ricky D. King
Marketing Manager	Stephanie Huffman
Executive Editor	David Shepherd
Page Composition	TF Designs, Greenbrier, Tennessee

Introduction to

Jeremiah

English historian Lord Macaulay wrote:

It is difficult to conceive any situation more painful than that of a great man, condemned to watch the lingering agony of an exhausted country, to tend it during the alternate fits of stupefaction and raving which precede its destruction, and to see the symptoms of vitality disappear one by one, till nothing is left but coldness, darkness, and corruption.

Yet Jeremiah of Anathoth found this exact fate thrust upon him! All of the Old Testament prophets ministered during crisis periods in their nation's history. Jeremiah, however, faced not only personal opposition and emotional trauma but physical discomfort and pain as well. Like our Savior, Jeremiah grieved over the sins of his people. The prophet wore these scars as badges of bravery, credentials of consecration, and tokens of triumph. Jeremiah combined in his life and ministry the salient features of both our Redeemer and his greatest interpreter.

As you prepare your mind and heart to teach this book, you will find God sent more than a series of sermons to ancient Judah. He sent a man! In these fifty-two chapters you will meet a prophet who delivered God's message not just with his lips but with his heart and his life. May the Lord bless as you prepare to share his message with those whom you lead.

THE WORLD IN WHICH JEREMIAH LIVED

The prophets of Israel wore "two hats." They foretold, but these men of God also served as "forthtellers." With keen accuracy, inspired by the Spirit of God's holiness (Hebrew concept of Holy Spirit), they predicted events centuries before these happenings occurred. But these men of God did even more. They spoke to their own generation about the evils of society.

To interpret Jeremiah's sermons, one must know of the major movements and trends in the political and economic world of that day. In Judah five different kings sat on the throne during Jeremiah's forty-plus years of ministry.

Josiah (639–608 B.C.), a good king who honored Yahweh and sought to do his will. Josiah brought reform and revival to the land, seeking the aid of Jeremiah in calling the people back to observance of the Mosaic law. But in his latter years he became involved in international politics. He tried to stop Egypt from going to help Assyria against Babylon at the Battle of Carchemisch and met his death in 608 B.C. (2 Kgs. 22:1–23:30a; 2 Chr. 34:1–35:27).

Jehoahaz (reigned three months), son of Josiah. Jehoahaz was a wicked king whom the people put on the throne after Josiah's death. Neco, king of Egypt, deposed and imprisoned him and placed Jehoiakim, a second son of Josiah, on the throne (2 Kgs. 23:30b–33; 2 Chr. 36:1–3).

Jehoiakim (608–597 B.C.), son of Josiah, a wicked king. Jehoiakim was the opposite of his father in almost every way. He reversed all the godly policies of Josiah and made Jeremiah's life miserable. Reviving the pagan practices of Manasseh, a former king, Jehoiakim began the final process that led eventually to Jerusalem's destruction and captivity. In 597 B.C. Nebuchadnezzar, Babylon's king, unseated, imprisoned, and probably killed him (2 Kgs. 23:34–24:5; 2 Chr. 36:4–8).

Jehoiachin (reigned three months), son of Jehoiakim. Jehoiachin followed Jeremiah's advice and surrendered to Babylon. Nebuchadnezzar imprisoned Jehoiachin in Babylon but treated him well. Thirty-seven years later, Evil-Merodach, then king of Babylon, released him. He also gave Jehoiachin a stipend and a degree of dignity for the rest of his life (2 Kgs. 24:6–16; 25:27–30; 2 Chr. 36:9–10).

Zedekiah (597–586 B.C.), third son of Josiah to rule over Judah. Zedekiah was weak and compromising. He vacillated between doing God's will as he received it from Jeremiah and following the demands of people who controlled him. During Zedekiah's reign, Nebuchadnezzar invaded Judah and Jerusalem three times (605, 597, 586 B.C.). On the third and final invasion, he destroyed the temple, burned the city, and carried all but a few people into captivity (2 Kgs. 24:17–25:21; 2 Chr. 36:11–21).

DATES AND EVENTS

To study the Book of Jeremiah effectively, one needs to keep in perspective several important events that occurred during the prophet's ministry.

639 B.C.: Accession of Josiah to Judah's throne.

621 B.C.: Cleansing of temple and discovery of law book, probably the Book of Deuteronomy or portions of it. Beginning of great reformation.

608 B.C.: Battle of Megiddo. Death of Josiah.

608 B.C.: Accession of Jehoiakim to Judah's throne after the brief reign of Jehoahaz.

605 B.C.: Battle of Carchemisch. Babylon defeats Assyria, who was probably helped by Egyptian forces. Assyrian Empire absorbed into Babylonian Empire.

605 B.C.: First invasion of Judah and Jerusalem by Nebuchadnezzar.

597 B.C.: Second invasion of Judah and Jerusalem. Death of Jehoiakim. Nebuchadnezzar takes ten thousand captives, mostly skilled workers, to Babylon.

597 B.C.: Accession of Jehoiachin to throne of Judah. After three months, he surrenders to Nebuchadnezzar and is carried to Babylon.

597 B.C.: Accession of Zedekiah to Judah's throne.

586 B.C.: Third invasion of Judah and Jerusalem. Temple burned and city destroyed. Almost all remaining inhabitants carried to Babylon. Jeremiah given his choice to go to Babylon or remain in Judah with the few people left there; he chooses the latter. Later, Nebuchadnezzar appoints Gedaliah as governor of those still in the land of Judah. Ishmael kills Gedaliah. A remnant flees to Egypt and forces Jeremiah to accompany them. Last recorded account of Jeremiah is in Egypt.

CHRONOLOGICAL ARRANGEMENT OF JEREMIAH'S LIFE AND PROPHECIES

A person who approaches the Book of Jeremiah will soon notice its lack of chronological arrangement. For its readers, it is a "jigsaw puzzle" that requires careful attention. The book contains prophetic discourses, biographical material, and historical narratives, arranged without apparent chronological sequence. The fifty-two chapters cover a period of more than forty years. It seems impossible to detect any principle of arrangement. As a result, those who attempt to read the book straight through may find themselves in a state of confusion.

The material begins with an account of the prophet's call and earlier prophecies. The successive chapters, however, wander hither and thither over the long and rugged course of Jeremiah's active life. Without warning, the scene shifts. The same chapter may contain sections that belong to widely different periods in the prophet's ministry. In other sections, the reader may not find any specific indication about the situation or period of the prophet's life reflected in the portion he is reading.

As an illustration of the chronological disorder, consider some of the chapters that are definitely dated in the text. Chapters 21 and 24 are designated as occurring during the reign of Zedekiah. Chapter 25, on the other hand, though appearing later in the text, is dated "in the fourth year of Jehoiakim . . . king of Judah." Chapters 27 and 28 belong to Zedekiah's reign, but chapters 35 and 36 go back to the time of Jehoiakim. The latter chapter goes as far back as the fourth year of that king. The Jewish captives carried to Babylon by Nebuchadnezzar are addressed in words of comfort several chapters before the announcement by Jeremiah to Jehoiakim that the event was about to happen. The prophecies relating to the foreign nations form the bulk of the book's latter portion. Most of them were delivered long before the final overthrow of Jerusalem and Judah.

Chapters 26–45, for the most part, contain biographical material. Normally one would expect that if any kind of writing should be chronological, it would be biographical data. But the last chapter in the "Biography of Jeremiah" contains the description of an event that occurred at least twenty-one years earlier than those in the immediately preceding chapter.

When the writer of this commentary began graduate work, his major professor came to him with a suggestion. He said, "We need a doctoral thesis dealing with the chronology of Jeremiah's book. The problem with all works of this type is that the writers end up denying some of the material was written by Jeremiah. We need someone who holds to the integrity of Jeremiah's authorship with reference to the entire book. Yet we want this writer to do an objective and exhaustive study of the background related to every passage in the book. Would you accept the assignment?"

The product of a three-year study by this writer was a thesis entitled "A Chronological Reconstruction of the Life and Prophecies of Jeremiah." Part of the thesis was to arrange the prophecies and other material in chronological sequence. Another result was to investigate why the material in the book is not in chronological order. The conclusion was that the book is a collection of separate documents dealing with Jeremiah's ministry. They were gathered either by Jeremiah himself; by Baruch, his secretary (see chs. 36 and 45); or by someone else. They were placed side by side to form the present canonical book, but no effort was made to integrate them into chronological order.

SUMMARY OF JEREMIAH'S CAREER

Most Old Testament students agree that Jeremiah was called to be a prophet in 626 B.C. They do not know his age at the time. He called himself a "child" (Jer. 1:6). The normal Old Testament meaning of the word translated "child" is a young boy. Other meanings of the word are lad, youth. While admittedly the word is used in the Old Testament for Joshua when he was forty-five years of age (Exod. 33:11), the subsequent ministry of Jeremiah leads us to believe that Jeremiah was a very young man.

When God called Jeremiah to be a prophet "to the nations," Judah's light was flickering, and the entire region of which Judah was a part was in turmoil. During the prophetic ministry of Isaiah (740–700 B.C.), the nation had almost gone under. Because good king Hezekiah had taken his troubles to the Lord's house and spread them before him, however, God delivered his people.

But that was another day and another century. Hezekiah's good reign had been followed by fifty-five years of Judah's most wicked king—Manasseh. During his reign, Manasseh sought to undo all the good Hezekiah had done through his religious reforms. He brought the land to a worse condition than when Joshua led the Israelites into the land of Canaan.

In the eighteenth year of his reign, Josiah launched a reformation, based on a book of the law discovered in the temple when it was being cleansed. It was probably the Book of Deuteronomy or a part of it. The young prophet enthusiastically supported the king. Later, however, when Josiah's reform movement turned into a nationalistic crusade rather than a spiritual movement, Jeremiah became disillusioned.

In 608 B.C., Egypt under Pharaoh Neco started north to aid Assyria against Babylon in a battle at Carchemisch. Josiah and his army tried to stop Egypt at Megiddo, and Josiah was killed. The people of the land chose Jehoahaz, son of Josiah, as king. But Neco deposed him and placed Jehoiakim, another son of Josiah, on the throne. That's when Jeremiah's severe troubles began.

Jehoiakim was one of the most wicked men ever to sit on Judah's throne. He exploited the people unmercifully for his personal gain. In addition, he led the people to reestablish the pagan religious practices of Manasseh's day.

Jeremiah opposed Jehoiakim. After the prophet's famous temple sermon (chs. 7 and 26), Jehoiakim banished him from the temple area.

Following God's orders, Jeremiah wrote in a book (36:1–32) the messages he had delivered since the beginning of his ministry. When it was brought to Jehoiakim's attention, he cut it to pieces and burned it. Jeremiah rewrote it and added more. This is the first record we have of Jeremiah's prophecies being gathered for future generations. Jeremiah continued his preaching during Jehoiakim's reign. His messages grew increasingly pessimistic about Judah's future.

In 605 B.C., the third year of Jehoiakim's reign, Babylon defeated the combined forces of Assyria and Egypt at Carchemisch. Having become master of that region, Nebuchadnezzar immediately invaded Judah and Jerusalem. He carried a number of captives to Babylon. In addition, he levied an annual tribute or tax on Jehoiakim and Judah. During this time, Jeremiah continued to preach but could not come into the temple area.

In 597 B.C., Nebuchadnezzar made a second visit to Jerusalem. This time he came to punish Jehoiakim for withholding tribute money. He carried ten thousand captives to Babylon. They were mostly the leadership of the land and skilled workers. Jehoiakim met his death during this chaotic period, and his son Jehoiachin became king. The young monarch submitted to Babylon, was taken to Babylon, and was treated kindly for his cooperation with Nebuchadnezzar. Zedekiah, a third son of Josiah, became king. He ruled until the final fall of Jerusalem in 586 B.C.

Zedekiah's main problem was his indecisiveness. From all appearances, this king wanted to do right. His deficiency of character lay in his inability to do what his better self told him was for his country's political and spiritual good. Zedekiah ran first to one group and then to another. He seemed incapable of making a decision and standing by it. As he began reigning, he took an oath of allegiance to Babylon, but the pro-Egyptian party would not let him enjoy peace of mind. Rather than fulfill his vow and hold fast his loyalty to Babylon, Zedekiah chose another course. He sought to determine which action was politically expedient. This policy eventually resulted in national suicide.

During the early years of Zedekiah's reign, Jeremiah's task was twofold. He sought to convince the people who remained in Judah that the future of the Jewish nation lay in those who had been carried into Babylon. Second, he insisted that those in Babylon should settle down for a long captivity, but he promised the nation would eventually be restored to their land.

At first, Zedekiah allowed Jeremiah freedom and even came to him for advice. The prophet advised surrender to Babylon. But Zedekiah chose to obey the strong nationalists who demanded that he hold out against the enemy. Babylon, however, refused to let up on Judah. Late in Zedekiah's reign, Nebuchadnezzar threw a siege around Jerusalem that, with one brief respite, lasted for more than eighteen months.

The major crisis of Jeremiah's life and ministry was the siege of Jerusalem. In the siege, the prophet of God was brought to the level of his people. He shared their dangers and duties, their heartaches, and hunger. If his faith did not waver and his judgment remained mature, his opportunities for service were great.

As events unfolded, Jeremiah's crisis grew progressively worse. The siege was temporarily interrupted because of the approaching Egyptian army. Jeremiah left the city and started for his home, Anathoth, a few miles away, to transact some personal business. He was accused of deserting to the Babylonians and arrested. At first, he was more or less under house arrest in the "courtyard of the guard" (37:21).

Later, Jeremiah was thrown into a dungeon. This was actually an underground cistern. An Ethiopian eunuch rescued him. Jeremiah then persuaded Zedekiah to put him back in the "courtyard of the guard" (38:13). He remained there until Jerusalem fell to the Babylonians.

Drained and desolate, Jerusalem's day of destruction finally arrived. The Babylonian army broke through the wall. King Zedekiah fled. The Babylonian army caught him in the plains of Jericho. They sent him to King Nebuchadnezzar. The Babylonians killed the king's sons, executed the leaders, put out Zedekiah's eyes, and carried him in chains to Babylon.

What about the people? Nebuzaradan, captain of the Babylonian guard, carried them to Babylon. He left only the poor of the land and gave them the vineyards and fields to tend as vassals of Babylon. These events and other details are found in 39:1–10 and 52:1–34. The latter is a historical appendix added to the book containing an account of Jerusalem's fall. The same material in 52:1–34 is found also in 2 Kings 24:18–25:30.

What about Jeremiah's future? One final chapter of his ministry awaited him. Chapters 40–44 contain the remaining record about the life of Jeremiah.

The material is chronological with the exception of 39:15–18, which is the promise made to Ebed-Melech, the Ethiopian eunuch who rescued Jeremiah from the dungeon.

This was a difficult period for Jeremiah. He faced a traumatic emotional adjustment when he saw the temple go up in flames. Jeremiah loved the temple. He had condemned it only because of the perverted worship that had been carried on in it.

When Nebuchadnezzar captured Jerusalem, he commanded his general, Nebuzaradan, to release Jeremiah. The prophet was committed to Gedaliah, the Babylonian governor of Judah, and he lived with his own people. Jeremiah was later given a choice. He could go to Babylon and be treated favorably, or he could stay with the people who remained in Judah. He preferred to remain with his people.

Later chapters tell of the prophet's further difficulties. Conspiracy seized the land. Gedalilah was murdered by Ishmael. Johanan then became the people's leader. Chapter 42 tells how the people decided they would go to Egypt. Under the guise of seeking advice, they went to Jeremiah. Actually, they wanted a confirmation of their decision.

Jeremiah told the people they had no need to fear the Babylonians, and he advised them to remain in Judah. They ignored his advice and went in a group to Egypt. The last picture we have of Jeremiah is his brief ministry with the people in Egypt. He continued to warn the people of coming judgment because they had rejected God's will.

JEREMIAH THE MAN

Jeremiah's greatest teachings came out of his heart. Early in his ministry he was alarmed because he felt certain judgment was coming immediately. He spoke of being in pain: "Oh, the agony of my heart! My heart pounds within me, I cannot keep silent" (4:19). When reform swept the land, he was carried away with its enthusiasm. But he snapped back to reality at the death of Josiah and saw the tragedy of a nation deceived by a shallow religious program.

The bitter days of Jehoiakim's ungodly reign brought a rapid maturity to the prophet. During those days he learned the true meaning of prayer. The prophet discovered through his prayer life the world's chief problem is a heart "deceitful above all things and beyond cure" (17:9). He came to possess in his heart a fire shut up in his bones that made holding back from delivering the divine message an impossibility.

During the time of Zedekiah, Jeremiah urged the captives in Babylon to submit to and support their captors. With the group left in Judah, he pleaded for surrender to the invading army. The prophet was convinced that Judah's hope for the future did not lie in seeking to defend a country guided by a corrupt leadership. It consisted rather in finding Yahweh by seeking him with their whole heart (29:13).

The destruction of Jerusalem and the burning of the temple prepared Jeremiah to understand a truth he had partially understood throughout his ministry: fellowship with God is the greatest good. As he absorbed this truth into his ministry, he could speak authoritatively of the divine ideal. It is a community of people on whose hearts God's will is written (31:33).

Underlying all of Jeremiah's thinking and preaching was his faith in the future. Even when Jerusalem was surrounded by the Babylonian army, he purchased a piece of property in nearby Anathoth. By doing this, he affirmed, "Houses, fields and vineyards will again be bought in this land" (32:15).

COMMENTARY ON JEREMIAH

This commentary is designed for those who teach the Word of God to laypersons. For that reason, we will avoid some of the issues that scholars deal with when they approach Jeremiah.

Few writers approach the Book of Jeremiah from a chronological standpoint. This approach requires an exposition of the material in a way that traces the spiritual development of Jeremiah's life as he served and preached. This commentary will make a concentrated effort to do this very thing. It will present each Scripture passage against the background of the time and the occasion when it was delivered. This will be done in order to show the prophet's growth from a young zealous, almost fanatical prophet, to a mature, godly statesman. But he remained unyielding in his convictions and refused to compromise his message. This approach will require some subjective decisions. No claim is made for absolute certainty in every case.

The study will be based on an unqualified acceptance of the words often spoken by Robert G. Lee about both the Old and New Testaments. He described the Bible as "supernatural in origin, divine in authorship, human in penmanship, infinite in scope, inspired in totality." The fact that we find progress in Jeremiah's understanding of God's will and purpose in no way dilutes his authority at any stage of his prophetic career.

At the close of this book, you will find a bibliography. It lists a number of works you are encouraged to explore. These books will increase your appreciation for the prophet whom many people consider the greatest in the of Old Testament.

Jeremiah 1:1–19

Jeremiah's Calling to a Twofold Task

I. INTRODUCTION
Nothing Ever Happens Around Here

II. COMMENTARY
A verse-by-verse explanation of these verses.

III. CONCLUSION
God's Last Voice to a Dying Nation

An overview of the principles and applications from these verses.

IV. LIFE APPLICATION
Responding to God's Call

Melding these verses to life.

V. PRAYER
Tying these verses to life with God.

VI. DEEPER DISCOVERIES
Historical, geographical, and grammatical enrichment of the commentary.

VII. TEACHING OUTLINE
Suggested step-by-step group study of these verses.

VIII. ISSUES FOR DISCUSSION
Zeroing these verses in on daily life.

Jeremiah 1:1–19

Quote

"*It* is most comfortable to stride unknown through the world, without being known to His Majesty the King. . . . To be known by God in time makes life so acutely strenuous. Wherever He is, there every half hour is of tremendous importance. But to live in that manner is not endurable for sixty years."

Soren Kierkegaard

IN A NUTSHELL

When God called Jeremiah to be a prophet, he told Jeremiah he had known him since before Jeremiah was formed in his mother's womb. Before the prophet was born, God had a plan and ministry for him. Jeremiah attempted to avoid God's call to service, but God addressed his inadequacies and spoke directly to his fear. Then the Lord made a threefold promise and issued a threefold challenge to the prophet.

Jeremiah's Calling to a Twofold Task

I. INTRODUCTION

Nothing Ever Happens Around Here

John McCutchen, the famous illustrator, drew a cartoon for the one-hundredth anniversary of Abraham Lincoln's birth. The drawing shows two men standing on the edge of a snow-covered forest in Kentucky on a cold February morning in 1809. A man in the general store asks, "What's the news around here?" The other man answers, "Nothing much. Oh, there's a new baby over at Tom Lincoln's. That's all. Nothing ever happens around here" (Grant, *The Way of the Cross,* 137–38).

Many important events in history began with the birth of a baby. The names of Isaac, Samuel, Samson, John the Baptist, and Jesus quickly come to mind. But the account of Jeremiah's call takes us back to before his birth—to his development in his mother's womb. Indeed, the story goes even farther back—back to the mind of God.

II. COMMENTARY

Jeremiah's Calling to a Twofold Task

> **MAIN IDEA:** *The days demanded a forceful messenger from God warning his people of imminent danger. To function effectively, he must possess a twofold nature—conviction and compassion for the task of destroying and rebuilding.*

The Time of Jeremiah's Call (1:1–8)

> **SUPPORTING IDEA:** *Timing plays a vital role in everything. Jeremiah was a man for whom the time was ready.*

1:1. Jeremiah came from the priestly family of **Hilkiah, one of the priests at Anathoth.** An old cliché says that a person who wants to train a boy to become a man should begin with his grandfather. The spiritual roots of Jeremiah, however, go back at least three centuries before his grandfather.

The history of this priestly family dates back to the time of David and Solomon.

Anathoth was located in the small territory possessed by the Benjamites. This put Jeremiah in the same geographical family as Saul, the first king of Israel. It also identified him genealogically with Saul of Tarsus, the persecutor, who became the great Christian apostle. This tribe's territory included a small amount of land, stretching only about twenty-six miles in length and twelve miles in width. Judah bounded it on the south and Ephraim on the north. Jeremiah's home lay about three or four miles northeast of Jerusalem.

1:2–3. God called Jeremiah to be a prophet in the **thirteenth year** of Josiah's thirty-nine-year reign. This means the prophet received his call in 626 B.C. According to the Scriptures, he prophesied until the eleventh year of Zedekiah's reign.

Jeremiah's prophetic ministry, therefore, spanned at least forty years. He served as both an official and an authentic messenger of Yahweh until the destruction of both the temple and the city. But he did not cease to minister as a prophet when the city of Jerusalem fell. When some of the survivors migrated to Egypt, Jeremiah went with them. We have no record of how long he remained as spiritual advisor and counselor for the people or even whether he remained in Egypt.

1:4–5. At this point the record changes from a third-person account, which might be labeled as a title introduction, to an autobiographical version. The prophet told of the call in his own words. A sudden change of person takes place frequently in the book. It occurs most often in Jeremiah's prophetic oracles. One has difficulty determining when the prophet is speaking and when the words are directly from Yahweh. The prophet so identified with Yahweh that his word actually became Jeremiah's word.

According to Jeremiah 1:5, God had been at work in the life of Jeremiah before he was born—indeed, before he was even conceived. A series of four verbs points to God's work before Jeremiah's birth: God **formed** him, **knew** him, **set** him **apart**, and **appointed** him. The biblical teaching is consistent and constant: God is involved in the forming and shaping of the preborn in the womb. Job testified to this truth (Job 10:8–12). But nowhere is it stated more eloquently than by David in Psalm 139:14–16. God personally weaves the preborn child together in the secret place of the womb. He causes the development of the bodily frame.

But more than just forming the preborn, God said to Jeremiah, **I knew you**. A careful reading of verse 5 indicates the knowing actually came before the forming: **Before I formed you in the womb I knew you**. God took an interest in and had an intimate knowledge of Jeremiah even before the first cells and sinews began to develop. There is more. For Jeremiah, before he was born, God set him apart. God put Jeremiah in a special category. He was consecrated or sanctified to God's service. And then, still before he was born, God appointed Jeremiah to a particular service—to be a prophet for him, to be a prophet to the nations.

In verse 5, the Hebrew word translated "formed" is the same one used in Genesis 2:7. The root idea is to be straitened or distressed. From this comes the meaning of "to form, fashion, make." Another derivation is "to devise, meditate." The nouns *maker, creator,* and *potter* come from the participle form of this verb. As a composer constructing the instrument on which the music will be played, God created Jeremiah to be a spokesman for him.

The word translated "knew" has a broad usage. It indicates more than factual knowledge, meaning experiential knowledge as well as sexual intimacy. It is consistently used for physical intercourse. In this present context, the verb indicates a relationship. God chose Jeremiah and set him apart before he was born to share a special affinity with his Creator.

The expression "to the nations" poses no problem for the person who knows the political climate of that time. Jeremiah's call coincided with the death of Ashurbanipal, king of Assyria, and the beginning of Assyria's decline as the dominant power in the Middle East. Babylon, under Nabopolassar, was entering the struggle for world domination. Egypt was watching with hopeful eye the decadence of the Assyrian Empire. Jeremiah was called that year to be a prophet. How could one with the broad insight he would develop be anything less than a prophet "to the nations"?

1:6–8. The dialogue that took place between Jeremiah and Yahweh parallels in many ways that of Moses and Yahweh. Jeremiah, like the great Lawgiver, protested that he was not able to speak, but he also pointed out his tender age. Where Moses may have felt he was too old for such a task, Jeremiah felt he was too young.

The Hebrew word translated **child** covers a broad range. It is used of Moses when he was a baby (Exod. 2:6) and of Joshua when he was a seasoned soldier in his mid-forties (Exod. 33:11). The normal usage, however, is of a youth, a very young man.

Yahweh refused to accept Jeremiah's plea of inadequacy. He repeated his commission and command. He gave no opportunity for the young man to come up with other reasons for refusing to accept the assignment. God combined his mandate with a word that served as an assurance to Jeremiah: **Do not be afraid . . . for I am with you.**

🅱 Yahweh's Touch on Jeremiah (1:9)

SUPPORTING IDEA: *The touch of God transforms mediocrity into excellence.*

1:9. All four of the major prophets received a divine touch, but two were transformed by it. Isaiah and Jeremiah present a marked contrast in the effect of God's touch in their call experience. Jeremiah did not respond as enthusiastically as Isaiah. Many writers have commented on the difference. Jeremiah did not volunteer for service. He was drafted. All his life, he remained an unwilling spokesman. The lad did not want to begin, and often he wanted to quit. But he had the marks of a true prophet: In one moment of despair, he said, "If I say, I will not make mention of him, nor speak any more in his name, then there is in my heart . . . a burning fire shut up in my bones, and . . . I cannot contain" (see Jer. 20:9 ASV).

The problem of Jeremiah differed from that of Isaiah. Both prophets received God's touch, but he had a different purpose for each. Yahweh touched Isaiah's mouth for cleansing. He was a young man with a consciousness of unclean lips. Yahweh touched Jeremiah's mouth for empowering. He was a child with a consciousness of inadequate lips.

The prophets Ezekiel and Daniel had similar experiences. The former was given a scroll with the message of God for the people. He was told to "open thy mouth, and eat that I give thee" (Ezek. 2:8 KJV). He did, and "it was in my mouth as honey for sweetness" (Ezek. 3:3 KJV). Daniel's experience came later in his ministry but was no less vivid and vital. In his vision of the son of man (Dan. 10), the prophet fell with his face to the ground when "one in the likeness of the sons of men touched my lips" (Dan. 10:16 ASV). All four major prophets thus received a divine touch. Isaiah for cleansing, Jeremiah for empowering, Ezekiel for food, Daniel for strength.

Yahweh's Task for Jeremiah (1:10)

SUPPORTING IDEA: *All effective work for the Lord consists of a twofold thrust—positive and negative.*

1:10. God next made Jeremiah's task explicit. It consisted of two essential elements. He must **tear down**. He must **build** up. Good preaching is always thus divided. Today's secular world cries loudly and insistently for the "positive approach." It resents the condemnation of anyone who refuses to recognize the value of pluralism and diversity. But God called Jeremiah first to **uproot** and to **destroy and** to **overthrow**. Then, of course, he called him also **to build and to plant**.

The Tree's Message for Jeremiah (1:11–12)

SUPPORTING IDEA: *God's "got the whole world in his hand," and he never comes too early or too late.*

1:11–12. These verses give a beautiful interpretation, in metaphorical terms, of Yahweh's first specific words to the prophet. Jeremiah was in a rural section. As he walked along, he saw the bud **of an almond tree**. This was one of the first signs that spring was approaching. Yahweh asked, "Jeremiah, what do you see?" The lad replied, "A *shaqad*." The Hebrew word *shaqad* means "to be awake, keep watch." Its root also produces the word for "an almond tree." Yahweh replied, **You have seen correctly, for I am watching to see that my word is fulfilled**.

This message gave great assurance to Jeremiah. He understood that God is active in the affairs of history. He is willing to intervene to help his people. God is awake (*shaqed*) and watching (*shoqed*) over Judah's destiny.

Yahweh would make certain his word would not return void. It would be **fulfilled**. After a long spiritual freeze, Judah's springtime was approaching. God's activity was about to begin. It might be an activity of judgment or of mercy—depending on the people's response. God was ready to act—either for Judah's deliverance or doom.

The Boiling Pot's Warning for Judah (1:13–16)

SUPPORTING IDEA: *Judgment awaited Judah because of the people's rebellion against Yahweh and his moral requirements.*

1:13–16. Jeremiah was passing by a cottage. God directed his attention to a seething pot or boiling cauldron, a common object near every house. On three sides, stones stood in place. The fourth side remained open as a spot from which to feed the fuel. The pot tilted away **from the north**, that is, toward the south. Its scalding liquid contents were about to boil over. This showed that God intended to send fierce judgment on Judah.

What was the significance of "north" in the vision? The contour of the land of Judah almost demanded that any invasion must come from the north. The adjacent land on the east and south was barren desert. On the west lay the Mediterranean Sea. Almost always invasion came from the north.

J. A. Thompson says, "Many of Israel's troubles had originally come from the north over the centuries, from the Philistines, the Assyrians, and the Arameans. The *north* was a symbol for dark powers often of uncertain origin" (p. 479). Robert Davidson agrees and adds, "The vision, and the expanded reference in verse 15 to 'all the people of the north and their kings,' do not clearly identify the northern peril. As Jeremiah's ministry progressed, however, it became even more clear that the foe from the north was to be identified with neo-Babylon empire." We will discuss this subject more thoroughly in commentary material on subsequent chapters.

Verses 15 and 16 contain words conveying the same general thought as Yahweh's words through his prophet, Habakkuk. Jeremiah's contemporary said, "Look at the nations and watch—and be utterly amazed. For I am going to do something in your days that you would not believe, even if you were told. I am raising up the Babylonians, that ruthless and impetuous people, who sweep across the whole earth to seize dwelling places not their own. They are a feared and dreaded people; they are a law to themselves and promote their own honor" (Hab. 1:5–7).

One undeniable truth comes to us from Yahweh's words to Jeremiah. Judah's God visits with stern punishment those who transgress his laws. Earlier prophets had spoken when hope of recovery still existed. But God called Jeremiah to a nation that had almost exhausted his patience. In the prophet's ministry, he would address people who were totally rebellious and facing complete disaster. The day called for every measure of effort to awaken, convince, and turn them back from the certain judgment that awaited such conduct. This advanced stage of moral deterioration called for severe messages and extreme action.

In this lesson from the boiling cauldron, Yahweh conveyed to his prophet a truth he remembered as long as he lived. Punishment is the inevitable consequence of sin. He regarded the nation's coming calamities as the visitations of God. But he did not think of Yahweh as just a vengeful deity who rejoices in vindicating his majesty through the discomforts of his people. Jeremiah understood punishment as an integral part of God's moral character.

Yahweh and Jeremiah both knew this message of impending disaster would not be a popular one for that day. Jeremiah must accept the fact that he was not to court popularity or be concerned with the nation's political future. He was to be God's prophet, and he must deliver God's message regardless of the cost.

F Yahweh's Promise of Eventual Triumph (1:17–19)

SUPPORTING IDEA: *Jeremiah's greatest legacy would be not his personal fame but his dedicated faithfulness.*

1:17–19. These two visions were "strong meat" for a small lad. We can easily understand why he recoiled and insisted he was not equal to the task. But Yahweh's concluding words assured him of divine resources for the struggle. Yahweh declared, **Get yourself ready! Stand up and say to them whatever I command you. . . . Do not be terrified by them, or I will terrify you before them. . . . They will fight against you but will not overcome you, for I am with you and will rescue you.**

Again, the call of Isaiah comes to mind as a contrast. Isaiah was cautioned against optimism while Jeremiah was comforted against pessimism. Isaiah was told he would fail. But he succeeded in a sense because Jerusalem was saved from Assyria's armies, to a large extent because of his ministry. Jeremiah was told he would succeed. But he failed in a sense because Jerusalem fell to the Babylonian armies, in spite of his ministry and his warnings. In his last days, though, Jeremiah was a hero, and he probably died a peaceful death in Egypt.

Yahweh prefaced his remarks to Jeremiah with a command, followed by a warning. "Strip yourself for action. And do not be paralyzed with fright before them, or I will make you paralyzed with fright before them." This meant whatever attitude Jeremiah took when the enemy came against him, Yahweh would intensify and make it of an even greater degree. "Be strong and I will strengthen you more. Grovel before them, and I will make you grovel even more." This sounded like a harsh warning, but it was realistic. If Jeremiah panicked when opposition arose, he would be totally discredited. As

Yahweh said to Joshua, so Yahweh said to Jeremiah, "Be strong and of good courage" (Josh. 1:6 NKJV).

In verses 18 and 19 God made a threefold promise to Jeremiah. First, God promised to strengthen the prophet. In this promise God used three comparisons. He promised to make the prophet like **a fortified city, an iron pillar and a bronze wall**. The first of these images speaks of a city with high walls and strong towers that render it inaccessible and impenetrable. Against it even great multitudes would battle in vain. The second term points to Jeremiah as a man of steel. He would be firm and unmovable, a tower of strength. The third term, "a bronze wall," involves the toughest metal known to the ancients. Bronze was an alloy of copper and tin, not an alloy of copper and zinc, like modern brass. Jeremiah would not be a wall of wood, which fire could burn down, or a wall of stone, which battering rams could knock down. He would be solid bronze, against which all weapons were ineffective.

Second, God promised Jeremiah, **They will fight against you but will not overcome you**. The prophet was to go to the front in a war zone. He would be under constant attack by seemingly overwhelming forces. But God assured Jeremiah that his side would win.

Third, God promised the prophet, **I am with you and will rescue you**. God did not promise to keep Jeremiah from experiencing difficult times; the Lord promised to be with Jeremiah as he faced difficulties from **the kings of Judah, its officials, its priests and the people of the land**. Notice the pronouns. God said it would be "they" against "you," but "I" who would be with "you." *They* would be many and powerful. *You*, Jeremiah, by nature are weak, frail, and alone. But *I*, the invincible Lord, will be with you and will rescue you.

To obey Yahweh's summons to service meant Jeremiah would plow a lonely furrow, with almost every segment of Judah's society against him. He was destined to learn later that he would not even have a wife to serve as companion and comforter.

In verse 19, Yahweh used a strong verb translated **rescue** to indicate the extent of his involvement with his prophet's need. It is the same one used to describe his promise to deliver Moses from the clutches of a powerful foe who would try to destroy him (Exod. 3:8; 18:4,8–10).

Yahweh's call made clear to Jeremiah that he must give up any thought of prosperity, popularity, or fame. Every prophet in every generation succeeds only if he is faithful in declaring God's will to the people of his own time.

Yahweh's call to Jeremiah was a real summons to a real world. The record of it is not just the recital of a dialogue; it is the description of a dynamic and authentic encounter with God. The account stands with moral authority as a certification of Jeremiah's right to speak for God. These words have meaning for us today. God is alive and active in the world in our generation. He is at work in nature as seen in the almond tree and at work in history as shown by the boiling pot. He is at work in human hearts as proven in the life of the young prophet.

MAIN IDEA REVIEW: *The days demanded a forceful messenger from God warning his people of imminent danger. To function effectively, he must possess a twofold nature—conviction and compassion for the task of destroying and rebuilding.*

III. CONCLUSION

GOD'S LAST VOICE TO A DYING NATION

In every crisis God has one or more voices that stand out above the crowd calling the people to repentance. He has never left himself without a witness. In every generation, he calls on people to forsake their sinful lifestyles and, by doing so, delay the coming judgment.

When the people were slaves in Egypt, God raised up Moses to bring words of assurance and supernatural deeds that led to deliverance. During the Philistine crisis, Samuel served as Yahweh's spokesman. He was the last of Israel's judges. And, though not the first to be called a prophet, he began the prophetic movement in Israel.

The last generation before Jerusalem's fall, however, produced one who, in many ways, was the greatest prophetic word of all. For forty years, Jeremiah exhorted, warned, begged, implored, and pleaded with his fellow countrymen to turn from their spiritual harlotry. When they refused, he called for peaceful surrender to Babylon, the nation God had chosen as his agent of discipline. His counsel was rejected, and as a result Judah paid a great price—seventy years of exile in a foreign land.

Jeremiah shared many of the common characteristics of his fellow prophets. He was also unique. Midway in his ministry, he suffered a midlife crisis. This was brought about, in many ways, by his complex personality. Tough-minded but tenderhearted, Jeremiah was the most introspective of all the prophets. He dared to dialogue, even debate, with God. This great man never wanted to preach. Only the fire shut up in his bones kept him from quitting.

PRINCIPLES

- God is involved in the forming and developing of the preborn in the womb.
- Too often, when God calls people, they respond with excuses emphasizing their weaknesses rather than relying on his strength.
- When God calls people to his service, he equips them for the task.
- The main reason people are slow to respond to God's call is fear.
- Those who serve God sometimes must tear down what needs to be removed before they can build and plant the new.
- God is aware of what is going on in his world and how people are responding to his message.
- Those who speak for God do not speak on their own authority but God's.
- Those who declare God's Word can expect opposition.
- God promises to be with his servants who obediently serve him.

APPLICATIONS

- Consider the issue of abortion in light of God's knowing and having a purpose for persons even before they are conceived.
- Write a brief description of how you now understand God's plan for your own life.
- List some reasons you have offered God to avoid his call to service.
- Evaluate the validity of those reasons.
- Make a comparison of your inadequacies with God's adequacy.

- Describe circumstances in which God has called on people to tear down what is in opposition to God's ways.
- Recall words of positive rebuilding you have recently spoken.
- List some people you have known who faced opposition for upholding or declaring God's word.
- Evaluate the extent to which you rely on the Lord's promise that he is with you.

IV. LIFE APPLICATION

Responding to God's Call

John Wesley, the founder of Methodism, was born into the home of a devout high-church Anglican minister in Epworth, England, in 1703.

When John was six years old, the rectory at Epworth caught fire and burned down. John appeared at a second-story window amid the flames and was rescued by neighbors. Thus from early childhood, Wesley felt the call of God was upon him. He referred to himself as "a brand plucked from the burning."

At seventeen Wesley entered Oxford University. In 1726 he was elected a fellow of Lincoln College at the university. Two years later he was ordained to the Anglican ministry even though his own conversion—his Aldersgate Street experience—did not occur until May 24, 1738.

In the England of Wesley's day, conventicles, or meetings of small groups, were forbidden by an Act of Parliament. Church of England ministers preached only in churches, avoided emotional "enthusiasm," and limited their ministry to their designated parishes. In February 1739, when George Whitefield began to preach in the open fields near Bristol to hardened coal miners who never darkened the door of a church, God blessed Whitefield's preaching, and many became believers. Whitefield pleaded with Wesley to come to Bristol and follow his lead of preaching in the open fields.

Wesley wrote in his journal for March 10, 1739: "I had no thought of leaving London, when I received . . . a letter from Mr. Whitefield . . . intreating me, in the most pressing manner, to come to Bristol without delay. This I was not at all forward to do, and perhaps a little less inclined to it."

Wesley, who never dreamed of doing such open-air preaching, continued to struggle with accepting God's call. On March 29 he recorded: "I could scarce reconcile myself at first to this strange way of preaching in the fields . . . having been all my life so tenacious of every point relating to decency and order, that I should have thought the saving of souls almost a sin, if it had not been done in a church."

By June, Wesley had made a breakthrough. He accepted God's call. He wrote in his journal: "I looked upon all the world as my parish. . . . I judge it . . . my bounden duty, to declare unto all that are willing to hear, the glad tidings of salvation. This is the work which I know God has called me to; and sure I am, that his blessing attends it."

From that time on Wesley preached to prisoners in jails, to wayfarers in inns, to passengers on ships, to people in fields and on hillsides. He proclaimed the Word of the Lord to small groups and to gatherings of thousands. During his lifetime he traveled 250,000 miles in England, Ireland, and Scotland—much of it on horseback—proclaiming God's Word. Indeed, the world was his parish!

Jeremiah, like John Wesley, was conscious of God's call upon his life from the time he was a child (vv. 6–7). Both men resisted God's call initially. Jeremiah's reason for resisting God's call turned out to be the same as John Wesley's—fear. And their reason turns out to be the same reason so many believers today resist God's call—fear. But our Lord has promised to be with us (Matt. 28:20). We should not be afraid to accept his call and the assignments he has for us. He supplies all we need to accomplish the work to which he calls us.

V. PRAYER

Eternal God and Father, who knew us before we knew you, help us to respond to your call to service not with excuses but with readiness of heart and mind. Remove all our fears. Put your word in our mouths and make us bold to speak for you, knowing when to tear down and when to build up. May your name be praised in all nations. Amen.

VI. DEEPER DISCOVERIES

A. Josiah, Son of Amon (1:2)

Many Old Testament students consider Josiah, Judah's fifteenth king, as the nation's greatest king. Like Uzziah and Hezekiah, his zealous predecessors, he sought to restore Judah to the glory days of David. Josiah came to the throne at the age of eight, following the assassination of his father Amon (2 Kgs. 21:19–23; 2 Chr. 33:21–24), who reigned only two years.

In Josiah's eighteenth year, 621 B.C., a book of the law was discovered in the temple. Most scholars agree it was the Book of Deuteronomy or at least a part of it. He consulted with some of his religious advisors and learned how Judah had violated God's will as revealed in the book of the law. Using this book as his guide, Josiah began an extensive reform movement. Jeremiah, the young prophet, joined the king's team and promoted the program vigorously.

The Bible is silent for much of this period. It picks up again, however, with a reference to the king's military campaign against Egypt's Pharaoh Neco in 608 B.C. Josiah set out to engage Neco in battle as Neco rushed to help Assyria against Babylon. Josiah was killed, and Jeremiah lost a friend and spiritual ally.

Josiah left an enviable legacy. The sacred historian wrote, "Neither before nor after Josiah was there a king like him who turned to the LORD as he did—with all his heart and with all his soul and with all his strength, in accordance with the Law of Moses" (2 Kgs. 23:25).

B. Prophet (1:5)

Old Testament writers used three Hebrew words to denote those men of God who directed, encouraged, comforted, chided, and warned Israel for centuries. The first two words, *roeh* and *hozeh,* are translated "seer." They are associated with the ecstatic group who preceded the mainline prophets designated by the Hebrew word *navi.*

Scholars disagree about the meaning of *navi.* Some claim it means "to effervesce." Others insist it indicates "one who was called." Most, however, believe it means "to speak." A large majority add the thought "to speak with authority." This would, of course, be influenced by the concept of having been called by Yahweh.

Although the prophetic succession seems to have begun officially with Samuel, such men as Abraham and Moses were also called "prophets." They stood equally along with other such personalities as Elijah, Elisha, Hosea, Amos, Micah, Isaiah, Jeremiah, and the other canonical spokesmen for God.

The prophets interpreted the law and called the people back to obedience of the law. Mingled with these messages demanding repentance and change of lifestyle were predictions about future events. God gave the prophets amazing insight into his purposes of redemption and knowledge of some minute details. These could only have been perceived by a person in unique fellowship with Yahweh. Among these detailed revelations were the birthplace of the Messiah and his virgin birth.

The prophets' messages were always spoken within the context of Israel's spiritual need. They condemned sin, warned of certain judgment, but always saw beyond the punishment to ultimate victory for God's people.

C. "Before you were born I set you apart" (1:5)

Jeremiah felt strongly that God had brought him into the world for a special purpose. He labored incessantly under this conviction. The Scriptures support the truth that God sets people apart to special tasks without their prior knowledge of it.

Theologians discuss at length the relationship of predestination and foreknowledge to a person's capacity to choose. Centuries of dialogue and debate have not solved this problem to everyone's satisfaction, nor will the matter ever be completely settled. Both are true though our limited minds cannot see how. The emphasis in this verse, however, is on God's foreknowledge and predestination. God chose Jeremiah, called him, and he obeyed.

VII. TEACHING OUTLINE

A. INTRODUCTION

1. Lead Story: Nothing Ever Happens Around Here

2. Context: The year of Jeremiah's call was 626 B.C. Judah was facing what would be its last forty years as a kingdom. The dominant world power was Assyria, but that was about to change. Babylon would usurp that position. God was planning to send one final prophetic voice to the nation. God had chosen Jeremiah, before his birth, to give the nation a final opportunity for repentance.

3. Transition: When Jeremiah was a youngster, God called him into his service. The prophet, like many of the great biblical figures, was reluctant to accept God's call. Jeremiah suggested reasons he was not equipped and adequate for the tasks God wanted him to do. God

addressed the prophet's fear and promised he would be with him, protect him, and deliver him. Then the Lord challenged Jeremiah to stand up and speak for him.

B. COMMENTARY

1. The Time of Jeremiah's Call (1:1–8)

2. Yahweh's Touch on Jeremiah (1:9)

3. Yahweh's Task for Jeremiah (1:10)

4. The Tree's Message for Jeremiah (1:11–12)

5. The Boiling Pot's Warning for Judah (1:13–16)

6. Yahweh's Promise of Eventual Triumph (1:17–19)

C. CONCLUSION: GOD'S LAST VOICE TO A DYING NATION

VIII. ISSUES FOR DISCUSSION

1. When does a fetus begin to be a human person? To what extent is God involved in the development and formation of the preborn? How does a person's theology affect his or her view of abortion?

2. What excuses do believers offer to God to avoid his call to service? How does God respond to these excuses?

3. From a Christian perspective, what types of thinking, values, and arguments do Christians need to be involved in tearing down, uprooting, and overthrowing in our post-Christian, postmodern society?

4. In a world of endless opinions, suggestions, and ideas, how important is it for believers to speak God's Word?

5. Why do people ridicule, reject, and persecute those who speak God's Word to them?

Jeremiah 2:1–4:4

Can a Bride Forget?

I. INTRODUCTION
Emma and Charles

II. COMMENTARY
A verse-by-verse explanation of these verses.

III. CONCLUSION
In Spite of Everything, God Still Loves

An overview of the principles and applications from these verses.

IV. LIFE APPLICATION
From Newlyweds to Divorce Court

Melding these verses to life.

V. PRAYER
Tying these verses to life with God.

VI. DEEPER DISCOVERIES
Historical, geographical, and grammatical enrichment of the commentary.

VII. TEACHING OUTLINE
Suggested step-by-step group study of these verses.

VIII. ISSUES FOR DISCUSSION
Zeroing these verses in on daily life.

Quote

"Like a woman unfaithful to her husband, so you have been unfaithful to me, O house of Israel,' declares the Lord"

Jeremiah 3:20

Jeremiah 2:1–4:4

IN A NUTSHELL

Jeremiah used a marriage metaphor to accuse Judah of adultery. God likened himself to Judah's husband and Judah to his bride. Beginning with the early period of their marriage, when Israel was devoted to her husband, Jeremiah traced Judah's downward course from bride to adulterous wife to prostitute. In a court of law, the Lord laid out his charges against his unfaithful bride and detailed her affair with other nations and with the Baals. The Lord pleaded with his sinful wife to acknowledge her guilt, turn from her wandering, and return to him. He promised to forgive her for her waywardness.

Can a Bride Forget?

I. INTRODUCTION

Emma and Charles

*E*mma Rouault was a beautiful and charming young woman. No wonder Charles, a respectable young doctor, fell in love with her. Soon they decided to marry. After their marriage, all Charles's efforts were devoted to pleasing Emma. He adored her.

But Emma did not feel the same way. She did not find in her marriage the bliss, passion, and ecstasy that she had read about in romance novels. She began to look for a more exciting life.

Opportunity soon presented itself to Emma in the person of Rodolphe, a true lady's man and man of the world. Soon Emma was deceiving Charles and going for rides around the countryside with Rodolphe, who wooed her with avowals of his love.

Then Rodolphe began to lose interest in Emma. To keep his interest, Emma began to spend money uncontrollably. Soon she was heavily in debt. Emma schemed to run away with Rodolphe, but he left a letter telling her he loved her but was leaving her for her own good.

Emma fell into deep depression. Charles neglected his medical practice in spite of the bills that were piling up and stayed by Emma's side.

One day Emma ran into Leon, a younger man whom she had known previously. His suave manners and dress impressed her. Soon Emma gave herself to Leon. Since Leon could not afford to entertain Emma in grand style, she often gave him the money or paid herself. By now Emma was even pawning some of her possessions to support her extravagant lifestyle. She was consumed with her thirst for romance. Living only for sensation, Emma fell deeper and deeper into depravity.

At last it all caught up with Emma. The banks refused to extend her a loan. In despair over her hopeless situation, she committed suicide with a dose of arsenic. Sometime after Emma's death, Charles discovered the love letters from Rodolphe and Leon in Emma's desk. He was crushed and disillusioned. It wasn't long before he died—a broken man.

As in the story of Emma and Charles Bovary from Gustave Flaubert's 1857 novel *Madame Bovary,* Jeremiah began his sermon in chapter 2 of his book with the story of newlyweds and the period of their honeymoon. Likening Israel to his bride, the Lord said, "I remember the devotion of your youth, how as a bride you loved me and followed me through the desert" (v. 2).

As a faithful bridegroom, God watched over his beloved bride. In the early days of their marriage, Israel was a loving wife, and God was a faithful husband. Unfortunately, as with Emma and Charles, the honeymoon didn't last.

II. COMMENTARY

Can a Bride Forget?

MAIN IDEA: *Jeremiah depicted Judah's defection from God and pointed out that a bride always remembers the early days of her love and marriage. Judah should feel that way and return to her husband, Yahweh.*

A Description of the People's Depravity (2:1–37)

SUPPORTING IDEA: *The people had turned from the God of their early days and become addicted to other gods who were, in reality, not gods at all.*

2:1–3. At God's command Jeremiah began his message with a reminder of the people's purity at the beginning of their existence as a nation. They had been obedient and dedicated. This was indeed a honeymoon experience.

In a second metaphor the prophet spoke of the nation as a "firstfruit." **Firstfruits** were the choice crops harvested first and offered to God. It also suggested that other fruit would follow—probably speaking of other nations. God's protective care assured the nation that any who opposed or sought to harm the people would be dealt with sternly.

2:4–9. Taking a fresh start with a command to listen, the prophet challenged the people with a question: What had happened to cause the people to turn so far away from God? He replied to his own question with an explanation that was an accusation. The first sin the people committed was ignoring God's blessings. Yahweh had redeemed them from bondage and brought them into a good land. They had rewarded him by defiling it. The religious leaders, both priests and prophets, took part in the disgusting conduct. For that reason, he would punish them.

2:10–12. The Lord challenged his people to go west as far as Cyprus (**Kittim**) and east to **Kedar**. Judah had done something not even heathen nations had done. She had left her God. To make matters worse, Judah was the only nation who had the true God. All the other nations had false, empty gods with no life. Yet the nations with the gods that were actually "no gods" had remained faithful to their gods.

2:13. People never live in a vacuum. If they give up one type of lifestyle, they will always adopt another. God presented his people with an unforgettable picture to help them see what they had given up and what they had put in its place. **They have forsaken me, the spring of living water, and have dug their own cisterns, broken cisterns that cannot hold water.**

A cistern was a reservoir into which rainwater could drain from a roof, tunnel, or courtyard. Cistern water was less than satisfactory. Jeremiah contrasted the cisterns with the springs that produced clear, pure water. Anyone living in the Middle East would recognize this exchange of a spring for a cistern as a bad deal.

2:14–19. Perplexed by the people's conduct, Jeremiah asked why they were acting like slaves. People in the ancient world, including the Israelites, usually became slaves in one of three ways. Either they were born in that state, or they suffered financial adversity and sold themselves or their children into slavery, or they were captured by a foreign power and enslaved by their conquerors. Jeremiah's rhetorical question begs for a negative answer. Of course, they weren't born slaves. Why, then, had they become **plunder**?

The **lions** of verse 15 referred to Assyria while **Memphis** and **Tahpanhes** in verse 16 were two cities in northeastern Egypt. The **Shihor** in verse 18 referred to a branch of the Nile River in Egypt and **the River** designated the Euphrates in Assyria. This last territory later came under the control of Babylon.

God's people had become vulnerable to these lions because they had forsaken God. They no longer held him in awe. In verse 19, Jeremiah reminded his people that sin is its own executioner. God can and will forgive the guilt of sin, but he doesn't remove it consequences.

2:20–28. Yahweh summarizes Judah's departure from him and their addiction to evil. Judah is like an ox that has broken its **yoke**. They had come to think of the covenant they adopted at Sinai (Exod. 24:3–8) as too restrictive. In Moab the people first encountered Baal worship. In verse 20, Jeremiah spoke of the people's sin as revolting against the lordship of Yahweh, preferring a "marriage" to Baal. The Hebrew word translated "Baal" means "lord" and is often translated "husband." The expression **On every high hill and under every spreading tree you lay down as a prostitute** (v. 20) described Canaanite worship acts. It appealed to the lower nature of those who participated.

Jeremiah, in verse 21, drove home his point with another familiar figure of speech. Vineyards abounded in the country. A century earlier Isaiah (Isa. 5:1–7) pictured Israel as a vineyard from whom the husbandman expected good grapes. At harvest time, however, he found only "stinking" grapes. God had given Israel stability, but they had squandered their heritage.

Judah's guilt was so ingrained that no human cleansing agent could eradicate it (v. 22). The Hebrew word translated **soda** and the one translated **soap** both refer to an alkali or salty chemical used in substances designed to cleanse and remove stain. The nation needed the forgiving work of Yahweh himself!

Anticipating the people's defense (v. 23a) and perhaps having even heard it, Jeremiah refuted their words with additional comments. The direct reply begins in the latter part of verse 23 and continues through verse 25. His reminder to the people of their behavior **in the valley** referred to the Valley of Hinnom. Located south of Jerusalem, this was a place where both Baal and Molech worshippers practiced child sacrifice as a part of their religious rituals. Many people of Judah joined in these sinful practices, especially during Manasseh's reign.

Changing figures of speech, Jeremiah compared Judah to animals in **heat**. This language is brutally frank and may be offensive to some people today, especially if read in public. The Old Testament prophets and other writers were graphic and earthy in their dealing with the matter of sexual relationships.

In verse 26 Jeremiah called the people back to sanity with a sober thought: such conduct brings, to a rational person, humiliation and self-contempt. The text suggests that many people on the king's staff, as well as some of the religious leaders, were participating in the sinful indulgences.

They in verse 27 included those religious leaders, both prophets and priests, who had sold out to the pagan worship. This depiction is strikingly modern. It describes professing Christians today who surrender to a degenerate lifestyle. They come to church on Sunday and pretend to be worshippers of the Lord. This type of religious hypocrisy is as old as time itself.

In verse 28, Jeremiah issued a challenge to the people. In essence, he said, "If the gods you have accepted in Yahweh's place are powerful, why don't they appear now and meet your needs? After all, you have an abundance of them! They average one to a town!" Since Judah had many small villages, that would have been a large number.

2:29–30. The prophet drew his defense to a close with a question and then a pronouncement. His question was, "How dare you accuse me of mistreating or failing you? Actually, you took the first step of misconduct when you dared to oppose me and revolt against my will for your life."

Though God had chastised the people to bring them back to him, they, like the people of Amos's day, refused to return. No amount of reprimanding seemed to be effective against the stubborn people. The people not only refused to heed Yahweh's prophets, but they treated them with more than just disrespect. Like a devouring **lion**—perhaps a reference to Assyria's cruelty—the people heaped physical violence on them. It was bad enough to turn a deaf ear to God's word. To kill the messenger who bears the divine tidings, however, "scrapes the bottom of the barrel" in wickedness. There was little hope for such people.

2:31–37. The remaining words of the prophet in this chapter contain God's final description of Judah's moral depravity. The concluding material of the larger unit (3:1–4:4) presents an open door for Judah to repent and escape the judgment that seemed inevitable.

The three questions in verses 31 and 32 should be understood as rhetorical. They express both surprise and dismay. Jeremiah could not understand why such favored people would turn against the God who had blessed them so bountifully.

In the first question, Jeremiah probably referred to the forty years Israel spent in the **desert.** God forced the people to wander because they lacked faith to move immediately into Canaan. True, God had been forced to discipline them rigorously, but he had not forsaken them. With all the hardships they endured, they were still much better off than during their days of slavery in Egypt. The reward of their patient endurance had been a land of fertile crops and other blessings. They could not claim that God had mistreated them.

The second question implied the people's stupidity. Who in their right mind would prefer a false autonomy to a servant relationship with the God who loved them unreservedly? The freest people in the world are those who choose to obey laws that are designed for their benefit.

The most beautiful of all the images in this section is that of the **bride** and her **jewelry**. In verse 32, the prophet stated an irrefutable fact about young ladies: They love tokens of affection from their sweetheart, groom, or husband. Symbolically, Yahweh had been Israel's groom, but she had **forgotten** every blessing he had sent as a proof of his love. The expression **days without number** means her ingratitude had existed almost continuously since he had given them to her. How could she be so selfish and presumptuous!

According to verse 33, the sinful people had done even worse. Like an unfaithful wife turned into a harlot, the nation had solicited immoral relationships. The prophet even went so far as to say they could give the worst of all women lessons in how to be unfaithful. How much lower could they stoop in sin?

Switching the explicit emphasis, in verse 34 Jeremiah spoke of the people's greed. They had exploited the poor so unmercifully that **the lifeblood of the innocent poor** was on the clothes of those who did the exploiting. The prophet might have even meant to be taken literally since he followed it with a statement, **You did not catch them breaking in**. This was a reference to the Mosaic law. A man could justify killing a person who stole only if he caught him forcing his way into his home (Exod. 22:2).

Verse 34 closes with a fresh charge that continues into verse 35. Jeremiah pointed out that the people had refused to accept responsibility for their wrong deeds. They insisted God was not displeased with them. But verse 35 closes with the prophet's sharp reply. He refuted their claim of immunity to punishment because they had **not sinned**. Punishment would come from God whether they believed it or not.

The prophet had one final word of condemnation and warning. Verses 36 and 37 contain a rhetorical question, followed by a divine pronouncement. Jeremiah did not actually expect an answer to his probing inquiry. He was amazed that the people had not learned a lesson from the failure of **Assyria** to be their true ally in previous days. He warned they would be as disenchanted and frustrated by the inability and unwillingness of **Egypt** to help. When would they learn the other nations only "used them" and never intended to give them any kind of freedom!

Jeremiah warned the people that Egypt would disappoint them just as Assyria had done in a previous century. Scholars differ on the significance of **with your hands on your head**. Some contend it was a position the people would assume as they went into Babylonian captivity. Others insist it was the indication of mourning and shame for having done a foolish thing.

The Babylonians did as the Assyrians did: they treated their captives harshly. But Jeremiah seems to be referring to embarrassment and disappointment rather than physical suffering in this passage. His point was the folly of making alliances with other nations. This action meant a failure to trust Yahweh and a lack of commitment to his moral demands.

Those who ignore the resources God offers and seek for aid elsewhere will come away empty handed. Perhaps Jeremiah still had in mind the "swift she-camel running here and there" (2:23). God's people in every generation need to learn that God is "a rewarder of them that diligently seek him" (Heb. 11:6 KJV).

☒ Plea for the People to Repent (3:1–4:4)

> **SUPPORTING IDEA:** *Judah's only hope for deliverance is to forsake her sinful lifestyle and come back to God.*

3:1. This section begins the second main division of Jeremiah's "inaugural sermon" to Judah. In the first (2:1–37), the prophet portrayed Judah's moral corruption. He said little about a return to Yahweh. In this chapter and continuing through verse 4 of the next chapter, he issued a call for the people to repent and turn back to the Lord. This verse gives an illustration that, though interpreted a bit differently by various students, make his case clearly. God is ready, even eager, to receive the people if they will **return** to him.

According to Deuteronomy 24:1–4, if a man divorced his wife, he forfeited his right to remarry her if she married another man. This was true even if she later became marriageable through the death of her second husband or if he divorced her. After quoting the Deuteronomic law, Jeremiah made a statement or asked a question, depending on the way one translates the Hebrew text.

At first reading of Jeremiah's words, one would be inclined to conclude consistency with the analogy meant Judah could not return to Yahweh. This, however, was not what Jeremiah meant. To say Judah cannot return to Yahweh would make all the future invitations of the prophet inappropriate. Indeed Jeremiah pleaded with Israel to do this very thing: Come back to your Lord!

The laws of Israel gave the woman no right to sue for a divorce. This was only the man's prerogative, and the requirements were simple: he could put her away for any unseemly act (and many of the rabbis were quite liberal in interpreting that word *unseemly*). God had not initiated the "divorce" with his people even though they had forfeited their rights to the marriage relationship by their sinful conduct. God had a right to extend grace and mercy, which he did.

Understood in this light, we understand this passage as a compassionate appeal to the people. They are guilty, but Yahweh is merciful. He is waiting to see the first sign of repentance. If they will take one step toward him, he will take ten steps toward them.

3:2–5. In these verses Jeremiah brought three facts before the people in an effort to show that they needed to repent and seek the Lord. Individually, each fact should have been convincing. Taken together, they left the people without excuse.

In verse 2, Jeremiah called on the people to observe **the land**. All the unproductive and fruitless hills testified of the immoral excesses in which the people had engaged. The evidence could be seen all around. Shrines existed everywhere, indicating the people had engaged in the kind of immoral rites practiced by the Baal cult. The lifestyle resembled the Arabs who waited in ambush to attack a trade caravan. The difference was that the people of Israel were **waiting** to engage in an adulterous relationship with a prostitute of Baal worship.

The parallel is not exact, of course, since the prostitutes were willing to engage in the sex acts. It was the major part of their profession. Jeremiah insisted that behavior such as this **defiled** the land.

The prophet's second affirmation (v. 3) dealt with the drought that Yahweh had sent as a disciplinary action. A number of Old Testament passages emphasize that God frequently withheld **rains** to register his disapproval of his people's conduct.

The water of the land consisted mainly of two rainy seasons, one in the fall and another in the **spring**. They are usually referred to as the "early rains" and the "latter rains" or "later rains." The early rains produced the firstfruits of the land, celebrated by the Feast of Pentecost, fifty days after Passover. The later rains produced the usually abundant fall harvest, celebrated at the Feast of Tabernacles. In verse 3, **the showers** probably refers to the early or fall rains that were usually lighter than those in the spring.

If either of these rains failed to materialize, a crisis occurred. If both failed in the same year, the land was in serious trouble. On such an occasion, the religious leaders usually called a special day for prayer and fasting as a symbol of repentance for wrongdoing.

Such a situation had occurred in Jeremiah's day, perhaps more than once. But rather than showing any sign of sorrow for their sins, the people remained unconcerned. The irony was that participation in the fertility cult rituals was supposed to produce the rains that ensured an abundant harvest. This was the reason Jeremiah expressed their unconcern by describing them as having the **brazen look of a prostitute**. They were incapable of registering any shame by such a simple thing as blushing. They had no consciousness of sin.

This attitude led the prophet, in verses 4–5, to present his third fact that served as a demand for repentance. Their relationship with God consisted of overemphasizing his unconditional love. They heaped up words of praise for him, assuring themselves that he accepted them as they were and, therefore, demanded no change in their lifestyle. Soon he would reverse himself and send blessings rather than adversities.

3:6–18. For some reason the prophet seems to have interrupted his sermon with a "side reference" to the Northern Kingdom (Israel). According to an earlier record in Scripture, these ten tribes were virtually destroyed and taken into captivity (2 Kgs. 17:1–40). Yet Jeremiah seems to speak as though they were still in existence.

In verses 6–10, Jeremiah addressed the Southern Kingdom (Judah) with words describing Israel's conduct and her refusal to repent and return to him. The prophet's message was, in essence, "Judah should have profited from witnessing the sin of Israel and the doom to which it led that kingdom."

Unfortunately Judah had learned nothing from the example of those who sinned and incurred God's punishment. Jeremiah did admit that Judah took a superficial step toward repentance, but he stated frankly that it was not sincere and won no favor with God. Could Jeremiah have been speaking of the revival in the days of Hezekiah? Was he suggesting the people never actually took those reforms seriously or they would not have reverted so quickly to pagan worship under Manasseh?

Verse 11 serves as a transition from Jeremiah's condemnation of Judah for learning nothing from Israel's moral failure. His contention was that Judah had the example of Israel to observe and was, therefore, more guilty than her sister kingdom. This statement may have been designed as "shock therapy" for Judah. It might perhaps serve as a means of leading the people to repentance. It also served as a basis for another appeal to the remnant of Israel left in the land and also to those in captivity. God still had a future for them if they were willing to turn to him. Verses 12–18, though addressed to the Northern Kingdom, contain a promise to both divisions of the once united monarchy. They could experience forgiveness and enjoy reunification.

In verse 12, the word **return** could be considered as having a strong imperative thrust. The expression that follows, **faithless Israel**, argues strongly for this interpretation. But the two promises that follow soften the command into more of an invitation. First, the Lord through his prophet promised he would no longer show a disapproving spirit toward Judah. Second, he would not remain enraged or infuriated toward them. Why? Because Yahweh is compassionate. He delights in forgiving his people.

Verse 13, however, contains the requirement for receiving the grace God offered. No cheap grace! No simplistic solution! God is Father, but he is not a doting grandfather who refuses to discipline his offspring and lead them to repentance. What had the people done for which they needed to repent? Jeremiah named three sins, but the first is actually the cause, the other two are the results.

First, the people had demonstrated a spirit of insubordination. Most versions translate the Hebrew word as **rebelled**. Two other excellent renderings are "revolted" and "trespassed." The Hebrew verb used here is probably the strongest word in the Hebrew language for wrongdoing or sinning against God.

Second, the result of such conduct was the confusion of one's priorities. This, in turn, led to giving allegiance to those things that were opposed to all that God commanded. Jeremiah's words mirrored the Canaanite sexual orgies with the expression **scattered your favors to foreign gods**. He then detailed it further with explicit language as he said **under every spreading tree**. He came only a bit short of actually using sexual language. This would not have been inappropriate since physical immorality was the essence of Canannite worship.

Third, these things resulted in the people's failure to observe the guidelines and keep the commandments God had given them. The prophet described it succinctly with the simple words, **have not obeyed me**.

Did Jeremiah actually travel to the Northern Kingdom and speak to those remaining in the land who had not been deported by Assyria? Did he contact some who had been exiled to distant lands? Either is possible. But most interpreters believe he spoke rhetorically to them through his words to Judah.

No matter which interpretation we accept, one thing is likely: Beginning with verse 14 and continuing through verse 18, Jeremiah spoke God's message to both groups, Israel and Judah. Though the situation had never looked darker, Jeremiah refused to lose faith for the future of both nations. He changed the object of his address from **Return, faithless Israel** to **Return, faithless people**. He meant to include both groups, all God's people.

In the Hebrew text the words translated **faithless people** read literally "backsliding sons" or "faithless children." The verb *turn* and the adjective *backsliding* have the same root. It means "to turn or return." This is a wordplay in the Hebrew that is difficult to express in the English language.

The Hebrew text also reads literally, "I, I am your Lord." When the personal pronoun occurs in addition to being in the verb stem, it emphasizes the pronoun. A good translation would be "I, myself, am Lord over you."

The word translated **husband** is also a wordplay in the Hebrew language. It means husband, and it also means lord or master. Using the word *Baal* as a verb, God was saying through his prophet, "I am both your husband and your Lord." The One who called Israel to be his bride is her Lord. Israel is Yahweh's servant but a servant whom he loves with the love a devoted husband has for his wife.

The **one from a town and two from a clan** (v. 14) should not be considered mathematically as though choosing representatives to a congress. The words suggest an exile. The Northern Kingdom was already in exile though a few people remained in the land. Jeremiah anticipated an exile of the Southern Kingdom, even this early in his ministry.

Jeremiah's words about the bringing of a few people from each district and family emphasized the doctrine of "a remnant shall return." Isaiah had preached this promise more than a century before. He had even given one of his sons that name (Isa. 7:3). Both of these great prophets were convinced that judgment would come to their nation. But they both preached just as strongly another important truth: God would still accomplish his redemptive work through his chosen channel, the descendants of Abraham and David.

In verse 15, Jeremiah gave one word about the restored people's future leaders. The word **shepherds** comes from a verb that means primarily "to feed" and was used for those who pastured a flock. The verb also meant "to lead, rule, govern." This word was used not only in the sense of spiritual guidance but also was applied to political rulers. In this sense these men were responsible for encouraging those whom they governed. One of Israel's problems through the years was the lack of leaders with integrity who had the best interest of their people at heart.

Verses 16–18 form a unit. Most Old Testament students agree they point to a time after the days of Jeremiah. But they disagree sharply about their meaning. Before one attempts to interpret the verses, he should look at what Jeremiah said to his audience.

In verse 16, Jeremiah stated the time as being **when your numbers have increased greatly in the land**. This would refer to the Jews and would obviously be after the return from the Babylonian captivity. The prophet did not say how great the increase would be, nor did he say how long after the return. But he did say that **the ark of the covenant** would cease to be of importance to the people. No one knows what happened to the ark of the covenant when the temple was burned by the Babylonians in 586 B.C.

In verse 17, Jeremiah stated, **They will call Jerusalem The Throne of the LORD**. "They" most likely refers to the Jews—at least those who heard Jeremiah speak would certainly have interpreted his words that way. But Jeremiah followed with two other affirmations. First, **all nations will gather in Jerusalem to honor the name of the LORD**. Second, they will no longer **follow the stubbornness of their evil hearts**. This "they" probably refers to the nations although it could include the Jews as well.

In verse 18, Jeremiah saw a merging of the two major groups of Jews existing in his day. He describes them as both coming from **a northern land** to the land God gave their **forefathers as an inheritance**.

Jeremiah prefaced all these remarks in verses 16–18 with a fresh affirmation. These statements are from the Lord. Translators render the prophet's words, **declares the LORD**. This comes from a Hebrew expression recognized as the strongest prophetic formula in the Old Testament. Some scholars render it, "oracle of the Lord."

Those who lived during Jeremiah's day would, if they seriously considered his message, have seen it as applying to national Israel. God will, even yet, restore the glory of the Davidic days. He called Abraham and promised to bless his seed and to bless all peoples through Abraham's seed. Nothing will thwart that plan.

As to the long-range significance of this passage, serious students of the prophet are divided. One group has a viewpoint that closely resembles that of national Israel during Jeremiah's day. The only difference is they immerse it into the Christian message. According to this viewpoint, when Jesus returns, the Christian community or church will be taken out of the world. A messianic kingdom will be established on earth.

The other school of thought sees passages such as this one and contends the promises to national Israel were fulfilled in Jesus Christ. Christians today are spiritual Israel. No other name but Jesus has been given whereby people can be saved.

Jeremiah believed in a glorious future for God's people. Yahweh would not forsake his redemptive program for the world because of their shortcomings. The same truth is still with us today. God will continue with his plans, with us if we permit, without us if we insist.

3:19–4:4. At this point Jeremiah returns to the thought from 3:5. In verse 19, God is the speaker. He maintains he would **gladly** give the people all the blessings they desired. One requirement they have overlooked: they must remain faithful to him. This included, of course, repenting of their sins and refraining from future defections.

In verse 20, however, the prophet came back to one of his earlier contentions and charges. He once more compared the people's conduct to that of an immoral wife. Jeremiah, in verse 21, suddenly seemed to interrupt the thought. He referred to a noise he heard in the distant hills. People were crying and lifting their voices in entreaty. Why this sudden outpour of concern? Jeremiah said, **because they have perverted their ways and have forgotten the LORD their God**. At first reading one assumes this is a picture of genuine repentance. But further study of the following verses raises a question about exactly what Jeremiah meant.

Was the prophet describing what he actually heard? Was he stating an ideal situation that he urged the people to accept? Did he hear the people crying to the false gods to deliver them? All three suggestions have been offered.

Old Testament students disagree about what Jeremiah meant when they read his sharp words in verse 22. The prophet called the people **faithless** and demanded that they return to Yahweh. In the same verse they then replied to his demand, assuring the Lord they would return to him.

Who is speaking in verse 23? Are the people admitting their Baal worship is a false approach to true religion? Since verses 24 and 25 seem to continue the people's repentance and confession of their wrongdoing, this seems to be the case. Yet the first four verses of chapter 4, which close this section, contain words that express the prophet's doubt. He indicates they need to realize that repentance must be sincere to be meaningful and effective.

However one interprets this section, he will have reputable and dependable scholars giving support. One of the best discussions of the options in interpretation of these verses is given by F. B. Huey Jr. in *Jeremiah, Lamentations,* in The New American Commentary. After listing five possible ways of viewing these verses, he concludes with an excellent summary:

> The Israelites seemed to be admitting everything God wanted to hear—that their idol worship had been a deception and that salvation was found only in the Lord (3:23). From their "youth" (when the covenant was established at Sinai) they had wasted their resources of cattle, grain, and even their children as useless sacrifices to their "shameful gods." The people appeared to be taking full responsibility for their folly and disobedience. "Let us lie down in our shame" suggests they were overwhelmed by guilt. If these words had been an expression of sincere repentance and return to God, the rest of Jeremiah's ministry would have been unnecessary. True repentance requires admission of sin but more than that. There must be sorrow for the sin (Ps. 51:17) and genuine turning away from it (Jas. 2:4).

In 4:1–2 we see God's insight. He recognized the people's feigned repentance. In verse 1, God insisted only if they turned away from their disgusting idol worship would he accept their actions as genuine. To God these sexual orgies connected with the worship were detestable. Uncleanness, especially in the sexual realm, is as far from God's holiness as one can fall.

The prophet emphasized other requirements for a godly life (v. 2). They dealt more with the ethical nature of Yahweh's demands. The three adjectives, **truthful, just and righteous**, occur many times in the Old Testament. They combine to define the character required for a covenant relationship with Yahweh.

The fact that a person lives a clean sexual life does not permit him to be greedy, manipulative, and overbearing in other areas of life. Pure religion is not only keeping oneself free from the taints of sexual impurity. It also involves showing compassion to the weak and equal justice to everyone (Jas. 1:27). We cannot separate these two sets of virtues. Repentance involves the whole person.

Jeremiah closed this lengthy discourse with a twofold metaphor describing true repentance (4:3–4). He addressed it to **the men of Judah and to Jerusalem**. It was an urgent call and the final one from an enthusiastic young preacher. Yet its truth applies to any audience in any situation in any century.

First, Jeremiah turned the people's attention to agriculture. The Hebrew word translated **unplowed ground** refers to land first broken up—virgin soil. Ground that had been previously tilled and cultivated contained thorns and thistles. The custom was to collect and burn the thorns after the harvest. The next year, when a new crop was planted, sowing preceded plowing.

Judah's previous "religious field" was so infested with thorn seeds of evil deeds that her only hope was to reclaim new ground. The nation's future was threatened by the legacy of its past. Only a radically new beginning would save Judah. Unfortunately, even the national collapse and the Babylonian exile were inadequate. Jeremiah saw later that only a new covenant had the dynamic required to fill the vacuum and meet the need (31:31–34).

Second, Jeremiah used a ritual with which the people were familiar—circumcision of the males. The prophet injected a new meaning into this custom. God did not give Abram this ancient symbol as just an outward sign. It was the witness to an inward reality—the removal of the hardened matter around the heart. The Hebrew word usually translated "heart" referred not to the emotion, intellect, or will alone. It stood for the totality of a person's inner life.

In the closing part of verse 4, Jeremiah issued a solemn warning about the consequences that would come to the nation if its disobedience continued. Throughout both the Old and New Testaments, God's prophets often described God's judgment in terms of **fire**. Sometimes, of course, it was purifying in nature and resulted in cleansing so that pure service would be forthcoming. With Israel this was always God's purpose and hope. Individuals, nevertheless, were consumed in it. This would happen to many people in Jeremiah's day.

> **MAIN IDEA REVIEW:** *Jeremiah depicted Judah's defection from God and pointed out that a bride always remembers the early days of her love and marriage. Judah should feel that way and return to her husband, Yahweh.*

III. CONCLUSION

In Spite of Everything, God Still Loves

Jeremiah never met the prophet Hosea in the flesh. But he was greatly influenced by this eighth-century prophet. The latter's domestic tragedy served as the major motivation for his ministry. If, as one student suggested, Hosea's ministry was a "succession of sobs," Jeremiah's became a "tunnel of tears."

The parallels between this inaugural sermon of Jeremiah and Hosea's call to ancient Israel are amazing. They include not only religious concepts but literary form and structure as well.

What was the one thing these two men of God shared above all others? The assurance of God's love, as voiced by the apostle Paul, centuries later: "God demonstrates his own love for us in this: While we were still sinners, Christ died for us" (Rom. 5:8).

The young preacher who delivered this sermon recorded in 2:1–4:4 grew and matured in his ministry, but two things he never lost—his hatred of sin and his love for the sinner. From the beginning of his ministry until its conclusion, more than forty years later, Jeremiah never changed. He begged, pleaded, and exhorted his fellow countrymen to repent and come back to the God of their youth. He would have agreed completely with one modern preacher who said, "If you feel God is not as close to you as he once was, which one do you think has moved?"

PRINCIPLES

- New converts and young believers often are fervent in their love, devotion, and obedience to the Lord.

- When you follow what is worthless, you become worthless.

- The Lord holds priests, teachers, and prophets—those who are responsible to guide his people—accountable.

- Turning from the Lord and seeking a substitute for him is sin.

- No person can remove his own guilt before God, no matter how hard he tries.

- People's sins keep them from experiencing God's blessings.

- Religious talk does not justify evil actions.

- For sinners to return to the Lord, they must acknowledge their guilt and rebellion.

APPLICATIONS

- Make a comparison of your love, devotion, and obedience to the Lord now and when you were a new convert.

- Consider your current pursuits and evaluate them as to whether they are highly worthwhile or worthless.

- Tell a fellow believer of responsibilities for which you believe God will hold you accountable.

- List persons you can turn to when you need help.

- Evaluate you friendships in terms of whether they are bringing you closer to God or causing you to compromise your relationship with God.

- Describe any barriers you now feel between God and yourself that prevent God's blessing in your life.

- Recall times when you have used religious language as a cover up for wrong actions or motives. Acknowledge this to God.

- As you tell God of ways you have sinned against him, hear and trust wholeheartedly his word of mercy and forgiveness to you.

IV. LIFE APPLICATION

From Newlyweds to Divorce Court

Kate Chopin's opening scene in her 1899 novel *The Awakening* is of a caged parrot that kept repeating over and over *"Allez vous-en! Allez vous-en! Sapristi!"* ("Get out! Get out! For God's sake!"). One soon learns the caged bird is symbolic of Edna Pontellier, an attractive young woman married to a successful businessman and caring husband.

Edna soon tired of the responsibilities of motherhood, marriage, and the fashionable lifestyle provided by her husband and allowed her erotic desires to blossom. She went from one disastrous affair to another, seeking freedom and fulfillment. Religious activity became oppressive, restrictive, and stifling. She became more and more restless as she sensed life was passing her by.

In the end, rejected by the man she desired and in continued rebellion against the tyranny of social boundaries, Edna cut off all hope for herself and committed suicide by swimming out into the ocean. Among her last thoughts were that no one "could possess her, body and soul," and that she possessed "the courageous soul that dares and defies."

Edna Pontellier is not unique. She stands in a long line of wayward, wandering, betraying, and philandering spouses—from Potiphar's wife to Hosea's wife Gomer and beyond. These women closely parallel the figure of Judah in Jeremiah 2–3, who moved from being a loving newlywed bride to one who strayed from her loving husband.

Whether in cases of physical or spiritual adultery, what is needed is spiritual restoration. Such spiritual restoration begins with the desire to return. It includes acknowledging one's guilt and rebellion (3:13). But it involves more than just words. It involves action—"if you will return . . . return to me" (4:1). The conditional nature of Jeremiah's sentence leaves the action necessary to initiate renewal of the relationship with the one who has departed from the relationship. It involves repenting, returning, and committing to no longer go astray.

There are no guarantees that a broken relationship will be restored to what it was before—or even to better than what it was before—there is only the guarantee of cleansing and forgiveness for those who return to the Lord with all their heart and cleave to him only. To repent and return or not to repent and return was up to Judah—and it is up to us.

V. PRAYER

O my Divine Lover, our heavenly Spouse, forgive our straying heart and feet. Forgive us for our willfulness, waywardness, and wandering. Cleanse us from the pollution and defilement of our debauchery. Awaken and restore our love for you, and embrace us in your tender arms so that we stray no more. O thou Eternal Lover of our souls, cure our backsliding and grant us the peace and rest of being faithful to you. Amen.

VI. DEEPER DISCOVERIES

A. "Holy to the Lord" (2:3)

The basic idea of the word *holy* or *holiness* came from the verb that originally meant to cut off, separate, devote, consecrate. Like so many words, both verbs and nouns, it derived its broader meanings from the situations and contexts where it was used.

In the Bible *holy* has four distinct meanings. First, it depicts "to be set apart." This referred to any place God dwelt or was present, such as the temple and tabernacle. It applied also to things and persons related to these places and to God himself.

Second, *holy* designates persons or things free from pollution or impurity. This leads to the idea of spiritually superior to or above and, therefore, summoning, eliciting, or inspiring praise, awe, or reverence. The concept pertains primarily to God but also to godly people. This is the reason we today call an especially godly person a saint or holy person.

A third suggestion in the word is that of something or somebody who commands great awe, even fright, almost beyond belief. This is primarily a part of the application when people consider God as so terrible in majesty that they cringe before him in terror.

This idea leads to the final meaning of holiness—to be filled with superhuman and potential power to exert totality on a person or thing. Fire is the symbol of God's holiness. Related to it closely are jealousy, wrath, remoteness, purity, majesty, and glory.

In a special sense, Jeremiah considered Israel as dedicated to God. Since Yahweh was "other than," Israel must also place herself in that category. This meant the people were under Yahweh's personal protection and those who opposed them faced danger, even doom.

B. "The prophets prophesied by Baal" (2:8)

When the Israelites invaded Canaan under Joshua's leadership, they encountered a new phenomenon. The Hebrews had spent forty years in the region of Sinai, wandering and worshipping their God Yahweh. The code of conduct was strict. Their sexual life was rooted in fidelity to marriage vows and family life.

The Canaanite religion was diametrically opposed to that of Yahweh. The people of Canaan, agriculturally oriented, depended on plentiful and fruitful crops. They needed proper weather, including sufficient rainfall. To secure an abundant harvest in the spring and fall, they participated in rituals that symbolized life and fertility. A major part of their worship ceremonies consisted of securing the approval of the Baals or lords of fertility.

The men engaged in sexual relations with women dedicated to this pagan concept of worship. Then they gave a fee to the women, which was turned in to the Baal religious hierarchy or priests. This was supposed to assure them of a bountiful harvest.

How did the Israelites respond to this religion? It "caught on" quickly. The fact that it appealed to their lower nature and lustful impulses heightened and enhanced its appeal. Best of all, they could "worship" at any time and at any spot they chose. For centuries Yahweh worship competed with Baal rituals and ceremonies, but Baal increased in popularity. At times Baal almost drove out all loyalty to Yahweh.

True prophets of Yahweh stood aghast at such practices. Wicked kings silenced the prophets with royal decrees, but for some this was unnecessary. Both prophets and priests voluntarily joined the apostasy from Yahweh. They reveled in the material benefits it produced when combined with what had been true Yahweh worship. These religious orgies so contaminated the Northern Kingdom that God commissioned Assyria to decimate the land.

Judah almost suffered the same fate at the hands of Assyria, but God gave the Southern Kingdom one more chance. Jeremiah was the last prophetic voice to speak to God's people. He condemned the sin of Baalism and pleaded with the people to put away this moral cancer and turn back to Yahweh.

C. Cisterns (2:13)

Since Palestine had limited rainfall, storage of this precious resource was essential. The large number of cisterns that exist in the land today give evidence of the effort to conserve surface water.

The Hebrew language contains a word that means "hole," "pit," or more often "well." We often cannot distinguish between the terms *cistern* and *well*. The Palestinian cistern was usually a bottle-shaped or a pear-shaped reservoir. Water could drain into it from a roof, tunnel, or yard. One problem encountered was the spongy or absorbent limestone out of which cisterns were dug. It allowed much of the water to escape.

Archaeological records indicate the people began to plaster the cisterns a short time before 1000 B.C., giving a more efficient way of storing water. Sometimes they covered the mouths of cisterns with stones, often adding crude filters to trap the debris.

Jeremiah's hearers understood easily his symbol in 2:13. Every property owner wanted to have a flowing spring on his property. This would relieve him of the task of digging a cistern in the limestone hills and plastering the inside. Besides, even if he made a cistern, it could develop cracks and leak water, leaving him without this life-giving resource.

Yahweh was the divine spring that gave living water. But the people rejected him and turned to worthless substitutes that left them with unmet physical and spiritual needs.

VII. TEACHING OUTLINE

A. INTRODUCTION

1. Lead Story: Emma and Charles

2. Context: In the early years of his ministry, probably during King Josiah's reign, Jeremiah denounced Judah for her sin. Chapters 1–6 probably were originally a separate scroll that circulated independently before being incorporated into the Book of Jeremiah as we have it today. This section is an emotionally charged call from the young prophet for the people to forsake their wicked ways and return to the Lord.

3. Transition: Likening himself to a loving and faithful husband and Judah to a bride, the Lord accused the nation of adultery. She had turned to other nations as her suitors and played the harlot with the debauched Baal worship of the land. After making his charges against Judah, the Lord brought forth his evidence to prove his case. Finally the Lord appealed to his wayward wife, pleading with her to repent, to turn from her sinful ways, and to return to him. If she would do this, he would forgive, cleanse, and restore her.

B. COMMENTARY
1. Description of the People's Depravity (2:1–37)
2. Plea for the People to Repent (3:1–4:4)

C. CONCLUSION: IN SPITE OF EVERYTHING, GOD STILL LOVES

VIII. ISSUES FOR DISCUSSION

1. Describe the love relationship between newlyweds. How can the first love of marriage partners be preserved and extended?
2. What stages do marriages go through? How important is faithfulness in a marriage? What are the similarities between physical adultery and spiritual adultery?
3. If God were to bring charges against you in a court of law, what would they be? If God were to bring charges against today's church in a court of law, what would they be?
4. Why do we fail to learn from the examples of others who have experienced God's judgment?
5. What is the cure for backsliding? What are the steps of repentance? What role does confession of sin and acknowledgment of guilt have in repentance?

Jeremiah 4:5–6:30

God's Chastising Punishment

I. INTRODUCTION
The Lions Are Coming! The Lions Are Coming!

II. COMMENTARY
A verse-by-verse explanation of these verses.

III. CONCLUSION
The Debasing Power of Sin

An overview of the principles and applications from these verses.

IV. LIFE APPLICATION
Here I Stand!

Melding these verses to life.

V. PRAYER
Tying these verses to life with God.

VI. DEEPER DISCOVERIES
Historical, geographical, and grammatical enrichment of the commentary.

VII. TEACHING OUTLINE
Suggested step-by-step group study of these verses.

VIII. ISSUES FOR DISCUSSION
Zeroing these verses in on daily life.

"*If* gold rust, what shall iron do?

For if a priest be foul, in whom we trust,

No wonder that a sinful man will rust."

Chaucer

Jeremiah 4:5–6:30

IN A NUTSHELL

Having spoken as a husband to his errant wife in chapters 2–3, God now declares war on Judah. In chapters 4–6 he warns that invaders are advancing and calls upon the people to flee from the coming disaster. In these chapters both God and Jeremiah speak. The prophet agonizes over the wickedness, evil, and moral and religious corruption that abounds in his society, and he writhes in pain over the judgment God is about to bring upon it (4:19). Yet the people refuse to return to walking in God's ways or to listen to the prophetic warning (6:16–17). The Lord has rejected them (6:30).

God's Chastising Punishment

I. INTRODUCTION

The Lions Are Coming! The Lions Are Coming!

*T*hrough the movie *The Ghost and the Darkness,* American moviegoers became familiar with the story of the race to build a railroad across Africa and what happened in 1898 when two man-eating lions slaughtered 135 Indian workers in Tsavo, East Africa.

In one scene, after a brutal attack by the lions, the railway station is jammed with workers. A train has pulled into the station, but you can hardly tell it's a train. All you can see are workers climbing on the train. As the train pulls out of the station, more and more workers chase after it. Many are pulled onto the train by those already aboard. The roofs of the flatcars are full of people. Everyone is leaving!

Such is the response that Jeremiah's message in 4:6–6:30 should have created. Jeremiah alerted his people, "A lion has come out of his lair; a destroyer of nations has set out. He has left his place to lay waste your land. Your towns will lie in ruins without inhabitants" (4:7). Again Jeremiah warned, "A lion from the forest will attack" (5:6). Therefore, he proclaimed, "Let us flee to the fortified cities!" (4:5). But the people of Jeremiah's day were not as wise as the workers of Tsavo. They persisted in what they were doing and refused to heed Jeremiah's warning.

God declared war (chs. 4–6)! Invaders were coming! Evil, wickedness, and moral corruption had spread through all levels and classes of society: the king and royal officials, priests and prophets, the great and the poor. Thus God announced he would pour out his wrath on the children, the young men, husbands and wives, and even the old (6:11).

When moral evil infects any culture, society, or nation, the people should be prepared for the word of warning that comes from the Lord: The lions are coming! The lions are coming!

II. COMMENTARY

God's Chastising Punishment

> **MAIN IDEA:** *The people of Israel and Judah needed to sound the alarm that an enemy was on the way that would devastate the land. God would send this destroying enemy because his people had forsaken him and adopted a lifestyle that conflicted with his will for them.*

A Disaster Is on the Way (4:5–31)

> **SUPPORTING IDEA:** *God warned the people, through his prophet, to take refuge from the avenger he had chosen to be his executioner of a sinful people.*

4:5–9. This section introduces ninety-two verses of passionate warnings and pleadings of Jeremiah to the people of Judah and the remnant of Israel. This prophetic material is almost entirely in poetry. It contains vivid imagery and the traditional Hebrew parallelism. Jeremiah spoke as though the invader was almost literally at the door, ready to break it down. We sense the panic of a young man who senses that devastation of his nation is imminent.

Most Old Testament interpreters feel certain that Jeremiah, fresh from his call experience, was still visibly moved by his vision of the "boiling pot" (1:13–15). In that earlier encounter with Yahweh, Jeremiah saw the cauldron "tilting away from the north." He also heard the Lord say, "From the north disaster will be poured out on all who live in the land. I am about to summon all the peoples of the northern kingdoms." Yahweh said further that their kings would set up seats of government and rulership at the entrances of Jerusalem's gates. In addition to attacking the capital's walls, they would destroy all the smaller towns in the surrounding area.

In verse 5, Jeremiah called upon those responsible for warning the people to **sound the trumpet throughout the land!** He followed with a command to **raise the signal to go to Zion!** The horn was used to summon the people to worship or to flee for safety. The context indicates that this order was given because the people were in danger. An enemy was on the way. When the shofar sounded, the people knew immediately that a state of emergency existed. The people would quickly seek safety behind the walls of their **fortified cities**.

In verse 6, the Hebrew word translated **signal** can also be rendered "standard." We cannot be sure to which the prophet referred. It might have referred to a fire signal that was lit on a hill to transmit news of an emergency to areas farther "up the country." This type of communication was used before better means of communication were established. Archaeologists have found in the ruins of Lachish, a city in southern Judah, a message that reads: "We are watching for the signals of Lachish according to all the indications which my lord has given for we cannot see Azekah." This was dated about the time of Nebuchadnezzar's third invasion when these two cities were still standing (Thompson, 220).

Jeremiah's language shows how serious he considered the crisis. He used nine verbs as imperatives in staccato-like fashion. This was more than the overreaction of a youthful preacher. A crisis was at hand, and God had sent his prophet to warn the people.

The enemy is further described in verses 7–8. Jeremiah uses the figure of predatory animals to convey how cruel the invader would be. Lions were often associated with Assyria. But reference to the **lion** doesn't assure that Assyria was the enemy Jeremiah had in mind. Other powers were on the scene that could have easily done the job. Jeremiah's advice to the people in verse 8 was not only to repent but to put on garments indicating their change of heart. The coarse cloth used as a garment for mourners was usually worn on the hips or under the garments.

4:10–12. These verses contain dialogue between the prophet and Yahweh. Students disagree about the proper way to interpret Jeremiah's boldness in his confrontations with the Lord. But our own personal experiences convince us he was no different from us. He was merely bold and honest enough to vocalize his questioning of how God runs the universe.

When Jeremiah accused God of deceiving the people (v. 10), did he express his own feelings or what he had heard the people say? Some interpreters even contend he was quoting what the false prophets were saying. These spiritual advisors who had sold out to evil had been assuring the people that everything was fine. They had been declaring that **peace** was present when Jeremiah knew danger lurked in every place.

Verses 11–12 continue the transition and dialogue. Most students agree that Yahweh speaks at this point with a forecast of what the people could expect. The wind that would come against the people would not be the kind that separated the chaff from the wheat at harvest time. Neither was it designed to purify the air or refine the people. It would be like the deadly sirocco. That wind often lasted for a week or two and devastated everything. In other words, things would not get better, only worse.

4:13–18. In verse 13, the prophet called on the people to see the enemy coming quickly like a swift hurricane. These invaders rode animals that were moving faster than birds of the heaven. After shouting a pessimistic word of alarm, he called on the people to make a deathbed repentance in order to escape the certain doom. The expression **wash the evil** is a figure of speech for a genuine change of heart leading to a new lifestyle.

Jeremiah issued a dramatic monologue as he announced the direction from which God's avenging agent would come. The tribe of Dan was originally placed by Joshua in the southern part of Palestine in the general vicinity of the Philistines. Not able to cope with these fierce people, Dan had later relocated. At the time Jeremiah spoke, **Dan** lay at the northern extreme of Palestine. The prophet, in his dramatic vision, called on a runner to move southward and announce the coming foe. With a little creative imagination, one can envision the enemy striking first at Dan, descending from the Golan Heights, and pressing on to Mount Ephraim. This was the territory stretching from Shechem to Bethel. Soon the enemy would reach the province of Judah and descend on Jerusalem.

What had brought this terrible calamity on the land? The answer is so obvious we almost stumble on its simplicity. The people had forsaken God and turned to their own sinful desires.

4:19–22. Scattered throughout the Book of Jeremiah are a number of passages scholars have labeled the "Confessions of Jeremiah." They deal with the inner life of the prophet. These passages contain words Jeremiah spoke to Yahweh in his moments of anguish, when he felt overwhelmed. These verses are considered by a few scholars as one of his "confessions." More will be said about the "confessions" when we consider the material in 11:18–12:6.

The first few verses are a "refined translation" of the Hebrew text. The literal reading is "My bowels, my bowels." The Hebrew word translated **anguish** meant "intestines, bowels, gut, belly, womb, viscera." In a number of cultures of that day, the seat of emotion and affection was located here and in the kidneys rather than in the heart. In Hebrew thinking, the heart was the seat of intelligence and will rather than the emotional part of a person's nature.

Having heard the **battle cry** and a noise indicating the invading army was on the way, Jeremiah saw nothing but catastrophe for his people. He knew everything in sight would soon be destroyed unless someone or something intervened. He considered that unlikely. So he posed a question to Yahweh. He needed assurance from his Lord. God responded but not in the way his prophet hoped. His voice rose above the noise of approaching tumult.

The grammatical structure shows the emphasis. The literal Hebrew text reads, "Me, they do not know." When a person "knew" God, this fact touched the whole personality and lifestyle. It influences and even permeates every part—mind, emotion, and will. The people of that day had only a superficial understanding of God's holiness. Their skills consisted of performing **evil**. They knew nothing of practicing moral and ethical deeds. Behind the coming judgment were ignorance and stupidity. All the suffering they were about to experience would be appropriate and deserved.

4:23–26. These four verses are one of the most graphic and powerful descriptions of God's avenging hand in the Bible. It reveals the outpouring of divine anger at whatever opposes and slanders God's holy character. Having described the moral and spiritual deterioration of the people, Jeremiah turned to the physical world. In a vision he saw the entire cosmos had reverted to chaos, the inevitable result of its evil. He pictured this phenomenon in four ways.

First, using the same words as the author of Genesis, he saw the **earth** as "without form and void" (KJV). No light could be seen as described in Genesis until God gave his first command.

Second, the **mountains** "moved lightly" (KJV). The Hebrew verb indicated "lightness." In spite of their massive weight, they swayed as though they lacked the heaviness usually associated with them. The point of this imagery seems to be that those things that have always been symbols of stability are giving way. The people can no longer feel secure or safe.

Third, every sign of **people** living on the earth had disappeared. Even birds had deserted the scene. No one could survive under such conditions, and none of those creatures that made their home in the heavens chose to be around such an empty vacuum.

Fourth, no vegetation survived, and no organized community life existed. Everything was rubbish and rubble. Solitude and desolation had replaced the former **fruitful land**. Everything stood in sharp contrast to the creation account, at which God looked and said, "It is good."

4:27–31. The last four verses of this chapter give Jeremiah's interpretation as revealed to him by Yahweh. After reaffirming his decision to devastate the land on which Israel lived, Yahweh gave a comforting promise (v. 27). He would not totally destroy it because he had an irrevocable covenant with Israel. Yahweh would continue to work his redemptive purposes through a remnant.

In verse 28, Jeremiah, quoting Yahweh, returned to his basic thesis. The earth faced havoc and desolation. On this point God would not change or negotiate. The verb translated **turn back** is rendered in many contexts as "repent." This expresses the idea of changing the mind and, therefore, one's course of action. God would not change his decision. It was nonnegotiable.

Panicking when they heard the approaching enemy riding swiftly and carrying their instruments of destruction, the people fled in all directions (v. 29). This left the villages and larger towns deserted. In verses 30 and 31, Jeremiah brought his argumentative message to a close with two illustrations. They both involved the picture of a woman. The first personified Judah decked out as a harlot. The second symbolized the nation as a woman in labor.

The first symbol was appropriate since the Canaanite religion had strong sexual elements. The figure bordered on being a literal analogy. Jeremiah's point was that the harlot had no love for her customer. In fact, she despised him. He was just a source of revenue for her. So it was for those who served as priestesses for the Baal worshippers.

The second symbol was perhaps the most literal of all the images the prophet used to describe Judah's coming suffering. A woman delivering a child is helpless, and she suffers great pain. What a graphic way to bring this section of Jeremiah's message to a close.

B Reason for Judgment (5:1–31)

SUPPORTING IDEA: *God set forth through his prophet the basic reasons for the coming judgment, followed by a renewed statement of his determination to send the deserved punishment.*

Old Testament students are divided about whether 5:1 continues a long discourse begun at 4:5 or whether it is a new oracle. Regardless of how one interprets this matter, one thing is certain. The prophet took a fresh look at what is chapter 5 in the text. In the previous material considered (4:5–31), the prophet emphasized coming judgment. In this material under consideration (5:1–31), the emphasis is on the causes for the coming judgment.

5:1–6. God's command resembles the negotiation between Yahweh and Abraham over the fate of Sodom (Gen. 18:16–33). But in that circumstance Yahweh's final offer was to spare the city if ten righteous people could be found. God's offer to Jeremiah, however, was to spare Jerusalem if Jeremiah could find one person "who deals honestly and seeks the truth." This suggests that Jerusalem in Jeremiah's day was more wicked than Sodom of Abraham's day.

Verses 1 and 2 contain the first of a number of symbolic acts Jeremiah used to illustrate his point. Both he and Ezekiel communicated through "enacted parables." The format is basically the same in both of them. God commands the prophet, and he immediately does it. God then gives the interpretation to the prophet, who passes it on to the people. These acts got the people's attention quickly.

In verses 3–5 Jeremiah learned a great lesson. Why did he go to the poor people first? Perhaps he felt they were more likely to be humble and obedient to God. But he was disappointed. His reasoning changed, and he decided they were limited in their understanding. He next went to the leaders thinking that surely they knew God's ways. But again he was disappointed. The concluding words in verse 5 set forth the figure of an ox that has broken loose from his yoke. This is what the leaders had done. They had also broken off the yoke and torn off the bonds.

5:7–9. Jeremiah referred to the people's promiscuity with some of the strongest language in the Old Testament. Like a group of hungry **stallions**, they gathered lustily at the house of **prostitutes**. In their passion they even stooped so low as to force themselves on the wives of other men. Who could fault Yahweh for the destructive punishment he sent on such people?

5:10–13. Having established that punitive measures were justified, Yahweh commanded that Judah's vegetation be almost completely destroyed (v. 10). Their disloyal and deceitful conduct had caused them to commit two grievous sins (vv. 12–13). First, they accused Yahweh of being inactive and even impotent. Second, they accused the prophets who condemned them as being nothing **but wind**. These two sins summarize the height of arrogance to which rebellious people stoop when they defy the Lord.

5:14–19. In replying to the charges of the people, the Lord first (v. 14) defended his prophets whom the faithless crowd had attacked. Rather than being empty and meaningless words, God promised to vindicate them and make their declaration a burning fire. The heat of their pronouncements utterly **consumes** those who dared to show disrespect to Yahweh's messengers.

Yahweh's promise to **make my words in your mouth a fire** is an interesting companion statement to Jeremiah's later words. In a deep depression during the dark days of Jehoiakim's reign, he must have remembered the words in this verse. The disenchanted prophet said, "But if I say, 'I will not mention him or speak any more in his name,' his word is in my heart like a fire, a fire shut up in my bones" (20:9).

Having dealt with the opposition to his prophets, Yahweh then enlarged on his divine purpose to deal with those who mocked him and his moral demands. In verse 15, he gave a brief description of the avenger. Many Old Testament scholars believe the description refers to Babylon. Others insist the words could apply to any of several groups, including the Scythians.

These invaders are strong and skilled in the art of war. **Their quivers are like an open grave.** They will bring a path of destruction that will level **fortified cities.** The economy will suffer ruin, and lives will be lost. Into the darkness and despair, Yahweh said he would not allow the people to be completely destroyed (vv. 18–19). Even failures have a future! Standing within the stern words of Yahweh are words of comfort and grace. He would later say more about God's redemptive plan and Israel and Judah's part in it.

5:20–25. The command that God gave the people through his prophet began with what Old Testament scholars call a "prophetic formula." This emphasized its importance, even urgency. Some suggest the reference, in verse 21, to "seeless" eyes and "hearless" ears refers to a recent drought in the land, causing a crop failure. They point to verses 24 and 25 as support for their claim. The people were unable to understand what God was doing among them.

In light of God's omnipotence, the people should have stood in awe of him. The Hebrew word used in verse 22 and translated **fear** is quite often translated "reverence." The word translated **tremble** comes from a Hebrew verb that means "to turn about, twist, whirl, dance, writhe, be in pain." It can mean "to shake or be brought forth." The cumulative effect of these two verbs is that the prophet felt God's people should behave carefully and respectfully toward God. Verse 22 closes with a metaphor, the sea. Even this great body of water obeys the limits God has set for it. But the people of Jeremiah's day exalted themselves above any restrictions God had set for them. What arrogance and folly!

In verse 25 Jeremiah told the people the same thing other men of God had told their generation for several centuries. Sin produces nothing good. Only evil things come to those who defy God's purpose for their lives. God is not merely neutral. He wants to bless, but to bless those who ignore him and rebel against his standards would cause him to act against his moral character. God is holy, and this cannot change.

5:26–29. In these verses the prophet charged the people with conduct similar to what he had described in parts of the temple sermon (7:1–8:3). In verse 26, he described the men with a Hebrew adjective that comes from a verb meaning "to act wickedly, unjustly, impiously." These wicked men had set out with one goal in mind—to trap and exploit their fellow countrymen. The bird catcher metaphor continues into verse 27. As a result of their treachery and deceit, they had become wealthy people with great authority and influence.

The first line of verse 28 describes their outward appearance as **fat and sleek.** The first word suggests fertility and prosperity. The second word means to be made smooth, bright, polished, hence to shine. This contains the idea of shallow, superficial, even phony. Today we might describe these people as "slick." The people had left God with one choice. **Should I not punish them for this? . . . Should I not avenge myself on such a nation as this?**

5:30–31. The last two verses in this chapter summarize the depravity of that day. Jeremiah used two words to characterize the conditions. The first one, a noun, translated **horrible,** comes from a verb meaning "to be desolate, laid waste, astonished, perishing."

The word translated **shocking** comes from a verb not used in the Old Testament. It probably means "to shudder." An adjective, *horrid* or *bad,* comes from this verb root. It is used in 29:17 to describe the "bad figs" of Jeremiah's vision. Some translate it "blighted." A similar Arabic word carries the meaning of "to infect with a contagion." The feminine form of the adjective, used here, has been translated "horrible" These two words are not entirely interchangeable, but they touch each other at several points.

The lifestyle carried on by the people had become normal with them. In God's eyes, it was disgusting and shocking. God's holiness and justice demanded punishment. Verse 31 places the blame exactly where it belongs—at the feet of the religious leaders—the **prophets** and **priests**. They had formed a coalition to promote wrongdoing in the land.

A final contribution to the rebellious conduct came from the people. They were content to have conditions as they were. In fact, they relished the idea. Jeremiah shot a probing question at them: **But what will you do in the end?** Jeremiah's question to Israel is as relevant today as when he delivered it to Israel and Judah. When the end comes, how will it be with you?

C Picture of Jerusalem's Siege (6:1–30)

SUPPORTING IDEA: *God's prophet warns the people of coming divine judgment and calls them to repent and be spared.*

In chapters 4 and 5, Jeremiah warned his people of the impending disaster and then warned them to take refuge in the fortified cities. He then, in imagination, pictured the invaders' progress until the various areas were conquered and they were ready to besiege Jerusalem. Chapter 6 opens with the certainty of Jerusalem's fall.

6:1–8. The clarion call in verse 1 came to three groups of people: those in **Jerusalem**, where the temple stood; **Tekoa**, home of Amos the prophet; and a city whose location is uncertain. Some interpreters feel since Jeremiah was from the tribe of **Benjamin** that he spoke specifically to his own tribesmen when he urged flight from the city. But others contend since Jerusalem was in the territory allotted to Benjamin that he spoke to all the inhabitants of the city.

Scholars have not been able to identify the town of **Beth Hakkerem** with certainty. Some lean toward a site west of Jerusalem or one on the road from Jerusalem to Bethlehem. Many identify it with a conical-shaped hill called the Frank Mountain, between Bethlehem and Tekoa. It was used for military purposes in the crusades. It is mentioned once in postexilic writings (Neh. 3:14).

In Jeremiah's call to **flee for safety**, he used a word that some interpreters have translated "put yourself under cover." The verb expresses the idea of hiding in a secluded place and also of carrying one's possessions along in the flight. The prophet equated the coming devastation with the "foe from the north." He addressed Jerusalem (v. 2) under the figure of a lady, beautiful and dainty. The advancing foe is described as **shepherds with their flocks**. The word *shepherd* often referred to political and military leaders.

Verses 4 and 5 can be interpreted in two ways. One view is that God is ordering the enemy to attack his people. An alternative interpretation is that the enemy is claiming to be fulfilling the words of Judah's God as Sennacherib did when he called on the people to surrender (Isa. 36:10). The normal time for beginning a battle was at the early morning hour. But the invader grew restless. As the day wore on, he decided to attack at night. The expression **this is what the LORD Almighty says** may be the prophet saying that God led the enemy to move early. On the other hand, the enemy could be speaking and justifying his action by claming the Jews' God Yahweh told him to follow this course of action.

The words **prepare for battle** read literally "sanctify for battle." It reveals that warfare in that day was considered a solemn religious act. Even today people in that area speak of a "holy war." Priests blessed the army before battle, and sacrifices were offered. Astrologers were called to give advice about strategy. Divination was used, and soldiers were restricted from having sexual relations. Even the Israelites used these methods in the early days of their national life.

Verse 6 gives a picture of preparation for siege warfare. To run battering rams against upper sections of the weak portions in a city's walls, the invader built a sloping ramp. The devastation of some hills in Palestine today probably dates back to this practice. The **trees** were used to build **ramps** or perhaps used for fuel, or both.

The latter part of verses 6 and 7 contains words of Yahweh explaining the reason he permitted such action. He had appointed pagans as his agents to discipline and even punish his people. The action would be partially punitive but hopefully corrective and redemptive. The corruption in the land flowed constantly, as though fed by an underground source. This evil on the part of his people angered God. He must respond.

6:9–30. These verses may be three separate fragments of Jeremiah's material placed side by side to follow the preceding exhortation. Most interpreters agree verses 9–15 record a dialogue between God and Jeremiah. In verse 9, Yahweh tells Jeremiah to let the invaders do their work. The idea is that he must give them free access and wait until they have finished. He then should come behind and see if any remained. If so, they would be the ones God considered worthy of being spared.

Jeremiah answered Yahweh with a pessimistic reply (vv. 10–11a). To attempt to salvage the nation would be impossible. No one would pay attention to him. They had already made up their minds; they would not be receptive to anything he said. His messages antagonized them. They considered him an affront and an insult and found no joy in listening to him. But in his complaint, the prophet insisted he was anxious to warn the people of coming judgment.

All age groups would be affected. Homes would be confiscated, and all means of survival would vanish. Yahweh placed the blame where it belonged—on the greedy laity and the professional religionists. The latter refused to address the issues of the day, ignoring the people's spiritual need. The people had developed seared consciences. Nothing embarrassed them. They had lost the capacity to be contrite or to feel guilty. Such people could look forward to nothing but desolation and doom.

Following the dialogue (vv. 9–15), Yahweh issued (v. 16) a fervent appeal for the people to reconsider their priorities and return to "the basics." He challenged them to recognize that the time had come for a choice. They needed to investigate the facts and inquire about the wise course of action. If they would pursue this policy, they would find tranquillity, calmness, and peace of mind. Unfortunately, they chose to ignore his plea.

Having been rejected, Yahweh had stern words for his people. He reminded them of the prophetic warnings (v. 17). God now had only one alternative. He called on the heathen world and even the forces of nature to pay close attention (vv. 18–19). He was about to demonstrate the end result of the course his people had chosen.

Anticipating their plea of defense, Yahweh refuted their argument before they even offered it (v. 20). He cared nothing about their formal religious rituals. Even if sweet-smelling offerings came from as far away as southwest Arabia or beyond, ritual without righteousness was meaningless to him.

Jeremiah presented his final "wrap-up" and summary (vv. 21–26). He delivered Yahweh's last warning and appeal (vv. 21–23), but he was interrupted, in verse 24, by a sudden outburst from the people. Sensing the critical urgency, they cried in panic. But the prophet immediately returned to issue caution and advice for their safety (v. 25) and then a heartfelt plea for repentance (v. 26).

Verses 27–30 contain words from Yahweh directed specifically to Jeremiah. We cannot be sure God intended for him to pass this message on to the nation. Yahweh told the prophet he had made him, in the words of John Skinner, a moral analyst of the people (v. 27). Their iniquities had caused them to become "fixed in concrete" (v. 28). Though God had attempted to purify them with severe discipline (v. 29), the work had not been successful. They remained a corrupted people. The last statement in this unit (v. 30) gives the final verdict. Yahweh called them **rejected silver** because he had rejected them.

> **MAIN IDEA REVIEW:** *The people of Israel and Judah needed to sound the alarm that an enemy was on the way that would devastate the land. God would send this destroying enemy because his people had forsaken him and adopted a lifestyle that conflicted with his will for them.*

III. CONCLUSION

The Debasing Power of Sin

Through Jeremiah's prophetic denunciation of Judah and Jerusalem, we see the pervasive nature of sin and moral corruption. Sin is never a single act committed in isolation. Sin is dynamic and progressive. It is remarkably generative. Sin yields more and more sin. It is a plague that spreads. Finally, the whole society—its beliefs, customs, dispositions, values, and traditions—are corrupt.

Sin in all its wickedness and corruption leads to judgment, destruction, and death. In four terse statements, Jeremiah described the ruin God was sending on his nation. In 4:23–26 each verse begins with the words "I looked." What did Jeremiah look at? He looked at coming devastation, destruction, and death that hearkened back to the primordial formless and empty world of Genesis 1:2. The coming destruction is pictured as cosmic and terrestrial. It will affect the entire world.

The stubbornness of this people is recorded in their twofold refusal in 6:16–17. First, such morally corrupt people and societies refuse to hear God's message. When counseled to return to the ways of God, they refused, declaring: "We will not walk in it" (6:16). Second, when urged to take seriously the prophetic warning, they refused even to hear the word of warning, stating: "We will not listen" (6:17).

PRINCIPLES

- God has built into his universe—the moral as well as the physical world—the great law of returns: you reap what you sow.

- When those who claim to be God's representatives—the prophets and priests—are corrupt, one can expect the entire society to be corrupt from top to bottom.

- People who have no shame and do not blush at loathsome conduct demonstrate how far they are from God.

- God's way is the only good way; it provides the peace and rest that people are desperately seeking.

APPLICATIONS

- Recount a time or times when you knew with your heart that a person reaps what they sow.

- Discuss what it means to presume on the grace of God and give examples where you have observed this.

- Ask God to increase your sense of his power and holiness.

- List some passages in the Bible that have been offensive to you or may still be offensive.

- Bring these passages to God and thank him for your awareness that they are offensive. Pray that his Spirit will take these offensive passages and do the work within you that God desires.

- At what times do you believe God's ways for you are best: never, sometimes, most of the time, always? Use this checkup to ask God to move you closer to seeing his ways are always best.

IV. LIFE APPLICATION

Here I Stand!

The story of Diogenes and his lamp is one of the best known antics of the ancient philosophers. He was a Cynic, a philosopher who lived in ancient Athens. Ancient literature tells us that "he lit a lamp in broad daylight and said, as he went about, 'I am looking for a man.'"

Salvator Rosa, a seventeenth-century Italian painter, depicted this scene in his painting *Diogenes in Search of an Honest Man.* We see the aged Cynic with a lighted lamp surrounded by a sneering and laughing crowd. But alas, they are commonplace people, idiots! They lack virtue and true reason. They are not honest. They do not represent the true humanity that Diogenes was searching for.

So it was for Jeremiah. God told the prophet: "Go up and down the streets of Jerusalem, look around and consider, search through her squares. If you can find but one person who deals honestly and speaks the truth, I will forgive this city" (5:1).

Today God is looking for those who will stand for righteousness in our society, for people who will take their stand for his Word and his ways. The challenge each of us faces as the light of his Word shines upon us is, Will I be an honest and true human being, or will I be shown to be a scoundrel and rogue?

V. PRAYER

Heavenly Father, help us to stand against the accepted practices and standards of our society that are ways of darkness and not ways of light. Help us to reject corruption at all levels, to avoid evil, and to shun all wickedness. We thank you that you have had those like Jeremiah who stood for you. Give us the strength and courage to stand for you today. Let us be persons of righteousness, of honesty, and of truth. Amen.

VI. DEEPER DISCOVERIES

A. "Disaster from the north" (4:6)

Old Testament students have an expression—"foe from the north"—by which they label the invader of which Jeremiah spoke in this passage. Reference to a "northern foe" appears in other messages throughout all of the prophet's recorded ministry. Who was this foe?

The ultimate adversary was Babylon under Nebuchadnezzar's leadership. Beginning in 605 B.C., Nebuchadnezzar made three visits to harass the land. In the first two incursions (605 and 597 B.C.), he invaded and carried a number of captives to his homeland. In the final assault, 586 B.C., he sacked the city, burned the temple, and carried almost all the remaining people to Babylon.

At the time Jeremiah spoke, however, around 626 B.C., Babylon was not a major power though she was beginning to make her presence felt. Other nations posed a much greater threat, and Jeremiah spoke excitedly as though his warning would be fulfilled sooner rather than later. Of whom was the prophet speaking? Scholars have had a field day discussing this dilemma. Some believe Jeremiah knew from the beginning the foe was Babylon. Others suggest various powers, the chief being Assyria and the Scythians.

Jeremiah showed profound wisdom in not identifying the foe who would conquer Judah. He realized the people might repent and be delivered. In fact, the revival under Josiah might have brought temporary respite. But the people under Jehoiakim reversed this good king's policies. Babylon turned out to be the true "foe from the north."

There is one other possible interpretation of this passage. Perhaps the concept of "disaster from the north" was a generic term used often because destruction almost always came from this direction. Look at a map of Palestine, and you will see this was almost the only way from which armies could come. Even if an enemy approached from the west through Philistine country, an attack on Jerusalem would almost require it to advance on it from the north. Jeremiah knew only judgment was coming. God had not revealed any more details to him, so he left the matter of "who" and "exactly when" alone. A good policy for today's prophets!

B. Prophets and Priests (5:31)

Prophet and priest, the two most important offices in the Old Testament, date back to Moses. At God's instruction, Moses appointed the family of Levi as the permanent priestly tribe and his own brother, Aaron, as high priest.

The office of prophet actually precedes the Levitical priesthood because God called Moses a prophet (Deut. 34:10). In fact, both offices go back to the days of Abraham. The Book of Genesis calls Melchizedek "priest of the most high God" (Gen. 14:18 KJV), and Abimelech recognized Abraham as a prophet (Gen. 20:7).

As Israel's religious life developed, the two offices took on separate and unique functions: Priests spoke to God for the people, and prophets spoke to the people for God. This definition contains much truth but is more simplistic than accurate. The truth is that members of each office often sought to usurp the authority and province of the other.

In Jeremiah's day, the two groups struck a bargain. They supported each other in compromising their spiritual convictions for the sake of material gain. Jeremiah, who combined both roles in his religious vocation, had sharp words of criticism for both groups. He said, "The prophets prophesy lies, the priests rule by their own authority" (5:31). He then added a third group to the evil coalition. Perhaps he shouted his message, "My people love it this way." His piercing question which followed targeted all three groups: "What will you do in the end?"

C. "I will not destroy you completely" (5:18)

At times, the prophets seem to be inconsistent and self-contradictory. When they condemned sin and told of the certain judgment awaiting the nation, their words seemed to imply nothing salvageable would remain. Yet, almost always, before the prophet finished the pronouncement, a word of hope would adorn the message. Old Testament students have a name for this phenomenon. They call it the "remnant."

Two facts form the basis for Old Testament redemptive theology. First, God chose Abraham to begin a family through whom the world would be blessed. He made a covenant with him, reaffirmed several times that he would honor it, and renewed the promise with Abraham's descendants. Second, God made a covenant with the descendants of Jacob at Sinai. This was "national Israel." He promised to make them a "kingdom of priests" (Exod.

19:6). The promise to Jacob's family, the twelve tribes of Israel, however, contained a condition. God said through Moses, "If you obey me fully and keep my covenant" (Exod. 19:5).

Several times God seemed on the brink of destroying Israel and starting over again, but he never followed through on that threat. Even as late as the ministry of Jesus, he made a striking statement through John the Baptist. "Do not . . . say to yourselves, 'We have Abraham as our father.' I tell you that out of these stones God can raise up children for Abraham" (Matt. 3:9). Many expositors contend the words "these stones" mean "the Gentiles." The covenant with national Israel was always conditional. The prophets warned them often. God never threatened to nullify his promise to Abraham.

What about the remnant? Almost every canonical prophet tempered his pronouncement of doom with a promise to save a seed through whom the nation would blossom again. Even the seventy years in Babylonian captivity did not extinguish national Israel's hope. Ezekiel assured the people that dead bones would live again (see Ezek. 37:1–14). That prophecy was gloriously fulfilled!

The remnant concept appears before the prophets. Noah and his family were a remnant that survived the flood (Gen. 7:1–23). Lot and his daughters were a remnant that escaped the destruction of Sodom (Gen. 19:29–30). God told Elijah that a faithful remnant still existed in Israel (1 Kgs. 19:18). But the canonical eighth-century prophets sharpened and developed this concept for Israel's future hope.

Prior to Jeremiah, *remnant* had two possible meanings. First, it included those who survived judgment because of God's grace (Isa. 1:9). Second, those who were in a right relationship to God because they deliberately made a right choice were a part of the remnant (Mic. 2:12). Jeremiah added a new dimension. His new covenant theology presented the vision of a remnant that entered into that new relationship with God. But they must wait for complete realization of this promise until the Messiah came.

VII. TEACHING OUTLINE

A. INTRODUCTION

1. Lead Story: The Lions Are Coming! The Lions Are Coming!

2. Context: In chapters 2–3 God spoke of the deterioration of Judah's relationship with him in terms of a husband and a wife. Now in chapters 4–6 God announces coming judgment on Judah in terms of an invading army from the north. God has declared war and is sending an invading army against his people because they have forsaken him and adopted lifestyles that conflict with his will. All of them are guilty—the king and his officials, prophets and priests, the great and small of society. There is not a righteous person among them—and they love it that way.

3. Transition: God called the people of Judah to return to the ancient paths, the good ways, and told them to walk in them. The people refused to follow God's ways and would not listen to his message. They persisted in their disobedience and affirmed the corrupt ways of their society. Therefore God became their enemy. He moved against them and their society to remove them. In the midst of that crooked and perverse culture, the Lord looked for anyone who would choose righteousness over wickedness. There wasn't one. Thus what the people were about to discover was that God is a punishing God as well as a forgiving God.

B. COMMENTARY

1. Disaster Is on the Way (4:5–31)
2. Reason for the Judgment (5:1–31)
3. Pictures of Jerusalem's Siege (6:1–30)

C. CONCLUSION: THE DEBASING POWER OF SIN

VIII. ISSUES FOR DISCUSSION

1. What areas of corruption, moral evil, and wickedness are prominent in our society today? What would God have to say about these things?

2. Why do people prefer to hear smooth falsehoods rather than stern truth?

3. What happens to the church and society when those who are sup-
    posed to serve God live more like their culture than as righteous peo-
    ple? What would happen if every believer in Jesus Christ stood out in
    our culture as righteous, honest, and true? What impact would they
    have?

4. Can God become the enemy of his people? What might be a situation
    that would cause this to happen?

Jeremiah 7:1–10:25

The Decay of Proper Worship

I. **INTRODUCTION**
When the Forts of Folly Fall

II. **COMMENTARY**
A verse-by-verse explanation of these verses.

III. **CONCLUSION**
"You Will Not Change"

An overview of the principles and applications from these verses.

IV. **LIFE APPLICATION**
No Brains at All

Melding these verses to life.

V. **PRAYER**
Tying these verses to life with God.

VI. **DEEPER DISCOVERIES**
Historical, geographical, and grammatical enrichment of the commentary.

VII. **TEACHING OUTLINE**
Suggested step-by-step group study of these verses.

VIII. **ISSUES FOR DISCUSSION**
Zeroing these verses in on daily life.

"*W*ould'st thou, my son, be wise and virtuous deem'd,

By all mankind a prodigy esteem'd?

Be this thy rule; be what men prudent call;

PRUDENCE, almighty PRUDENCE gives thee all.

Keep up appearances; there lies the test,

The world will give thee credit for the rest.

Outward be fair, however foul within;

Sin if thou wilt; but then in secret sin.

This maxim's into common favour grown,

Vice is no longer vice unless 'tis known.

Virtue indeed may barefac'd take the field,

But vice is virtue, when 'tis well conceal'd.

Should raging passions drive thee to a whore,

Let PRUDENCE lead thee to a postern door;

Stay out all night, but take especial care

That PRUDENCE bring thee back to early prayer.

As one with watching and with study faint,

Reel in a drunkard, and reel out a saint."

C h a r l e s   C h u r c h i l l

Jeremiah 7:1–10:25

I N   A   N U T S H E L L

*A*t the Lord's command, Jeremiah went to the temple and proclaimed a word from the Lord. He called on the people of Judah to repent of their wicked ways, their presumption of God's protection no matter what they did or how they lived, and their trust in the temple rather than in the Lord of the temple. He rebuked the people for their false confidence, false hope, and false sense of assurance based on their professed loyalty to the temple. Together with this temple sermon is grouped a series of similar announcements, pronouncements, and renouncements. Among these was Jeremiah's poetic declaration that the nation of Judah, like Israel, had disregarded God's law and turned from the true and living God to foolish idolatry.

The Decay of
Proper Worship

I. INTRODUCTION

When the Forts of Folly Fall

*I*mpregnable. Indomitable. Unassailable. Indestructible. These were the words used to describe Belgium's Fort Eben Emael. It was built in the 1930s at the junction of the Albert Canal and the Meuse River as a defense against a German invasion.

Row after row of barbed wire, steel antitank obstacles, and minefields encircled the walls of the fort. On the west side, a concrete-lined, water-filled moat blocked the approach to the fort's walls. Steel-reinforced concrete casements jutted from the walls. Sixty-millimeter antitank guns and machine guns poked through embrasures in the walls to destroy any enemy troops that attempted to scale them. The Belgiums had anticipated every possible enemy threat in the construction of the fort. They felt it could hold out indefinitely against any assault.

But Adolf Hitler had an idea. He conceived a plan of attack using a new military tactic—a surprise glider attack—and a new, untried military weapon—an explosive hollow charge called a *hohlladung*. This charge could be attached to the cupolas and casement defenses of the fort and blow a hole through the concrete, causing terrible death and destruction.

Thus it was that at midday on May 11, 1940, Fort Eben Emael came under unexpected German assault in the world's first glider attack. In twenty-eight hours, seventy-eight German glidermen in ten inexpensive gliders silenced the fort, defeated its ten-times superior numbered force, and led a mile-long column of Belgian soldiers out of the fort as prisoners of war.

The people of Judah in Jeremiah's day also believed they had an inviolable and sacred fortress, a structure that would guarantee their survival and preservation in face of all invaders—their temple.

The temple of Jeremiah's day was the temple Solomon had built in Jerusalem. God had chosen Zion to be his dwelling place forever (Ps. 132:13–14). The people of Judah knew they were God's chosen people, that Jerusalem was his chosen city, and that their great temple was his earthly dwelling place. At the Lord's command, Jeremiah went to the temple and proclaimed a message from God. This temple sermon, the first major prose section in the Book of Jeremiah, is summarized in chapter 7. Attached to it in chapters 8–10 is other material related by content.

Jeremiah accused the worshippers of having bought into a lie. The lie was their "temple theology." This theology is summarized in their words, "This is the temple of the LORD, the temple of the LORD, the temple of the LORD!" (7:4). The repetition of the words had become superstitious or magical to them. They placed their trust in the outward trappings of their religion. Jeremiah told the worshippers they were in for a rude awakening. They soon would lose both their city and their temple if they did not repent and turn back to God.

II. COMMENTARY

The Decay of Proper Worship

MAIN IDEA: *Hypocritical worship, combined with stubborn rebellion, produces an incurable state leading to inevitable doom for both individuals and nations.*

With the close of chapter 6, the chronological arrangement of Jeremiah's prophecies ceases. Any further meaningful examination of Jeremiah must take into account the historical background of that passage.

Old Testament interpreters agree almost unanimously that chapters 7–10 form a unit. They represent one stage in the collection of Jeremiah's prophecies and development of the book. Not all suggested scrolls can be so clearly identified. This one, however, must have been gathered at some time either by Jeremiah, his secretary Baruch, or someone familiar with the prophet's works. Most likely, this material in these chapters is arranged thematically rather than chronologically. The general motif is the fatal consequences of hypocrisy in worship.

The first unit in this section has been called the "temple sermon." How far does the temple sermon extend? Interpreters differ, but the most generally accepted position is through 8:3. For the purpose of this study and commentary, we will accept this arrangement. More will be said when we look at chapter 26.

🅐 Conduct Should Match One's Worship (7:1–8:3)

SUPPORTING IDEA: *God will not accept the worship of a nation that honors its ritual requirements but ignores its ethical demands.*

7:1–2. These verses give the setting for Jeremiah's message to the people and further identifies the prophet's words as being delivered with God's authority. The parallel passage in chapter 26 locates the time as "early in the reign of Jehoiakim." Since Jehoiakim began reigning in 608 B.C. and Babylon's first invasion was in 605 B.C., this sermon was probably preached sometime before 605 B.C.

The place where Jeremiah preached the sermon was the temple in Jerusalem. God commanded the prophet to **stand at the gate of the LORD's house**. There he would speak to people on their way to **worship**. The word *worship* comes from a verb that means "to bow down or prostrate oneself before one who ranks higher." This powerful word picture is appropriate to characterize the proper attitude required of an Israelite approaching Yahweh.

7:3–8. Jeremiah prefaced his words to the people with a firm declaration of his authority. Yahweh had given him the words he was about to utter. He then gave a summary of what he was about to say in more detail. **Reform your ways and your actions, and I will let you live in this place** (v. 3).

Reciting magical formulas or holy words with hypocritical lips could not give immunity from the dangers that threatened the nation. Enchanted phrases mouthed in rhythmic unison would not provide certainty of God's presence. Nothing less than transformed conduct would meet his approval. Yahweh could fellowship with his people in the temple only if they were compassionate for the weak and helpless. Magical, sentimental expressions of loving ardor for the temple but lacking in concern for the unprivileged and helpless would find no approval from God. He required—even demanded—positive action to correct the abuses under which the weak were suffering.

What were the specific areas of conduct Jeremiah accused the people of ignoring? They had divorced morality from religion as completely as in the earlier days when worship was accompanied by sexual immoralities. Students of Jeremiah have difficulty determining how much of their worship was superstition and how much was hypocritical.

The prophet set forth the conditions under which Yahweh would allow the people to remain in the land. The overall requirement was a revision of their lifestyle and priorities. The specifics included: (1) practice fairness and impartiality; (2) cease exploitation of the weak, including **the alien** dwelling among them; (3) desist from violence; and (4) refrain from allegiance to deities whose moral standards were opposed to those of Yahweh.

These were Yahweh's terms, and he would settle for nothing less. He was under no obligation to allow a corrupted people to continue in the land. This fact had been a part of the covenant made at Sinai and reaffirmed forty years later before the people entered the promised land. He demanded they face realistically their refusal to be honest with themselves and with him.

7:9–11. Jeremiah followed his stern statement of the facts with two questions. The answer to each question is so obvious they are virtually rhetorical in nature. The prophet's question was, Will you continue to do these things and claim to be followers of Yahweh? To do so was utter hypocrisy.

Jeremiah climaxed his tirade against the people with one of the boldest metaphors he could have used. This temple that the people revered had become a hiding place for marauders and thieves. What was the basis for such a figure of speech? Pagan temples were places where criminals could find retreat from law enforcement officers or even enemies who wished to plunder their illicit gains. As lawbreakers in the nation found safety in the isolation of pagan strongholds, so the people of Jeremiah's day considered themselves **safe** in Yahweh's temple.

7:12–15. With his case established, the prophet proposed an object lesson in history. He challenged his hearers to look at a parallel event in Israel's past, the destruction of another worship place, the sanctuary at **Shiloh**. Shiloh was the place where Israel's worship center was located from the time of Joshua when the Israelites entered Canaan until it was destroyed about 1050 B.C. by the Philistines.

Though we lack all the facts about how Shiloh was destroyed, one thing we know for certain: those who abuse the holy name of God face certain judgment. The way the prophet led up to this announcement deserves careful study. The analogy between the people of Eli's day and that of his own day was striking. The religious leaders had no answer for the prophet but threatening him with physical force. Chapter 26, which we will investigate later, shows how intensely people are moved by religious hatred, especially when it interferes with their financial gain.

7:16–20. Some Old Testament students contend that Jeremiah's temple sermon ends with verse 15. They see the remainder of chapters 7–10 as made up of fragments from many sources of Jeremiah's ministry. In my judgment this is a serious error. At this point we have Jeremiah's account of his dialogue with Yahweh about his future message to the people. I believe these four verses are a parenthesis before Jeremiah takes a fresh start in the temple sermon.

God told Jeremiah, **Do not pray for this people.** He pointed to the people's behavior. God recognized Israel had gone so far in their repeated rebellions that they had lost the ability to recognize their wrongdoing. He was always ready to forgive, but his acceptance is contingent on our repentance. As God viewed the situation, he felt the people no longer had the ability to turn away from their God-dishonoring lifestyle.

The people had sold out (vv. 17–18) to one called the **Queen of Heaven.** She was a goddess venerated primarily by women though assisted by the husband and children. She was worshipped to assure fertility and stability of the marriage. Scholars are not certain which goddess was revered. The words could be interpreted as meaning "stars of heaven" or "heavenly host." The preferred meaning, however, is "Queen of Heaven."

This goddess is thought to be Ishtar, a Mesopotamian goddess of fertility and war. She was sometimes identified with the planet Venus. The worship was sexually oriented, though the exact nature of the ritual is unknown. Part of the worship form consisted of making **cakes**, probably with Ishtar's image, offering **drink offerings**, and burning incense. Many scholars believe this worship was introduced to Israel by King Manasseh.

Addicted to this worship, the people had grown incapable of changing their lifestyle back to Yahweh's demands. For that reason Jeremiah understood God's dictum, "Don't even pray for them. They are hopeless!" Archaeologists have uncovered many images of nude goddesses from sites occupied by the Israelites. One can understand why Yahweh and his prophet protested so vehemently against such worship.

Yahweh asked Jeremiah a rhetorical question. We might paraphrase his question in this way: "Whom do they think they are hurting? Me? No way! They are only bringing disgrace and damage, injury and shame to themselves." Frustration and exasperation would be the reward for their ungodly conduct. Judah's evil had caused them to pass the point of no return. The only fate awaiting them was the full measure of Yahweh's wrath on the people and the land.

7:21–26. Yahweh said in effect, "Go ahead. Have it your way." He did not mean for Israel to accept his words literally any more than Jesus did when he said we must hate our parents to follow him. He had given commandments about burnt offerings and sacrifice at Sinai, but this was not his primary message. What he wanted was wholehearted devotion and unimpeachable fidelity to everything he required.

Yahweh informed the people they might as well **eat** all the **sacrifices** themselves. He desired none of it since it was offered by hands stained with unethical conduct. Rather than heeding Yahweh's commands and call to return, Israel had gone even deeper in rebellion. From the early days of their exodus from Egypt, God had sent spokesmen to them, but they had ignored these godly messengers. Each succeeding generation had grown worse and more militant in their defiance.

7:27–29. These verses record another private word from Yahweh to Jeremiah. Things would get worse. Judah would refuse to heed the message or honor the messenger. Jeremiah was to tell them exactly who and what they were—**the nation that has not obeyed the LORD its God or responded to correction**.

Yahweh directed his command in verse 29 to the people, not to the prophet. The cutting of hair symbolized grief. The Hebrew texts reads literally, "Cut off your crown." Growth on the head was considered as more than a headdress. It was a diadem. To cut the hair brought down one's pride. But more might be involved in this action. The Nazarite's long hair symbolized his consecration to Yahweh. The removal of his hair indicated the abandonment of his vow.

To Jeremiah, the nation, or what was left of it, had forsaken its dedication to Yahweh and no longer deserved the diadem that long hair symbolized. Another analogy manifested itself in Yahweh's command. He ordered the people to **lament on the barren heights**. This was where a large number of the wicked deeds had been committed.

Jeremiah's closing statement in this section resembled his conclusion of the long unit (4:5–6:30). For this reason a few Old Testament students see the temple sermon ending here. In my judgment the discourse continues a bit further. Jeremiah has one final word about Israel's flagrant sins and their consequences.

7:30–34. In the first two verses of this final section, Jeremiah pictured perhaps the most disgusting of all Israel's sins. The people had not only worshipped idols, but they had been bold enough to set them up in the temple in Jerusalem. One writer speaks of it as a "supreme act of defiance and a gross gesture of sacrilege" (Thompson, 293).

The people had stooped to another activity, equally disgusting to the prophet and to Yahweh. They had built "fireplaces" in a valley south of Jerusalem. The expression **Ben Hinnom** meant "son of Hinnom" probably a former owner of the valley. The term **Topheth** was probably a Hebrew word-play on "shame." This indicated the humiliation or embarrassment of doing such an awful thing in the name of Yahweh worship.

In this "high place" pagan ceremonies were conducted. They included, among other things, human sacrifices, especially of children, during the reign of Manasseh. They may have temporarily ceased during Josiah's reformation, but they reappeared when his successors came to the throne.

The last few words in verse 31 could indicate the people had convinced themselves that such practices were approved by Yahweh. Notice the words of Micah about child sacrifice (Mic. 6:7). Of course, Yahweh had commanded earlier the consecration of firstborn males. But he had never suggested or approved of offering them as human sacrifices. In fact, he insisted, it was **something I did not command, nor did it enter my mind.**

The days are coming indicated a future but unspecified date. The "when" of arrival often depended on the people's choice of conduct and lifestyle. Yahweh revealed (v. 32) the location's name would be changed. Rather than **Valley of Ben Hinnom**, it would be called **Valley of Slaughter.** The high place would be so full of dead bodies that many would lie unburied. Verse 33 pictures the scavengers having free access to devour any way they desired. No one would disturb them in their greedy plunder.

One other change would take place in the people's condition. Jeremiah warned that all types of mirth and joy, including wedding festivities, would disappear in Jerusalem and the smaller towns. Devastation and barrenness would characterize the land. The prophet presented nothing for which the people might be optimistic.

8:1–3. These three verses present the final humiliation of the people for their flagrant defiance of Yahweh's commands. To the Jewish mind, desecrating a person's grave and exposing his bones to the elements were among the worst insults anybody could heap upon the deceased. But the Lord pronounced these this very things would happen. Bodies of the dead would be allowed to lie like garbage scattered on the ground.

Invading armies often desecrated the graves and bodies of those they had conquered to show contempt for them. This was a form of gloating over their victory. When the people faced such cruel tactics and crushing experiences, they often preferred death rather than such humiliation.

This warning to the people concludes the temple sermon. Jeremiah offered a ray of hope that the people would return to Yahweh, but he did not seem optimistic. Chapter 26 records the response he received from the nation's religious leaders.

B The Letter of the Law Is Not Enough (8:4–13)

SUPPORTING IDEA: *True worship of God requires more than obedience to a law, repetition of a creed, or participation in a ritual. It requires a proper spirit.*

Most Old Testament students agree that chapters 7–10 contain a separate collection of Jeremiah's oracles. The first and longest unit has been considered. It prefaces and serves as the basis for the remaining sermons or units. As we study these units, we ask, "What method did the compiler use to determine how the material should be arranged?" We have no difficulty recognizing some natural units. This unit, however, seems to be a miscellaneous collection of sermons delivered toward the early days or years of Jehoiakim's reign or Josiah's last years. Two themes pervade all of them—Israel's stubborn rebellion and her inevitable doom.

The section being considered here reflects an overconfidence the people had in their spiritual superiority because of Josiah's reforms. Did Jeremiah support the king's reforms, or did he oppose them? Some passages indicate the former and others the latter.

The answer seems to be twofold. At first the young preacher upheld and promoted everything the king advocated. He toured the country, preaching on behalf of the reform and urging everyone to "get on the bandwagon" for the king. Later, however, he saw the reform movement was deteriorating into a campaign of intense nationalism. The spiritual element was minimal or nonexistent.

The climax that revealed to Jeremiah the full picture was the battle of Megiddo. Pharaoh Neco of Egypt started north where a battle between Assyria and Babylon was about to take place. Josiah attempted to stop him, and they clashed at Megiddo. Josiah was killed, and the bubble of Jewish nationalism burst.

The prophet now saw clearly what had been happening in Judah during the closing years of Josiah's reign. What had started out as a good reform movement had become a "front" for a political power play. The people put Jehoahaz on the throne, probably because he shared his father's views. Egypt sent a contingent to Jerusalem, deposed the new king, and sent him to Egypt in chains. Neco chose Jehoiakim, another son of Josiah, to rule in his brother's place. These events, in my judgment, formed the background against which the next two sections (8:4–13; 8:14–9:1) were delivered.

8:4–7. In verse 4, Yahweh asked the people, through Jeremiah, two rhetorical questions. No reply was expected. The words expressed the exasperation of the Lord. The prophet knew the answer was, "Yes, the nature of people is to learn from their mistakes and seek to correct their errors." Yahweh followed, in verse 5, with two additional rhetorical questions. "Why do these inhabitants of Jerusalem not follow the same course as normal people?"

Two statements define their irrational conduct. First, the people's holding to **deceit** may mean their disloyalty to Yahweh, or it may characterize the idolatry to which they were addicted. Of course, the two ideas would overlap since becoming attached to false gods was a form of disloyalty to Yahweh. Second, being unwilling to repent was a form of hypocrisy in worship, seeking to pretend one kind of life when they were living the opposite.

In a previous section (2:6–10) Jeremiah contrasted Judah's conduct with that of the other nations. In these verses he compared their behavior to two different animals. First, the impetuous plunge of the **horse** is more than a gentle turning aside. It is a headstrong, intentional, and energetic action. This pictures Judah's willful rebellion. Second, Jeremiah turned to the **stork** and **dove** as illustrations. God has endowed these creatures with an intuitive knowledge of the proper time for their activities. They reply automatically to this built-in radar system.

8:8–9. When the people boasted, **We are wise, for we have the law of the LORD,** they were probably referring to Josiah's reform movement. It was based largely on the law book discovered in the temple. Most scholars agree that it contained part, if not all, of the present Book of Deuteronomy.

Unfortunately, interpreters disagree on the meaning of Jeremiah's reply. He accused the **scribes** of having a **lying pen**. This is the first mention in the Old Testament of the scribes as a special class. Though we lack sufficient facts to know all the details, one truth is obvious. A rivalry existed between the priests and prophets for the conveying of religious truth. Since he was from a priestly background, Jeremiah, at first, tended to side with their approach to worship. But his disillusionment with the final result of Josiah's reform movement caused him to adopt the prophetic approach. During the remainder of his life, he functioned as a prophet, not a priest.

In verse 9, Jeremiah stated the fate of these self-designated **wise** people. They would become victims of their own illusions because they had refused the true wisdom of Yahweh. Only a dreary and desolate future awaited them.

8:10–12. Even a cursory examination reveals a number of parallels between these verses and 6:12–15. Jeremiah was probably citing material he had used before in other speeches. Notice two specific chastisements that would come to all those involved in God-dishonoring activities. Their wives would be taken by other men, and their remaining possessions would be confiscated. Beginning with the expression **from the least to the greatest** in verse 10 and extending through verse 12, Jeremiah repeated almost word for word the accusations he made in 6:12–15. He felt strongly about the sins of these corrupt people, especially the leaders. They could expect full retribution for their greed and immorality.

8:13. This final verse deals with the food supply. The **harvest** would be taken away. God had provided his people with a land of milk and honey—a land with vineyards they didn't plant. Somehow they had lost sight of the source of all their blessings. The absence of food would be a painful reminder of the Lord, whom they had forsaken.

Empathy for People Crushed by Catastrophes (8:14–9:1)

SUPPORTING IDEA: *Those who know the Spirit of Christ should always identify with those who are going through difficult days.*

This section falls into two natural divisions. In verses 14–17, some disastrous event has occurred that traumatized the people. Jeremiah felt the crisis and was alarmed. The material in 8:18 to 9:1 consists of a dialogue between Yahweh and Jeremiah. At certain places, however, interpreters have difficulty determining who is speaking.

What was this crisis? The most logical conclusion is the one proposed and supported by John Skinner. He contends this morale-shattering event was the battle of Megiddo which took place in 608 B.C. In this conflict Josiah attempted to interfere with Pharaoh Neco's northward march. He planned to participate in the battle of Carchemisch, in which Babylon and Assyria were about to engage. The winner of this battle would be the powerbroker of that region. Egypt most likely planned to help Assyria, though some translations render 2 Kings 23:29 as "against" rather than "to help" the king of Assyria. Neco killed Josiah, throwing Judah into panic.

8:14–15. Jeremiah seems to have joined the disturbed people. He called for everyone to take residence in the cities, which were strongly reinforced. The prophet admitted that he, at first, had expected to be safe. But because of the existing circumstances, he had come to doubt this was realistic.

8:16–17. Everything about the situation pointed to doom. Egypt, with its strong cavalry, stood poised for attack. Neco had set up headquarters on the Orontes River and could easily come by **Dan** and the Golan Heights to Judah. Jeremiah even understood God to be telling him that catastrophe would engulf the land as reptiles, serpents, and other such creatures harassed the people. This segment closes on a miserable and pessimistic note.

8:18–19. The speaker in verses 18–19a is Jeremiah himself echoing his words and the words of the people. He urged Yahweh to heed their **cry** and bring relief to the grief-stricken community. In verse 19b, the Lord first answered with what are two rhetorical questions. The reply expected was, "Of course God, the true king, is still in Jerusalem even though the earthly monarch is dead."

The final question, rhetorical since the answer is obvious, placed the blame where it belonged—at the people's feet. Their depraved lifestyles and stubborn wills explained their immoral choices. Since they detested Yahweh's demand for holy living, they created gods in their own image and worshipped them.

8:20–9:1. Jeremiah never viewed his people's sufferings without identifying with them passionately. In verse 20, he either voiced the anguished cry of the people or recorded it. The wheat harvest had **ended** without any reaping.

The time had arrived for the gathering of the summer fruits. The first season lasted from April to June. The latter harvest came in late September and October. When both failed, the people faced a crisis. The words Jeremiah spoke may have been those of a popular proverb used in daily life to express frustration over any famine. If so, he certainly used it with greater intensity.

Jeremiah sensed a twofold tragedy in the situation. The people faced a serious food shortage for the remaining summer months. This led to a second feeling of desperation. Their God had forsaken them. Since the people suffered severely, so did their prophet. He looked for their physical healing and could think of no better place than soothing balsam found in **Gilead**, east of the Jordan River. Surely resources were there to meet that need.

This therapy of Gilead, however, could provide no cure for the people's spiritual needs. As long as they remained rebellious and unregenerate, chastisement and suffering would continue from the God of holiness. This thought brought uncontrollable **tears** to Jeremiah's eyes. If he had the resources, his grieving would be unlimited and unending. This expression in 9:1 probably serves as the main reason he is called the "Weeping Prophet."

One textual matter that is relevant for this unit and also for the one to be considered next should be mentioned here. The first verse of chapter 9 in most English versions is the last verse of chapter 8 in the Hebrew text. This means the next large unit of study will begin with verse 2 of chapter 9 in most English versions. A few, however, make the adjustment and run parallel with the Hebrew text.

Ⅾ Depraved People Face Punishment (9:2–26)

SUPPORTING IDEA: *People can go so far in sin that they lose the perspective that enables them to repent and turn from their wicked ways.*

Chapters 9 and 10 consist of three self-contained units. They probably existed independently before being incorporated into the larger scroll of chapters 7–10. Also, all three may have been a part of the original scroll of prophecies that Jeremiah dictated to Baruch in chapter 36. Another possibility is that one or all three may have been part of the "many similar words" added to the original scroll that Jehoiakim burned (36:32).

When was this message (9:2–26) brought to the people of Judah? Various students have suggested different dates in the prophet's ministry. In my judgment the most logical occasion for the original delivery is about the same general time frame as the two preceding ones (8:4–13; 8:14–9:1). But they probably came early in Jehoiakim's reign. Another view is that Jeremiah preached these words at a later time when Babylon became the new foe from the north. The situation is the same as later when Babylon was on the scene with a strong military contingent and threatening to invade the land. The presence of this message with the other material argues strongly for a similar historical context for the original preaching of this sermon.

An analysis of the prophet's words suggests five segments in the flow of thought: 9:2–9,10–16,17–22,23–26; 10:1–16,17–25. The exposition of Scripture will be based on these divisions.

9:2–9. The first verse of this section begins identically with the last verse of the preceding one (9:1). But this does not indicate any organic connection between the two segments. In the previous one Jeremiah expressed his compassion while in this one he conveyed his disgust. The inn for which he longed would have been a crude, isolated place with none of the amenities offered by today's hotels. Jeremiah longed to get away from the people who were depraved and rebellious. He never wanted to see them again. They had disappointed him because they had defied and even disgraced Yahweh.

In verses 3–6, the prophet painted a graphic scene of the iniquity that pervaded the land. He referred to the tongue as a **bow** drawn **to shoot lies**. Reality, integrity, and honesty played no part in their successes and achievements. Moving quickly from one corrupt transaction to another, they refused to give God credit for any success. They worked hard and even wore themselves out with their lies and deceptions.

Verses 7–9 contain Yahweh's response in light of the people's appalling conduct. Summarizing the major cause for their wickedness, God proposes a rhetorical question couched in a parallelism. Does he have any option but to **punish** his people? How can he retain his own integrity if he allows such sinful activity to go unpunished?

9:10–16. Verse 10 contains the words of Jeremiah. He will mourn aloud for the desolation that will come soon to his land. In verse 11, the prophet gives direct words of Yahweh. In verse 12, he speaks again himself with a question directed to the people. The remainder of this segment (vv. 13–16) contains words of Yahweh, delivered by Jeremiah to the people. In my judgment this interpretation, generally though not universally accepted by Old Testament students, helps us understand this passage.

Of what value to the people was a message such as this? It would help the people understand the reason for their plight. Hopefully, it would serve as a motive for their repentance at a later time when they thought more soberly.

Who did the prophet have in mind as the executioner of God's will? Scholars differ widely at this point. They include four possible ethnic groups: the Assyrians, Scythians, Babylonians, Egyptians. The further my own studies carry me, the deeper my feeling that Jeremiah felt the nation was in great danger from the Egyptians at this time. The Scythian threat had passed, Assyria was in no position to wage an offensive war, and Babylon needed to defeat Assyria before she could take on Judah.

Egypt was free to return and punish Judah unmercifully for attempting to interfere with her trip northward to join the conflict between Assyria and Babylon. Jeremiah, as a young prophet, felt divine judgment would take place immediately against Judah. No reason exists for denying that this zealous though slightly immature and youthful preacher felt Egypt would strike quickly and decisively.

9:17–22. In the Judah of Jeremiah's day, and in some areas of the Middle East even today, people hired professional mourners to give status to their funerals. Archaeologists have found Egyptian tombs showing boatloads of women with disheveled hair and garments accompanying a corpse at a funeral (Thompson, 316). Speaking for Yahweh, Jeremiah called for the "professionals," urging them to their task. This indicates he felt the situation was urgent and deaths were imminent.

On this occasion, however, Jeremiah felt the ordinary retinue of paid grievers would be insufficient. So tragic would be the situation that even the professionals would be affected, perhaps through the loss of their own children. The coming death toll would be so numerous that dead bodies would remain unburied. Jeremiah's analogy was graphic. He compared the corpses to grain ready for the harvest, already fallen to the ground, but with no laborers on hand to put it into containers.

9:23–24. Some scholars see these verses as an interruption of the context. In my judgment this is an unwarranted conclusion. What is more natural than for Jeremiah to close this oracle with a warning to the people to refrain from trusting their own abilities and accomplishments?

The three things Jeremiah warned the people against continue to be great values of life that become our greatest stumbling blocks. The prophet never denied the value of these qualities. But they are not the ultimate goals we should seek. **Wisdom**? Yes, but not human wisdom. **Strength**? Certainly, but not to promote one's own agenda and ignore the weaknesses of others. **Riches**? Unquestionably, but not in order to insulate oneself against the poor and needy.

In what should humankind delight? Above all, in an intimate relationship with the Lord. From this come all the virtues that make for character, security, and happiness. The three words listed in verse 24—**kindness, justice and righteousness**—which Yahweh perfectly revealed in our Savior's life on earth are the values that bring happiness and fulfillment.

9:25–26. These two verses are more than a misplaced fragment as a few scholars contend. They represent the logical conclusion to a message warning Judah that their continued rebellion would result in punishment. This punishment, however, would include more than Judah.

The words about circumcision and uncircumcision confuse some interpreters. This is because they try to be certain about which nations, besides the Israelites, practiced this rite. Some expositors suggest the prophet listed **Judah** between **Egypt** and **Edom** because records show these two countries practiced circumcision.

What was Jeremiah's point in this message? In my judgment he was declaring one important truth. Physical circumcision contributes little, if anything, to one's spiritual life. This was not a new thought in Jeremiah's preaching. Earlier in his ministry he had already commanded the people to "circumcise yourselves to the LORD, circumcise your hearts (4:4).

Even before Jeremiah appeared on the scene, the people had already been told to "circumcise your hearts, therefore, and do not be stiff-necked any longer" (Deut. 10:16). Paul later used this same figure of speech. He said the true circumcision is "inwardly; and circumcision is circumcision of the heart, by the Spirit, not by the written code. Such a man's praise is not from men, but from God" (Rom. 2:29).

These words of Jeremiah about circumcision bring us back to the essence of everything he emphasized in his temple sermon. A religious "rite" does not make us pleasing to God but by being "right" in our heart. This is the same truth Paul taught so vehemently in another of his letters. He wrote, "Neither circumcision nor uncircumcision means anything; what counts is a new creation" (Gal. 6:15). Jesus called this experience being "born again" (John 3:3) or "born of the Spirit" (John 3:8). How marvelously the gospel of Christ is "in the Old Testament concealed and in the New Testament revealed."

Ⓔ Idol Worship Is Idle Worship (10:1–16)

SUPPORTING IDEA: *Those who engage in idol worship are practicing futility. These man-made things, since they have no life, will lead their devotees to emptiness and doom.*

Since Jeremiah saw invasion as imminent, he sent a warning to the people. In exile they would face many temptations to adjust by compromising with the people among whom they were living. The prophet cautioned them not to do so.

10:1–5. "Do not let the religious lifestyle of the heathen people who capture you become your goal." This was Jeremiah's message to people whom he knew would be taken captive when their land was invaded. The entire sixteen verses form a stinging satire designed to be preventive maintenance for his fellow Israelites.

In verses 2 and 3, the prophet describes how a piece of wood becomes an idol. Another prophet (Isa. 44:9–20) gave a similar description of the process. In verse 5, the prophet climaxes this segment with several striking statements. They express truths about the idols that he wished to impress upon the people to make them realize the foolishness of worshipping idols.

First, he spoke of an idol as **a scarecrow in a melon patch** without the ability to carry on a conversation. Second, he described idols as immobile. Rather than being a lift to the worshipper—the proper role for a deity—they were a load to be **carried**. Third, since idols have no life, they are without power to **harm** or to help. These "not gods" possessed no ability to change anybody.

10:6–10. These verses contain words of Jeremiah addressed to Yahweh. The prophet spoke them for the people's edification and benefit. He emphasized two major attributes he felt should motivate the people to reconsider and return to the living God. First, he possessed strength. Second, he is wisdom. He is supreme, unique, and unequaled.

In light of Yahweh's superiority, Jeremiah felt that every person should recognize the obligation to **revere** Israel's God. He contrasted Yahweh's wisdom with that of **the wise men of the nations**. Any knowledge they claimed to have was without foundation. Its source lay only in the worship of idols made from material substances. The **Tarshish** from which the silver came was probably located in Spain, considered the western limit of the ancient world. Since we do not know the location of **Uphaz**, some scholars suggest it was somewhere in the eastern limit of the known world. If so, perhaps this was the prophet's way of saying, "Everyone in the entire world is stupid except those who worship Yahweh."

The prophet's description of the clothing did not enhance the images of lifeless deities. The **blue** and **purple**, reserved only for the most expensive garments and usually for royalty, added nothing to the lifeless images. They remained impotent and worthless. Yahweh was the only God. To arouse his fury, indignation, and rage brought a person into a precarious position. The **earth** itself felt the tremor of his **wrath**.

10:11–16. Verse 11 represents a transition. It is written in prose rather than poetry and in Aramaic, a variation of Hebrew. My own judgment is this expression was made by Jeremiah to reaffirm God's authority for all that had been written and that which followed.

Jeremiah describes the threefold basis of God's work in creating the world. He set them in contrast to the characteristics of the idols the people had manufactured. The words translated **wisdom** and **understanding** contain some parallels in meaning, but they might be distinguished in one essential way. The connotation of the first is moral and spiritual while the second indicates skill, ability, and confidence.

Verse 13 describes the effect of God's presence in what the secular world today calls "the natural forces" and declares he controls them. The prophet knew who brought all things into being and maintains ultimate authority over them.

God's spokesman devoted two verses to a final stinging criticism of those who participated in idol worship. The expression **when their judgment comes** included final judgment when **everyone** stands before God, but it also refers to the here and now. When the testing time comes, Yahweh will be vindicated in the eyes of all people. The Hebrew text contains the idea of sudden visitation upon the people. Jeremiah always preached God was about to act in history to demonstrate his power, manifest his holiness, and vindicate his name. When this occurs, those who have opposed him will face destruction and ruin.

The Hebrew text of verse 16 reads literally, "not as these, the portion of Jacob." The order of words indicates the prophet's emphasis. He wished to draw a sharp distinction between those who belonged to God in a special way and those who did not enjoy that relationship. God loved all the nations, but he had chosen Israel as the agent of his redemptive purpose. Through this people he promised to send the Messiah, our Savior.

The prophet's final word was to declare the **name** of the Lord, who cared so much for them but demanded so much from them. The expression LORD **Almighty** means literally "Lord of hosts." This may refer to the commander of the hosts of heaven, the stars, or it may refer to an army on earth. It eventually became a designation for God's power. This satirical commentary on idolatry paved the way for Jeremiah's last word in this larger section of messages.

F Judgment Is Coming—and Soon! (10:17–25)

SUPPORTING IDEA: *Late or soon, by night or noon, God has the last word. Israel faces the fruit of the seed she has sown.*

These last nine verses present a perfect climax for this unit. In these verses Jeremiah has pleaded, warned, entreated, beseeched, and even cried as he delivered Yahweh's communications. Now he sees the enemy knocking, even banging, at the door. What a vindication for the young preacher who has seen so much in such a short time!

10:17–18. During the Great Depression, people sang a little ditty that went like this: "Pack up your troubles in an old kit bag and smile, smile, smile." If those lyrics had been present in Jeremiah's day, he would have changed the last three words to "run, run, run." He saw nothing but gloom and doom, and he envisioned it as occurring immediately.

The Hebrew text does not specify exactly what type of blockade or confinement the people faced as Jeremiah spoke. Neither does it identify the foe who was harassing and threatening the people. At least four possibilities stand out as candidates. The eventual power that conquered and enslaved the people was Babylon; but shortly after the battle of Megiddo, the most likely foe to threaten Judah's security was Egypt.

10:19–22. Who is the speaker in these verses? Perhaps the best approach is to recognize that Jeremiah identified so completely with his people that he equated their sufferings with his own feeling of anguish. As the nation felt pain, so did the prophet. How like Jesus, who took on himself our sins and even the penalty we deserved. In many ways Jeremiah was more like Jesus than any of the prophets. In all their afflictions, he was afflicted.

In verse 19, the prophet's words applied directly to his own emotional hurt. When the shadow of sorrow and the pain of suffering fell on him, he expressed his intensity but recognized one inescapable fact: The heartbreaking grief belonged to him, and he must bear it. Verse 20 applies more specifically to the nation though Jeremiah also shared in the emptiness that came when his words were fulfilled. The word **tent** should probably be understood as referring to Jerusalem while the **sons** symbolized the citizens of that glorious city.

In verse 21, the prophet used the term **shepherds** to designate the rulers. Both Jeremiah and Ezekiel viewed the kings as Yahweh's special representatives. He placed them in charge of guarding the covenant as they reigned. Yahweh expected them to continue the work of Moses, Joshua, and the judges, all of whom ruled by their charismatic personalities. As they failed to be faithful to their assignment, the nation suffered.

Jeremiah must have put his hand to his ear as he, in verse 22, summoned the people to hearken and heed the noise he heard. When the two major invasions finally came in 597 and 586 B.C., widespread destruction and looting resulted. This favorite expression of Jeremiah, **a haunt of jackals** (see also 9:11; 49:33; 51:37), found literal fulfillment in many places. Archaeologists have confirmed the biblical records, showing many towns were destroyed in this area. Some devastated places were never rebuilt. Others were inhabited again but only after long periods of abandonment. There is no indication that any of the smaller towns in Judah had continuous occupation during the Babylonian exile.

10:23–25. The last three verses of this section show the two sides of Jeremiah. First, in verses 23–24, we see the tender and spiritual part of his personality and character. He recognized that all things are in God's hands, and we should never attempt to set his agenda. In God's will is our peace—and nowhere else. Jeremiah knew Judah needed a correction. But he pleaded for God to **correct** his people with **justice**—not in **anger**. The prophet admitted if the full force of God's punitive action fell on all of them, they would be destroyed.

Verse 25 closes this section and the four chapters of this study unit with an exclamation that reveals another side of the prophet. With all his spiritual strength and power, he was still a human being. Similar expressions and prayers appear in other parts of the Old Testament, especially some of the psalms. In such entreaties the person praying asks for strong revenge.

How does the Christian deal with such attitudes? In the light of New Testament teaching, to seek revenge is wrong. Let God avenge! This is the Christian viewpoint, as taught by both Jesus and Paul.

MAIN IDEA REVIEW: *Hypocritical worship, combined with stubborn rebellion, produces an incurable state leading to inevitable doom for both individuals and nations.*

III. CONCLUSION

"You Will Not Change"

In the movie *The Godfather* there is a classic scene near the end. Former war hero and new don of the Corleone family Michael Corleone decides to settle all family accounts with his enemies after his father's funeral.

Michael is asked by his sister Connie and her husband to be their baby's godfather. The baptism is held in a cathedral with a priest and cardinal presiding. The camera alternates between Michael and various Mafia hitmen preparing their machine guns and shotguns. During the ceremony the priest asks Michael if he believes in God, Jesus Christ, the Holy Ghost and if he renounces Satan and all his works? To each question the godfather responds, "I do," as the camera cuts to another assassination scene.

The priest concludes the baptismal ritual, blessing it all "in the name of the Father, and the Son, and the Holy Spirit" as three of the murder scenes are flashed back onto the screen. As the camera returns to Michael, the priest concludes the ritual by saying, "Go in peace, and may the Lord be with you. Amen." Michael Corleone leaves the cathedral surrounded by his family and followed by the priest and cardinal.

Like Michael Corleone, the error many people make today is to continue on course, to persist in disobedience, even when they know they are doing wrong. The Lord said of the people of Judah, "They go from one sin to another" (9:3). Jeremiah said of his hearers, "They cling to deceit; they refuse to return" (8:5). He asked, "Are they ashamed of their loathsome conduct?" Then he answered his own question, declaring, "No, they have no shame at all; they do not even know how to blush" (8:12).

In *The Godfather III,* years later Michael Corleone has a conversation with Cardinal Lamberto, the man who will become Pope John Paul I. Michael tells him it has been thirty years since his last confession. The cardinal encourages Michael to confess his sins. Michael asks the cardinal, "What is the point of confessing if I don't repent?" Finally, as a bell tolls in the background, Michael acknowledges that he has betrayed his wife, betrayed himself, killed men, ordered men to be killed, and even killed his own brother. The cardinal states that Michael's sins indeed are terrible. He tells him, however, that his life still could be redeemed. But then he says to him directly, "You will not change."

And so it is for many people today.

PRINCIPLES

- Because people go to a place of worship does not mean that they are living as they should.
- Faith in God calls for righteous actions and behaviors in social relationships.
- God is aware of the actions of people, especially of those who claim to be his people.
- People have selective memories about God's judgment and think it never applies to them.
- When people do not honor God as they should, they harm themselves.
- Repentance is the way to experience God's blessing.
- God values integrity in his people.
- The tendency toward idolatry resides in all human hearts.
- The Lord God is the creator and sovereign ruler of all things.
- People's lives are not their own, and people are not the masters of their ways. They belong to the Lord.

- God's justice is either corrective or destructive. His disciplinary justice is based on his mercy. His destructive justice is based on his anger and wrath.

APPLICATIONS

- Take some time to assess your motives for going to church.
- Evaluate the extent to which your faith in God is expressed in social relationships.
- If you come up short in your evaluation, ask God to show you steps to take in connecting your faith with words and deeds.
- As part of your quiet time with God, consider the reality of his judgment of nations and individuals. Imagine your own encounter with God at judgment and allow that to shape your attitudes and actions for the next day.
- Bring into your conversation with God one or more attitudes and actions that are preventing a happy relationship with God.
- Be specific in your naming these attitudes and actions.
- Focus on the depth of God's mercy toward you and the extent to which he has gone in Christ to break down all that separates you from him.
- Look at the strongest idol in your life in light of what you could lose in clinging to it rather than to God.
- For a day, stop every hour and evaluate who has mastered your life in the last sixty minutes. Talk with God about what you have observed.

IV. LIFE APPLICATION

No Brains at All

After Dorothy and her dog Toto were blown into the land of the Munchkins by a cyclone, Dorothy learned that she would have to travel to the Emerald City to meet the Great Wizard of Oz so she could ask him to help her get back to Kansas. As Dorothy traveled the yellow brick road, she met a scarecrow. She informed him she was going to the Emerald City and planned to ask the Great Oz to send her back to Kansas. When the scarecrow asked Dorothy where the Emerald City was and who Oz was, she expressed her surprise that he did not know. He answered sadly, "I don't know anything. You see, I am stuffed, so I have no brains at all."

What Scarecrow knew about himself—that he had no brains at all—the people of Judah had not learned about their idols. In fact, Jeremiah, in rebuking the people for their idol worship, used this same analogy: "Like a scarecrow in a melon patch, their idols cannot speak" (10:5).

In 10:1–16 Jeremiah exposed the foolishness of idolatry. The poetic section alternates between verses in which idols and their worshippers are condemned (vv. 2–5,8–9,11,14–15) and verses in which God is praised (vv. 6–7,10,12–13,16). The impact of this can be felt dramatically when two groups alternate reading the sections as an antiphonal response. When Jeremiah stated, "No one is like you, O LORD" (v. 6) and "there is no one like you" (v. 7), he was not just affirming that God is the greatest when compared to other gods. Jeremiah was emphasizing the Lord's uniqueness. The Lord God is totally different from all other gods. He is in a class by himself.

We of the modern age may find it quaint that these people fell down and worshipped what they had made with their hands. We readily acknowledge their idolatry was foolish and their idols were nothing, that their idols gave their worshippers no help and no hope. Yet deep in the human heart is a propensity toward idolatry. The idols of our modern age are not necessarily carved and gilded images or statues. They are whatever takes first place in our lives. Our modern idols may be money or power, an activity or pleasure, a hero or an institution. Anything that substitutes for God is an idol.

V. PRAYER

Almighty Lord, maker of all things, King of all nations, the only true and living God, forgive us for trusting in the outer trappings of our religion, its rituals, and its services rather than in you. Forgive us for attempting to domesticate you so we would feel safe in our sins and loathsome conduct. Help us to turn from all idols and from all that is worthless. Cast out the idols from our hearts. Grant that we will obey you from the heart and with all of our heart. Amen.

VI. DEEPER DISCOVERIES

A. "What I did to Shiloh" (7:14)

Shiloh's importance was in the fact that God chose this site to locate Israel's worship center or religious headquarters when they entered the promised land. During the nomadic days of wilderness wandering, a tent served as a provisional sanctuary where God met with his people.

Upon arriving in Canaan, God decreed this city would be the place where all articles and other matters related to worship would be deposited. The structure that housed these items was probably not elaborate or ornate, but it was more fixed and firm than the tent in the wilderness and, therefore, served for a number of years. Shiloh was the "early Jerusalem," serving as the place for the tribes to make pilgrimages for the annual feasts.

The Scriptures contain no explicit information about the time of Shiloh's destruction. But archaeological evidence indicates it was destroyed about 1050 B.C. Supporting this is the fact that when the Philistines returned the ark to the Israelites, they housed it in Kiriath-Jearim rather than Shiloh. Whatever caused the destruction of Shiloh, Philistine armies or some other phenomenon, the destruction seems to have been complete.

B. Scribes

The word *scribe* stood for those who "wrote" for the king or anyone who could afford their services. Unfortunately, we do not have records about the development of this profession. By the time of the divided kingdom, however, the scribes had become a class, almost elitist. Since Israel, in spite of her defections, took the law of Moses seriously, the scribes were the ones who guarded and copied the texts. As a result, a rivalry arose between the priests and the scribes over who were the authorities in religious rituals and other matters.

Many think the law book discovered in the temple by Josiah's "cleanup crew" had been edited, perhaps considerably, by the scribes. If the rivalry between the priests and scribes became intense, it developed more so between the scribes and the prophets. To their credit the scribes were the ones who kept the law preserved during the Babylonian exile. To their discredit, they, both before and after the exile, claimed to be the authorities in teaching and interpreting the law.

By the time of Jesus, the scribes had become arrogant with their claim to near infallibility in their opinions. Most of the scribes tended to associate themselves with the Pharisees. The latter had a propensity toward accepting the intensely oral interpretations and traditions that had attached themselves to the law. Their claim to complete authority brought both groups into conflict with Jesus as he attempted to put spirit into the law.

Because Jeremiah was so much like Jesus in his approach to religious concepts, he likewise met opposition from the scribes. This was reflected in the prophet's words, "How can you say, 'We are wise, for we have the law of the LORD,' when actually the lying pen of the scribes has handled it falsely?" (8:8).

C. "High places of Topheth" (7:31)

The Israelites lived in a world obsessed with idol worship. Jeremiah recoiled at all such activities, wherever practiced, but one location brought exceeding irritation and condemnation. The Valley of Hinnom lay near Jerusalem. It holds a rather unglamorous position in Old Testament history. Pagan worshippers, especially those of Baal and Molech, practiced child sacrifice, especially at a place called Topheth located in this area. The word *Topheth* carried the meaning of "fireplace," from either the Aramaic or Hebrew language. Jewish scribes changed its meaning, however, to "detestable, abominable, shameful thing" because of the worship ceremonies carried on there.

This area became the city's garbage dump. In New Testament days people referred to the Valley of Hinnom, or "Ben (son of) Hinnom" by the Greek name *Geenah*. Jesus used the picture of the never-ending and unquenchable fires of the garbage dump as a symbolic picture of eternal punishment for sins (Matt. 5:22).

VII. TEACHING OUTLINE

A. INTRODUCTION

1. Lead Story: When the Forts of Folly Fall
2. Context: In the years before the end of the nation of Judah, the people of Judah believed that no harm could come to them because they

were God's chosen people, Jerusalem was God's chosen city, and their temple was God's earthly dwelling place. The people felt completely safe and believed God would protect them no matter how they lived since they perpetuated and participated in the temple rituals. Jeremiah criticized these presumptuous views, called on the people to repent and obey God, and warned of the coming judgment.

3. Transition: Going to the temple courtyard, Jeremiah preached against the people's domestication of God and their confidence in the temple. He told his hearers they were in for a rude awakening and that they soon would lose their temple, their city, and their nation. He sought to appeal to their consciences, to their reason, and to their history— all to no avail.

B. COMMENTARY
1. Conduct Should Match One's Worship (7:1–8:3)
2. The Letter of the Law Is Not Enough (8:4–13)
3. Empathy for People Crushed by Catastrophes (8:14–9:1)
4. Depraved People Face Punishment (9:2–26)
5. Idol Worship Is Idle Worship (10:1–16)
6. Judgment Is Coming—and Soon! (10:17–25)

C. CONCLUSION: "YOU WILL NOT CHANGE"

VIII. ISSUES FOR DISCUSSION

1. Why do people go to church or participate in worship services when it doesn't make any difference in how they live each day?
2. Why is participating in religious rituals more attractive to many people than obeying God's Word and living according to his ways?
3. Why is the human heart so prone toward idolatry? What modern idolatries capture so many hearts today?
4. Based on the names and titles for God in 10:1–16 (Lord, King of the nations, the true God, the living God, the eternal King, the Portion of Jacob, the Maker of all things, the Lord Almighty), discuss the nature and works of God and the impact he should have on people's lives.

5. What does the Bible mean by the anger and wrath of God? How are these different in God than in human beings? How do the concepts of God's corrective justice and his mercy contribute to your understanding of his anger and wrath?

Jeremiah 11:1–12:17

Covenant: Our Relationship with God

I. INTRODUCTION
Convincing People to Accept the Covenant

II. COMMENTARY
A verse-by-verse explanation of these verses.

III. CONCLUSION
A Lamb Led to the Slaughter

An overview of the principles and applications from these verses.

IV. LIFE APPLICATION
The Enemies Within

Melding these verses to life.

V. PRAYER
Tying these verses to life with God.

VI. DEEPER DISCOVERIES
Historical, geographical, and grammatical enrichment of the commentary.

VII. TEACHING OUTLINE
Suggested step-by-step group study of these verses.

VIII. ISSUES FOR DISCUSSION
Zeroing these verses in on daily life.

Quote

"*The* absence of anger, especially that sort of anger which we call indignation, can, in my opinion, be a most alarming symptom. And the presence of indignation may be a good one. Even when that indignation passes into bitter personal vindictiveness, it may still be a good symptom."

C. S. Lewis

Jeremiah 11:1–12:17

IN A NUTSHELL

Jeremiah 11–12 arises out of the background of King Josiah's reform after the book of the law, the book of the covenant, was found in the temple and read to the people in 621 B.C. At this time King Josiah led his people in renewing the covenant and pledging to live according to it (2 Chr. 34:8–33). In support of Josiah's reform, the Lord instructed Jeremiah to travel throughout Judah and Jerusalem and remind the people of the terms of the covenant that the nation had entered into with God at Sinai in the time of Moses. Jeremiah's message is summarized in 11:1–17. When the people of Jeremiah's home village heard his denunciations about their covenant-breaking and his announcement of God's plan to uproot the nation, they plotted to kill Jeremiah. God revealed the assassination plot to Jeremiah, and this led to his voicing a complaint to God and God answering his questions (12:1–17).

Covenant: Our Relationship with God

I. INTRODUCTION

Convincing People to Accept the Covenant

*W*hen World War I ended in 1918, Woodrow Wilson was cheered by many Europeans as the savior of the Western world. At the Paris Peace Conference in January 1919, Wilson led the Big Four nations that dominated the conference (Italy, Britain, France, and the United States). Wilson also opposed any imperialistic parceling up of the conquered territories by the victorious European nations.

Wilson, who had embraced the idea of a League of Nations, was chosen as chairman of the committee that drafted the league charter and agreements (referred to as Covenant). This league would manage and modify peace settlements, outlaw future wars, provide mandates for liberated colonies, and promote social justice. By mid-February 1919, Wilson had persuaded the Paris Conference to make establishing the league an integral part of the final Treaty of Versailles.

On his return from Europe in July 1919, the president submitted the treaty in person to the Senate. But his plan for a League of Nations was bitterly opposed in the Senate. He went on a whirlwind tour to generate support for the league—a move that eventually caused Wilson to suffer a stroke and failed to move the nation to his point of view.

During Wilson's incapacitation, the Senate attached fourteen reservations onto the treaty. Wilson could not compromise his covenant. With such reservations attached, he urged senators to vote against the treaty. The treaty and its league were defeated on November 19, 1919, and again on March 19, 1920. Wilson had asked the nation to accept this covenant in total or not at all. In his view it was an all-or-nothing agreement, and he got nothing.

Not content with the defeat of his beloved league, Wilson pushed the Democratic Party into making the 1920 election a "solemn referendum" and true mandate on the league. Wilson, his party, and their candidate suffered overwhelming defeat. The Republican candidate, Warren G. Harding, promised a return to "normalcy" for the nation and was swept into the presidency by a tidal wave of votes. Wilson's covenant, the League of Nations, was dead in America.

Like Woodrow Wilson, Jeremiah the prophet went around among his people urging the people to listen to and affirm a covenant. The Lord told Jeremiah, "Listen to the terms of this covenant and tell them to the people of Judah and to those who live in Jerusalem" (11:2). And again, "Proclaim all these words in the towns of Judah and in the streets of Jerusalem" (11:6).

The covenant and its terms that Jeremiah was to remind his people about was the covenant the nation entered into with God at Sinai in the time of Moses (v. 4; Exod. 19–24). The heart of this covenant was obedience.

Eight times the Hebrew word rendered "listen" and "obey" is used in 11:2–11. For those who would obey the covenant terms, there was blessing—both spiritual and material (11:4–5). For those who persisted in disobedience, there were curses, just as for the original hearers (11:3,8; Deut. 27:15–26).

But the hearts of Jeremiah's hearers were not touched. And as with Woodrow Wilson, the consequences of his nation's refusal to accept the obligations of the covenant and the attitudes of his fellow countrymen toward him personally wreaked havoc on Jeremiah and his spirit.

II. COMMENTARY

Covenant: Our Relationship with God

MAIN IDEA: *God expects those who enter into covenant with him to take it seriously and be faithful to his demands.*

A God's Command to Proclaim the Covenant (11:1–8)

SUPPORTING IDEA: *Those who have made a commitment to God need to be reminded constantly to honor it.*

11:1–8. Students of Jeremiah encounter difficulty when they seek to understand why certain chapters follow one another. Chapters 11 and 12, however, give no problem, since they "hang together" as a unit. Both are related to the great reformation under Josiah. They probably existed, at one time, as a separate scroll or units of scrolls before being incorporated into the present Book of Jeremiah.

Most Old Testament students view this momentous reform movement as beginning in 621 B.C. when workers who were cleaning the temple discovered an ancient law book. The result of this discovery was a royal decree revamping the nation's religious life, based on commands in this book.

Jeremiah participated in and supported the king's reform program. As a result he met opposition from many sides, even the people from his own hometown, Anathoth. The problems these happenings caused in Jeremiah's emotional and spiritual life pervade these two chapters. Those who enjoy seeing clear-cut outlines to units of biblical material can be quite comfortable with these two chapters. A simple yet comprehensive organization presents itself on first reading.

This first main division of Scripture (vv. 1–8) consists of two subsections. The first five verses record Yahweh's words to Jeremiah about his responsibility. The Lord ordered the young prophet to tell the people about the serious nature of the covenant he had made with their ancestors at Sinai.

To what covenant did Yahweh refer? No reason exists for denying this newly discovered material was the product of Moses. It was probably only a part of the complete Book of Deuteronomy that we have today. Those scholars who suggest chapters 12–26 are probably correct. This Deuteronomic material represents an amplification and enlargement of the material in Exodus 21:1–23:33. The people at Sinai adopted these commands given in a solemn ceremony, recorded in Exodus 24:1–8. The Mosaic covenant was undoubtedly the one to which Yahweh referred in his words to Jeremiah.

What did Yahweh promise the new generation after their fathers had died in the wilderness? He would give them this new land "flowing with milk and honey" (Jer. 11:5). This gift of the land came with conditions. Israel must be faithful to him. Yahweh repeated this promise and warning many times through Israel's history. He chose Jeremiah to voice his last warning to the nation.

Was this covenant conditional? Absolutely! What part of it? The part that referred to the land and to national Israel. Not God's original promise to Abraham. He would bless the world through Abraham's seed. That remained irrevocable. It was gloriously fulfilled in Jesus Christ.

These two subsections (vv. 1–5,6–9) contain essentially the same message, but it is expressed in different ways. The first five verses are written in the third person except for the last four words that give the prophet's reply to

Yahweh's words. The last four verses are written in the first person with Jeremiah telling of Yahweh's command to him.

How soon in the reform movement did Yahweh speak to his young and newly called prophet? Let us review some dates. God's call to Jeremiah came in the thirteenth year of Josiah's reign (1:2). The law book was discovered in the temple in the eighteenth year of Josiah's reign (2 Kgs. 22:3–10). Old Testament students generally agree that these dates were 626 and 621 B.C.

What did Jeremiah do during those five years? Although records are not available, he probably spent them in and around Anathoth where his family ministered, assisting in the worship of that day. The religious rituals were mostly carried on at the local shrines in Anathoth. In the judgment of many interpreters, the prophetic utterances in 2:1–4:4 and 4:5–6:30 were composed and delivered during those years. The young priest-turned-prophet probably became an outstanding religious personality.

What about events related to Josiah and the king's reform movement? According to the account in 2 Kings 22:11–23:25, Josiah moved quickly in the religious reform.

One of the chief events was the celebration of Passover. John Skinner writes, "Not since the day of the judges who led Israel, nor throughout the days of the kings of Israel and the kings of Judah, had any such Passover been observed." Skinner imagines how it might have been:

> In the spring of that year, a rumor reaches the village of the discovery in the Temple of an ancient law-book, said to be that of Moses, which had caused the gravest concern to the king because of the glaring disparity between its requirements and the existing state of things in matters religious and moral. This is speedily followed by a summons to the local elders to a great national convention at Jerusalem at the approaching Passover season.
>
> When the delegates return they have a thrilling story to tell—of a Passover such as had never been observed in Israel before, of a Solemn League and Covenant entered into by the king and heads of the people to make the newly found law the basis of public religion, and to extirpate everything inconsistent with it, of a cleansing of the temple from idolatrous emblems, the ejection of sacred prostitutes and the whole crew of diviners, astrologers and wizards from the Temple

precincts, and many other startling demonstrations of reforming and iconoclastic zeal (Skinner, 89–90).

Something similar to this must have occurred at every town throughout the land. One can visualize the people's resentment when they saw their holy places torn down. Think for a moment how the "old-timers" felt when they gazed on the ruins of their holy places. Along with this ignominy, the priests knew they would receive little offerings in the future.

What part did Jeremiah play in this program of reform? According to 11:6, the Lord ordered Jeremiah to go throughout **the towns of Judah and in the streets of Jerusalem** urging the people to **listen to the terms of this covenant and follow them.** This would include centralizing worship in the temple and eliminating worship at the local shrines. To understand the problem fully, one must read the two lengthy passages in Exodus and Deuteronomy mentioned above (Deut. 12–26; Exod. 21:1–23:33).

Notice carefully, in verses 6–8, the way Yahweh presented his warning. Rather than threatening the people, he spoke of how he had sent **the curses of the covenant** upon the disobedient people. This included every succeeding generation up until that present day.

B Opposition to Jeremiah and His Preaching (11:9–17)

SUPPORTING IDEA: *People who have their own agenda resent anyone disturbing it, especially when their income and livelihood are affected.*

11:9–17. A period of time elapsed between God's first word to Jeremiah about the covenant and this new one. Most students believe Jeremiah went on a trip throughout the area, doing exactly what God commanded him. No record exists to inform us about the success or failure of the prophet with the small villages. The one exception was Anathoth, his hometown.

What is the relationship of 11:9–17 to 11:1–8? Does the second unit relate historically to the first? If so, does it follow the first chronologically? If so, how much time intervened between the two? All three of these questions need to be considered.

Most Old Testament scholars believe these two passages are closely related historically. Likewise, the large majority believe one follows the other chronologically, but the remaining question is, How quickly?

Here is one way of integrating these two passages. The young preacher, sensing God's call and enthusiastically supported by the king, made a tour of cities and villages in and around Judah. He urged the inhabitants to close down their local worship places and come to the temple with their sacrifices. His last stop was probably his hometown, Anathoth. His reception outside Anathoth was mixed but mainly unenthusiastic, perhaps even negative. The people and especially the priests did not want to make the change. The former loved the convenience, and the latter loved the revenue.

What about the conspiracy in verse 9? This probably referred to all the cities that Jeremiah visited, including Anathoth. They rejected him so completely and thoroughly that the young prophet felt a conspiracy had been formed against him. In the next segment (11:18–12:6), Jeremiah spoke of some evil plot formed against him at Anathoth of which the Lord gave him knowledge. This might have been a part of the general conspiracy, but it was probably more intense since it was in his hometown.

What was the style of worship in which the people of the towns and villages were engaged? With the limited evidence we have, we cannot speak with certainty. Verses 10–12 indicate idolatry abounded. Jeremiah spoke, in verse 13, of their having as many gods as there were cities. This certainly means they had sold out to many pagan deities. What about the temple at Jerusalem? From other accounts, corruption abounded there also. The conclusion we must reach is that very little pure Yahweh worship existed in either place.

In verse 14, Yahweh spoke a strange word to the prophet. We presume he meant for him to pass it on to the people. "No need to intercede for these people any more! They have passed the place of no return. I refuse to hear their supplications or entreaties!"

How literally should we interpret these words? Does anyone ever go so far that God refuses to heed and forgive? An earlier prophet helps us at this point. Isaiah spoke of the people in his day as those who "call evil good and good evil, who put darkness for light and light for darkness, who put bitter for sweet and sweet for bitter" (Isa. 5:20). They had lost the spiritual capacity to distinguish between right and wrong. This led them to a position of being unable to repent. Someone expressed it as being "morally color-blind." When that happens, God *will not hear* because they *cannot* repent!

The conclusion seems obvious. Whether in "big church" at Jerusalem or the "little congregations" out in the villages, worshippers and religious leaders alike had made worship of Yahweh a sham. What was the result? No need to bring any offerings to Yahweh. He sees through your hypocrisy.

In verses 16–17, Jeremiah brought this segment to a sharp conclusion. Like Hosea, he likened the nation to an olive tree. Two things made this an attractive literary image. First, its natural beauty. Second, it was a symbol of affluence since olive oil was a precious commodity. Jeremiah once more focused on the days of the nation's youthful devotion, her bridal love (v. 2).

Jeremiah did not actually say much in these two closing verses that he had not declared previously in earlier addresses. But one thing set these words apart from his previous ones. We get the impression that the end is near. An indicator of this is the fact that the prophet used the prophetic perfect in the last two verbs of verse 16. Jeremiah was so sure of his prophecy that he spoke of the event as having already happened.

Verse 17 is a supplementary parallelism. It reinforces what was said in verse 16 but adds a parallelism to verse 16. This should probably be called a supplementary parallelism since it added new thoughts. The jury is no longer deliberating. The verdict is in. Judah's sin has not only been found out; it has found her out. Payday is close. Perhaps a little further off than the youthful and zealous preacher felt but very near.

Ⓒ God's Servants Can Expect Opposition (11:18–12:6)

SUPPORTING IDEA: *Often our closest friends, even our family, are those who oppose us the most severely.*

11:18–12:6. The scene changes. These verses contain a dialogue between the prophet and Yahweh. We must not press the literary style used today as a guideline for this prophetic work. In verses 18–20, Jeremiah explained what he learned and how he learned it. First, it came as a direct revelation from Yahweh. Whether God spoke vocally or gave Jeremiah the insight to figure it out for himself is not relevant. The prophet learned about the **plot** because Yahweh provided the knowledge.

From the previous segment, we know a coalition formed against Jeremiah's preaching. This was true among all the small villages as well as in the big city of Jerusalem. In the Hebrew text, "plot" does not appear in verse 18, but for some reason many interpreters insist on putting this word in their translation. The original reads literally, "And Yahweh caused me to know and I kept on knowing."

The Hebrew text is difficult at this point, but the point is clear. At first, Jeremiah had been naïve about this conspiracy against him. The old cliché "to the pure all things are pure" seems to fit him at this point. Often highly idealistic people do not realize how evil some people can be. Jeremiah was perhaps sheltered in his early life from the cold, hard facts about man's inhumanity to man.

The first part of verse 18 probably refers to all the towns the prophet had visited. Obviously, he faced a cool reception everywhere. At his home village, however, the violence must have been more intense. This causes us no surprise, especially if we are familiar with the life of our Savior. The most serious threat on his life came early in his ministry from those of his hometown (Luke 4:16–30).

From Jeremiah's own words we learn the people had deceived him, perhaps by pretending that they were receptive to his message at first. This occurred also with Jesus when he preached in the synagogue at Nazareth (Luke 4:22). But as Jeremiah continued, opposition to him mounted. He spoke of his simplistic understanding with a phrase that we also find in another prophet's writings to describe our Savior's voluntary sufferings in the redemptive work at Calvary: **like a gentle lamb led to the slaughter** (v. 19; Isa. 53:7). This was probably a current expression in the prophet's day, but it reached undying fame when it was incorporated into God's redemptive activity.

The record does not state exactly when Jeremiah learned of this plot that had apparently been in progress for some time. Jeremiah alluded to the event that disclosed the hidden danger rather than indicating and describing it. Clearly, however, the prophet knew nothing about it until it was ripe for execution.

Jeremiah followed his confession by uttering, in verse 20, a prayer that is one of the infamous imprecatory prayers of the Old Testament. He called on God to pour out wrath and retribution upon these cruel people who had done such a terrible thing to him. His vindictive spirit certainly violated everything Jesus taught about what our attitude should be toward those who oppose us. How do we as Christians handle such an outburst from a prophet whom we admire for so many other qualities?

Jeremiah took the content of his heart to the right place—to Yahweh. He did not deny the anger and the desires of his heart fueled by that anger. Jeremiah was appealing to the sovereign Judge who never errs. Justice rather than personal justification and revenge was the motive of his heart. That's why he brought his desire to the God who sees all things clearly.

Did Jeremiah know before Yahweh's reply recorded in verse 21 that the inhabitants of his hometown had led in the plot against his life? If he did, this might help explain the severity of his complaint in the previous verses. But in verse 22, Yahweh assured Jeremiah that he would not be disappointed. Those of his hometown who plotted against him would be dealt with properly.

The second section of this material (12:1–6) contains some of the most heartrending words in the entire Book of Jeremiah. It consists of a spirited complaint from Jeremiah and a frank answer by Yahweh. Charles Edward Jefferson suggests an excellent summary of the Lord's answer to Jeremiah could be, "Cheer up, the worst is yet to come" (Wood, 51).

Jeremiah acknowledged Yahweh's righteousness. The prophet then raised a question that has disturbed interpreters through the centuries: "Why do evil people live free of adversity while those who seek to serve the Lord constantly face reverses and hardships?" Or to state the question in the more popular format: "Why do the righteous suffer and the wicked prosper?"

The prophet had no questions about Yahweh's power. But he wondered about the fairness of some of his decisions. Because he knew that his heart was an open book before the Lord, he expressed what the Lord already saw within him. Jeremiah felt if he could not reconcile the confusions that haunted him, he could no longer function as an effective prophet of God.

Jeremiah had a simplistic solution. Impatient minds always think that way. The prophet required only a few words to sum up the entire matter. Only one solution! Wipe them off the face of the earth with one stroke. Deal with them as they had intended to treat him.

Interpreters encounter difficulty when they try to understand verse 4. At first glance, it seems to interrupt the context. Some students take the easy road and suggest a rearrangement of the text. A few go so far as to delete it completely. But such drastic action doesn't solve the problem. Surely those who compiled the book would have adjusted the material as they compiled it if they thought this were necessary. Public speakers, especially preachers, often switch subjects suddenly without laboring their conclusion after making a strong point.

No interpretation for this verse is accepted by everyone, but one seems to rise above the others. The prophet asked a rhetorical question. Rather than seeking to answer it directly, he reminded the people of the relationship between the people's moral life and nature's productivity. The implication of Jeremiah's words seems to be that he did not believe the situation was fair. The land was suffering because of the general population's wickedness, but the righteous people were also suffering in the process.

This interpretation supports the position for which Jeremiah had been contending. God should destroy the wicked people and then the good people, like himself and others, could live at peace.

God's answer to Jeremiah, in verses 5–6, contains a word of warning. Further heartaches and perils await the young prophet. In verse 6, Yahweh revealed to Jeremiah the most shocking news yet. It was the third of three progressive steps informing him how intensely opposition to him had developed. First, he found out a plot had developed against him. Second, he learned it began and was centered in his hometown. Third, God informed him, **Your brothers, your own family—even they have betrayed you.** This was the most unkind cut of all. They had played the game of pretend, and Yahweh warned, **Do not trust them, though they speak well of you.**

How much can one take without wanting to quit? In verse 5, Yahweh used two metaphors to let the prophet know what was ahead. The first metaphor comes from athletic competition. If foot-racing exhausts the prophet, what about trying to run as fast as the swift horses? Problems and conflicts are ahead that will make the present ones minor by comparison.

The second metaphor contains two possible applications, based on how one translates the Hebrew text. The KJV reads, "How wilt thou do in the swelling of the Jordan?" Modern versions render it **thickets by the Jordan** or "thicket of the Jordan" (NASB). What is the difference?

The "swelling" would probably refer to the flooding season when the Jordan River overflows in certain areas. The "pride" or "splendor" would probably refer to the region surrounding the Jordan, which was a place of jungle growth. It had become a lair or hideout for lions.

This is quite a picturesque locality. Down the broad valley of the Jordan there runs a winding strip of green that marks the course of the river. It lies deep below the general level of the valley, as deep in places as two hundred feet, and is a tangle of thick bush and driftwood that the river overflows in time of flood. This jungle is spoken of as the pride of Jordan. For instance Jeremiah speaks of a lion coming up out of the pride of Jordan, and it is held by many that in our text he is simply contrasting this jungle with more settled country.

But there is one problem with this interpretation. The Septuagint or Greek version translates the Hebrew by a Greek word that expresses the prancing of spirited horses. This is not a major problem. George Adam Smith, who prefers to translate the expression "jungle" or "rankness," comments wisely in his *Historical Geography of the Holy Land:* "It is floods which have made the rankness, they fill this wider bed of Jordan every year" (p. 485).

What do all these facts mean as we seek to interpret? The phrase "in the swelling of the Jordan" works well as a translation. The Hebrew phrase of which it is a translation has several meanings. Some of them are "to grow up," "to increase," "to be lifted," "exalted," "majestic." From this comes such meaning as pride, haughtiness, even arrogance.

What was the Lord's final and summary message for Jeremiah? First, his own family members were his greatest enemies. Second, greater problems and dangers awaited him in the future. He must love everybody but trust nobody, only God.

Did Yahweh's words satisfy Jeremiah? At least, they kept him in the prophetic ministry to which God had called him. His days of depression were not over. Scattered throughout the remainder of the Book of Jeremiah, we shall see other times when Jeremiah entered the valley of depression and despondency. But the "fire in his bones" still burned.

D God's Instrument of Punishment (12:7–17)

SUPPORTING IDEA: *Using less righteous people as his agent and then punishing them, God will then offer salvation to them.*

12:7–17. Old Testament students disagree on where to place this "seeming fragment." It concludes the scroll containing Jeremiah's preaching during the reformation of Josiah. Many interpreters contend the verses are a message added to this collection because it had no other place to go.

These scholars divide mainly into two camps. One group places this oracle during the early part of Jehoiakim's reign. The basic support for their position is found in 2 Kings 24:1–2. This historical book reads:

During Jehoiakim's reign, Nebuchadnezzar king of Babylon invaded the land, and Jehoiakim became his vassal for three years. But then he changed his mind and rebelled against Nebuchadnezzar. The Lord sent Babylonian, Aramean, Moabite and Ammonite raiders against him. He sent them to destroy Judah, in accordance with the word of the Lord proclaimed by his servants the prophets.

The "wicked neighbors" are the "enemies" mentioned by Jeremiah in this passage.

The second group feels the opening verses of Jeremiah's words suggest a calamity of greater magnitude than the 2 Kings passage. The forsaking by Yahweh, they say, can hardly refer to anything less than the fall of Jerusalem in 586 B.C. They think this prophetic passage was delivered later, after the invasion of Jerusalem in 597 B.C. This incursion was when Jehoiakim met his death. At that time indignation was still felt against the surrounding nations for their participation in the land's devastation. This passage might even belong in the brief three-month reign of Jehoiachin or more probably the early years of Zedekiah's reign (597–586 B.C.).

A few students see a third option. Among this latter group is an outstanding scholar, Rabbi H. Freedman. This school of thought points out the verbs are, in the Hebrew text, the "perfect" or "completed" form. He contends they should be considered as "prophetic perfects." According to him and others of this school, the prophet was so certain the incidents would happen that he spoke of them as already completed. They contend that Jeremiah delivered this section during the days when Josiah or Jehoahaz reigned, no later than the very early days of Jehoiakim's tenure.

In verses 7–13, Jeremiah spoke with alarm. This could reflect the youthful exuberance of a young prophet. To him, God was about to wrap it up. This attitude is often true of a young, immature preacher. Added to this, Jeremiah had been hurt. For a number of years, Josiah's reformation had seemed to be successful. Then suddenly the bubble burst. He saw the intense nationalism that developed, killing the religious spirit. Added to this was the attempt to kill him. Jeremiah became once more the flaming "hell fire and brimstone" preacher of his early years.

Jeremiah presented these words that he had received from Yahweh to the people in the form of a poem. The Lord was ready to give up on Israel and Judah. They had deserted him and refused to keep the covenant vows of their forefathers. God no longer felt obligated to them and was justified in turning them over to their foes. This would be the same thing he had done with the Northern Kingdom, delivering it over to Assyria several years before.

The words **house** and **inheritance** in verse 7 are probably used as part of the larger parallelism rather than "house" referring to the temple. The Jewish commentary known as the Targums softens the word **hate** in verse 8 to "expelled." This was probably so as not to conflict with **the one I love** in verse 7. The literal meaning, however, is "hate."

The two vivid figures of speech in verse 9 convey the innermost feeling of God. He pictured the nation as a **speckled bird**, symbolized by its beautiful plumage. While this could represent the people's pride, the more probable meaning lies in the bird's visibility and appeal to enemies. In this dramatic and creative poem, the prophet warned the people of the doom awaiting them because of their sinful lifestyle.

The word **shepherds** (v. 10) is used often by Old Testament writers as a figure for rulers of Israel and Judah. A few suggest this is the meaning here. Bu in this context almost all interpreters contend the meaning is "the leaders of Israel's enemies." In verse 12, they are also called **destroyers**. Although the same Hebrew word is not used, the parallel is obvious.

The prophet's picture (v. 11) of the land's blight caused by **the sword of the LORD** (v. 12) presents a difficulty for some interpreters. The meaning is that God will operate in this century the same way he did in the preceding century. When the Northern Kingdom became rebellious, he chose a foreign power, Assyria, as his agent of destruction. Verse 13 indicates the people, meanwhile, will continue their normal pursuits. They will plant wheat and other crops as usual. But they will not harvest what they have sown. When they become ashamed of their crop failure, they will need to remember the reason: They have been unfaithful to Yahweh.

Verses 14–17 give one final truth about Israel's God, Yahweh. Since he is the supreme ruler of the world, he has his compassionate eye on everyone. He must punish the wicked nations even though he uses them to punish his people. But after that punitive action has been completed, he will restore his people to their land. He will offer them a chance to embrace him as Lord. Yahweh's ultimate goal is the blessing of all peoples.

MAIN IDEA REVIEW: *God expects those who enter into covenant with him to take it seriously and be faithful to his demands.*

III. CONCLUSION

A Lamb Led to the Slaughter

Jeremiah was the son of a priest from Anathoth, a priestly village (1:1). Amazingly, it was the men of Anathoth who plotted against Jeremiah and sought to kill him (11:21). Jeremiah couldn't believe it. He likened himself to "a gentle lamb led to the slaughter" (11:19). Verse 18 informs us that Jeremiah only came to a realization of the plot when God revealed it to him. That Jeremiah learned this by revelation is repeated twice for emphasis.

Their plan was to "destroy the tree and its fruit," to "cut him off from the land of the living," and make it so "his name" would "be remembered no more" (11:19). The first phrase alone indicates total destruction. But Jeremiah's foes were not satisfied with that. They didn't want him to be remembered.

Jeremiah cried out in the first of his laments against those who plotted against him. He called on God for "vengeance" (11:20), and in a fitting parody of having declared his previous position as "a gentle lamb led to the slaughter" (11:19), exclaimed, "Drag them off like sheep to be butchered! Set them apart like sheep for the day of slaughter" (12:3).

The Lord answered Jeremiah's complaint and promised to punish the wicked men along with their sons and daughters (11:22–23). He announced that "the sword of the LORD will devour from one end of the land to the other; no one will be safe" (12:12). But the Lord also announced a word of compassion and hope to those who would confess and learn his ways (12:15–16).

PRINCIPLES

- Covenants, once entered into, are to be honored and kept.
- People do not like to be rebuked when they are in the wrong. Often they reject the messenger as well as the message.
- It is fitting to bring hard questions to God for his answers and to voice our honest frustrations and complaints to him.
- God himself knows very well our most disappointing and hurtful experiences.

- Those who respond properly to God's chastisement find him to be a God of compassion.

APPLICATIONS

- Make a list of the covenants you have entered into and review the expectations of these covenants for the parties involved.
- Evaluate how well you are fulfilling each of these covenants.
- Where you find yourself not living up to the covenant, acknowledge that to yourself, to God, and to other parties in the covenant.
- Take actions needed to fulfill what you have promised to be and do in these relationships.
- Describe your reaction the last time you were rebuked. Assess the reasons you reacted as you did and whether corrective action is needed in the way you take criticism.
- Next time you become angry, bring that anger, frustration, and complaint into God's presence and notice the difference it makes sharing it with him rather letting it smolder inside.
- Based on the whole of the biblical truth, describe God's expression toward you.

IV. LIFE APPLICATION

The Enemies Within

Henry II (reigned 1154–1189), king of England, was a good and able king. He ruled the largest territory of his time, from Ireland to the Pyrenees. He is said to have been imaginative, energetic, and commanding, and to have had an alert and ready mind. It is said of him that his hands were never empty, that he always held a book or a bow. He restored the royal authority and renovated the financial, military, and judicial aspects of the government, and he established the supremacy of common law under royal control. Henry was married to Eleanor of Aquitaine.

By the late 1170s Henry had imposed his will in virtually all matters of the kingdom. Obstacles had been overcome, defeated, or outflanked. His achievements lulled him into a sense of security. He ignored warnings of trouble, brushed aside items he should have been alert to, and minimized problems that were brought to his attention.

From 1173 until his death, Henry had to contend with his quarrelsome wife, whom he imprisoned, and his four troublesome sons and their territorial ambitions. Their tragic story is presented in the Academy Award-winning movie *The Lion in Winter.* Eleanor of Aquitaine aligned herself with the French to ensure her oldest son's position as heir to the throne. King Henry favored his youngest son. None of the sons cared for either of the parents but only sought to obtain personal power.

A contemporary, Gerald of Wales (1147–1216), royal chaplain, archdeacon, and prolific writer, recorded that Henry ordered one space in the painted chamber of Winchester Castle to be left blank. When Henry later had it filled in, he had an eagle painted with four young ones perched on it—one on each wing and another on its back, all tearing at the parent with talons and beaks, and the fourth eaglet sitting on the parent's neck waiting to peck out its parent's eyes. When King Henry's close friends asked him the meaning of the picture, he replied that the four young eagles represented his four sons who would like to see him dead.

Just two days before he died, Henry, learning his remaining sons had united in opposition against him, said, "Enough, now let things go as they may; I care no more for myself or for the world. . . . Shame, shame on a conquered king."

Reports of plots and treachery from within one's own family must be the hardest of all to accept. This must be especially true when a person has only done right by his own people and has sought nothing but good for them. But such was Jeremiah's fate, according to 11:18–12:6.

V. PRAYER

Dear Lord, help us not to be discouraged to the point that we fail to proclaim your word when your people are unfaithful to the covenant obligations they have entered into with you, when they do not obey you completely, when they fail to do everything you have commanded. Help us to take our grievances and frustrations to you, knowing you are always righteous. And, dear Lord, even if those who are closest to us do not understand us and go so far as to turn against us, help us to trust in you from our heart. Amen.

VI. DEEPER DISCOVERIES

A. Covenant (11:1)

The Hebrew word translated "covenant" represents a concept rooted deeply in most religions and cultures of the ancient Eastern world. Some modern synonyms in the English language are *league, pact, alliance, agreement*. This is because the word contains several shades of meaning. The covenant is a unifying theme in biblical literature. Those recorded in Scripture, however, do not represent something brought into the world solely by Jewish thinking or practice. They were built on agreement models in the larger world of politics and economics, especially among the Hittites and Assyrians. These covenants consisted of contracts or arrangements between nations or individuals of equal or unequal authority.

Any person interested today in a detailed study of these ancient treaties can find copies of them among records of both the Hittite and the Assyrian empires. The former contains a larger number, and they date during 1400 to 1200 B.C. The few existing among the latter come from 850 to 650 B.C.

Neither group entered into covenants containing fixed and firm forms, rigid and unchangeable in structure. The Hittite treaties or covenants, however, whether between king and vassal or two kings of equal authority, were more likely to be monolithic. A number of Old Testament passages, especially Deuteronomy and Joshua 24, show Israel was familiar with these treaty forms and used them often.

The Old Testament concept of making these agreements was "cutting a covenant." A sacrificial ceremony accompanied making the covenant and usually the eating of a sacrificial meal.

Following Israel's delivery from Egyptian bondage, Yahweh presented a covenant to the redeemed people. It demanded complete faithfulness to him. The people accepted it, but almost immediately they broke it and entered into covenant with other nations who served other gods. The prophets, especially Hosea and Jeremiah, called the people back to covenant obedience.

The climax in Old Testament covenant history was Jeremiah's prophecy of a new covenant. Jesus Christ fulfilled that promise. This invalidated the Mosaic covenant that was conditional from the start, but not the one with Abraham. Through his seed, Jesus Christ, the world is being blessed today.

B. Anathoth (11:21)

When Joshua divided the newly conquered land of Canaan, he assigned the city of Anathoth to the Levites (Josh. 21:18). As a Canaanite town, it had probably been the shrine of their goddess Anath. Thus a pagan place of worship was transformed into a priestly city of Yahweh.

Before reaching its highest prestige as Jeremiah's home, Anathoth enjoyed distinction as the birthplace of two military heroes in David's army—Jehu and Abiezer. This small town lies almost hidden in the list of cities in Sennacherib's pathway as he marched toward Jerusalem (Isa. 10:30). It may have been one of the thirty-eight walled towns which the Assyrian general boasted that he captured. Though conquered, and no doubt depopulated, by Babylon in 586 B.C., 128 men returned from exile and resettled Anathoth (Ezra 2:23; Neh. 7:27). After the exile, the Benjamites occupied the city. Jeremiah held title to some land in Anathoth (37:11–12). Any of his nephews or cousins returning to the city probably reclaimed it when they returned from Babylon.

Where is the ancient Anathoth today? For many years archaeologists were almost unanimous that it was located on a site now occupied by modern Anata. This village, about two miles northeast of Jerusalem, stands on a high ridge about 737 yards above sea level. It is composed of three hills connected by low saddles. But in the early twentieth century, scholars began to call this location into question. Two alternates were suggested, Ras el-Kharrubeh and el-Isawiyew.

Regardless of which location is the correct one, when we enter the area, we walk in the vicinity of where Jeremiah lived, and we can still breathe the air of the ancient village in which he lived. We can look on the rocky shelves down which the central range of Palestine declines through the desert to the valley of Jordan, and we can gaze as Jeremiah did from his home and see the land fall away in broken, barren hills to the north end of the Dead Sea. Jeremiah knew the stern, sober, stabilizing discipline of the desert.

C. "Why does the way of the wicked prosper?" (12:1)

Why would a person ask this question? Because we look around and see that many evil and corrupt people seem to have far more of this world's goods than the righteous people. Many of them are liars, cheats, and phonies. We often conclude that they have these advantages because of their lifestyle. In other words, it often appears that "the wages of sin is *not* death."

To answer this profound question completely is impossible. To do it in a few words is even more so. Three simple statements might not solve the problem, but perhaps they will shed a little light on the subject.

First, God disciplines his own children. The writer of Hebrews say, "My son, regard not lightly the chastening of the Lord, nor faint when thou art reproved of him; for whom the Lord loveth he chasteneth, and scourgeth every son whom he receiveth" (Heb. 12:5–6 PHILLIPS).

Second, we learn great lessons from the reverses of life. Often the benefits that accrue to us when we make mistakes more than offset the inconvenience because of our errors. The suffering of the righteous can mean greater glory for someone else in some other place. Remember Jesus suffered—although he was without sin. His redemptive love and suffering have blessed the world.

Third, the present condition is not the last chapter. We haven't seen all of this life yet, and none of us has seen the life to come. Give God a few years. The best might be just ahead. God can restore even those years the locusts have eaten (Joel 2:25). Heaven is a place where God will wipe away every tear and death shall be unknown. Our present distress is temporary and trifling when we realize what is in store for us.

Why do the wicked prosper? Why do the righteous suffer? They don't always! What about when they do? Have faith! God has "the whole world in his hands."

VII. TEACHING OUTLINE

A. INTRODUCTION

1. Lead Story: Convincing People to Accept the Covenant
2. Context: Some time after 621 B.C. when the book of the covenant was found in the temple, reform broke out under King Josiah. The Lord instructed Jeremiah to travel throughout Judah and Jerusalem and remind the people of the terms of the covenant that the nation had entered into with God at Sinai in the time of Moses.
3. Transition: Jeremiah was faithful to fulfill the assignment the Lord gave to him, but instead of responding positively to his message, those closest to him planned to assassinate him. When God revealed the assassination plot to Jeremiah, this led Jeremiah to voice his com-

plaints to God in strong imprecatory language and to demand vengeance from God.

B. COMMENTARY

1. God's Command to Proclaim the Covenant (11:1–8)
2. Opposition to Jeremiah and His Preaching (11:9–17)
3. God's Servants Can Expect Opposition (11:18–12:6)
4. God's Instrument of Punishment (12:7–17)

C. CONCLUSION: A LAMB LED TO THE SLAUGHTER

VIII. ISSUES FOR DISCUSSION

1. How do people today feel about promises they make, obligations they enter into, and their covenant pledges? What consequences come from failing to honor such agreements?
2. Does there ever come a time when Christians should no longer pray for lost sinners? How would one determine such a time? If such a time exists and believers pray for the lost anyway, does God still hear their prayers?
3. What biblical figures uttered imprecatory complaints against others? Are such utterances unchristian, or do they teach us valuable lessons about being honest and forthright in our complaints before God? What might some of these lessons be?

Jeremiah 13:1–27

Pride: Vice of Fools and Ruin of Nations

I. **INTRODUCTION**
The Great Sin

II. **COMMENTARY**
A verse-by-verse explanation of these verses.

III. **CONCLUSION**
"Why Will Ye Die?"

An overview of the principles and applications from these verses.

IV. **LIFE APPLICATION**
Becoming MADD

Melding these verses to life.

V. **PRAYER**
Tying these verses to life with God.

VI. **DEEPER DISCOVERIES**
Historical, geographical, and grammatical enrichment of the commentary.

VII. **TEACHING OUTLINE**
Suggested step-by-step group study of these verses.

VIII. **ISSUES FOR DISCUSSION**
Zeroing these verses in on daily life.

Quote

"*Pride* is a vice that ill suits those that would lead others in a humble way to heaven. Let us take heed, lest when we have brought others so far, the gates should prove too narrow for ourselves. For God, who thrust out a proud angel, will not tolerate a proud preacher, either. For it is pride that is at the root of all other sins: envy, contention, discontent, and all hindrances that would prevent renewal."

Richard Baxter

Jeremiah 13:1–27

IN A NUTSHELL

By means of symbolic object lessons of a ruined linen belt and smashed wineskins, the Lord announced through Jeremiah that the nation of Judah and the people of Jerusalem had become useless. While the people's sins were many, the chief reason for this judgment on the nation and its people was their pride. Jeremiah announced that a foe was coming from the north that would carry Judah into exile.

Pride: Vice of Fools and Ruin of Nations

I. INTRODUCTION

The Great Sin

C. S. Lewis called pride "the essential vice, the utmost evil." He pointed out that "it was through Pride that the devil became the devil." He asserted: "Pride leads to every other vice: it is the complete anti-God state of mind." Lewis said, "Pride is spiritual cancer: it eats up the very possibility of love, or contentment, or even common sense." Lewis asked and answered, "What is it that makes a political leader or a whole nation go on and on, demanding more and more? Pride again." Lewis concluded, "It is Pride which has been the chief cause of misery in every nation and every family since the world began. Other vices may sometimes bring people together . . . but Pride always means enmity—it *is* enmity. And not only enmity between man and man, but enmity to God" (Lewis, *Mere Christianity*, 108–14).

Pride was a problem for Judah and Jerusalem. It was "because of your pride" (Jer. 13:17) that Jeremiah announced God's judgment on Judah and Jerusalem. He warned them, "Do not be arrogant" (v. 15). And told them, "This is what the LORD says: 'In the same way I will ruin the pride of Judah and the great pride of Jerusalem'" (v. 9).

Three different Hebrew words for *pride* are used in Jeremiah 13. Together these words provide insight into this great sin.

In verse 9 the word rendered "pride" means "height," "eminence," and "majesty." It is this word that is used when God announced, "I hate pride and arrogance" (Prov. 8:13). It is this word that is used in the announcement, "Pride goes before destruction" (Prov. 16:18). This was the sin of Sodom (Ezek. 16:49), Egypt (Ezek. 30:18), Babylon (Isa. 14:11), Moab (Jer. 48:29), the Philistines (Zech. 9:6), the Assyrians (Zech. 10:11), and Israel or Ephraim (Hos. 5:4–5; 7:9–10).

Another term for pride in Jeremiah 13 is found in verse 15. This word is rendered "arrogant"—"Do not be arrogant." This word means "to be high," "to be lifted up," "to be exalted," or "to be haughty." This word is often used in the Old Testament to describe how people exalt themselves by claiming power over circumstances that are beyond their control. As king, Uzziah thought he could assume the role of priest and offer sacrifices in the temple (2 Chr. 26:16). Likewise, this was Hezekiah's problem (2 Chr. 32:24–26). An arrogant attitude is an abomination to the Lord, and it precedes a person's destruction (Prov. 16:5,18).

The third word for pride in Jeremiah 13 is found in verse 17. This word is used only three other times in the Old Testament. This is the type of pride Elihu spoke of to Job (Job 33:17) and that characterized Nebuchadnezzar before God humbled him (Dan. 4:37).

II. COMMENTARY

Pride: Vice of Fools and Ruin of Nations

MAIN IDEA: *If prosperity has slain its thousands, pride has slain its tens of thousands.*

A God's Command and the Prophet's Obedience (13:1–7)

SUPPORTING IDEA: *When God commands us, we must obey immediately even if the assignment seems strange and we do not understand it.*

A person who seeks to interpret Jeremiah's prophecies must be aware of the historical situation that provides a platform for his public messages and private meditations. The latter includes also the prophet's dialogues, which were often in the form of his confrontations with Yahweh.

Interpreters should also bear in mind the compilation of the book. Sometimes groupings of prophetic messages and historical events were made chronologically and sometimes topically. Often the reasons for gathering certain passages into a unit are very obvious, but other times such a determination is difficult, almost impossible.

The next collection of prophetic material presents the most difficult task thus far in our study. A new unit definitely begins at chapter 13, and another most certainly begins at chapter 18. This leaves chapters 14–17 as a separate block that could be considered as a self-contained unit or could be joined to chapter 13. In this study we will consider the material as two separate scrolls of messages from Jeremiah. This means we will treat chapter 13 as an independent component or unit. As we will see, the chapter deals with pride and contains two symbolic sermons or parables concerned with this first of the seven deadly sins.

Combining all the features of this account, we might call these two passages "acted out parables with great symbolic truth." The prophets, especially Jeremiah, often communicated their messages in this dramatic way. As in all parables, to seek a hidden meaning in every detail is an exercise in futility. But several parallel truths do exist in this account. In other words, the story contains one primary truth, but several other suggested analogies seem to be present.

13:1–2. Translators render the Hebrew word *ezor* in verse 1 differently. Some of them are: **linen belt**, girdle, waistcloth, loincloth. But the exact type of garment is not as important for the message as the fact that it was made of linen. This story abounds with symbolism. Students of Jeremiah have made many suggestions about why Yahweh specified it be made of linen. The practical nonsymbolic reason would, of course, be because it was cooler. Another is because it would be more readily ruined by dampness than leather. But the most generally accepted is because of its symbolic teaching. Israel was called to be "a kingdom of priests."

Yahweh gave Jeremiah no reason why he should refrain from putting the girdle in the water. Expositors have come up with many suggested symbolisms. In the absence of a divine explanation, perhaps the best course is to leave it alone. If one must speculate, the simplest and easiest approach might be that God wanted to keep in focus the original purity of Israel.

13:3–5. God came **a second time** with a message to Jeremiah. The immediate truth we glean from this statement is that we must obey God's initial command about a matter before he gives us further revelation. Another way of saying this is, we must enter one door into the room of obedience before he sets a second door before us.

To what geographical location did God order Jeremiah? Older translations render the word "Euphrates." But most contemporary translations transliterate the Hebrew letters and read **Perath**. This presents a location problem. Where is this latter site? We find the answer in Joshua 18:23. It is an old village a few miles outside Anathoth, one of the towns occupied by the Benjamites, probably the modern Wadi Farah. This location meets all requirements of the verse, having a lavish fountain, a broad pool, and a stream. They all soak into the sand and fissured rock of the surrounding desert.

One must admit this explanation gives credence to the biblical text and makes good sense. Which would impact Jeremiah's audience most: a seven-hundred-mile journey to a distant land, with a return visit "many days later" (v. 6) or a similar trip a few miles from town? Most of us would vote for the latter.

Old Testament scholars, however, disagree. Even some modern students cling to the traditional view. They insist that hiding the "girdle" in the Euphrates carried implications for the Chaldeans or Babylonians being the enemy who would invade the land of Judah and carry away captives. These interpreters find another symbolism. Influences from this area, the land of Assyria and Babylon, had corrupted the worship of both Israel and Judah. This was especially true during the reigns of Ahaz and Manasseh. They imported many worship rituals from these regions.

13:6–7. Jeremiah took precautions to make sure no one would accidentally discover the belt. He covered it over with earth. When he retrieved it, the people knew immediately that this was the same article as the one he had buried. The corruption spoke the message and gave the lesson without a lengthy sermon from the prophet. Nothing is more useless than something contaminated with filth and impurity. God can use any vessel in his service provided that vessel is clean.

Israel and Judah had been in the process of deterioration for a long time. Israel had reached the point of no return in the eighth century, and God had given her over to Assyria. Judah had come dangerously close to the same fate at that time. But God had spared the Southern Kingdom, perhaps partially because of Hezekiah's good policies and humble attitude. Manasseh's fifty-five-year reign, following Hezekiah, had changed everything in Judah for the worse. Once more Judah hovered over the precipice leading to total destruction.

B God's Pronouncement Through His Prophet (13:8–11)

SUPPORTING IDEA: *The people's pride had led to a condition of refusing to hear and obey God's mandates.*

13:8–11. This segment of Jeremiah's ministry bears no date, but the evidence leads most scholars to place it during the early years of Jehoiakim's reign. Pharaoh Neco put him on Judah's throne after deposing Jehoahaz, who succeeded Josiah.

Until he became puffed up with pride and destroyed himself, Jehoiakim was in an enviable position. He had the good will of Egypt because he was Neco's appointee. He had Assyria's backing because they were an ally of Egypt against Babylon. Jehoiakim had virtually unlimited autonomy.

Jehoiakim followed the habit of egotistic tyrants. Intoxicated with pride, he "feathered his own nest" in an effort to gain financial security. That period formed the historical background of this prophetic message from Jeremiah.

Through Jeremiah, Yahweh brought three charges against his people. First, they had not listened to him. Second, they adopted as their lifestyle their own wishes and desires with a stubborn, headstrong, and inflexible arrogance. Third, they adopted the values of the gods they had erected to the inappropriate desires and lusts of their carnal minds.

What had been the result of Israel's infidelity? She had become without value. Her net worth was nothing. Yahweh had chosen her for a purpose, and she had not measured up. This purpose was twofold. First, to be a kingdom of priests, a holy nation (Exod. 19:6) showing God's holiness to the world. Second, through Israel God would send the Messiah to redeem the world. Israel had failed in the first segment of her assignment. How could she fulfill the second phase of it? Like the linen belt, Israel had lost her value.

To further develop the image of the linen belt, the belt bound the garment to the body. Yahweh wanted his people to be identified with him in loving fellowship. In this way, they would serve a fourfold function. The literal Hebrew text suggests this fourfold result. They would be his unique people, be identified by bearing his name, become an object of his praise. The final result would be they would become a beautiful adornment reflecting his character. They refused to obey him, thus failed in their assignment, and therefore, must forfeit their privilege.

Continued Sin Brings Even Deeper Darkness (13:12–17)

SUPPORTING IDEA: *The more people sin against God, the less they are able to change their pattern of living.*

The person or persons gathering the messages and historical records of Jeremiah obviously placed this material following the previous unit because of their thematic parallel. Both refer to punishment that will come to the people because they have defied God's command for righteous living. In all probability, however, both units came in the early years of Jehoiakim's reign. This unit might have been a little later.

13:12. Old Testament prophets often used a social occasion as a platform from which to deliver an urgent message to the people. Perhaps this circumstance might have been a function at which drinking of a strong beverage was a main attraction. Jeremiah began with a simple statement, **The LORD . . . says: "Every wineskin should be filled with wine."**

Translators vary on whether the rendering should be "wineskin" or "jar." The word *container* is suggested here because it might be a good compromise. Robert Davidson insists the wine jars were made of earthenware and were easily broken in the course of a drunken party. This would be similar to an affair today when wine glasses are smashed. Yahweh knew the people would give a curt reply. People absorbed in their own revelry almost always respond with a worldly wise statement when a spiritual messenger arrives on the scene. Those who are "under the influence" always try to act cute on such an occasion. They delight in acting haughtily and putting God down with a sarcastic reply.

13:13–14. Yahweh gave Jeremiah an answer in advance. He said he would fill both the leaders and the people with drunkenness. Just as the natural law of gravity works, so this spiritual law operates. Sin produces death, both in a physical and a spiritual sense. When Christ intersects our life and enters our inner self, we begin to operate within the realm of another law. Paul calls it the "law of the Spirit of life" in Christ Jesus (Rom. 8:2).

How is this related to Jeremiah's words about God filling the people with **drunkenness** and smashing together **fathers and sons**? The prophet meant when people sell out to the Evil One and his way of life, they enter the realm of sin and death. They are caught in Satan's vise and cannot escape. Evil begets evil, and that evil begets even greater evil. Does God do it? Yes and no. God sets up the system. God permits it. Each individual makes his own choice. The result is that a person becomes incapable of making right choices because he is trapped or enslaved. Only divine intervention can move a person from the "law of sin and death" into the "law of the Spirit of life" in Christ Jesus.

How are we to interpret the words, **I will allow no pity or mercy or compassion to keep me from destroying them** (v. 14)? Read Jeremiah 18:1–10. When God makes such a statement, the conditional element is always present. If the people will return to God, he will return to them.

13:15–17. These three verses are an ideal conclusion for this larger oracle or unit (vv. 1–17). It consists of the two symbolic messages that begin with the first verse of this chapter. These verses show God rarely delivers an unconditional message of doom. Implicit in most of God's warnings is the possibility of avoiding the threatened punishment, if repentance comes from the persons who are confronted with their sin. In my judgment, all the verses in this chapter hang together as one unit of Jeremiah's preaching.

When were these messages delivered? Probably during the first period of Jehoiakim's reign. The new king was still basking in the prosperity and the exuberance brought about by Josiah's strong nationalism. But dark days were ahead for Jehoiakim because he would not be loyal to his covenants. In a few short years, Babylon would return and take a large number of captives from Judah. This occurred in 597 B.C. In the melee, Jehoiakim would die. At the time of these messages, however, Jehoiakim was still living. He was a proud young ruler, and the people were arrogant toward Yahweh's demands for holy living.

Jeremiah began his summary and final appeal with a warning, but in verse 15 he preceded it with a twofold call to attention. The verbs translated **hear** and **pay attention** reinforce each other and give intensity to the prophet's command. Jeremiah's words served as a final plea to the proud, self-willed people who had treated every prophetic message with contempt. He is saying, in essence, "Don't be too proud to repent."

The Hebrew word translated **arrogant** means "to be high, lofty, lifted up, exalted." Some synonyms today are insolent, presumptuous, overbearing. All of these meanings were probably in Jeremiah's mind as he warned the people of their evil conduct.

In the remainder of this verse, the prophet took Israel through a metaphorical journey in order to send the people a warning. He pictured a man lost in a forest. Mistaking the dusk for twilight, indicating the dawn of a new day, he thinks he only needs to wait for a short time. Everything will then be bright. But what he does not know is that the thick darkness of night will soon approach. Old Testament prophets often used darkness to symbolize invasion by a foreign power and the exile that followed.

Jeremiah preferred to preach Yahweh as a God of love and to base his appeals on that divine trait. Any true prophet of God feels the same way. Sometimes, though, people have become so enslaved by sin and blinded by its appeal that a spokesperson for God must resort to other motivations. A true prophet of God must also be willing to make even fear the basis of his calling people to God. Our Savior warned people of impending judgment if they persisted in defying God.

What was Jeremiah's attitude toward the bleak and desolate future awaiting the nation if the people refused Yahweh's message? It was certainly not one of glee. As he reflected on the people's doom if they persisted in rebellion and immorality, he broke into tears.

Translators see several possibilities in verse 17. The ambiguity centers on the Hebrew word *mistarim,* which means "hidden places" or "hiding places." Some versions read, "If you will not listen in these deep glooms" while others translate, "In secret my soul shall weep." Either choice reveals the prophet's tender heart and his compassion for those to whom he preached. One thinks of Jesus weeping as he approached the city of Jerusalem (Luke 19:41).

As Jeremiah thought about the doom facing his people, he felt it so strongly that he conceived of it as already having happened and used the Hebrew verb form that expressed completed action. Jeremiah had virtually accepted the inevitability of his people's refusal. The prophet's insight on a human level gives us at least partial insight into understanding God's foreknowledge as related to our free choice.

Verse 17 thus seems to be the logical place to end this unit. Jeremiah condemned the people's sins, expressed his compassion, and hoped for their renewal. Yet deep in his heart he doubted they would change. Already he could see evidence that judgment had begun, and he saw greater sufferings for the people. The more they sinned, the greater the odds that they would not change.

God had given the nation every chance to repent, but they had refused. Time had run out. More than a century earlier, Amos had warned the Northern Kingdom, "Prepare to meet your God, O Israel" (Amos 4:12). They scoffed at the idea and paid the price. Now the Southern Kingdom was about to follow in their steps.

Final Word to the King and the Nation (13:18–27)

SUPPORTING IDEA: *The time had arrived for God's judgment to begin.*

Israel's new king needed to realize that he could not resist the agent God had appointed as his tool. The same applied to the entire nation.

Old Testament students differ in their approach to these final ten verses in chapter 13. Some of the more radical interpreters contend that the section consists of several short fragments from the prophet added with no cohesion or unity. In my judgment this is a simplistic but erroneous approach. This section is a logical conclusion to the two parabolic messages that Jeremiah brought to the people during the last days of Jehoiakim's wicked reign. Israel's king had become puffed up with pride and had led the people in the same direction.

After several years of building his power base following the battle of Carchemisch, Nebuchadnezzar of Babylon had become powerful enough to control the international scene. In his exalted conceit, however, King Jehoiakim of Judah felt he could ignore reality and refuse to recognize Babylon's lordship over him. He withheld the annual tribute levied on Israel. As soon as Nebuchadnezzar was strong enough at home, he set out to make this rebellious king an example to other nations.

The events in Jehoiakim's life serve as a basis for understanding Jeremiah's words to Jehoiachin, the king's son and successor. The historical books give the factual information (2 Kgs. 23:36–24:14; 2 Chr. 36:5–8). Several other words from Jeremiah about this king supplement the historical accounts. A review of what we do know is in order.

In 608 B.C., Pharaoh Neco of Egypt set out to take part in the battle between Assyria and Babylon. The Babylonians had already conquered the Assyrian capital, Nineveh, in 612 B.C. Usually, when the capital of a kingdom or empire fell, this meant the entire structure dissolved. But with Assyria this didn't happen. The army regrouped and continued fighting. The battle scene would be Carchemisch.

On which side did Neco plan to fight? Some translations of 2 Kings 23:29 read, "Pharaoh-nechoh king of Egypt went up against the king of Assyria"

(KJV). Others read that he went "to help the king of Assyria." Why the difference? The Hebrew preposition can be rendered either "against" or "on the side of." An example in English is when something is "against" something, it is "on the side" of it. Egypt was helping Assyria block the growing power of Babylon in the international power struggle.

Josiah set out to stop Neco. At Megiddo the Egyptian king killed Josiah, and the people placed Jehoahaz on the throne to follow his father. Neco replaced him with Jehoiakim, another son of Josiah. He sent Jehoahaz to Egypt in chains, and we hear no more about him. This all took place quickly. Jehoahaz reigned only three months (2 Kgs. 23:31; 2 Chr. 36:2).

In 605 B.C., Babylon routed the Assyrian army and became undisputed ruler of the Middle East. Nebuchadnezzar lost no time asserting his power. Babylon invaded Jerusalem the same year (Dan. 1:1–7) and carried away captives.

For several years Jehoiakim seems to have had a free hand. Nebuchadnezzar was occupied dealing first with matters at his home base in Babylon and then asserting his authority over Egypt. Whereas Egypt had levied an annual tax on Judah when she placed Jehoiakim on the throne, the situation was reversed. Babylon placed a levy on Judah in 605 B.C. Jehoiakim submitted to it at first, but after a short time he rebelled, withholding the annual tribute.

The death of Jehoiakim is clouded in mystery. To be dogmatic about exact dates is impossible since we do not have sufficient information. After Jehoiakim's break with Babylon, the Lord led Babylon to send troops from various nations it had conquered to deal with the troublesome vassal. They overran the whole country. The land and the people were reduced to misery. This was shortly before 597 B.C. During the period of confusion that followed, Jehoiakim came to a sudden and violent death. How did it happen? Either in a battle with some of his many foes or because of an uprising among his oppressed subjects. Most scholars accept the date for this event as 597 B.C.

Jehoiachin, son of Jehoiakim, came to the throne, inheriting a bad situation. After the young king had reigned only a short time, Nebuchadnezzar appeared before Jerusalem. Against this background we approach this final section in chapter 13 of Jeremiah's prophecies.

13:18–19. Jeremiah had a message for the young king: "Surrender! Do not try to pit yourself against the might of Babylon." The prophet included the **queen mother** in his message. Two facts seem to be evident by this action.

First, the queen mother was a position that exerted great influence in the palace and throughout the nation. Second, this must have been especially true in the case of Jehoiachin. He was only eighteen years old and probably unmarried. The fact that Jeremiah gave her name, Nehushta (2 Kgs. 24:8), may indicate that she was a strong personality with power over her son.

Although Jehoiachin ruled only three months, his character was evident. The historian says of him, "He did evil in the eyes of the LORD, just as his father had done" (2 Kgs. 24:9). How did Jehoiachin respond to Jeremiah's message? The record tells us, "Jehoiachin king of Judah, his mother, his attendants, his nobles and his officials all surrendered to him" (2 Kgs. 24:12). Later, Jehoiachin was treated well in Babylon and probably experienced a natural and peaceful death (Jer. 52:31–34).

Jeremiah gave the young king three reasons he should surrender. First, if he refused, he would be deposed. When this occurred, both the king and his mother would lose the **crowns** that set them apart as royalty. Second, the cities of the **Negev** or south country already had been or soon would be conquered. If the king expected any help from the area south of Jerusalem, he might as well forget it. Third, the nation would be taken into captivity. The **all Judah** may be a hyperbole, but certainly a large percentage of the nation would be carried away. In other words, Judah was doomed.

In verses 20–27, Jeremiah wrapped it up with a prophetic warning. The message included counseling, advice, and exhortation. The prophet's words began as though they were directed to the king as the nation's leader. But they broadened into a plea for the entire nation to realize the serious nature of the situation.

13:20. Jeremiah asked the king a specific question, portraying him as a shepherd. New Testament writers picture the pastor of the local church as a "shepherd" of the flock. But in the Old Testament, the king was often thought of as one who should fulfill this role.

13:21–22. In verse 21, Jeremiah moved toward a larger audience with his words. The question with which this verse begins could be directed toward either the king or the nation as a whole. The second question in the verse seems to be pointed specifically toward the latter.

When security problems arose, the kings of both Israel and Judah had generally sought their protection and deliverance through alliances with other nations. The prophets had warned them that this was a dangerous policy, but they usually ignored the Lord's messengers. In earlier days, Syria, Egypt, and Assyria had proved to be frail and ineffective as well as downright deceptive. In Jeremiah's day, Judah had depended on Babylon, but the day was not far off when this nation would also prove untrustworthy.

The "foe from the north" had ceased to be indefinite in verse 20. By now, the Scythians were off the scene, Assyria was nonexistent, and Egypt was impotent. No doubt about it, Babylon, Judah's most recent ally by treaty, loomed on the horizon as the true threat. Both in politics and religious rituals, the king and the people had allied themselves with Babylon. The time was rapidly approaching when they would reap what they had sown.

The second question in verse 21 is even more striking. Few pains are sharper than those of a woman giving birth. But the analogy does not give the entire picture. The mother-to-be looks forward to her newborn child. Judah could only look forward to devastation and captivity. No pain hurts so much as the one we know we deserve because of our wrong actions. This is exactly where Judah stood. The prophet answered the question before the nation asked it.

In verse 22, the prophet was not actually saying *if* but *when* as he inquired about what Judah's response would be when the judgment came. The punishment had already begun, but much more would shortly follow. Judah's sin had not been just found out; her sin had found her out. Jeremiah intensified the picture of torn skirts and mistreated bodies in verse 26.

13:23. Verse 23 is a rhetorical question that Jeremiah used to make an affirmation. He posed his question to emphasize the depth of Judah's sin. The people had lived in rebellion against God so long and so arrogantly that it had become a lifestyle. One might even use the word *addictive* in speaking of their slavery to iniquity. It was impossible for them to change. Their condition was hopeless.

What was Jeremiah's point with these two metaphors? God made the Ethiopian and the leopard the way they were. They did not want to change. In a similar way, the people, by their continued choices, had made themselves into hardened sinners. Now they had no desire to change their lifestyle. One Old Testament student says, "Play with sin long enough and it takes over. The outcome of Judah's sin could and would be total disaster for the nation" (Robert Davidson, 116). How can people in any generation repent unless they have has a desire for change?

13:24–27. Judah would become nothing as God blew upon them. The nation would float away like worthless debris from the threshing floor. Yahweh would bring shame and disgrace on them by making them into the very thing they had been worshipping.

The expression **pull up your skirts over your face** has a sexual connotation. This is because the pagan worship into which Israel had fallen involved sexual orgies. One of the ways God punishes sin is by turning the sinners over to their sin, letting it take full course in their lives. The punishment is matched to the sin.

The final half of verse 27 ends the discourse with a question that can be translated two different ways. Perhaps Jeremiah with his language skill meant it that way. Some interpreters contend that it means, "How much longer will God allow this to go on before he suddenly comes in judgment?" Others assert just as strongly that Jeremiah meant, "How much longer before you will become dissatisfied with your sin, repent, and be delivered?"

These two factors are always present in a message that condemns sin and declares imminent judgment. However we interpret the prophet's question, one thing is certain: Jeremiah meant the people should stop asking why they were experiencing judgment. They must admit that they had brought it on themselves.

MAIN IDEA REVIEW: *If prosperity has slain its thousands, pride has slain its tens of thousands.*

III. CONCLUSION

"Why Will Ye Die?"

Words from the prophets have more than an application to the nation that God had chosen to be his agent in bringing the Savior. They apply to individuals as well. In a country church where I served as pastor during school days, one of their favorite songs contained these striking lines: "Why will ye die, why will ye die? / When the fountain of life is flowing nearby / Why oh why will ye die?"

What a message for our world today! How long before we turn to him who is not only the way and the truth but also the life? At the risk of being oversimplistic, a short answer could be given which summarizes the matter:

We can be saved when we abandon our pride and turn to him who is Savior and Lord.

PRINCIPLES

- Those who lose their close spiritual bond with the Lord—and thus no longer bring him renown, praise, and honor—become useless to him.
- Alcohol destroys people and nations. Drunkenness results in conflict, chaos, ruin, destruction, and death for all who indulge in it. Because of this, God's judgment on people and nations may be likened to the results of inebriation and intoxication.
- Pride is a great sin—a deadly sin—that keeps individuals and nations from knowing God, and it will result in their destruction.

APPLICATIONS

- Assess your spiritual bond with the Lord.
- Evaluate the dangers of alcohol and other addictions in your life. Talk with God about these and consider disclosing these to friends and asking for their help.
- Recall the last time you were aware of sinful pride in your thoughts, words, or deeds. Thank God that you were aware of this. Ask God's forgiveness and cleansing. Humbly trust him to forgive you and to cleanse you of this spiritual poison.

IV. LIFE APPLICATION

Becoming MADD

Why would the Lord say to Jeremiah, "I am going to fill with drunkenness all who live in this land . . . and all those living in Jerusalem" (13:13)? The answer is because it was part of his judgment on that society. God's "all who live in this land" and his "all those living in Jerusalem" included five specific classes of people—kings, priests, prophets, fathers, and sons.

"Every wineskin should be filled with wine" (v. 12) was a popular saying. It personifies wineskins as the party drinkers. Every wineskin—every drinker—was to be filled with wine. Because this was a familiar saying, Jeremiah's hearers mockingly would come back with, "Don't we know that every wineskin should be filled with wine?" (v. 12).

At this retort, Jeremiah was told to put a double twist into the saying. The Lord told Jeremiah to tell his hearers that the "wine" they were going to be filled with was God's potent wine—"I am going to fill with drunkenness all who live in this land" (v. 13). God's potent wine is the wine of his wrath. Jeremiah was to inform them that everyone would be filled with God's wine to destruction. Just as men at a drinking party bump and bounce themselves into and against one another, so God would cause them to smash into one another until they burst. So the Lord would dash all in the nation against one another until all was ruined and destroyed.

Thus this wine passage in Jeremiah 13:12–14 is not really about drinking and drunkenness. It is about judgment and destruction from God. Nevertheless, the analogy is only valid because inebriation and intoxication result in such chaos, ruin, destruction, and death.

In 1979, Laura Lamb and her mother Cindi were struck head-on by a repeat drunk driver traveling at 120 miles per hour. Little five-and-one-half-month-old Laura instantly became one of the world's youngest quadriplegics. Within a year thirteen-year-old Cari Lightner was killed by a drunk driver, who two days earlier had been released on bail for a hit-and-run drunk driving crash. This driver already had two drunk-driving convictions and a third one that he had plea-bargained to reckless accident.

Candace Lightner, Cari's mother, and her friends in California formed MADD—Mothers Against Drunk Drivers. By the end of 1981, Lightner and Lamb, who had been waging a war against drunk drivers in Maryland, joined forces. In 1984 MADD modified its name to Mothers Against Drunk Driving. The present mission of this "Voice of the Victim" organization is "to stop drunk driving, support victims of this violent crime, and prevent underage drinking."

Today, with more than three million members and supporters in six hundred chapters and community action teams in all fifty states, Guam, Canada, and Puerto Rico, MADD is the largest crime victim's assistance organization in the world. MADD's activism resulted in the federal law that required states to raise the legal drinking age to twenty-one or lose their highway funding.

Since MADD's founding, alcohol-related traffic fatalities have declined 43 percent.

Currently, only 7 percent of all traffic crashes involve the use of alcohol, but 38 percent of fatal crashes involve alcohol use. Traffic crashes remain the greatest single cause of death for persons ages six through thirty-three. Almost half of these fatalities are alcohol-related crashes. Three in ten Americans will be involved in an alcohol-related crash. In fact, enough alcohol-related traffic deaths occur in the United States each week that it is the equivalent of two jetliners crashing week after week. What carnage alcohol produces—and this is just in traffic fatalities! Nothing has been said about the economic cost of alcohol abuse, other alcohol-related violent crimes, or the human cost on the families of those who drink and their victims.

There's no debate about it: drunken people destroy one another. Indeed, drunkenness and all manner of smashing against one another that comes with it—whether as a judgment from God or merely as the result of human actions—is a blight on the land.

V. PRAYER

Dear Lord, forgive our pride, arrogance, and self-exaltation. Bind us close to you. Help us to be humble in heart and to exemplify in our lives the humility that was in Jesus and that is a distinguishing mark of your true children, so that you may receive all the renown and praise and honor. This we humbly ask in the name of Jesus. Amen.

VI. DEEPER DISCOVERIES

A. "I will ruin the pride of Judah" (13:9)

Throughout God's Word, writers emphasized pride as the first step downward in the life of nations and individuals. Only a few hours before Simon Peter denied the Lord, he boasted, "Even if all fall away on account of you, I never will" (Matt. 26:33). A few minutes later, after Jesus had warned him of what would happen, Peter reaffirmed his statement. He boasted even more, saying, "Even if I have to die with you, I will never disown you" (Matt. 26:35). The other ten disciples present declared an equal loyalty. Yet look at what happened. Before morning they all "deserted him and fled" (Matt. 26:56).

Of the five kings who sat on Judah's throne during Jeremiah's ministry, Jehoiakim was the most exalted in his opinion of himself. Josiah began his reign as a humble servant of God. As his reform movement progressed, however, he became more self-confident. This resulted in his trying to stop Pharaoh Neco from going to Carchemisch in order to help Assyria against Babylon. This burst of unhealthy self-reliance cost him his life.

Jehoahaz and Jehoiachin ruled only three months each, before and after Jehoiakim. From the limited information we have, only a superficial evaluation of them is possible. Jehoiachin seems, however, to have been similar to his father in both attitude and greed. His willingness to follow Jeremiah's advice and surrender to Nebuchadnezzar, however, speaks well for him. Zedekiah, Judah's final king, was not so much proud and overbearing as he was weak and indecisive. Completely dominated by a strong nationalistic group in Judah, he was actually only a puppet in their hands. The remaining king, Jehoiakim, had possibly more pride than all the others combined. He caused Jeremiah to utter some of the sharpest words against a political leader to be found in the Old Testament.

Throughout centuries of recorded history, things have not changed much. In a recent cartoon the artist depicts the ruins of a great city destroyed by a nuclear explosion. No living human is in sight, but two apes are surveying the scene of utter desolation. One remarks to the other: "I hear they were remarkably clever."

What a commentary on the contemporary situation: millions too clever to believe God, too clever to follow Jesus Christ, too clever to repent and turn from theirs sins. Not too clever, however, to escape the judgment of God.

B. "Why has this happened to me?" (13:22)

The greatest cry of the human race through the centuries has been to know the truth about God. The second is probably to know the "why" of suffering. The two answers are inseparably joined.

One minister points out three attitudes toward this dilemma. (1) Some say all suffering comes from God. (2) Some say all suffering comes from sin. (3) Some say all suffering is imaginary. All three of these have an element of truth, but no one contains the full truth. Whatever the cause, suffering hurts.

About the first, God does sometimes send suffering, but he always has a good reason for it. For instance, God may send limited and temporary suffering to prepare us for a great task. He wishes us to learn something about suffering before allowing us to enter a labor where we will experience greater adversity and pain.

In the verse under consideration, however, Judah's suffering will be caused by her own sins. The law of sin and retribution takes over when we violate God's precepts and commandments. Sin carries with it the seed of its own destruction. Any system or individual that denies God will eventually disintegrate of itself.

Jeremiah's word to the people of his day was, "When the suffering comes, don't ask why it has come. You individuals will suffer because of your own personal sin. The nation will suffer because of its corporate sin." Nothing can change this truth. One man put it this way: "We may deny the suffering will come. Sometimes we can even delay it. One bitter fact, however, remains. We cannot escape it. Sin will remain sin whether we recognize it or not."

VII. TEACHING OUTLINE

A. INTRODUCTION

1. Lead Story: The Great Sin
2. Context: God had bound the nations of Israel and Judah to himself. They were to be his people and bring him renown, praise, and honor. But these nations refused to listen to God. Just as Israel earlier had been taken into exile, so a great force was coming from the north to carry proud Judah into exile.
3. Transition: The Lord told Jeremiah to illustrate the uselessness of the nation of Judah to God by means of a symbolic action. Jeremiah was told to take a waistcloth or belt, which symbolized the nation that had been closely bound to God, and take it far away and bury it. After some time, Jeremiah was told to retrieve the useless belt. As the belt, so had Judah become completely useless. The Lord also told Jeremiah to announce at a drinking party that he was about to bring judgment on the nation, which would be smashed and destroyed as wineskins or containers are destroyed when they are smashed together.

B. COMMENTARY

1. God's Command and the Prophet's Obedience (13:1–7)
2. God's Pronouncement Through His Prophet (13:8–11)
3. Continued Sin Brings Even Deeper Darkness (13:12–17)
4. Final Word to the King and the Nation (13:18–27)

C. CONCLUSION: "WHY WILL YE DIE?"

VIII. ISSUES FOR DISCUSSION

1. Is it possible for a believer to become totally useless to God?
2. What should God's people do today to bring him renown, praise, and honor in our society?
3. What can you do to help address the problem of the destruction and broken relationships that occur because of alcohol?
4. Why has pride been called the greatest sin? Do you think it is? Why or why not?

Jeremiah 14:1–17:27

Past the Point of No Return?

I. INTRODUCTION
Rescue at the Falls

II. COMMENTARY
A verse-by-verse explanation of these verses.

III. CONCLUSION
God Is God

An overview of the principles and applications from these verses.

IV. LIFE APPLICATION
A Single Servant

Melding these verses to life.

V. PRAYER
Tying these verses to life with God.

VI. DEEPER DISCOVERIES
Historical, geographical, and grammatical enrichment of the commentary.

VII. TEACHING OUTLINE
Suggested step-by-step group study of these verses.

VIII. ISSUES FOR DISCUSSION
Zeroing these verses in on daily life.

"*Life* at best is very brief
Like the falling of a leaf,
Like the binding of a sheaf,
Be in time.
Fleeting days are telling fast
That the die will soon be cast,
And the fatal line be passed,
Be in time."

Anonymous

Jeremiah 14:1–17:27

IN A NUTSHELL

Jeremiah 14–17 contains a collage of materials designed to show that God was determined to punish Judah. Occasioned by a devastating drought and severe famine, the people repeatedly petitioned in the Lord's name, acknowledged their sins, and asserted confidence in the covenant God. But the Lord responded "no" to their pleas and instructed Jeremiah not to intercede for them (14:1–15:9). This revelation is followed by a section on Jeremiah's personal crisis and God's comfort, warning, and strengthening of the despondent prophet (15:10–21). A further autobiographical section (16:1–13) reveals that the Lord ordered Jeremiah to remain single and childless and to avoid socializing or participating in the normal joys and sorrows of his people. Jeremiah's personal situation and isolation pictured the Lord's judgment on the immoral nation. The section closes with instructions about proper observance of the Sabbath and national survival (17:19–27).

Past the Point of No Return?

I. INTRODUCTION

Rescue at the Falls

*N*iagara Falls. The very name speaks of honeymoon couples, sightseers, romance, breathtaking natural beauty, and awesome power. The Niagara River, forming a portion of the boundary between the United States and Canada, is the natural outlet from Lake Erie to Lake Ontario. Slightly above the falls Goat Island splits the Niagara into two parts. The larger division plunges 170 feet over Horseshoe Falls on the Canadian side; the rest of the water flows over the rockier American Falls before continuing on for seven miles through the Niagara Gorge.

On a beautiful summer Saturday morning, James Honeycutt took his friend's children, seventeen-year-old Deanne and her seven-year-old brother Roger, for an outing on the Niagara River in his fourteen-foot aluminum runabout. The inexperienced skipper seemed unconcerned as he continued to head his craft downriver. A mile or so above the falls they passed the long breakwater that evens the river's flow. Now the Niagara was roiled, water was slapping against rocks, and the thunderous pounding of the water grew louder as they plunged perilously toward the falls.

When Honeycutt decided to bring his runabout's bow around, it was too late. The small motor could not make headway against the strong current. Suddenly the struggling motor whined and raced wildly—the propeller pin had sheared. Smashing against rocks in the rapids, the stern flew up into the air. All three passengers were thrown into the water. Honeycutt and Roger plunged over the lip of Horseshoe Falls.

Just as Jim Honeycutt and the Woodward youngsters had passed the point of no return, so had ancient Judah. How tragic it must have been for Jeremiah to hear the Lord tell him, "Do not pray for the well-being of this people" (14:11). A prophet was supposed to pray for his people. But the Lord announced, "Although they fast, I will not listen to their cry; though they offer burnt offerings and grain offerings, I will not accept them" (14:12).

Judah had passed the point of no return. They were marked for death, the sword, starvation, and captivity (15:2).

John Hayes and his wife happened to be visiting Niagara Falls for the weekend and saw the aluminum boat flip over. Spotting Deanne's life vest, Hayes raced to the river and reached out his hand to her. Deanne failed to grasp it. Hayes ran down river ahead of Deanne and leaned farther over the rail. As she swept past him, she grabbed his thumb. Hayes and another tourist pulled the girl over the rail just feet before the falls! Deanne was safe. Below the falls, Clifford Keech, captain of the *Maid of the Mist II*, spotted Roger's orange life vest. Using the full reverse power of his vessel's engines to hold his position against the current, he and his crew rescued Roger and united him with his sister and their parents.

Tucked away in the midst of Jeremiah 14–17 is another word from the Lord, a bright announcement. "The days are coming" (16:14), the Lord declared, that another exodus—one from Babylon—would eclipse Israel's exodus from Egypt in people's memory. There would be a great rescue: "I will restore them to the land I gave their forefathers" (16:15). The words "as surely as the Lord lives" shows this prediction is an oath. And the formula identifies the guarantor of the oath—Yahweh himself.

While Judah had passed the point of no return and could not help itself, a rescuer stood ready to reach out his divine hand and pull those who would grab hold of him to safety.

II. COMMENTARY

Past the Point of No Return?

MAIN IDEA: *Even though people go so far in sin that they become virtually incapable of repentance, the true prophet of God still loves them.*

An astute and perceptive student of Jeremiah discovers many chapters that "hang together" as a unit. They existed as separate components before being incorporated into the fuller compilation of material. Some, however, seem to be independent blocks of material and fit no collection of messages. This seems to be the case with chapters 14–17. Several units seem to be present within these chapters. They can be outlined as follows.

The first unit extends from 14:1 to 15:9. It begins with a description of a severe drought that has come to the land, bringing suffering and economic hardship (14:1–6). Interpreting this phenomenon as a judgment of God on the people because of their sins, Jeremiah interceded for them. He asked God to have mercy and forgive them. The remaining material (14:7–15:9) records three dialogues between the prophet and God. In them, Jeremiah begged God to forgive the people and remove the judgment. In each case God rejected Jeremiah's request.

The second unit begins with a bitter complaint of the prophet against God (15:10–18). It continues and concludes with his rebuke of the prophet (15:19–21).

The third unit (16:1–21) consists of an extended discourse in which the Lord revealed what his will for the prophet would be as a result of the sinful conditions in Judah. Yahweh disclosed further the people's fate but concluded this declaration with a promise of return to the land. He then returned to the picture of judgment. The chapter closes with Jeremiah's response to Yahweh's words (16:19–21).

The fourth unit (17:1–18) presents a problem to many expositors. They see a number of fragments without any logical relationship to one another. But in my judgment, all of this material can be considered as one message. It gives a final composite picture of moral conditions in Judah and Jeremiah's perplexity because of the situation.

The fifth and final unit (17:19–27) concludes the larger section with a message about proper observance of the Sabbath. Many scholars consider it an independent oracle, having no connection with the larger context.

◢A◣ Description of Nature in a Time of Drought (14:1–6)

SUPPORTING IDEA: *When the blessings of God are absent in a land, both people and animals are reduced to the point of starvation and death.*

14:1. The phrase that begins this prophecy differs from the common ones we find elsewhere. It occurs only four other times in Jeremiah's prophecies (1:2; 46:1; 47:1; 49:34). The Hebrew text reads literally, "that which was a word of the Lord to Jeremiah." This might have been a special way to call attention to a passage and to affirm that it was indeed a divine oracle.

The material that follows in the next few verses is not so much a prophetic oracle as it is a description of the **drought** and its effects. The definite article preceding the noun combined with its plural form may indicate this was a severe drought remembered widely or even a series of droughts.

14:2–4. With short, crisp, almost abrupt words, Jeremiah, in verse 2, pictured the scene. The cities had weakened and deteriorated. A moaning wail ascended as the people cried out to Yahweh. The prophet pictured the cry as going **up from Jerusalem** because this is where the people gathered for prayer to God. Individual entreaties went forth also from people throughout the entire land.

In desperation the leaders sent for water (v. 3). The word translated **nobles** comes from a Hebrew word that means "glorious." It stood for the people of great status and influence. The word translated **servants** means literally "little ones." No one was left untouched by this drought.

The only place the servants might have hoped to find water was where it was stored. Finding none there, they felt they had failed their masters and expressed their grief through a mourning ritual. Their response, showing their shame by covering their heads, probably lay in a current belief of that day. A messenger who brought "bad news" of any kind considered himself to be an "unworthy servant." Verse 4 continues the description of the land's desolate and disheartening condition.

14:5–6. The drought's effects extended its reach even to animal life. Jeremiah mentioned two in particular to emphasize the enormity of the emergency.

Few animals of the field show as much tenderness toward their young as the female deer. Only a major crisis would cause a mother, human or beast, to forsake a newborn. Yet this was the situation in Judah. Wild donkeys, possessed with an unusual ability to sniff moisture in the air, stood equally frustrated. They roamed the hillsides and stood on the cliffs seeking for some trace of rain, without any success.

🅱 First Intercession of Jeremiah (14:7–12)

> **SUPPORTING IDEA:** *Interpreting the drought and its effects as Yahweh's punishment of the people for their sins, Jeremiah pleaded for Yahweh to deliver his people.*

14:7–9. Jeremiah attributed Judah's suffering to her sin. He called on Yahweh to act on the nation's behalf. He included himself among those responsible for the crisis. In verse 7, he spoke of **our sins** and **our backsliding**. He then spoke with an active verb, saying **we have sinned**, asking for no mercy because of extenuating circumstances.

Calling on God to **do something for the sake of your name** was a significant statement. It appealed to Yahweh on the basis of what other nations might think of him if he refused to make things right for his people. They would think that God was too weak to restore his people. Furthermore, if he showed mercy to his own people, the nations might be led to see that love is a stronger force than stern justice.

In verses 8 and 9, Jeremiah recognized the nation's only prospect for redemption was in Yahweh. A Jewish commentator compared the Hebrew word translated **hope** with an Arab cognate and suggested a better translation would be "strength." The Hebrew word translated **Savior** means to deliver (Freedman, 101).

The four questions Jeremiah presented to Yahweh are actually two, each having two parts. Each of the two inquiries is presented as parallelism.

The prophet first compared Yahweh to a mobile deity, who would not remain long at a time with his people. The Hebrew word translated **stranger** is the same word the poet used when he asked, "Who shall abide in thy tabernacle?" (Ps. 15:1 KJV). It meant, in that context, "who shall stay temporarily" in contrast to the one "who shall dwell in thy holy hill." The word translated **traveler** or "wayfaring man" in some versions comes from a verb that means "to journey, be on the way." Such people have concern for those among whom they dwell temporarily.

Jeremiah then, in verse 9, compared Yahweh to an impotent military commander caught unawares by an enemy army. In addition, the one in charge was unable to wage a successful campaign against the foe because of limited resources. The prophet knew the shortcomings of his people. Yet he knew God had chosen Israel to be his representatives to the nations. Faced with this dilemma, he could only plead for God's mercy and forgiving love.

14:10–12. Yahweh replied to the prophet with a firm refusal. The people showed no sign of repentance. Jeremiah might have waved his hand back and forth to demonstrate how the people meandered back and forth from one pagan idol to another. They had lost all capacity for long-term commitment to any person or cause.

Yahweh could not extend his blessing to such people. In verse 11, he instructed Jeremiah to stop interceding for them, and he refused to give them a hearing. Why did God ignore their pleas? In verse 12, Yahweh gave the reason. The people's worship was empty, without meaning. They went through the motions of worship, even bringing the prescribed offering, but these religious actions did not affect their lifestyle.

Ⓒ Second Intercession of Jeremiah (14:13–18)

SUPPORTING IDEA: *Blaming the people's sins on the false prophets who advised them, Jeremiah continued his plea for the people.*

14:13. Jeremiah relentlessly pressed his case. He was so close to Yahweh, so surrendered to his will, and so concerned about the people that he dared to question the Almighty. Jeremiah expressed his questions not in a spirit of revolt, but with a heart of genuine concern for those to whom he ministered.

14:14–16. Yahweh spoke immediately, pointedly, and clearly about those who preached in his name without his commission or authority. Verses 15–16 give the fate of these phony preachers. When the bitter judgment of Judah came, these false prophets would suffer along with the others. In fact, in some cases, their shame and pain might be even worse!

14:17–18. A few Old Testament students have suggested the first five words of verse 17 should be included in verse 16. This would make the remainder of verse 17 and verse 18 part of a prayer Jeremiah uttered when he thought about the suffering in store for Judah. But most students contend the five words represent a fresh command to Jeremiah. They constituted a message Yahweh wished the prophet to deliver. As God considered the coming judgment, he was not cool and aloof. His heart was broken.

The expression **for my virgin daughter** in verse 17 confirms that these are Yahweh's words. This was a favorite way he expressed his relationship to Jerusalem. Expositors find two possible applications of the word *virgin* to Jerusalem. First, God had conceived the city as a special place for the worship of him and the construction of the temple. Second, the city had never been "raped" by a foreign army.

Scholars have disagreed about the expression **has suffered a grievous wound, a crushing blow.** Some see this as an action that had already taken place, since the verb tense is perfect, indicating completed action. Of course, both Yahweh and the prophet could have seen it in a vision as having already happened and spoken of it that way. The verb in verse 18, translated **have gone to a land**, is definitely a perfect form. It too may be a prophetic perfect. On the other hand, it might refer to the attack of Nebuchadnezzar in 597 B.C. when a number of the leaders in Judah were transported to Babylon.

Whatever else these verses teach us, one truth stands out: God suffers when his people suffer. A true prophet of God feels the same way. Even if those we love deserve the punishment they receive for sinful acts, we empathize with them.

Ⓓ Third Intercession of Jeremiah (14:19–15:9)

SUPPORTING IDEA: *Persisting in his plea with Yahweh, Jeremiah receives a final negative response.*

14:19. Heartbroken when he viewed the distress and agony of his native land, Jeremiah once more approached God. He refused to believe Yahweh had completely and unequivocally rejected his people.

A true prophet always identified so completely with his people that he stayed with them, regardless of how much they rebelled against God or him personally. Yet a time comes when one must face reality. The false prophets never agreed with this fact but continued to lead the people astray. Jeremiah was rapidly coming to the time when he must accept God's assessment. The people had gone so far in sin that they had grown incapable of true repentance. Yet he made one final effort on their behalf.

14:20–22. Was this prayer one that Jeremiah prayed for himself? It was for himself but also for the people. He was framing words of contrite repentance, but in reality the people, when they uttered such words, were not sincere. They could bring their offerings, perform the rituals, and say empty words of praise to God without any intention of changing their lifestyle.

All of these things Jeremiah had said before in petition to Yahweh. Perhaps the only new element was his total and unqualified admission that the people were completely lost without Yahweh since he is the only true God.

15:1–4. Yahweh replied to Jeremiah's plaintive cry with the strongest and most irrevocable statement he had made up to this point. The two examples he gave represented two of Israel's most notable intercessors: Moses in Exodus 32:11–14,30–32; Numbers 14:13–19; Deuteronomy 9:13–29; and Samuel in 1 Samuel 7:8–9; 12:19–25. Each had called on God to forgive the nation when the people had sinned by pursuing foreign deities. They had called on God to restore the people to their covenant relationship.

Anyone who feels that Yahweh's response to Jeremiah's intercession was cruel and harsh should remember the historical facts. For centuries Yahweh, through his prophets, had warned Israel and Judah of what would happen if they did not change their lifestyle. Yet they had continuously rejected him and his messengers. The stubborn people had exhausted God's patience.

The Hebrew verb translated **send** is the same word Moses used in Exodus 5:1 when he ordered Pharaoh to "let my people go." Jeremiah may have used an intentional play on words. But in this context, the verb had a dismal and foreboding meaning. It was like a stern order to "send" or "drive" them away.

Jeremiah must have suffered traumatically when he came to the conclusion that nothing could turn away the coming judgment for Judah. God's firm refusal in this context planted the seed for Jeremiah's later declarations to Zedekiah. When Babylon surrounded Jerusalem a few years later, Jeremiah told Judah's final king that he should quit resisting Babylon and accept the judgment Yahweh had decreed. This, Jeremiah insisted, was the king's only hope for survival and the only way Jerusalem could avoid total destruction.

In answering the people's inquiry about what course they should pursue in light of God's declaration, Jeremiah immediately delivered God's word for them. Four possibilities were open. The first three—**death, the sword, starvation**—would be immediate, while the fourth—**captivity**—would be a living death.

Yahweh outlined the four instruments he would use to demolish the people. The sword would bring immediate destruction, but Yahweh would use three other tools to finish the job. **Dogs**, the animals Jews held in such contempt, would congregate to haul their dead bodies out of sight. Winged creatures from the skies and animals from the earth would gorge themselves on their remains. Even their enemies and other neutral nations would look upon them with disgust.

Though the immediate reason for the coming judgment was the people's stubborn rejection of Yahweh's way for them, another factor was present. The wicked king who had led Judah away from God for more than half a century had sown the seed for Judah's wickedness. The fact that Jeremiah mentioned Manasseh's father, Hezekiah, might have contained a subtle innuendo. God originally planned to take the good king home to be with him earlier, but the monarch pleaded for more time on earth. Yahweh granted the ruler fifteen additional years. During that time Manasseh was born. We often bring sorrow on ourselves and others when we ask God to change his plans to suit our personal wishes.

15:5–9. These verses contain a poem describing the fate that awaited Jerusalem. Most of the verbs in verses 6–9 are in the perfect tense, implying completed action. Some interpreters see them as referring to a recent event already taken place, while others contend they are in prophetic perfect tense and translate as events yet to come. Most of those holding the former view identify the recent tragedy as the 597 B.C. invasion by Nebuchadnezzar. The latter view identifies the events with the invasion of 586 B.C. Some students see these verses as an independent poem placed here by compilers because they continue the theme of Yahweh's preceding words (vv. 1–4).

Verse 5 expresses a doleful, heartbreaking thought. No one cared enough about devastated Judah to have any feeling for her. The great city had passed off the scene of national importance. In the next verse Yahweh reaffirmed the cause for the devastation he had sent. Judah's sinful conduct was more than one or two missteps. She had continued her sinful deeds over many years. This forced God to act in judgment.

The prophet combined two previously used figures of speech (v. 7). The separating of the grain from chaff and other undesirable elements occurred regularly in the agricultural community. The leaders of the walled towns gathered at the **city gates** to conduct official business. Combining these two figures, Jeremiah pointed to one of Judah's basic sins. Corruption in the nation's legal system violated the principles of integrity and equity that Judah's holy God demanded from his people. The nation faced death, destruction, and devastation because they refused to change their sinful conduct.

Who suffers the most when military force seizes a nation? Women and children! Jeremiah pointed this out with explicit words. In verse 8, the hyperbolic statement about the **widows** and the **sand of the sea** emphasized loss of countless men in combat. **At midday** showed the eagerness of the soldiers to attack. They did not even wait for the darkness to launch their bitter campaign. **Suddenly** pointed out the element of surprise while **anguish and terror** indicated the severity of Babylon's cruelty.

Verse 9 continues the picture of mistreated and abused women. **The mother of seven** indicated a woman with a large household. The number seven spoke symbolically of fullness or completion. The mothers with great responsibilities, still in their prime, would be treated mercilessly. Those who were fortunate enough to survive would not escape death. The executions would take place publicly as an example of what sin does to a nation.

E The Prophet's Complaint and Yahweh's Response (15:10–21)

SUPPORTING IDEA: *Discouraged and despondent, Jeremiah bemoans his state and calls on God for deliverance and vindication.*

Scattered throughout the Book of Jeremiah are several poems dealing with the inner life of the prophet. They provide insight into his character and feelings. Old Testament scholars call them the "Confessions of Jeremiah." The generally agreed upon confessions are: 11:18–12:6; 15:10–21; 16:1–3; 17:9–18; 18:18–23; 20:7–18.

These confessions were probably never delivered publicly and were most likely never published in Jeremiah's lifetime. The prophet's confessions were sometimes monologues but more often dialogues with God. They laid bare the innermost thoughts and agony of his life. This included his fears and his conflict with adversity, doubt, and temptations. In short, they contained his reaction to a world that threatened to crush him. He faced a huge task that overwhelmed his sensitive nature.

15:10. Though most of the confessions were directed to Yahweh, this one began with an exclamation of anguish to his mother. Jeremiah did not blame his mother but only regretted that he had been born. His complaint is similar to Job's (Job 3:1). Jeremiah was probably familiar with Job's plaintive wail.

15:11–14. Yahweh, in verse 11, assured his prophet that everything happening to him was a part of his divine plan. The time would come when his opponents would entreat him to make petition in their behalf (v. 11). This happened on several occasions as Babylon later tightened the noose around Judah's neck. During the eighteen-month siege of Jerusalem, the king himself begged Jeremiah to intercede for him to Yahweh.

At present, however, Jeremiah needed to learn a lesson. He had been rebellious toward God. His insubordination had not been in following the Baal cult but in his questioning of the ways of the Lord. Again a parallel with Job is evident. The ancient patriarch eventually admitted that he had spoken of "things I did not understand, things too wonderful for me to know" (Job 42:3). Jeremiah needed to learn this same lesson.

Verse 12 means Yahweh informed Jeremiah that human strength could not defeat the "foe from the north." God would do it his own way and in his own time. Verse 13 suggests that Jeremiah was not a poor man. Perhaps he had already inherited some of the family wealth. Later he left Jerusalem during a temporary lifting of the siege by the Babylonians "to go to the territory of Benjamin to get his share of the property among the people there" (37:12).

Yahweh concluded the matter with a strong statement. Jeremiah himself would share the people's enslavement in a foreign land. This would happen unless he repented and showed a different attitude toward Yahweh.

15:15–18. Jeremiah showed proper respect for Yahweh, but at the same time he continued to press his case. His tone became a bit more conciliatory, and his words took on the form of a heartfelt plea. He realized he was dealing not only with an omnipotent God but with an omniscient God who was aware of everything about him.

The Hebrew verb translated **understand** in verse 15 contains a variety of meanings in addition to the usually rendered "know." In this context it meant "to be aware of" or "call to mind." The word translated **remember** meant more than recollection. It carried the idea of recapturing the past in such a way as to influence present action.

Having recognized Yahweh's omnipresence and omniscience, Jeremiah moved to what he considered Yahweh's greatest trait—mercy and forgiving love. But Jeremiah still had a spirit not quite up to New Testament standards. He wanted Yahweh to give him vengeance against those who had persecuted him.

The **long-suffering** of which Jeremiah spoke probably referred to Yahweh's delay in punishing those who had opposed the prophet and his ministry. Jeremiah felt that Yahweh, in failing to reprove his enemies, had prolonged the suffering he was enduring. He reminded Yahweh of how he had suffered and was continuing to do so for him. Was it asking too much when he called upon Yahweh to vindicate him by removing his enemies?

In verses 16 and 17, Jeremiah gave three reasons why Yahweh should grant his request. First, he had accepted Yahweh's **words** when they came to him. Second, he avoided the shallow entertainment of the day because it led to things that dishonored Yahweh's name. Third, he chose to spend time in solitude, meditation, and prayer. In this way he could maximize his fellowship with Yahweh and the spiritual things required for a dedicated life.

Jeremiah closed his plea to God in verse 18 with two questions that were probably rhetorical, but he felt Yahweh should answer them. The prophet felt he was suffering greatly. His own people had turned against him, and an outside foe was always a personal threat to him as well as a potential peril to the entire nation. He knew if Nebuchadnezzar conquered the land and raped the people, he might be among the casualties.

Add to these facts the isolation he endured because he had been set apart as a prophet of God. Jeremiah was human. He had all the desires of an ordinary person to have friends and be accepted among his peers. He had suffered severely—if not physically, certainly in the spirit.

The second question bordered on rebellion against Yahweh. He accused Yahweh of being fickle, undependable, false, almost hypocritical. The Hebrew word translated **deceptive brook**, to which he compared Yahweh, meant literally "a liar." The word *brook* is not in the Hebrew text. The translator supplied that because Jeremiah had this in mind since he followed it with **a spring that fails**. The brook or *wadi* dried up in the summer when the rains stopped. Jeremiah's figure of speech meant that Yahweh was unreliable.

15:19–21. Yahweh did not even bother to answer Jeremiah's questions or defend himself against the prophet's accusations. He spoke sharply. Jeremiah had called upon the people to repent. Now Yahweh called on the prophet to **repent**. Only if Jeremiah changed his attitude could he attain the favor that he had previously enjoyed with Yahweh.

Yahweh reminded Jeremiah that since he had been called to speak words for him, he must be careful of his own **words**. This included those spoken to Yahweh as well as those directed to the prophet's audience. Rather than allowing the congregation to influence him toward evil attitudes, he must be the one that motivated them for good.

When Yahweh called Jeremiah to be his prophet, he promised to be a tower of strength against those who opposed him. Rather than suffering defeat at their hands, the prophet would be victorious over them. The only way he could realize that promise was to adopt God's viewpoint. Yahweh wanted to deliver Jeremiah, and he would do so if he met Yahweh's terms.

This ends Jeremiah's second confession. He began it with a complaint to his mother which was actually a protest to God. Yahweh ended it with a mandate to the prophet.

F Coming Disaster and Future Restoration (16:1–21)

SUPPORTING IDEA: *God must punish Judah because of the people's sin, but because they are still the group through whom the Messiah will come, he will restore them.*

A few scholars contend the first few verses of this section continue the confession of Jeremiah that began in the preceding chapter (15:10). But most see this entire chapter as a separate prophecy or oracle. In my judgment the latter view seems more reasonable. In verses 1–13 Yahweh pictured a bleak future for Judah. He ordered Jeremiah to practice a rigidly disciplined lifestyle in light of the coming woeful conditions. But beginning with verse 14, Yahweh assured the prophet that he would later deliver Judah from their approaching captivity and return the people to their homeland. This section continues through verse 18. Verses 19–21 contain a brief dialogue between Yahweh and Jeremiah that ends the chapter and the message.

16:1–4. Yahweh gave Jeremiah a stern order. He **must not marry and have sons or daughters**. He explained that future conditions would be so terrible that the prophet should not subject a family to them. **Deadly diseases** would spread everywhere. Funerals would be nonexistent. Dead bodies would rot **on the ground**, exposed to the elements. To Jewish people this was one of the worst disgraces possible. Every person deserved an honorable burial.

16:5–7. Yahweh went even further. He ordered Jeremiah to refrain from showing any comfort to people in mourning. This seems to be cruel, but God sought to impress on his prophet how disgusted he was with the people's sin. We should never forget how terrible and dishonoring to God sin is and should never minimize it.

16:8–9. Yahweh added another dimension to his prohibitions for Jeremiah. He must not enjoy himself socially. To do so might indicate he approved of the people's levity and enjoyment. Because of the present crisis and further woes ahead, the people needed to get serious about their moral and spiritual need. An active social life discouraged such an attitude.

16:10–13. Yahweh concluded this portion of his message to his prophet with a word for the people when they asked for an explanation for their sufferings. The answer to their question was twofold.

First, their parents had started them on their downward course. This could have meant the generation of Manasseh, or it could have referred to the collective generations of the past several centuries. Second, the generation to whom Jeremiah spoke had done even worse. He told them frankly that they had **behaved more wickedly** than their **fathers**.

What would be the result of their wickedness? Exile **into a land** unfamiliar to them. This was Babylon. The Northern Kingdom had already fallen to Assyria; perhaps some of them had been taken into Babylon from captivity in Assyria following the battle of Carchemisch. Judah, however, knew nothing about Babylon. This nation was even farther away from them than Assyria. It was bad enough to be taken into exile, but to be taken to a land of which they were completely ignorant was even worse.

16:14–15. Beginning with verse 14 and continuing through 15, Yahweh suddenly "changed gears" as he looked into the future. His redemptive plan remained in effect. He would not desert those whom he had chosen to be his instrument for implementing it. Their banishment to a foreign land would not be permanent. At the proper time he would restore them to their land.

These verses, placed within the context of reprimand and warning, show that God never regards his wrath toward his people as the last word. He made a covenant with Abraham to bless the world through Abraham's seed. That promise would be fulfilled. Actually, the day would come when the return from Babylon would be a greater fact in Yahweh's program of world redemption than the exodus from **Egypt**.

16:16–18. Having inserted a word of hope, Yahweh returned to the present situation. The imminent discipline of his people would be thorough. God used two figures of speech to illustrate his point. The analogy of a fisherman gathering fish into his nets would have been familiar and meaningful to the Israelites. The imagery of the hunter reflected a Persian military strategy. Forming an unbroken line of soldiers, they would march from one end of an island to another seeking their victims. A few scholars have identified these two pictures with the successive Babylonian invasions of 597 and 586 B.C.

16:19–21. These last three verses of this section contain a brief dialogue between Yahweh and his prophet. The most logical approach is to interpret verses 19 and 20 as words of Jeremiah and verse 21 as coming from Yahweh himself. The Lord's words opened the door of understanding for Jeremiah. He saw that nations from all over the world would turn to Yahweh and acknowledge that he alone is Lord.

Jeremiah realized that previous generations of his countrymen had wandered far from the true God. They had made **worthless** deities that had no value and offered no security. The question and answer in verse 20 record the prophet's conclusion. Anything or anyone beside Yahweh is insufficient to meet the needs of the people. In verse 21, Yahweh gave his verdict and promise. Since Jeremiah had decided to be his dedicated vessel, Yahweh would work with him and empower him. As the two worked together, people from every nation would come to know the salvation that Yahweh offered.

Ⓖ Picture of the Moral Condition in Judah (17:1–18)

SUPPORTING IDEA: *Reflecting the seriousness of the crisis, Jeremiah poured out his soul to the people and then turned to Yahweh for help.*

At first glance the messages in this section seem to be unrelated. But further study shows a thematic unity. They serve as a microcosm of Jeremiah's ministry, especially his days of service during the reign of Jehoiakim. Whether they are a collection of small, independent sermons or one lengthy discourse is not important. In my judgment the first thirteen verses contain words of Yahweh, and the last five give us Jeremiah's response.

17:1–4. These words show the spiritual bankruptcy of Judah. The revivals under Hezekiah and Josiah had not slowed the nation's downward plunge. Judah's sin was so thorough that Jeremiah pictured it as deeply ingrained. He used the metaphor of a stylus or diamond **point** set in **iron**. Such tools were used in ancient times for writings like the Moabite Stone. The nation needed radical heart surgery, not just a soothing ointment. Even the sacred places such as the altar **horns** of the temple reflected the nation's iniquity.

No security for Judah remained. Though a superficial tearing down of the Baal altars had occurred, the practice of idolatry had been so widespread that it was still remembered by the **children**. People do not remove their sin by frivolous and shallow external deeds or ceremonies.

Verses 3–4 bear a strong resemblance to 15:13–14. The words **my mountain** probably refer to Jerusalem, Yahweh's unique treasure. Jeremiah warned that Yahweh would give the enemy not only Judah's great religious shrine, but her **wealth** as well. Scholars do not agree whether Jeremiah spoke of the 597 B.C. invasion or the final raid in 586 B.C. Actually, his words applied to tragic occurrences that took place both times. Jeremiah did not announce the exact time of the final tragedy or how many invasions awaited Judah before the final blow fell.

Jeremiah seldom pronounced a coming judgment without telling the people why punishment would come on them. He repeated in this context what he had said on other occasions. The **fault** was their **own**. Two results would follow. First, Judah would **lose the inheritance** Yahweh had promised the nation. Second, the people would be taken from their home and would spend time in another **land**. They would become servants of a foreign people and be subjected to the gods they worshipped (16:13).

17:5–11. These verses contain a poem that might have been composed at a different time, most likely earlier than the previous material (vv. 1–4). Jeremiah probably inserted it at this spot because the message was so relevant to what Yahweh had said to him in the preceding four verses. This poem is structured stylistically like the Wisdom Literature that began and flourished several centuries earlier in the United Kingdom during the reign of Solomon. The style and content were popular methods of writing.

The contrast between those who have confidence in their own resources and those who trust Yahweh for their strength was one of Jeremiah's basic themes. The metaphor he used to contrast two different types of people contains two contrasting pictures. One takes us to the hot desert where a stunted, prickly shrub struggles to eke out a bare existence. The other carries us to a brimming river where everything lives because of life-giving water. These scenes represent two persons. One diverts his attention from the God who loves and desires the best for his creatures. These people make flesh their arm (see KJV) and depart from the living God. The other group casts their needs, cares, sins, and sorrows upon God.

Verses 9–10 contain words of deep insight about the **heart**. This body organ refers to more than the emotional part of a person's makeup. It represents not only the seat of feeling but of understanding and volition. Some versions translate "desperately sick" rather than **deceitful**. This is not a false concept. Sin is a sickness. This is why Jesus compared himself to a physician.

This concept of sin as sickness includes the idea of rebelling against God. It also adds the end result that comes when people ignore his will for their lives. Sick people adopt morbid, distorted views of life that they would not embrace if they were well. This is because they do not **understand** themselves. This is exactly what God, through Jeremiah, said about the heart.

Verse 11 reflects a popular belief that the partridge sat upon eggs that were not her own. Many ancient writers denied the validity of this notion, claiming the partridge had many enemies who stole from her. The prophet's point in the metaphor was that those who enrich themselves by unjust means will have little enjoyment of their ill-gotten wealth.

17:12–18. The general verdict of scholarship is that Jeremiah's fourth confession begins at 17:9 and continues through verse 18. This would make all of these verses a part of that fourth confession. (See comments at the beginning of 15:10–21 about the confessions of Jeremiah.)

At this point, Jeremiah entered the dialogue. Verses 12 and 13 reflect his words to Yahweh rather than Yahweh's words to him for proclamation to the people. He begins with a tribute to Yahweh, indicating his respect for him as the sovereign God of the nation. Following that, he states that the people's security is in Yahweh. Those who refuse to follow him will suffer extinction.

In verses 14–18, we find Jeremiah's final plea to Yahweh. Begging for deliverance from the misery he is enduring, the prophet insists he has never been derelict in his duty, nor has he compromised his message. In his depression he calls on Yahweh to remove his enemies, even showing the spirit of retaliation and vengeance in demanding their **double destruction**.

Honoring the Sabbath (17:19–27)

SUPPORTING IDEA: *A nation's progress, security, and existence depend to a large extent on how its people observe the Lord's Day.*

Those who attempt to reconstruct the compilation of Jeremiah's messages experience great difficulty trying to fit this message into the total picture. Scholars have dated it everywhere from the early years of Josiah's reign to the days of Nehemiah. Each one offers strong evidence for his position. We will treat it as an independent sermon added to this scroll and make no attempt to assign a date for its original delivery. The message is relevant to any period in Jeremiah's life and appropriate for any generation.

17:19–26. Scholars suggest several different gates that might fit the description of the **gates** in verses 19–21. The point is that Yahweh wanted Jeremiah to be where the maximum number of people, including the leaders of the land, would hear him.

Yahweh commanded Jeremiah to make the message simple and direct. He wanted the people to reassess their observance of this day he had set aside as special. Obviously, the nation had grown lax in their observance of this day.

The command in verse 21 about the carrying of **a load on the Sabbath** had further implications than just this menial task. In verse 22, Yahweh extended it. He commanded the people not to **do any work on the Sabbath, but keep the Sabbath day holy, as I commanded your forefathers**.

The Old Testament records two reasons God gave for observing or remembering the Sabbath Day. Exodus 20:11 says that he "blessed the Sabbath day and made it holy" because he created the world in six days and rested on the seventh. In Deuteronomy 5:15, Moses told the people to observe the seventh day as a memorial of their redemption from Egyptian slavery. As Christians, we have these same two motivations with one exception—our redemption is from the slavery of sin through Christ's atonement.

Two extreme attitudes toward the Sabbath have often prevailed—legalism and libertinism. In an effort to remove the shackles of an overemphasis on rules, many people throw away all restraints. As a result, they fall into the "deep ditch" on the other side of the road. We should avoid the negative attitude of completely withdrawing from activity on the Lord's Day. Yet we need to make the Christian Sabbath or Lord's Day what God intended it to be—a "set apart" day.

17:27. Jeremiah closed this short oracle with a severe warning. If Judah failed to heed Yahweh's words, the people faced a terrible fate. Abraham Lincoln expressed this truth well for our nation. He said, "As we keep or break the Sabbath day, we nobly save or meanly lose the last and best hope by which man arises."

MAIN IDEA REVIEW: *Even though people go so far in sin that they become virtually incapable of repentance, the true prophet of God still loves them.*

III. CONCLUSION

God Is God

People who have lived their lives for themselves with no thought of God often experience a time of calamity or desperation, a day of disaster, such as the drought and famine experienced by the people of Jeremiah's day. When this happens they cry out to God. They assume that God will hear their prayers and give them relief. Such a viewpoint reduces the Almighty God of the universe to a cosmic servant. It presumes that God is obligated to respond to us and our needs when we want, as we want, to do what we want, no matter what.

But God is God. He is not subject to our desires and demands. Unless we approach him in true repentance and are willing to turn from our wicked ways, it does not matter if the most spiritual persons in the world were to intercede for us. God will not hear. He will not act on our behalf. He will not rescue us so we may continue to ignore him when our lives return to normal.

This is a truth the people of Jeremiah's day needed to learn. It is a truth we need to learn today as well.

PRINCIPLES

- Sooner or later if people continue to sin with impunity against the Lord, they will pass a point of no return.

- The Lord is not obligated to respond to our repentance and confession as we desire.

- Not everyone who claims to speak for God is his true spokesman.

- Sometimes God calls his servants to offer up their singleness to him and to forego participation in the normal activities of life so he can use them in his service.

- God's ultimate desire is not judgment and destruction but rescue and restoration.

- People who attempt to live in their own strength will not prosper, but those who trust in the Lord will never fail.

- Often, a person's obedience to God in what appears to be an inconsequential external matter reveals his true attitude toward God and his commands.

APPLICATIONS

- Perform a maintenance check on your "sin detector" to see if it may have become desensitized. Consider what happens to fire detectors that lack proper sensitivity to smoke.
- List some essential characteristics of those who speak for God.
- Imagine pursuing your own rights, desires, or plans and finding that you have moved away from God.
- Evaluate the view of God that is operative in your life most of the time and how well that view matches up with what the Bible teaches about God.
- From persons you know, contrast someone who is self-sufficient with someone who is strongly rooted in God.
- Ask some fellow believers what are some small matters that reveal the authenticity of faith in a person.

IV. LIFE APPLICATION

A Single Servant

The Lord had a special ministry for Jeremiah. It required him to remain single and to forego having children. Such was not Jeremiah's choice; the Lord commanded him not to marry and have children (16:2). The Lord forbade him from participating in societal events (16:5) and normal social activities (16:8).

"I hope no [one] will be as lonely as I have been," a single adult named Charlotte wrote in a time of despair. She had suffered the embarrassment of a broken engagement to a man from a well-connected family. She angered many of her coworkers and was constantly accused of trying to do a man's job. She earned a master's degree, served as principal of a school, advocated women's rights, and was reckoned as a major force in negotiating with the government. She gave her food away to help others who were starving because of a famine. Then she starved to death, weighing only fifty pounds at her demise.

When God's call came to Charlotte, better known as Lottie Moon, she answered and spent forty years as a missionary in China. She wrote, "I would I had a thousand lives that I might give them to the women of China!"

What makes people such as Lottie Moon give up their natural desire for marriage, family, and a normal social life? The call of God. God had a special ministry for her—and for countless others through the centuries. And because she was willing to offer up her singleness to him, she was able to fulfill her role in his plan.

V. PRAYER

Heavenly Lord, keep us from passing the point of no return. Save us. Rescue us. And draw us safely to your shore. Forgive us for presuming on your grace. Restore us and establish us in you. Help us to commit all the plans and desires we have for our own lives to you so you may use us in your service. And help us to obey you in all matters you have commanded. Amen.

VI. DEEPER DISCOVERIES

A. "Like a stranger in the land" (14:8)

Have you ever felt like you served an absentee god? One who comes and goes on a whim? An old cliché spoke of such a person as a "fair weather friend." In Jeremiah's depressions, he felt this way about Yahweh. He used a Hebrew word about him often translated in our language as "stranger."

Is our God an absentee god? Does he come and go, completely oblivious to our sufferings? If we find we must voice Jeremiah's prayer, the fault might be our own. Why should God associate with a person who has no desire to fellowship with him? Yahweh said of the people in Jeremiah's day, "They love to wander." Their indifference to spiritual things prevented Yahweh from associating with them.

God is *not* a traveling stranger who visits for a night and then moves on. When he had reflected for a moment, Jeremiah corrected himself. He said, "You are among us, O Lord, and we bear your name" (14:9).

God is permanently with us today. How? In Jesus Christ. At Bethlehem he became one of us and at Calvary he brought us unto himself forever. Through his Spirit, he maintains a constant fellowship with us until he returns to take us to be with him in the Father's house.

B. "Do men make their own gods?" (16:20)

The Bible tells us God made man in his image (Gen. 1:27). One person with keen insight said, "Before long, secular man 'returned the favor.' He began to create god in his image, and he has been doing it ever since."

Throughout our contemporary society, humans talk about God in two ways, reflecting two worldviews. One is concerned with what God wants man to be. The other focuses on what man wants his god to be. Much of the lack of reality in our religious experience comes because we fail to face this difference and the implications it brings for daily life. Many moderns do today what pagans did in ancient times. They make gods of food, drink, money, sexual indulgence, nationalism, and race.

Another great prophet painted a sarcastic picture of an ancient Israelite and his idolatry. He described how the man goes to the forest and cuts down a tree which he has previously planted. He takes part of it and warms himself with it. After that he makes a fire with which he bakes bread. After using most of the tree to satisfy his material need, he has a small amount left. The prophet said, "From the rest he makes a god, his idol; he bows down to it and worships. He prays to it and says, 'Save me; you are my god'" (Isa. 44:17).

C. "The heart is deceitful . . . and beyond cure" (17:9).

The KJV reads "desperately wicked" rather than "beyond cure." A few of the modern versions, however, strike a compromise with "desperately sick" (NASB, HCSB). This displeases some who view it as trying to "water down" the matter of sin by calling it only an "illness."

To be completely honest and objective, sickness and wickedness are not always exactly the same thing. But Jeremiah, in this context, used the word to designate moral infirmity. We may assume that he intended to include the idea of moral liability or at least spiritual shortcoming. The prophet intended to communicate one point to his audience: a person cannot trust his heart completely in major decisions, either morally or spiritually, if it is in a desperately unhealthy state.

This truth is applicable in all areas of life. An ill person usually takes a morbid, distorted view of a situation that he would view differently if he were well and healthy. Counselors say a person should never decide anything in a time of physical or emotional distress. We don't focus clearly in such a situation and fail to see the whole picture.

Jeremiah affirms this truth. In life's higher issues, the heart cannot be relied on for proper decisions if it is thinking improperly because of sin and guilt. The prophet added "who can understand it?" to enforce his point. The heart was not primarily the seat of feeling and emotion to the Hebrew mind. It was basically the seat of volition and judgment, in many ways the concept of the entire person.

The heart is the depth within us, completely impenetrable and unfathomable to the human mind. From it come aims, desires, fears, hopes, and joys. Within it lie our motives that are concealed even from our own discernment.

How can we obtain a heart that does "think straight"? The answer is in the old expression many of us heard as children, "Surrender your heart to Jesus." This means, of course, the entire life—another way of saying, "Receive Jesus Christ as Lord." The developmental struggle may be long and extended. It may involve many "growing pains," but this is the only way to rid ourselves of all shams, lies, and iniquity.

We sang a simple song as children: "Into my heart, into my heart. Come into my heart, Lord Jesus. Come in today. Come in to stay. Come into my heart, Lord Jesus." That's still the need in our postmodern world.

VII. TEACHING OUTLINE

A. INTRODUCTION

1. Lead Story: Rescue at the Falls

2. Context: A drought and famine caused the people of Judah to call on the Lord for relief. The Lord announced to Jeremiah that he would not answer their plea, and he used the situation to reveal he was determined to punish Judah.

3. Transition: God used Jeremiah's personal suffering and life situation to picture the immoral condition of Judah.

B. COMMENTARY

1. Description of Nature in a Time of Drought (14:1–6)
2. First Intercession of Jeremiah (14:7–12)
3. Second Intercession of Jeremiah (14:13–18)
4. Third Intercession of Jeremiah (14:19–15:9)
5. The Prophet's Complaint and Yahweh's Response (15:10–21)
6. Coming Disaster and Future Restoration (16:1–21)
7. Picture of Moral Condition in Judah (17:1–18)
8. Honoring the Sabbath (17:19–27)

C. CONCLUSION: GOD IS GOD

VIII. ISSUES FOR DISCUSSION

1. Why do people often turn to God when they are faced with natural disasters such as drought and famine?
2. Discuss whether God always forgives those who call on him and confess their sins. Are there conditions under which he may not? What are they?
3. Based on passages such as Jeremiah 16:1–9 and 1 Corinthians 7:32–35, identify advantages there might be for a servant of the Lord to remain single.
4. Should Christians observe a Sabbath, a weekly day of rest, in which they refrain from their normal work? What benefits might there be to such a practice?

Jeremiah 18:1–20:18

A Visit to the Potter's House

I. INTRODUCTION
Clay in the Potter's Hands

II. COMMENTARY
A verse-by-verse explanation of these verses.

III. CONCLUSION
Are We Still Pliable?

An overview of the principles and applications from these verses.

IV. LIFE APPLICATION
Two Victorian Poets

Melding these verses to life.

V. PRAYER
Tying these verses to life with God.

VI. DEEPER DISCOVERIES
Historical, geographical, and grammatical enrichment of the commentary.

VII. TEACHING OUTLINE
Suggested step-by-step group study of these verses.

VIII. ISSUES FOR DISCUSSION
Zeroing these verses in on daily life.

Quote

"All this of Pot and Potter—Tell me then

Who is the Potter, pray, and who the Pot?

Why, said another, Some there are who tell

Of one who threatens he will toss to Hell

The luckless Pots he marr'd in making—Pish!

He's a Good Fellow, and 'twill all be well."

Edward Fitzgerald

Jeremiah 18:1–20:18

 IN A NUTSHELL

Jeremiah used two symbolic actions involving pottery to instruct the people. First came a lesson from pottery-making (18:1–10). Then came a lesson from pottery-breaking (19:1–13). Following both symbolic acts, the Lord announced he was preparing or shaping disaster on Judah (18:11; 19:15). In both instances these announcements led to personal attacks against Jeremiah (18:18; 20:1–2) and to Jeremiah complaining to the Lord (18:19–23; 20:7–18).

A Visit to the
Potter's House

I. INTRODUCTION

Clay in the Potter's Hands

*H*er strict Presbyterian parents named her Sarah Addison Pollard, but this strong-willed girl did not like that name. She liked Adelaide better, so she adopted it. Adelaide was frail and suffered from a host of physical and psychological problems. She was diabetic. She experienced periods of deep depression. She suffered debilitating collapses that forced her to return to her family for long periods of recuperation. She attended healing services in an attempt to be cured of these maladies.

Adelaide's consuming desire was foreign missions—a calling that seemed constantly to slip away from her. When she finally did get to go to Africa, she was forced to leave after only a few months because of the outbreak of World War I. She spent the war years in Scotland and then returned to the United States.

During one of her periods of depression following her failed attempt to go to Africa, she sat in a prayer meeting too distracted to concentrate. In her dark mood she heard the prayer of an old woman: "It's all right, Lord! It doesn't matter what you bring into our lives; just have your own way with us!"

That evening Adelaide returned home. She meditated on Jeremiah 18:3–4. She thought, *Perhaps my questioning of God's will shows a flaw in my life, so God has decided to break me, as the potter broke the defective vessel, and then to mold my life again in "his own pattern."* As she bowed in renewed consecration to God and his will for her life, the words of a poem began to form in her mind:

> Have Thine own way, Lord! Have Thine own way!
> Thou art the potter, I am the clay!
> Mold me and make me after Thy will,
> While I am waiting, yielded and still.

Like Adelaide, the people of Jeremiah's day needed to be remolded by God. They were flawed vessels. Their lives were marred, and they needed to be reshaped according to the Divine Potter's design. Jeremiah announced the Lord's question: "O house of Israel, can I not do with you as this potter does?" (18:6). But if the nation hardened themselves and would not yield to Yahweh, they would be smashed beyond repair (19:10–11).

II. COMMENTARY

A Visit to the Potter's House

MAIN IDEA: *God can transform wrecked lives, but often the messenger who delivers this truth meets violent opposition.*

The material in these three chapters once existed as a separate unit before being incorporated into the Book of Jeremiah as it now exists. These chapters contain narratives, sermons, and dialogues related to one of the most difficult periods in the prophet's ministry.

What sets these chapters off as a unit? Many students suggest the two incidents about the potter's work led the compiler of the book to place them side by side. Most of them see only the first two chapters as forming a separate unit. In my judgment, a closer study shows that a thematic unity exists in the three chapters that includes but supersedes the two references to pottery.

The first unit (18:1–10) gives in narrative form an account of Jeremiah's visit, at God's command, to a potter's house. While the prophet observed the potter at work, Yahweh pointed out to him a great spiritual truth. As the potter reworked the clay when it was marred in his hand, so Israel was in God's hand. He would deal with the nation on the basis of her choices.

The second unit (18:11–17) records God's giving Jeremiah a message for the people (v. 11), followed by a warning (v. 12) that they would reject his word. Verses 13–17 contain a lengthy rebuke and warning that Yahweh commissioned Jeremiah to speak.

The third unit (18:18–23) contains a confession of Jeremiah. The first verse gives in prose form the effect Jeremiah's message from Yahweh had on the people and their plan to assault him. The remainder (vv. 19–23) gives a record of Jeremiah's plea with Yahweh to vindicate him by destroying those who were trying to do him harm.

The fourth unit (19:1–15) follows logically the preceding material. Yahweh gave instructions to Jeremiah following his complaint about those who opposed the prophet and their malicious plotting against him. He told the prophet to buy a clay jar and use it to illustrate a message of condemnation to the people, warning of future punishment.

The fifth unit (20:1–6) tells in narrative form the result of the prophet's emotionally charged sermon to the people. A priest ordered the arrest of Jeremiah. He went even further, authorizing his beating and putting him in stocks, perhaps on public display. After being released the next day, Jeremiah countered with a sharp message directed at the priest.

The sixth unit (20:7–18) concludes this section with the final confession of Jeremiah. His words reflect perhaps the most bitter complaint of his career. The physical pain Jeremiah suffered and the humiliation he experienced broke his spirit.

Ⓐ Jeremiah's Visit to the Potter's House (18:1–10)

SUPPORTING IDEA: *The Divine Potter has his hand on the material with which he works.*

18:1–4. Chapter 18 opens with a third-person account of God's Word coming to Jeremiah. Beginning with verse 2, the account is written in the first person; the prophet told the story in his own words. The expressions **Go down** (v. 2) and **went down** (v. 3) suggest that Jeremiah went to a lower part of the city, perhaps a valley. Many interpreters believe the incident took place somewhere near the Valley of Hinnom.

Jeremiah had probably seen a **potter** at work many times before the day recorded in this chapter. Either at this particular place or one like it, the prophet had often observed the skill and dexterity of the artisan. The potter produced various vessels for different uses to enrich the life of Israel's citizenry. Perhaps never before had Jeremiah been in such a contemplative mood observing a potter at work as on this particular day. He was deeply concerned about the nation's spiritual plight. He was ready to hear God's object lesson.

Most interpreters agree that verse 4 contains the heart of this story. We find in it two great truths. First, as the potter worked the product was disfigured. Second, the potter changed his purpose or direction and produced something other than what he had originally planned. This story, of all

Jeremiah's "acted out parables," has appealed to many subsequent writers. Paul's letter to the Romans uses it to illustrate spiritual truths.

One who interprets a parable must remember the nature of this literary device. It is not an allegory where every part has an application. He should look for the one essential truth the speaker or writer meant to convey. In this event Yahweh meant to reveal one supreme fact to Jeremiah that he was to pass on to the people. The work of Yahweh for Israel had been marred. He had meant for the nation to be a great theocracy, but this had not happened. The chosen people had refused to be faithful to the covenant they made with Yahweh at Sinai.

God must work in a different way to accomplish his redemptive purposes. He would not cast off his people entirely, but they must face chastisement and correction. Israel must regroup and reexamine her concept of God's nature. Crushed into shapelessness by the potter's hand, the clay was placed once more on the whirling **wheel**. Though broken and **marred** it could still be used. Likewise, reshaped to a new design, Israel would still be molded into a useful servant, **as seemed best to** the Potter.

18:5–6. Jeremiah added the words in verse 5 to assure his audience that the truths that followed were just as reliable as those coming after verse 1. He was as certain that Yahweh had spoken to him now as he was when God had told him to go to the potter's house. What was this message? **Israel** belonged to Yahweh in a very special way. He had called Abraham from Ur of the Chaldees to inaugurate a new era in the history of his dealing with the nations. Punishment of the sinful world by a flood had not changed human nature. People needed more than punishment. They needed redemption and the inward change that comes when one meets Yahweh and comes into a personal relationship with him. Through the seed of Abraham, God would bless the world.

Several centuries passed before Yahweh's chosen agent was ready to become active in this redemption process. Abraham's descendants spent four centuries in Egypt, much of the time as slaves. But under Moses, God redeemed his chosen people, gave them national identification, and made a covenant with them. Though Israel had broken the covenant, Yahweh had not cast her off. She was still his agent to implement his plan. He had his hand on Israel in a special way. As the clay was subject to the potter, so Israel was subject to him.

18:7–10. Jeremiah was a prophet who covered all the bases when he spoke God's will. He had made clear that Yahweh was in charge and would never relinquish his sovereignty. But he needed to point out the flip side of this coin. His message was no inflexible pronouncement of a rigid determinism that ignored human personality. Neither was Yahweh a deity who was enslaved by his previous decrees. Both he and his creatures have choices.

Unfortunately many fine Christians stumble on this paradox in God's nature. They cannot bridge the gap between two great theological truths— God's foreknowledge and our free will. A few oversimplify the matter of God's foreknowledge with the statement, "What is to be will be." This attitude is as far from reality as the opposite mind-set that denies God's omniscience, or knowledge of everything.

The basic problems expositors have had with these verses centers on the Hebrew verb about God that appears twice (vv. 8,10). In the older versions, translators rendered it "repent." If to repent means to feel sorry for sin, then God cannot repent because he never sinned. In an effort to deal with the matter of whether God can "repent," modern versions present it differently. The problem is that few versions agree on exactly what words to use in translating it.

Another, different Hebrew word is used in verse 8 to describe the action of any nation that turns from its evil deeds. It is also translated **repents** by some modern versions. In other words, a Bible reader today finds no consistency in the various versions. This, in my judgment, confuses students about which versions they should accept and which ones they should reject. In an effort to be fair, let us look at one of the standard Hebrew lexicons and see what they say about the word used in the original text.

In verse 8, the Hebrew text says literally, "If that nation turns from its wickedness which I spoke against." In Hebrew the verb translated "turns" appears first in the sentence for emphasis. The Hebrew means "to turn, turn back, return, to turn away, cease, desist." It was used by the prophets as a call to repentance, but the emphasis is on turning from walking in one direction to walk in another.

In verse 8 Jeremiah , speaking for Yahweh, continued to say, **I will relent** (NIV, NASB). The KJV renders the Hebrew verb "repent." In verse 10, the same Hebrew word is rendered **reconsider**. The NASB renders it "think better" while the KJV renders it "repent." In both verses, the Hebrew word is the same. It (*nacham*) means literally "to mourn, grieve over, feel compassion for, pity." A further meaning is to repent in the sense of giving up a previous course of action so as either to produce a change of conduct or of purpose or to free oneself of any displeasing object. Can God repent? Can he change? This is the question. Virtually all Christian theologians would say, "No. He is the Unchangeable One."

So what does this Hebrew expression mean? Scholars are trying to put the word into proper context for today's world so we might understand exactly what the original writer was saying. What is the basic truth for us? George Adam Smith says, "By figure and by word the Divine Sovereignty was proclaimed as absolutely as possible. But the Sovereignty is a real Sovereignty and therefore includes Freedom." God may change his course of action as circumstances change. But God does not change with regard to his essence, his attributes; he is the same yesterday, today, and tomorrow.

Discerning students see in this parable one other trait of God often overlooked or at least not proclaimed in proportion to its importance. To the traits of divine sovereignty and divine freedom, this parable introduces divine patience. The human potter did not immediately throw away the lump of clay that became marred. Even so, the Divine Potter had some fresh purpose for his clay beyond the ruined fragments in his hand. What a lesson for God's servants in all ages! This thought has been revolutionary to many people.

The key issue in this verse appears in verse 4. What is it? The relationship between the potter and the clay! The Divine Potter controls the clay and can do with it as he pleases. But he has chosen to delegate the outcome to the choice of nations and individuals. What Moses said on God's behalf to Israel, Jeremiah said for God to the Israel of his day: "I have set before you life and death. . . . Now choose life, so that you . . . may live" (Deut. 30:19).

B Commission, Warning, Rejection, and Reply (18:11–17)

SUPPORTING IDEA: *Judah has been deluded by false worship.*

18:11–12. Yahweh never left Jeremiah in doubt about his will for the people. Whether stated explicitly or not, he meant for every word his prophet spoke to ring with a "thus saith the Lord." Jeremiah was told to warn the people once more that they could not continue in their defiance of divine mandates. God is always on the field even when he seems invisible. If the people expected to survive the coming onslaught, they must repent.

Immediately following Yahweh's first word to the prophet, he provided another. This message resembled the one given to Isaiah in his call and inaugural vision (Isa. 6:9–10). "The people will not hear you! Their pride, along with other forms of wickedness, has infiltrated and saturated their lives. They have thus developed a stubbornness of heart which has immunized them against any kind of repentance. They not only will not repent, but they cannot repent." Nevertheless Yahweh said in essence, "Tell them this same thing another time. Give them one more warning."

18:13–15. With two rhetorical questions, Yahweh pointed out the people's stupidity. Their actions defied logic. Even the impersonal forces of nature consistently follow certain patterns of behavior. Take, for example, the beautiful mountains of Lebanon. They remain throughout all seasons covered with a coat of snow. One could depend on that every day of the year. Why? Because God had planted this fact in the structure of the universe.

This led to the second question. The Hebrew text is difficult at this point, but the NIV translation, in my judgment, renders the prophet's point as well as any version. It is a supplement or progressive parallelism related to the first question, strengthening the previous affirmation. The natural forces God has ordained operate with dependability and consistency.

Jeremiah knew the people understood the answer to both rhetorical questions was "no." So he did not labor the point but went immediately to the contrast. The people had abused the option Yahweh had given them and rejected the covenant their forefathers had made at Sinai. They had done foolishly, flaunting their freedom in Yahweh's face.

Wrong worship always leads to wrong conduct. People become like what they admire. They likewise admire what they worship. These two facts overlap, intertwine, and enslave people, driving them into habitual performance. We manufacture gods to personify and give credence to the things we practice. Israel's worship was not only vain and worthless; it reflected their stupidity.

Verse 15 begins with the primary cause of the people's turning from Yahweh. They had failed to remember the provisions of the past and the continued blessings of the present. This always leads to ingratitude. The latter part of verse 15 contains an insight into the effect of worship on conduct. Israel's perverted worship—engaging in the ceremonies associated with devotion to idols—had twisted their sense of ethics and morals.

The **bypaths** and **roads not built up** meant directions contrary to Yahweh's will for his covenant people. At first, such roads seem attractive, promising a more enjoyable life. But after only a short time, those who travel them find that these short-term pleasures lead to long-term sorrow. Eventually they discover that "the transgressors shall be destroyed together: the end of the wicked shall be cut off" (Ps. 37:38 KJV).

18:16–17. This section closes with a graphic description of Israel's fate. Yahweh dealt first with the land. This was an important matter to both God and the people. Yahweh had promised the land to Abraham, Isaac, and Jacob. He brought the Hebrew slaves out of Egypt in order to give them this place "flowing with milk and honey" (Jer. 11:5).

Moses described it as "a good land—a land with streams and pools of water, with springs flowing in the valleys and hills; a land with wheat and barley, vines and fig trees, pomegranates, olive oil and honey; a land where bread will not be scarce and you will lack nothing; a land where the rocks are iron and you can dig copper out of the hills" (Deut. 8:7–9). Now the land is about to be **laid waste, an object of lasting scorn**. How the prophet must have grieved as he delivered the message! All who viewed it after its destruction would gaze in disbelief. How could this happen to a land that was once wealthy and strong?

Jeremiah dealt next with the people. God had declared once that he would be "an adversary unto thine adversaries" (Exod. 23:22 KJV), but that was a conditional promise. They had broken the covenant, defied their Lord, and defiled the land. Like the sirocco, the hot dry wind blowing from the eastern deserts, the Babylonian army would come. God would make no move to help his people. They had refused to seek his face; now they must pay the consequences.

Ⓒ Jeremiah Asks God to Destroy His Enemies (18:18–23)

SUPPORTING IDEA: *Jeremiah pours out his heart to God concerning his enemies.*

18:18. The preaching of Jeremiah kindled the anger of both prophets and priests. They organized to "put him out of business." The priests officiated at the sacrifices and received revenue for performing their services. The prophets were the spokesmen whose mandate was to interpret God's will for the people. Unfortunately, most of them had "sold out" to the priestly system and were giving their approval to the people's current religious life.

The **wise** were probably the scribes who copied the laws and other religious sayings of the day. They often gave their interpretations to the people, putting them in close proximity with the two other groups. This three-unit coalition represented the establishment in Judah's religious life. They organized to silence Jeremiah's voice.

Notice these three groups did not approach the matter with physical force as the men of Anathoth had done earlier in Jeremiah's life (11:18–23). They were religious people and sought to destroy the prophet by discrediting him in the people's eyes. They avoided making a martyr of him and thus running the risk of strengthening his message.

Jeremiah's opponents decided on a two-pronged attack. First, they would launch a propaganda campaign against him. Through indoctrination and brainwashing they felt they could turn the tide of popular opinion against him. The second step in their attack was to ignore any suggestion he made for changing the present situation in Judah's religious life.

18:19–23. People, even good Christians, do strange things when depressed. Jeremiah is one of several examples of this truth in the Old Testament. His words represent not only his humanness but one of the lowest points in his ministry. He felt God had forsaken him. Jeremiah began by calling on Yahweh to **listen** as his opponents planned what he felt would be his demise. He then reminded Yahweh of his own faithfulness and, in verse 21, petitioned him with words that were probably rhetorical in nature.

This prayer represented everything Jesus condemned. The prophet wanted God's wrath poured out on these people who opposed him. He asked for revenge not only on the men but also on their **wives** and **children**. When God's people get out of control, they say strange things, even in their prayers.

These words of Jeremiah give the record of a struggling soul. They open a window on that battlefield with which no other conflict can be compared— the moral struggle of a person with himself. What makes it so significant is that this man was one of God's choicest servants. Unfortunately Jeremiah did not have two resources that Christians possess today—the Sermon on the

Mount and the divine power our Savior breathed into his followers in the upper room. God help us to use this power of the Holy Spirit!

🄓 Yahweh's Message to Jeremiah and the Nation (19:1–15)

> **SUPPORTING IDEA:** *Because the people have continued in abominable and degrading practices, Yahweh will bring catastrophic affliction.*

19:1–2. These verses and the ones that follow continue the prose narrative of chapters 18–20, which is interrupted briefly three times with poetical sections. The first (18:13–17) contains a message for Jeremiah to proclaim publicly. This is followed by two complaints (18:19–23; 20:7–18) of the prophet to Yahweh.

Verse 1 states that the command to Jeremiah was directly from Yahweh. This is the second illustration from the realm of the **potter** and his work. No evidence exists that this is an independent story added because it was similar to the first ten verses of chapter 18. This event, in my judgment, came as a direct response to Jeremiah's plea to Yahweh in the preceding verses (18:19–23).

In the previous chapter, Jeremiah received and taught his message from an unfinished product. In this chapter, God spoke to him through one already completed. In both, God emphasized his sovereignty to the prophet and the people. Yahweh told Jeremiah to take some of the **elders** and **priests** with him, most likely to be witnesses of what he would do and say.

The **Potsherd Gate** was one of several gates in various parts of the walled city. Each gate had a name that denoted its significance. Through the centuries these gates often took on new names as other events occurred at or near them. The word *potsherd* is the English rendering of a Hebrew word related to pottery. People probably attached this name to the gate because fragments of pottery were tossed there as refuse.

19:3–9. Since Jeremiah's audience consisted of elders and priests, why did Yahweh direct him to address the **kings of Judah and people of Jerusalem?** Perhaps this smaller group represented the larger gathering to which he would deliver his message later. The plural "kings" suggests a dynasty of kings, perhaps all the royal leaders through the more than two centuries the United Kingdom had been divided. Jeremiah's words could be considered a "dress rehearsal" to the nation's secondary leadership for a future time when he would have a larger audience.

Another possibility is that Jeremiah felt he would never have an opportunity to speak to the king personally. He expected the leaders to pass the word on to the king, probably Jehoiakim. In this message, Jeremiah said little or nothing he had not already stated on several other occasions. But each time he seemed to speak with greater urgency.

In verse 6, Jeremiah repeated his words about **Topheth or the Valley of Ben Hinnom** from his temple sermon (7:32). In the future it will be called the **Valley of Slaughter**. This helps in dating the material in this chapter and thus probably in all three chapters of this section.

Most interpreters believe Jeremiah was banned from the temple area after his infamous temple sermon (7:1–8:3). After dictating to Baruch the scroll of his prophecies, the prophet told his scribe, "I am restricted; I cannot go to the LORD's temple" (36:5). After the king burned Jeremiah's scroll of prophecies and he dictated it again, the prophet probably had to hide for a while. Thus during the period from the temple sermon until the dictation of the scroll, Jeremiah was forced to be away from the temple area. This was probably the period when he preached several symbolic messages. This would include the ones about the linen girdle and the wineskins (13:1:1–14) as well as these about the potter and his work. The time for these messages would be shortly before 605 B.C. (36:2).

Verse 7 describes the desperate strait that people would find themselves in when Judah's enemies attacked. Jeremiah said not only would their carcasses be given as food to the birds and beasts, but he added, **I will make them eat the flesh of their sons and daughters, and they will eat one another's flesh during the stress of the siege** (v. 9).

Are we to interpret this passage literally? Several passages in the Old Testament refer to this practice. Moses warned the people of a future time when parents would eat the flesh of their children (Deut. 28:54–55). The biblical historian records that this terrible thing occurred when Samaria was besieged by the Syrians (2 Kgs. 6:26–29). The Book of Lamentations attests that this same thing happened during the siege of Jerusalem in 586 B.C. Josephus wrote that the practice took place during the siege of Jerusalem in A.D. 70. D. J. Wiseman says this nauseating event was widely known in the Near East across many centuries.

The contemporary mind has difficulty thinking of such a practice. A number of scholars suggest the prophet, as well as all the other writers, was speaking symbolically. According to these scholars, the expression meant the parents exploited their children to the fullest. Yet the Scriptures record it, and who are we to deny that it happened exactly as the biblical record states?

19:10–13. Yahweh once more instructed the prophet to illustrate a message with an action the people would not forget. This demonstration was similar to but actually more dramatic than the words about the girdle and the wineskins in chapter 13. The prophet's "live act" paved the way for the words that followed.

One can feel the intensity grow as Yahweh unfolded the fate of Jerusalem and the areas nearby. Yahweh would deal a blow so severe that the city would never be the same again. Every home that had been a place of false worship would be visited by God's chastening hand.

19:14–15. Jeremiah chose the temple area as the location from which to deliver his words to the larger group of people. Does this mean he was not banned from this area after his temple sermon? Or did he defy the order and choose this place in spite of the prohibition? Whatever the reason for choosing this particular spot for delivering his message, the prophet took a bold step. Although we only have one verse describing his sermon, we can be certain he repeated the essence of what Yahweh had previously said to him.

Was the prophet foolish to speak so harshly when it was virtually certain he would be ignored? Not at all. He had a commission from Yahweh, and he must do as his Lord had ordered him whatever the cost.

Ⓔ Jeremiah's Reply to Pashhur (20:1–6)

SUPPORTING IDEA: *When people accept God's call to serve him and proclaim his Word, they must accept the results and adversities that follow.*

20:1–2. This clash between Jeremiah and Pashhur resembles, in many ways, that of Amos and Amaziah (Amos 7:10–17). A person who feels safely entrenched in the shelter of an institutional hierarchy often speaks boldly, even defiantly. Pashhur went even further than Amaziah when the latter confronted the prophet from Tekoa who came to Bethel.

Pashhur immediately threw this "Yahweh-hurled" man into confinement. He delivered the prophet to his cohorts for a beating—probably the customary forty stripes—and restrained his prophetic activities. Translators have trouble with the word rendered **stocks.** Many contend that Jeremiah was placed in a small room often used for short detentions. The verb root of the noun means "turn over," which has led to the translation of "stocks." A confined room, however, would just as well have kept a man in a crooked or fetal position.

20:3–6. We don't know what led Pashhur to release Jeremiah the next day. Perhaps he "cooled off" and decided he had more to lose than gain by destroying the prophet. Another alternative is that he had enough religious background to make him uncomfortable annihilating a prophet who spoke in Yahweh's name. Or perhaps he felt Jeremiah was correct in what he was saying. Pashhur must have realized that Babylon's armies were gaining strength. He refused to jeopardize his security by agreeing with Jeremiah publicly, but he was reluctant to harm him further.

Jeremiah had a harsh message for this man who was supposed to represent the people who believed in Yahweh worship. The prophet recognized him as one who had "sold out" for the sake of security. Observant students have found an interesting irony or subtle sarcasm in this account. As "chief officer in the temple of the LORD" (v. 1), Pashhur was an "overseer." When Yahweh called Jeremiah to the prophetic ministry, he said, "Today, I appoint you over nations" (1:10). The same Hebrew word is used to describe both men. Both were overseers. Two commissioned to the same task met in an ideological clash.

When Jeremiah pronounced a name change for Pashhur, this was no small matter. Often in the Scripture we read of a name being changed after the performance of a good or evil deed. Jeremiah was saying, in essence, "From now on people will recognize you as your own worst enemy." Pashhur would behold with his **own eyes** the judgment that would fall on the nation.

In addition, Pashhur would pay a terrible price himself. After taking the nation's **wealth**, Babylon would then turn on Pashhur and his loved ones. Jeremiah did not state as explicitly as Amos (5:17) the disgrace, ignominy, and shame that the wicked overseer would experience. What he did say, however, was enough for Pashhur to get the point.

F Jeremiah's Most Bitter Complaint to Yahweh (20:7–18)

SUPPORTING IDEA: *The mystery of undeserved suffering is neither perceived nor resolved by logical thinking or reasoning, but by faith in God.*

20:7–10. To doubt is not a sin, but continuous lack of faith is one of the worst spiritual shortcomings. When a person who is earnestly trying to follow

God's will meets with many reverses, resentment comes easily. This is what happened to Jeremiah, and we can sympathize with him. Yahweh had called this young man to an impossible task. His periodic confessions seem to have grown more bitter. This final complaint appears to be the most harsh of all.

These four verses represent the beginning of a three-point step in Jeremiah's resolution of his problem. The prophet uttered bitter words against Yahweh. He accused him of using force and violence to conquer his prophet. The first verb translated *overpowered* has sexual overtones. Its basic meaning is "to open wide," but from this comes the idea of persuade, entice, deceive, seduce.

Several translators see "seduce" as the best word by which to render the verb in this context. They point out it is used in an earlier law about seduction (Exod. 22:16). Some suggest Jeremiah conceived of his relationship to Yahweh as similar to a marriage even as he pictured Israel's relationship to Yahweh in the same way. The analogy would be that Yahweh had deserted him and was therefore guilty of infidelity.

The next part of this verse reads literally, **you overpowered me and prevailed**. Two different Hebrew verbs are used here, in contrast to the first part of the verse where the verb is repeated. These three verbs placed together constitute a strong and bold—almost arrogant—accusation of Yahweh from a prophet.

The third part of verse 7, combined with verse 8, gives another picture of Jeremiah's misery. In addition to his physical agony, Jeremiah suffered slurs and experienced mockery every time he spoke of coming judgment and punishment. He placed the blame for it on the fact that he was delivering what he felt was the message God had given him. The prophet was virtually saying, "I resign, Lord, effective immediately."

In the midst of his misery, Jeremiah reexamined his call. God's word was still **shut up** in his bones like a **fire**. He could no more quit preaching than he could quit breathing. He was tired of being silent. The prophetic voice within him must speak. Nothing could stop him, not even the accusations and murmurs of those around him. He knew his enemies wanted him to fail, but this strengthened him and renewed his determination to preach God's word. He could not hold back the message. It was burning within. Every truly called preacher today knows the feeling and shares the emotion.

20:11–12. Jeremiah's faith brought him courage, which produced a new resolve and even more faith. He envisioned God as a soldier on the field leading the troops against the enemy. He knew his foes would be conquered by Yahweh's irresistible power. Two words described their future—**disgraced** and **dishonor**.

Fortified by his faith and assurance, Jeremiah then became bold enough to pray for destruction of his foes. He felt justified in doing this because he was totally dedicated to doing God's will. This, in his opinion, carried privileges. Extermination of his opposition was one of them.

20:13. This verse contains the third and final stage of Jeremiah's inner conflict. As with so many other struggles of Old Testament saints, this prophet concluded with a word of **praise** to Yahweh. He never allows his children to suffer beyond their ability to endure. Jeremiah joined that long train of believers who moved from doubt to a stronger faith.

20:14–18. These verses contain one of the strangest paradoxes in the Scriptures. How could a man come out of the emotional pit to praising God and then immediately sink deeper than ever into the abyss? Scholars have tried many ways to explain this phenomenon. In desperation, some fall back on the old "escapist route." They contend we have here a misplaced fragment added because the compilers of the book did not know what else to do with it. To take such an approach opens the door to any kind of textual manipulation one wishes to make on any difficult passage.

F. B. Huey gives, in my judgment, one of the best explanations. He says, "It is not unusual for deep depression to follow on the heels of a mood of exaltation. Anyone who has experienced fluctuating moods in the midst of a difficult situation knows it is possible for people to praise God one moment and despair the next" (Huey, *Jeremiah*, 194–95).

In his "regression to abnormality," Jeremiah poured out a series of curses on himself. This section resembles Job's outcry (Job 3:1–16) but with one difference. Job expressed his disillusionment with everything about his life and the universe. Jeremiah focused on his own problems. His despair drove him to curse first himself and then all the conditions surrounding his existence. But he refrained from pronouncing an anathema against his parents or God.

Jeremiah even proclaimed harsh words against the person who announced his birth. This was another way of saying he wished he had never been born. Like Job, he grieved because he did not die in his mother's womb. One cannot sink much further into pessimism and despair!

The "Confessions of Jeremiah," as scholars call them, end here. We have no record of Yahweh's reply to the prophet. Further records of Jeremiah's life and activities, however, suggest that he resolved his grief and accepted his lot in life. Perhaps he recalled and relived his experience of God's call. God had promised to make him strong against his enemies. Jeremiah learned the lesson that many people have experienced: God often uses severe testing to strengthen our faith. The coming days of Zedekiah's reign would be difficult, but God's prophet would be fortified by an unshakeable faith.

MAIN IDEA REVIEW: *God can transform wrecked lives, but often the messenger who delivers this truth meets violent opposition.*

III. CONCLUSION

Are We Still Pliable?

From the illustrations of pottery-making and pottery-breaking, the nation of Judah was confronted with deciding whether they would be a nation that served God's purposes and conformed to his ways or they would be broken on the rocks of history. Judah's stubbornness made it like hardened clay. No longer pliable, they could not be reshaped.

Jeremiah's lessons challenge us in the same way. Are we still pliable? Can the Divine Potter still refashion us into a vessel for his service? Are we willing to submit to being reworked as he removes our flaws? Or are we determined to continue in our stubborn ways to become a hardened vessel that cannot be refashioned?

PRINCIPLES

- God puts to best use those who allow him to shape their lives according to his will. When we refuse to allow God to shape us according to his will, we are of no use to him.

- When those who minister are maligned by those they minister to, sometimes they become angry and bitter against those they seek to serve.

- Those who harden themselves against God and his Word will be broken and shattered.

- When God's servants become discouraged or are rejected by their hearers, they should take their complaints to the Lord.
- It is virtually impossible for those whom God has burdened with his message to refuse to proclaim his Word.

APPLICATIONS

- Imagine yourself as a piece of pottery, part of which needs to be refashioned.
- Place yourself in God's hands and ask him to refashion you as he wills.
- Tell God how you feel about those to whom you minister but who reject your ministry on their behalf.
- Make a list of areas of your life where you have hardened yourself against God's desires for you.
- Evaluate your pattern of complaining about those to whom you seek to minister and assess whether these patterns are productive or are making relationships more strained.
- Look at your level of desire to share God's message with others. If you find room for improvement, make this part of your regular prayer to God.

IV. LIFE APPLICATION

Two Victorian Poets

The most popular poem of the Victorian era was Edward Fitzgerald's *The Rubaiyat of Omar Khayyam*. While many today have never heard of this lengthy work, aphorisms from this poem are among the most frequently quoted lines in English poetry. The poem advocates a philosophy of life that is skeptical of divine providence, mocks the transience of all human accomplishments and existence, and concentrates on the fleeting pleasures of the moment, especially the love of wine.

The occasion for Fitzerald's reflections, like those of Jeremiah, was seeing a potter at his wheel: "I remember stopping by the way to watch a Potter thumping his wet clay." In the section called "The Book of Pots" Fitzgerald has a number of clay pots enter into conversation. One earthen vessel states that surely the Potter who formed him would not smash him to shapeless earth again. Another pot agrees that the Potter would never do such a childish thing as to destroy the vessel that he made in a fit of wrath.

Robert Browning, another eminent Victorian poet, responded to Fitzgerald with a poem of his own. Browning's poem challenged the hedonism Fitzgerald advocated. The opening words of Browning's *Rabbi Ben Ezra* are well-known today: "Grow old along with me! / The best is yet to be."

In his poem Browning also used the metaphor of the potter's wheel. He characterized those who lived only for the present as foolish. He instructed his readers, "Look not thou down but up! To uses of a cup." Browning declared, "But I need, now as then, Thee, God, who mouldest men." Browning affirmed that in the midst of the whirl of life he did not "mistake my end" for present, transient pleasures.

What a difference between those who seek to live their lives as they see fit and those who seek for the Lord to make them fit for life as he would have them live it. Fitzgerald or Browning? Judah or Jeremiah? Your stubborn will or God's divine will? The question about which type of vessel we will be and how we will respond to the Divine Potter is as old as the seventh century B.C., the nineteenth century A.D., or the twenty-first century.

V. PRAYER

Divine Potter, mold us into your servants. Reshape us as you see fit. Remove the flaws, defects, and imperfections that mar us and hinder us from being all you want us to be. But please, dear sovereign Fashioner, be gentle in reforming us, we pray. Amen.

VI. DEEPER DISCOVERIES

A. Making Pottery

Few people today understand exactly how the ancient potter worked with his crude equipment. Several scholars have attempted to describe the process. F. B. Huey in The New American Commentary (*Jeremiah*, 180–81) gives one of the best descriptions:

Jeremiah watched the potter at his "wheel" (literally, "two stones"). The lower stone was turned with the feet. It was attached by an axle to the upper wheel. As the lower wheel was turned, the upper wheel, on which the lump of clay was placed, rotated. As the wheel turned, the potter skillfully shaped the clay into a vessel by the pressure of his fingers against the pliable material. If the clay did not achieve the desired shape, he did not throw it away. Instead, he patiently reworked it until it became the vessel he wanted it to be. If it became misshapen as he worked it, it was not because of his lack of skill. The clay may have been of an inferior quality, may have contained defects or perhaps was not sufficiently moist and pliable.

B. "Not Pashhur, but Magor-Missabib" (20:3b)

In modern days we do not frequently change our name or anyone else's, except in a marriage when the bride takes the groom's family name. But name-changing often took place in Old Testament days by parents for their children or by people who felt Yahweh leading them to do it. Abraham, Sarah, and Jacob were among many in the Old Testament who experienced a name change.

Old Testament scholars have searched in many languages for the meaning of Pashhur, but no general agreement exists. Jeremiah took the ordinary Hebrew words for "Pashhur, the son of Immer, and produced 'Prosperity All Around,' the son of 'The Talker.'"

Whatever our name is, it stands for something. It identifies *us*. If we are "cheapskates," when people hear our name, they think of this characteristic. If we are fussy and ill-tempered, people think of this when our names are mentioned. If we are mean, dishonest, and dishonorable, sooner or later our name will come to suggest this each time it is spoken.

What about Jeremiah and Pashhur? They started out on the same level. Both were sons of priests, so they began with equal opportunities. We have no reason to believe either was superior to the other in ability. Pashhur, however, found popularity, ease, and overflowing success. In this context he had been appointed to a high office while Jeremiah remained ostracized by society.

Pashhur listened to the crowd and preached "smooth things" for them. Jeremiah listened only to the Lord. The former put the latter in jail; and when night came, he seemed to be the victor. But when morning came, the situation was reversed. Jeremiah became the one in charge. Many things change if we accept our situation, trust God, and wait!

What drives you? What name should be given to you?

VII. TEACHING OUTLINE

A. INTRODUCTION

1. Lead Story: Clay in the Potter's Hands

2. Context: The Lord instructed Jeremiah to visit a potter's house. From the example of the potter refashioning a marred pot that he was making, the Lord revealed to Jeremiah that he was about to bring disaster on Judah. If the nation turned from evil and became pliable in God's hands, he could remold them according to his will. If they continued in their hardness and stubbornness, they would be smashed like a clay pot.

3. Transition: One of the most important lessons nations and individuals can learn is that we are marred vessels. Each of us needs reshaping and refashioning by the Master Potter's hands. The greatest tragedy is when we become so hardened that he can no longer mold us but must cast us aside as useless.

B. COMMENTARY

1. Jeremiah's Visit to the Potter's House (18:1–10)

2. Commission, Warning, Rejection, and Reply (18:11–17)

3. Jeremiah Asks God to Destroy His Enemies (18:18–23)

4. Yahweh's Message to Jeremiah and the Nations (19:1–15)

5. Jeremiah's Reply to Pashhur (20:1–6)

6. Jeremiah's Most Bitter Complaint to Yahweh (20:7–18)

C. CONCLUSION: ARE WE STILL PLIABLE?

VIII. ISSUES FOR DISCUSSION

1. Based on the two symbolic actions related to the pot and the potter in Jeremiah 18 and 19, discuss what you understand the relationship is between divine sovereignty and human free will.

2. How should a person who serves God handle his complaints about the people to whom he ministers? What should the Lord's servant do when he doesn't like the people he serves or when he begins to see them as enemies?

Jeremiah 21:1–23:40

Leadership's Accountability

I. INTRODUCTION
Saddam, Uday, and Qusay

II. COMMENTARY
A verse-by-verse explanation of these verses.

III. CONCLUSION
Four Kings, Four Verdicts

An overview of the principles and applications from these verses.

IV. LIFE APPLICATION
Baghdad Bob

Melding these verses to life.

V. PRAYER
Tying these verses to life with God.

VI. DEEPER DISCOVERIES
Historical, geographical, and grammatical enrichment of the commentary.

VII. TEACHING OUTLINE
Suggested step-by-step group study of these verses.

VIII. ISSUES FOR DISCUSSION
Zeroing these verses in on daily life.

"Don't it s'prise you, de way dem kings carries on, Huck?"

"No," I says, "it don't."

"Why don't it, Huck?"

"Well, it don't because it's in the breed. I reckon they're all alike."

"But, Huck, dese kings o' ourn is reglar rapscallions; dat's jist what dey is; dey's reglar rapscallions."

"Well, that's what I'm a-saying; all kings is mostly rapscallions, as fur as I can make out."

—from *The Adventures of Huckleberry Finn* by Mark Twain

Jeremiah 21:1–23:40

IN A NUTSHELL

In 588 B.C. King Zedekiah sent a delegation to Jeremiah to inquire whether God would deliver Jerusalem from the Babylonian army's siege. Occasioned by this inquiry, chapters 21–23 present Jeremiah's evaluation of the last four kings of Judah—Jehoahaz (Shallum) (22:10–12), Jehoiakim (22:13–23), Jehoiachin (22:24–30), and Zedekiah (21:1–10). In the midst of his assessment of these evil kings, Jeremiah presented the basics of good government and the responsibilities of rulers. He identified justice and righteousness as the two key ingredients of good government (21:11–22:9). Jeremiah contrasted these evil rulers with the coming ideal righteous king (23:1–8). The section ends with Jeremiah's denunciation of false prophets (23:9–40).

Leadership's Accountability

I. INTRODUCTION

Saddam, Uday, and Qusay

*H*istory—both ancient and modern—is filled with rulers who were tyrannical dictators, psychopaths, malevolent megalomaniacs, and just plain "rapscallions." Late twentieth-century Iraq provides one example from the descendants of the conquerors mentioned in this section of Jeremiah.

As the world now knows, Saddam Hussein's rule was barbaric and brutal. His decade-long stalemate invasion of Iran cost a million lives on both sides. In that war he was responsible for using poison gas and executing thousands of prisoners of war. He practiced genocide against the marsh Arabs, draining and poisoning the marshes. He ordered the gassing of cities and mass killings of civilian Iraqi Kurds in the northern part of his country. In southern Iraq thousands of Shi'a Arabs were executed on his command.

Uday and Qusay followed in their father's steps. Qusay, the younger brother, was Saddam's heir apparent. Along with the elite Republican Guard, he controlled the intelligence and security network of police, informants, and thugs. He also supervised Iraq's biological and chemical weapons programs. Uday, the older brother, had a talent for murder, larceny, extortion, bribery, and rape. Uday, who also had a reputation for rage, ran the Fadayeen, an irregular paramilitary militia. They were notoriously violent.

All of this came to an end for the Husseins when the American-led coalition attacked Iraq, surrounded Baghdad, and defeated the Iraqi forces. Later Qusay and Uday were killed in a shootout with American forces, their mangled bodies put on public display, and Saddam himself was captured—a pathetic man hiding in a hole in the ground.

Jeremiah was given the task of announcing the Lord's assessment and evaluation of the last four kings of Judah—three brothers and a son. As Jerusalem was surrounded (21:1–10), we see each ruler measured against the Lord's standards for godly rule. Each fell far short. Each had oppressed, robbed, and done evil to his own people. They had set their eyes and hearts on dishonest gain, shed innocent blood, and practiced oppression and extortion (22:17). The principles of righteousness and justice had been abused as they built their luxury palaces, and they had exploited their countrymen's labor (22:13).

Because of all their wicked deeds, one would be handed over to his enemies after they breached the city, and he would be shown no mercy (21:7); another would never return from where he was taken captive but die in that place (22:11–12); still another, according to an announcement strikingly similar to Uday and Qusay's end, would have the burial of a donkey—he would be dragged away and left exposed (22:19); the fourth, in similar fashion to Saddam, would end up a despised, broken pot whom no one wanted. His children, much as Saddam's daughters who fled to Jordan, would be hurled out and cast into a land not their own (22:28).

II. COMMENTARY

Leadership's Accountability

MAIN IDEA: *A leader in any field, especially that of public service, must be willing to accept responsibility and be faithful in discharging it.*

A person who studies the Book of Jeremiah needs to stay in touch with the facts about all five kings who ruled during the prophet's ministry. Each of them played a distinctive role in the prophet's life and career. By studying the activities of the king, one is able to understand better the reaction of Jeremiah to each event that occurred during his ministry.

Chapter 21 begins a new phase of the recorded life and preaching of Jeremiah. Some have called chapters 21–45 the "Biography of Jeremiah." This is because these chapters major more on the events in the prophet's career, though prophetic discourses are by no means absent. This section, however, has the same problem as other parts of the book. No chronological markers exist by which to trace Jeremiah's life.

This section introduces a new king, Zedekiah, the last of Josiah's sons to reign over Judah. Virtually all the subsequent material in the book until the fall of Jerusalem relates to events that occurred while Zedekiah sat on Judah's throne. One seeking to understand Jeremiah's ministry to the fullest extent during this period should be familiar with the happenings during Zedekiah's reign. They are found in 2 Kings 24:17–25:21 and 2 Chronicles 36:11–21. But a much more detailed account of his reign and events surrounding his death is found in the Book of Jeremiah.

Chapters 21–23 should be considered as a separate unit in the Book of Jeremiah. They form an ideal introduction to the remainder of the larger section (chs. 24–45). Chapters 22–23 contain a collection of messages from Jeremiah to Judah's recent kings and a lengthy section to his contemporary colleagues, the current prophets.

Chapter 21 may have been placed by the compilers before the two following chapters as a preface to them. It serves in a twofold capacity. First, it introduces the siege of the city that would last for eighteen months. Second, it gives a preview of the type of king who would attempt to lead the city in its last chaotic days before being destroyed by Babylon.

Ⓐ The First Inquiry of Zedekiah (21:1–14)

SUPPORTING IDEA: *Earthly rulers often seem bold and self-sufficient when prosperous, but when a crisis arrives, most of them call a person of God for advice.*

21:1–2. History has no harder test for the character and doctrine of a great teacher or preacher than the siege of his city. In secular history, Archimedes in Syracuse, Pope Innocent in Rome, and John Knox in St. Andrews give striking illustrations of this truth.

What does a siege do for a person who seeks to speak for God? It brings him to the people's level. He shares their dangers, duties, heartaches, and hunger. If his faith does not waver, his opportunities for service are great. A siege can turn a prophet or quiet thinker into a hero.

During the siege of Jerusalem, Jeremiah advised King Zedekiah to surrender to Babylon. The account of his activities during the siege are scattered throughout the book. Was the prophet a traitor? Not at all. He lived on a different level and marched to a different drummer than the others. He heard voices no one else in Judah was spiritually equipped to hear. His was the same persuasion as the early Christians who refused to say, "Caesar is Lord." They knew only Jesus Christ deserved that distinction and honor. Jeremiah knew Yahweh alone had a grip on the situation, and only he knew the end from the beginning.

What about Zedekiah? To his credit, he meant well. To his discredit, he was weak willed. He became king in 597 B.C., following a brief, lackluster reign by Jehoiachin, who had succeeded his wicked father Jehoiakim. Zedekiah was an appointee of Nebuchadnezzar. The final ruler of Judah, Zedekiah was pulled between two forces: the diehard attitude of the nationalist party in Judah and the influence of Jeremiah. We might picture him as a young, inexperienced man running from one person to another, asking, "What should I do now?"

In the early years of Zedekiah's reign, the king came dangerously close to rebelling against Babylon as the ultrapatriotic group insisted he should do. Chapters 27 and 28 give some details of this near calamity. Several years later, however, Zedekiah grew bolder, and this was his undoing. He felt that Egypt under her new king, Pharaoh Hophra, would give Judah the strength to resist Babylon.

By late 589 or early 588 B.C., Nebuchadnezzar's legions arrived in Judah and began to suppress Zedekiah's revolt. They blockaded Jerusalem and began what turned out to be an eighteen-month siege of the city. Dividing the people in the city from the towns and cities outside it, they picked off the smaller places one by one. The incident, recorded in Jeremiah 21:1–10, took place during the blockade and before the actual siege of Jerusalem began.

Verse 1 records Zedekiah's sending two messengers to Jeremiah with an inquiry. Some scholars think the messengers were members of the pro-Egyptian party in Judah, but this is by no means certain.The first, **Pashhur**, son of Malkijah, should not be confused with Pashhur, son of Immer, who abused Jeremiah (20:1–6). But he was also opposed to Jeremiah's policies. Later (38:1–13) this Pashhur was one of a group that sought to have the prophet executed.

The second, **Zephaniah**, son of Masseiah, on the other hand, seems to have sympathized with Jeremiah. In his letter to the exiles in Babylon, Jeremiah referred to him as the "overseer" and spoke favorably of him (29:25–29). If he was the priest mentioned in 52:24, he was second in rank to the high priest or had attained the position by the time Jerusalem fell.

Since these men represented high-level leadership in Judah, why did Zedekiah send them to Jeremiah? Probably because he realized the prophet had accurately foretold events thus far, especially those related to his nephew Jehoiachin and the invasion of 597 B.C. By this time Jeremiah had probably become a man whom the administration did not like but dared not ignore.

Verse 2 gives a new picture of Jeremiah. Once a lonely prophet, maligned as a calamity howler, criticized as a negative thinker, and persecuted as a traitor, he has suddenly become a celebrity. The prophet is now the "last resort" of the despairing king. What greater honor than to have a royal delegation pleading with him to secure an oracle from Yahweh for the nation! No longer banned, the prophet is sought after by the "top brass." When weak people with authority are suffering from fright, they do strange things.

Pashhur represented the civic authority of Judah while Zephaniah represented the religious hierarchy. Both segments of Judah's society were scared to death. In fact, they were so frightened that they "went to church," or at least they went to see the preacher. This almost represented a deathbed inquiry. Even today some people seek God only from the motive of fear.

The king had a good reason for reacting to the present situation with alarm. King Nebuchadnezzar of Babylon was active in the area at the very moment Zedekiah's messengers were seeking a word from Yahweh. This verse contains the first reference to Nebuchadnezzar in the Book of Jeremiah. But their plea was not that of a humble sinner showing repentance by confessing his wickedness, vowing a new lifestyle, and seeking God's grace.

What was their word to the prophet? They wanted Yahweh to perform a miracle for them as he had done for his people before. Two great events must have been foremost in their minds: the deliverance from Egypt, and the more recent deliverance from Assyria when Sennacherib encircled the city. Unfortunately, they showed the attitude of many people today. In spite of their ungodly conduct, they wanted Yahweh to rescue them when their own resources failed.

21:3–10. Jeremiah bypassed the committee and directed his message specifically to the king, calling him by name. He did not even mention the fact that Zedekiah was king of the country. The exalted office meant nothing to the prophet. In the verses that follow (vv. 3–14), Jeremiah gave more than an answer to the two-person committee. He issued a three-pronged declaration—to Zedekiah, to the people, and to the entire royal house of David. The prophet's message was not only uncompromising but shattering.

Jeremiah destroyed all illusions the king or people might have cherished for a speedy deliverance. The expression **weapons of war that are in your hands** probably refers to the Judean troops or guerrilla groups that were operating outside the city walls. They were harassing the enemy to prevent their beginning an actual siege that would come a little later.

Most scholars agree the Hebrew word translated **besieging** does not accurately express the situation. The context indicates the siege had not actually begun. Perhaps a good translation would be "pressing hard" or even better "blockading." A few contend the prophet meant the enemy would confiscate Judah's instruments of warfare and use them in destroying the people.

In verse 5, Jeremiah stated a truth the people needed to understand clearly. Their real enemy was not Babylon but themselves and their wicked way of life. Nebuchadnezzar was only the agent of Yahweh. He was carrying out the Lord's death sentence against a people who had broken their covenant with him. God's sovereignty means he can choose any method he desires to reveal his holiness and his wrath against sin.

The figure of an outstretched arm is a familiar one in the Old Testament that pictures Yahweh delivering his people. Almost always, however, an ethical command to the people accompanies it. Here, the figure is reversed. Jeremiah used three nouns to describe God's emotional reaction to Israel's sin. The word **anger** comes from the word *nose*. This suggests breathing through the nose or breathing heavily. The word **fury** has the root meaning of "to be hot." The noun **wrath** comes from a verb meaning "to be bitter." The three words combined express Yahweh's emotional reaction to wrongdoing. To use another English word, it *infuriates* him. Verse 7 intensifies the prophet's message about the coming doom.

Beginning with verse 8, Jeremiah speaks directly to the people with an alternative. "Get out of town! Surrender to the enemy! Since the 'ship of Zion' is sinking, look for a lifeboat, even if it is nothing but a raft." One can't be much more specific than that.

Was Jeremiah a traitor or guilty of treason? The prophet did not need a special revelation from God to realize the situation was hopeless. An observant attitude and intellectual honesty would convince anyone that the nation had sinned away its day of grace. Surely not everyone in the city and larger area deserved the fate that awaited them. But here is a lesson we must learn. The price of living in a corporate society is that the innocent often must suffer along with the unrighteous when collective sin leads to national tragedy.

21:11–12. Two opinions exist among scholars about these verses. Some feel they begin a new section that extends through 23:8. This larger segment consists of messages delivered for and to the former kings and the current ruler of Judah. In my judgment, the best way to deal with these verses is to consider them Jeremiah's closing words to Pashhur and Zephaniah.

Having declared the fate awaiting Judah, the prophet added a window of hope, but with it came a stern demand. The king himself and his associates must come back to a lifestyle that is pleasing to Yahweh. Justice was Jeremiah's key point. Royal power was to be used in responsible leadership, not abused for personal gain. Yahweh meant for the king to protect those exposed to risk—widows, orphans, aliens.

21:13–14. The Jerusalem of Jeremiah's day was surrounded by three valleys. It was not located on a plain but on a **rocky plateau**. An enemy could not advance from any direction except the north. The people often boasted of their invulnerability. But Jeremiah warned them that Yahweh could send a fire of judgment at any time.

What form would this judgment take? The expression **kindle a fire in your forests** presents an apparent problem since, as far as we know, no forests existed in the area near Jerusalem. Some interpreters suggest the cluster of houses and buildings gave the appearance of a forest. But most contend the allusion is to the building called the Palace of the Forest of Lebanon (1 Kgs. 7:2).

Approximately a century earlier the Southern Kingdom faced a similar threat; and the king, Hezekiah, called on the Lord; and he spared Jerusalem. The question now was whether the people and king would show repentance and implore God to forgive them for their sinful ways. As Jeremiah spoke to them, the possibility looked bleak. The prophet was not optimistic about Judah's future, but he continued to warn the people.

Ⓑ Yahweh's Word to the King (22:1–9)

SUPPORTING IDEA: *The privilege of being a leader brings with it great responsibility. To whom much has been given, much will be required.*

Yahweh never intended for his people, Israel, to be ruled by a king. His plan from the beginning was a theocracy, guided politically by a charismatic leader to whom he would speak directly through spiritual fellowship. He chose the priesthood to conduct the religious element in Israel's life. Moses and Aaron were the two personalities whom he selected at the beginning of the people's identification as a nation.

For eighty years Moses and Joshua led Israel. For approximately 120 years, Israel existed as a loose federation, ruled by various military judges. During this time priests emerged as an influential force in the nation's political life. Samuel, a nonmilitary judge, served also in a limited way as a prophet. During Samuel's closing days, the people petitioned God through him for a king to rule.

Neither Yahweh nor Samuel wanted Israel to be ruled by a king, but both yielded to the people's wishes. God warned of the consequences of Israel's having a king (1 Sam. 8:9–18). The first king, Saul, was a bitter disappointment. The second, David, was in many ways a great king, but his personal life tragically sowed the seed for later rebellion in the kingdom. The third king, Solomon, through his excesses, led the unified kingdom to disruption. At his death in 931 B.C., two kingdoms came into existence: Israel, the ten northern tribes; and Judah, the two southern tribes.

Israel's history was hectic, volatile, and sinful. Of the nineteen kings who ruled, every one was wicked. Each seemed to exceed all the previous ones in ungodliness and sin. Finally in 722 B.C. the Northern Kingdom was destroyed by Assyria and the people were taken into captivity. Their exact fate is still unknown and still debated by scholars, many of whom call them "the ten lost tribes."

Judah's behavior was not quite as wicked as Israel's, but it grew progressively worse. One redeeming factor was that a direct descendant of David stayed on the throne through the years. That almost failed when Athaliah, daughter of Ahab and Jezebel, seized rule for six years (2 Kgs. 11:1–3). But the line was restored in Joash (2 Kgs. 11:4–12).

Yahweh sent several prophets to Judah in an effort to save her from the suicidal course she was pursuing. The final and greatest was Jeremiah. He made a heroic effort to halt Judah's downward plunge, but the people would not listen to his message. Chapters 22 and 23 of Jeremiah's book summarize his messages to the final four kings of Judah and the false prophets of that day. They are a warning to any privileged nation following the same path to destruction.

22:1–3. Jeremiah, speaking for Yahweh, "drew a line in the sand." He stated God's requirements as plainly and clearly as any place in the prophet's recorded messages. In his earlier years Jeremiah majored on the fleshly sins of the people as they engaged in abuses of the Canaanite religion. As he grew older and the Babylonians drew closer to Jerusalem, Jeremiah seems to have focused his emphasis on another type of sin. He declared God's disapproval of the nation's leaders and their exploitation of the common people, denying them social justice. Showing compassion toward weaker people is as much God's requirement as personal piety and sexual purity.

22:4–9. Speaking for Yahweh, Jeremiah made Judah's future depend on how the nation's leadership responded to God's message. Unless Judah heard and heeded Yahweh's mandate for equity and fairness in the nation, the palace of the king would become a ruin. Verse 4, however, came first in this context. Kings can continue to rule in the land and execute justice if the nation will repent and turn back to God's requirements. This general warning was given before the prophet became specific about each ruler who had sat on the throne since good king Josiah.

Ⓒ Futility of Mourning for King Shallum (22:10–12)

SUPPORTING IDEA: *There is no need to pray for those whom Yahweh has bypassed because of their unacceptability.*

22:10–12. This message about Jehoahaz (**Shallum** was his personal name before ascending the throne) stands first in a collection of four king-related passages that the compilers of Jeremiah's materials included in the book. Though we cannot be sure, perhaps they grouped them this way to show the prophet's relationships to Judah's kings. No direct words about Jeremiah's relationship to Josiah are recorded here, except a brief reference (22:15–16), probably because none existed. Jeremiah and Josiah probably remained personal friends. Some evidence does exist that the prophet became disillusioned with the reform movement toward the king's closing days.

This message about Jehoahaz was addressed to the people. They had placed this young man on the throne to succeed Josiah as king when Josiah was killed by the Egyptians at Megiddo (2 Kgs. 23:29–30). Jehoahaz was Josiah's youngest son. Some scholars contend this indicates he was probably more in sympathy with Josiah's policies than the other sons. This verse is an outburst by the prophet warning the people that their popular young hero who has been taken into exile **will never return** to Judah.

Verses 11 and 12, written in prose, give a further explanation about the short reign (2 Kgs. 13:1–8) of young Jehoahaz. If the people chose him as king hoping he shared the convictions of his father, they were disappointed.

First, the historian said, he "did evil in the eyes of the LORD" (2 Kgs. 13:2). Second, Pharaoh Neco carried him to Riblah in the land of Hamath and he died there, obviously never reaching Egypt. The Scripture does not tell how he met his death.

Ⅾ Greed of King Jehoiakim (22:13–23)

SUPPORTING IDEA: *Those who serve as leaders should not exploit their constituents for personal gain.*

22:13–14. Jehoiakim, Judah's next king, had a big appetite for wealth and prestige. Jeremiah's attack upon the king's buildings was not merely for their large and extensive nature. He called attention to two facts even more deserving of censure and reproach; either of them, in Jeremiah's eyes, made Jehoiakim unworthy of serving as king.

First, Jeremiah rebuked Jehoiakim for erecting his buildings by ignoring two great principles of Jewish faith—righteousness and justice. The two terms overlap at points in meaning though they are not exactly interchangeable. The effect of the prophet's words was a severe rebuke to the king. He was not just derelict in his duty but actually abused his privilege as the nation's leader. The king's responsibility was to guard the freedom and rights of every individual in his kingdom. The slavery of which he was guilty was an offense against covenant law.

Jehoiakim desired a spacious house. Modern archaeology has brought to light evidence of some large buildings probably constructed about the seventh century before Christ. They fit well the type dwellings of which Jeremiah spoke. A collection of stamped jar handles discovered contained some signs indicating royalty with the Hebrew letters *lmlk hbrn* ("belonging to the king"). They were in a fine brick fortress of this period, with a gate and a large building inside.

The second rebuke was in the record of Jehoiakim's words at the beginning of verse 14. The king said, **I will build myself a great palace**. Though the king lived there, the building belonged to the state. The way the king made the statement revealed his inner thoughts. J. A. Thompson pointed out, "Jehoiakim, who was only twenty-five years old when he began to reign and only thirty-six when he died (2 Kgs. 23:36), was evidently a thoroughly spoiled and self-indulgent young despot" (p. 479).

22:15–17. In these verses, Jeremiah spoke directly to the king. He asked two heart-searching rhetorical questions (vv. 15–16). In verse 17, he made downright accusations, declaring to the mighty monarch the exact nature of his sins and what caused him to do the evil deeds. What makes a truly great king? Jeremiah held before Jehoiakim the example of his father's life. Josiah was the model of true royalty.

Jeremiah asked a probing question. In essence, the prophet said, "Does having a large home with beautiful furnishings improve your status as a king?" He insisted Josiah had the necessities of life. Yet he never turned the other way to avoid seeing those who were without food or adequate lodging. Did that make him any less a great or successful king? The implication was obvious. The expression **all went well** meant he left a legacy of true greatness.

What does "to know the Lord" mean? Jeremiah gave the classic answer. He said nothing about an emotional experience but came to the heart of the matter. The formula is twofold. First, follow the command given in verse 3 and repeated in verse 15. See to it that one's personal conduct helps to eliminate the inequities among people. The second one was exemplified in the life of Josiah: defend **the cause of the poor and needy.**

22:18–19. These two verses contain Jeremiah's prediction of Jehoiakim's fate. The prophet stated three things about his death. First, no one would **mourn** for this once glorious king. Second, he would have a shameful **burial,** that **of a donkey.** Third, he would be **dragged away and thrown outside the gates of Jerusalem.**

Jehoiakim's death is clouded in mystery. About 598 B.C. he withheld tribute from Babylon, and Nebuchadnezzar sent troops to deal with him. They overran the whole country, reducing the land and people to the depths of wretchedness and misery. During the period of confusion that followed, Jehoiakim met a violent death. It occurred either in a battle with some of his many foes or because of an uprising of his oppressed subjects.

The author of Chronicles states nothing about Jehoiakim's death or burial. The author of 2 Kings states only that he "slept with his fathers" (2 Kgs. 24:6 KJV). The significant point is that neither of the historians gives us any details about his burial. There must have been something unusual about it because we have an account of the burial of every king who ruled over Judah except Jehoiakim and Hezekiah.

22:20–23. In these verses Jeremiah turned aside a moment to address all the people in Jerusalem about their plight. They had lost their **allies**. Who were these allies? Probably Egypt, mainly, but also included were those who staged the revolt recorded in chapter 27. Any person aware of recent happenings would have recognized that Nebuchadnezzar of Babylon was now in control.

The prophet told Jerusalem to shout the news as far off to the north as **Lebanon** and to the northeast as **Bashan** in Transjordania. They were also to make the message known in **Abarim**, a mountain range in Moab overlooking the Dead Sea.

Verse 21 gives the reason for Jerusalem's dilemma. Jeremiah reminded the people that they had ignored all the warnings. From their earliest days they had refused to obey the Lord. Perhaps many of them could remember the days of Manasseh. At that time Jerusalem and the temple were the center for all kinds of perverted deeds in the name of religion. Disobedience and defiance had become their lifestyle.

Concluding this section, Jeremiah used two metaphors to describe the judgment that would come on the land. In verse 22, he used a wordplay that may be translated, "The **wind** will shepherd your **shepherds**." Actually, the prophet was utilizing the twofold connotation of the verb that means literally "feed" or "pasture" when applied to a flock. The word takes on larger meanings as its usage increases. It was used in the sense of "to lead, guide, rule, govern." An even larger meaning then evolves: the verb can speak of devastation.

When totally defeated and without friends, Judah will stand stripped and humiliated. Those whom the people once considered their lovers and then their **allies** will be carried into captivity. All the resources Judah had depended on in days past will be gone. The last words in verse 22 give the reason for this condition: **because of all your wickedness**.

In verse 23, **Lebanon** probably refers to Jerusalem. Jeremiah must have spoken figuratively here. First, a number of the fine buildings, including the palace, used large amounts of cedar, which came from Lebanon. Second, the tall cedars of Lebanon represented security. Birds could nest safely in them. Likewise, citizens of Jerusalem felt secure amid the mountains.

The prophet used still another figure of speech. He compared Judah's coming suffering to the birth **pangs** of a mother before delivering a child.

How the people must have shuddered when the prophet used this illustration. The captivity by Babylon represented the birth pangs of a new era in Judah's history.

E Worthlessness of Jehoiachin (22:24–30)

SUPPORTING IDEA: *God is patient, but there comes a time when he acts decisively against those whose hearts are unrepentant.*

In some ways Jehoiachin—or Coniah, a shortened form of the name—may have shown good judgment. For instance, he probably surrendered willingly to Babylon. The hospitality he received from the Babylonian king many years after he went as a captive indicates this may be true (52:31–34; 2 Kgs. 25:27–29). On the other hand, he most likely had no option. To be charitable toward him, we could suggest Jeremiah may have had a part in his failure to resist Babylon. Since the prophet advised Zedekiah at the beginning of his reign to surrender, he may have recommended for Jehoiachin to do the same thing at an earlier time.

The Scriptures state that Jehoiachin was an evil man and an unsatisfactory ruler. His mother Nehushta is mentioned along with accounts of the young king. This may suggest that she wielded an important influence on the eighteen-year-old lad.

22:24–27. These verses indicate that Yahweh was displeased with Jehoiachin before he surrendered to Babylon. He probably began early to be in sympathy with his father's wicked policies. Yahweh's statement about rejection of the **signet ring on my right hand** suggests that Jehoiachin had already displeased him. His further words in verses 24–27 add evidence that the young man had already made clear his policies in governmental affairs. Jehoiachin seems to have been more than just a typical young, headstrong man. He had already become a habitual rebel against Yahweh's demands.

22:28–30. This section is poetry in contrast to the three preceding ones in prose. Jeremiah may have composed the short poem or song as an answer to queries from the people about Jehoiachin. Why would the prophet be called upon to defend his words that condemned Jehoiachin? Many scholars feel this short section reflects Jeremiah's answer to a group in Babylon and in Judah. They wanted to lead a rebellion and bring Jehoiachin back to his native land as king. They had asked Jeremiah why this should not be done and why he opposed it, and this was a part of his reply.

The two questions Jeremiah asked (v. 28) are a preface to the restatement of his original affirmation. The three verses are in poetical form. He used a shortened form of the king's name, Coniah, probably to fit the metrical structure. In essence, he says, "Why do I consider Jehoiachin as unqualified to serve Judah as a broken pot doing its kitchen work? Listen everyone to the Lord's word!" He then stated God's will and decree was that this man would never have a son to **sit on the throne . . . or rule anymore in Judah**.

Jehoiachin was not **childless**, in the literal sense of that word. Actually, he had seven sons (1 Chr. 3:17–18). Archaeological records show that rations apportioned to Jehoiachin by Evil-Merodach, the Babylonian king, included some for his children.

What about the promise made to David that he would always have a descendant on the throne of Judah? The answer is that Jesus Christ, the son of David, inherited that promise and sits on God's throne today. Jeremiah's prediction was correct. None of Jehoiachin's offspring succeeded in sitting on the throne of David to rule over Judah.

F God's Provision for Israel's Future (23:1–8)

SUPPORTING IDEA: *The failure of leaders to serve the Lord does not prevent God's redemptive program from succeeding.*

These verses contain the final message in this larger section (22:1–23:8) about the kings of Judah. This smaller section is about Zedekiah, though Jeremiah refrained from using his name. Perhaps the prophet avoided it out of respect for the king because the siege by Babylon was probably already underway. The eight verses contain three divisions. The first (vv. 1–4) deals with the wicked rulers whom the prophets spoke of as "shepherds." The second (vv. 5–6) announces the coming of a righteous ruler. The third (vv. 7–8) proclaims the return of those who have been banished—not only to Babylon but to other places as well.

23:1–4. Because Jesus used this figure as an illustration of his relationship to those who follow him, we have difficulty remembering the Old Testament's main usage. The kings—along with their helpers—were preeminently **the shepherds** of their people. Yahweh placed them in charge of the nation. They were not only to protect their subjects but also to provide for their day-to-day needs.

Jeremiah uttered sharp words of rebuke to the shepherds for neglecting their duty (vv. 1–2). In verse 2, the prophet used a play on words to enrich the picture he wanted to paint. The Hebrew word translated **bestowed care** is one that means "to visit," in either a good or bad sense. The Hebrew reads literally, "You have not visited them; behold, I will visit upon you the evil of your doings."

Verses 3 and 4 contain Yahweh's promise to restore his people and grant them the joy of a large **increase in number**. He will also give them rulers who will look after the people's interests rather than their own.

23:5–6. This short poetical piece announces as clearly as any in the Old Testament the coming of God's Messiah. The expression **days are coming** is general in nature and has no time reference. This was a way of calling attention to a solemn statement of some significant event that would surely occur. The Book of Jeremiah contains only a few messianic prophecies. Judah had failed to fulfill its potential. But God had determined that he would not fail and thus announced his intention to send **a righteous Branch**. He would carry out the ideals of the divine kingdom.

Jeremiah used an interesting metaphor. The word *Branch* comes from a verb that means "to shoot, sprout, grow up, spring up, arise." This same figure, though not expressed with the same terms, was used by Isaiah (Isa. 11:1) to predict the coming of the messianic Servant of the Lord. He would arise from the remnant of a crushed nation.

After the exile the word *Branch* became a classic word to descibe the expected ideal king. Actually, no political figure who approximated this predicted ruler ever arose. This prediction was fulfilled in Jesus Christ, our Savior and Lord, who became the true King of the Jews. But he was even more. God made him both Lord and Messiah. The Jews rejected their king because they did not recognize that the true Messiah was a spiritual deliverer, not a political ruler.

The interesting fact about this prophecy is that Jeremiah used a play on words to express his thought. Zedekiah's name meant "Yahweh is my righteousness." The One whom Jeremiah predicted would come was Yahweh's true **Righteousness**. Human kings had failed. The One divinely sent would not fail.

23:7–8. Yahweh, through his prophet, promised an even greater exodus than the one from Babylon. In what sense would this be true? The exodus from **Egypt** was probably larger in numbers than the one from Babylon, but the coming one would include a more extensive geographical territory.

Some see the exodus Jeremiah predicted as prefiguring a later exodus, perhaps the one the world has seen in modern days since 1948. Others contend the passage finds its ultimate fulfillment in the Christian context. They understand the larger exodus to be the people who are delivered from the slavery of sin to liberty and freedom in Jesus Christ. This school of thought points out that Jesus said, "I go to prepare a place for you" (John 14:2 KJV).

G Condemnation of the False Prophets (23:9–40)

SUPPORTING IDEA: *When prophets claim to be from God, they should be examples of integrity, morality, and perception in order to glorify their heavenly Father.*

Most students agree that this larger passage contains five shorter messages by the prophet. They were grouped together in this context because all deal with the subject under consideration. Since Jeremiah was in disagreement with the "false prophets" of his day, he suffered rebuke from them. They represented the opposite of everything Jeremiah taught. The divisions of Scripture for the segments are as follows: vv. 9–12,13–15,16–22, 23–32,33–40.

23:9–12. In this passage Jeremiah described his emotional distress because of the nation's sexual immorality. Judah's wicked behavior had produced in him a state similar to being in a **drunken** stupor. The word translated **heart** refers to the mind as much as one's feelings or emotions. Judah's apostasy shattered the prophet's ability to cope mentally with the situation and left him deeply disturbed. He attributed the land's barrenness to these sins.

Jeremiah went even further. He placed the blame on Judah's religious leaders, the prophets and priests. They had "sold out" to ungodly principles and even took advantage of their authority to commit unspeakable deeds in God's holy house. Such conduct would bring God's judgment. When the nation fell to an enemy, they would suffer for their part in bringing it upon the land.

23:13–15. Jeremiah called attention to the distinction and yet similarity between the Northern and Southern Kingdoms. Both nations displeased God with their wicked acts. Both were involved with sexual immorality though the expression is not used here with reference to Israel. Jeremiah pointed out that both kingdoms were like **Sodom** and **Gomorrah**. These two cities had a reputation for adultery and homosexuality.

23:16–22. In this section the Lord warned the people against listening to false prophets who told them that no harm would come to them or the nation. Yahweh classified these prophets as being insistent to the point of being obstinate, headstrong, and inflexible. Speaking **their own** thoughts rather than those from **the LORD**, they insisted nothing unfavorable about the nation would occur. None of these men, however, had received their message from Yahweh.

Verses 19–22 contain Yahweh's pronouncement of what the future held for those who persisted in wicked conduct. Judgment would come suddenly and irreversibly. Yahweh would not stop until he had achieved his redemptive **purposes**. In the meantime, those who trusted him must wait until later to fully comprehend the Lord's will. Verses 19–20 appear again in 30:23–24. By the time the latter message was brought to Judah, the people would be in a better position to understand the words Yahweh spoke.

Jeremiah summarized for Yahweh in verses 21 and 22 the basic truth of this section. God did not commission these false prophets, and the words they were saying did not represent his will. If he had sent them and they had delivered his message, conditions in Judah would be different.

23:23–32. In this oracle, God contrasted himself and his ability to reveal his will with the false prophets who claimed that power. Though the NIV translates only the first two verses as poetry, some students contend the entire section is metrical. Yahweh began this message with a firm declaration of his ability to see those **far away** as well as those **nearby**. In other words, no one can **hide** from him. His presence extends to the most remote spot on **earth**.

Beginning with verse 25 and continuing through verse 29, Yahweh stated that he was aware of the claims being made by the false **prophets** about their **dreams**. They imagined they could lull the people into a feeling of security. He compared them to the earlier false prophets who led the people to follow the Canaanite **Baal** cult rather than the true God. They will be no more effective in bringing security than **straw** can substitute for **grain** in satisfying the appetite. When a true prophet speaks, he does so with power and authority that comes from God.

In verses 30–32, Yahweh finalized his claim to ultimate authority. The false prophets only proclaimed what they heard others say. They had no message from God. Rather than helping the people, they led them **astray**. Yahweh opposed them and all they stood for.

23:33–40. To understand verse 33, one needs to understand the meaning of the word translated **oracle**. It means "burden." The oracle was a message that burdened the prophet so much that he felt compelled to deliver it. This verse means when the people asked Jeremiah, **What is the oracle of the Lord?** he was to reply with a play on the word's double meaning. "What burden? You are the burden! The Lord says he will **forsake you**!"

In the remainder of this section, Yahweh enlarged on this thought and concluded his entire message about the false prophets. Anyone who falsely claimed to be speaking a message from the Lord would face Yahweh's judgment and condemnation. The false prophets, in pretending to have an oracle from the Lord, were just stating their **own** words and opinions. Those who continued to do so would be dealt with severely.

> **MAIN IDEA REVIEW:** *A leader in any field, especially that of public service, must be willing to accept responsibility and be faithful in discharging it.*

III. CONCLUSION

Four Kings, Four Verdicts

From Jeremiah's critique of Judah's last four kings, we learn a number of principles from God's perspective about the political arena and those who govern. We learn that political leaders and rulers who live by God's judgments and standards are blessed over those who live extravagantly while ignoring God. We learn that rulers who do what is just and right are honored over those who practice injustice and greed. We learn that those who use their power to provide for the vulnerable members of their society are to be preferred over those who use their power to self-serving ends—profiteering and extortion—or to oppress others.

From Jeremiah's critique of Judah's false prophets in chapter 23, we learn a number of principles about those who claim to speak for God. Among these are that prophets' personal character and lifestyle are paramount. False prophets lie and live immoral lives. False prophets also speak a self-originated message, which they claim is a divinely originated message. False prophets proclaim a pleasing message and say what people want to hear. They offer false hope and deluded comfort. They strengthen the hands of evildoers rather than turn people from their wickedness. False prophets are of no benefit to their hearers, and they will be punished by the Lord.

PRINCIPLES

- When people are in trouble, they often turn to religious leaders and institutions.
- The Lord holds rulers accountable for their administrations.
- To do what is right and just is more important than to be rich and prosperous.
- Those who claim to speak for God should make sure they have a word from the Lord.
- Personal character is important for God's spokesmen. The lives of those who claim to speak for God should be consistent with the message of God that they deliver.
- True prophets of God seek to turn people from their evil ways and deeds.

APPLICATIONS

- Draw a graph of your spiritual life over the last ten years with the vertical axis indicating closeness to God at the top and distance from God at the bottom.
- Look at the low points and see if you can find some of the factors that contributed to these low states.
- Do the same with the high points, seeking to discover factors God may have used to draw you closer to him.
- Evaluate your voting patterns over the past five years and assess whether they are based on God's standards for those who govern or on those candidates that will best serve your personal interests.
- Make a list of your priorities. How many of them reflect a desire for comfort and material prosperity? How many of them reflect God's interests and his kingdom priorities?

- As you listen to teaching and preaching, seek to discern what is clearly based on God's Word and who is merely human opinion dressed in religious garb.

- Imagine that your church is in the process of calling a pastor. Make up a list of priorities your church's pastor search committee should keep before them as they seek a pastor.

- Next week perform the following experiment. On Wednesday, ask yourself what Sunday's sermon was about and then evaluate the extent to which that sermon has made a difference in your life the first days of the week.

IV. LIFE APPLICATION

Baghdad Bob

Mohammed Saeed al-Sahaf, known also as "Chemical Ali" and "Baghdad Bob," was the Iraqi information minister during the last days of Saddam Hussein's rule. He is best remembered for his skewed views and outrageous proclamations about the status of the war in Iraq. With great bravado Baghdad Bob made assertions that were at odds with the reality around him.

His announcements that the Republican Guard were in control and had surrounded and crushed the invading forces, that coalition forces were nowhere near the airport but were lost in the desert, that American forces were under siege and committing suicide by the hundreds on the gates of Baghdad, and that there were no Americans in Baghdad as tanks and armored personnel carriers rumbled into the city caused considerable amusement. Amazingly, many Iraqis and Muslims and Arabs throughout the Middle East not only listened to but believed his words.

The art of bravado—making outrageous proclamations, confidently promoting skewed views, and boldly asserting what is at odds with reality—is nothing new. Jeremiah faced such opportunists who filled his hearers with false hope about Judah's situation, who told the people no harm would come to them, and who declared that they would have peace. These false prophets told lies, declared visions out of their own minds, and prophesied their own delusions. Amazingly, the people listened to them and were led astray by their reckless lies.

Not everyone who speaks with confidence and authority is telling the truth. God's people need to examine carefully the lives and the words of those who claim to speak a message from the Lord. They need to be sure it is the Lord's servant and the Lord's message they are heeding. It is too easy to embrace a message we want to hear. It is much harder to hear, to heed, to submit to, and to obey the oracle or burden that comes from the Lord.

V. PRAYER

O righteous Ruler, we pray for the leaders and politicians of our country. Help them to act in right and just ways. Keep them from the temptations to use power in self-serving ways. May they seek to protect the vulnerable members of our society. May our leaders never exploit and take advantage of their positions of power and influence. May they realize that they must render an account for all the responsibilities they have been entrusted with. And bless all those who speak your Word and who remind us of our responsibilities as citizens of both an earthly country and a heavenly kingdom. Amen.

VI. DEEPER DISCOVERIES

A. "The Lord Our Righteousness" (23:6b)

God's righteous demands can never be attained by human effort, but a name like *Zedekiah* sets us on the path toward securing it. Messianic prophecy speaks of the ideal King as being completely righteous and having a passion for the spread of righteousness throughout his kingdom.

The rulers of both the ten northern and the two southern tribes had failed miserably to be the shepherds Yahweh intended. But God refused to give up on his redemptive program. Judah's last king was named Mattaniah, but he took the name Zedekiah, which means literally "Righteousness of Yahweh" or "Yahweh is my Righteousness." This was the last effort to establish God's righteousness through a political ruler.

Interwoven with the earthly attempt is the divine answer to humankind's failure. What man could not do because he was weak through the flesh, God accomplished by sending his Son, born of a woman. Jeremiah declared three profound yet simple truths about God's mighty act of deliverance as related to our need of and his provision for our righteousness.

The *source* of our righteousness is found in God the Father. Jesus Christ is the only complete answer to his own nature and to our problem of sin and guilt.

The *secret* of our righteousness lies in the truth revealed to us by this name. Martin Luther listed four kinds of righteousness: political, ceremonial, legal, and moral-spiritual. Outward forms of righteousness cannot change the inward state, but inward transformation can change radically the outward actions. The secret is Jesus Christ in us, the hope of our attaining the glory God desires for us and from us.

When we accept the righteousness of God through Jesus Christ as our only hope, we receive a remarkable *serenity* about both present and ultimate matters. Peace with God means the war is done. God has judged our sin upon Christ our substitute. He was so fully and completely satisfied with the sacrifice of Christ that he will eternally remain so. This gives us a new standing before God. In his righteousness we are righteous. He will never again take up judgment against us. The One who knew no sin was made to be sin in order for us to become righteous.

B. True Prophets and False Prophets

Informed students declare that the Hebrew prophetic movement remains, after centuries have passed, the greatest influence ever exerted in the world. But this office in the Jewish culture always stood in jeopardy and in danger of being degraded. This is true because direct inspiration from God is a rare thing, granted to exceptional people and often only for a short time and for a specific purpose. To make this claim of special revelation is easy. But it can be used for selfish purposes.

The spoils of asserting prophetic status cover a wide area. It was a ready means of flattering a foolish king or exciting a still more foolish mob. Reward from royal patrons, or the popularity that is so sweet to most of us, comes to people who use the name and influence of a prophet in this manner. Sometimes it was used, still more basely, for personal and monetary gain.

John Skinner and George Adam Smith have interesting discussions about the contrasting characteristics of the true and false prophets. Here is a brief summary:

- The true prophet had a personal relationship with God. The false prophet had no such relationship.

- The message of the true prophet was conditional, depending upon the response of the people. The false prophet was ultra-patriotic. He saw God as the unconditional ally of his people regardless of their character or attitude.

- The true prophet recognized and proclaimed the ethical and moral character of God and the corresponding demand for such character in the lives of his people. The false prophet saw no relation between religion and ethical demands for everyday living.

- The true prophet had unimpeachable integrity. He delivered the truth as it had been revealed to him regardless of personal desires or ambitions. The false prophet was a man of doubtful character, sometimes actually immoral. A time-server, he preached a pleasing and optimistic message at all times in order to be popular with his hearers.

VII. TEACHING OUTLINE

A. INTRODUCTION

1. Lead Story: Saddam, Uday, and Qusay

2. Context: The coming of a delegation to Jeremiah from King Zedekiah provided an opportunity for the Lord's evaluation of each of the last four kings of Judah.

3. Transition: How politicians and those who rule over people carry out the responsibilities of their offices and discharge their duties is important to God. The evaluations of the last four kings of Judah provide insights into God's expectations of those who wield political power and into his standards of judgment about how they fulfill the obligations of their office.

B. COMMENTARY

1. The First Inquiry of Zedekiah (21:1–14)

2. Yahweh's Word to the King (22:1–9)

3. Futility of Mourning for King Shallum (22:10–12)

4. Greed of King Jehoiakim (22:13–23)

5. Worthlessness of Jehoiachin (22:24–30)
6. God's Provision for Israel's Future (23:1–8)
7. Condemnation of the False Prophets (23:9–40)

C. CONCLUSION: FOUR KINGS, FOUR VERDICTS

VIII. ISSUES FOR DISCUSSION

1. Discuss what you understand to be the relationship between the political process in today's world and God's expectations for politicians.
2. In your opinion, can politicians live and act by God's standards of what is right and just in today's political process? Why or why not?
3. What are the main lessons Jeremiah 21–23 teach us about politics and power?
4. In today's society personal character seems to be not as important as the ability to get the job done. How do you feel about this issue? How does Jeremiah 21–23 shed light on this matter? How will your reflections relate to your evaluation of political candidates and to your actions on election day?
5. Discuss as many tests as you can name to determine if a person who claims to speak for God really has a message from the Lord.

Jeremiah 24:1–29:32

Who Speaks for God?

I. **INTRODUCTION**
Peace in Our Time

II. **COMMENTARY**
A verse-by-verse explanation of these verses.

III. **CONCLUSION**
Be Careful Whom You Listen To

An overview of the principles and applications from these verses.

IV. **LIFE APPLICATION**
The Lost Boys of Sudan

Melding these verses to life.

V. **PRAYER**
Tying these verses to life with God.

VI. **DEEPER DISCOVERIES**
Historical, geographical, and grammatical enrichment of the commentary.

VII. **TEACHING OUTLINE**
Suggested step-by-step group study of these verses.

VIII. **ISSUES FOR DISCUSSION**
Zeroing these verses in on daily life.

"*W*ho is in charge of the clattering train?

The axles creak, and the couplings strain. . . .

For the pace is hot, and the points are near,

And Sleep hath deadened the driver's ear;

And signals flash through the night in vain.

Death is in charge of the clattering train!"

E d w i n   J .   M i l l i k e n

Jeremiah 24:1–29:32

IN A NUTSHELL

*T*wo chronologically reversed chapters (chs. 24–25) place side-by-side Jeremiah's experiences following the first two deportations of Judeans to Babylon. Chapter 25 goes back to the earliest deportation in 605 B.C. during Jehoiakim's reign when Nebuchadnezzar took captive Daniel and other eminent young leaders among the Judean nobility. Chapter 24 follows the second wave of deportations in 598–597 B.C., which saw King Jehoiachin, his queen mother, palace officials, executives, artisans, community leaders, and the prophet Ezekiel led into exile and Zedekiah, the youngest son of Josiah, placed on the Davidic throne. For the twenty-three years preceding the first of these deportations Jeremiah had warned the people of coming judgment, but they would not listen (25:3). Then almost a decade later, after the second wave of deportations, the Lord gave Jeremiah a graphic illustration about the people of Judah. The Lord likened those who had already been taken into exile to good figs that would be protected and preserved and those who had been left behind in Judea to rotten figs that would be discarded. That both of these chapters following deportations to Babylon deal with the future of the people of Judah—those taken into exile and those who remained in the land—and with the future of the Babylonian conquerors is a common theme.

Chapters 26–29 provide vignettes from Jeremiah's life. Chapter 26 offers a fuller look at the temple sermon of chapter 7. Chapters 27–28 relate the story of the making and breaking of Jeremiah's yoke. Through this symbolic action Jeremiah counseled submission to the Babylonians. Chapter 29 contains Jeremiah's letter to the Babylonian exiles. The common theme for these chapters is how to decide who speaks the true word from the Lord.

Who Speaks for God?

I. INTRODUCTION

Peace in Our Time

*W*inston Churchill devoted the 1930s to warning his countrymen against the rising menace of Nazi Germany's unilateral remilitarization, which was being carried out in clear violation of both the Treaty of Versailles and the Treaty of Locarno. His numerous warnings and speeches fell on deaf ears. Churchill was ridiculed, mocked, and dismissed as an irrelevant babbler.

Adolf Hitler, the German fuehrer and chancellor, desired world domination. In March 1938 he annexed Austria. He next eyed Czechoslovakia with its more than three million German-speaking inhabitants.

Neville Chamberlain, the British prime minister, sought peace through acquiescence, accommodation, and appeasement. Much like the false prophets of Jeremiah's day (6:14; 8:11), Chamberlain sought peace at any price and refused to recognize the devastation and long disruption that were about to come upon his people's world. After his second trip to Germany, Chamberlain returned to England a hero—waving the joint declaration that stated their countries would "never go to war with one another again."

In March 1939 German troops marched into Prague. On September 1 German troops entered Poland, and German bombs fell on Polish cities. Two days later Britain and France declared war on Germany, and the world was at war again. On May 10 Hitler attacked Holland, Belgium, and France. Chamberlain resigned, and Britain installed Winston Churchill as prime minister and asked him to form a new government.

Much as Churchill, for years Jeremiah had been prophesying that disaster and destruction were coming. The prophet told his people that the city of Jerusalem would be devastated, as the Northern Kingdom's religious center, Shiloh (26:8–9), had been. And in his confrontation with the acquiescing and accommodating Hananiah, he said, "The prophet who prophesies peace will be recognized as one truly sent by the Lord only if his prediction comes true" (28:9). But as time soon showed, the clattering train of Judah was plummeting down a disastrous track. A spiritual sleep had deadened the ears of the national leaders. Prophets, priests, and political leaders missed all the flashing signals the Lord had been sending them through his prophets (28:7–8), and now death was in charge of the out-of-control nation.

II. COMMENTARY

Who Speaks for God?

MAIN IDEA: *Regardless of how discouraging a situation becomes, God is with his people. When the outlook gets dark enough, stars will come out.*

One of the big problems in studying the Book of Jeremiah is its lack of chronological arrangement. Another problem, perhaps even greater, is determining the rationale for the present arrangement. In my judgment the answer is that various independent scrolls were placed side by side with no effort to synthesize or integrate them. But one question remains: Where does one scroll end and another begin?

Thus far in this study, we have been able, with one or two exceptions, to see clearly the organization of material into scrolls. In addition, we have been able to recognize a theme around which we could organize our study. But the chapters before us here present the most difficult problem yet encountered. The two previous sections (chs. 18–20; 21–23) are easily discernible. The section following (chs. 30–33) is one of the most obvious in the entire book's material. Scholars almost unanimously call it the "Book of Comfort."

In order to get the picture here, we need to "walk through" these six chapters. In this way we can have an overview that should help in the study of this unit and determine, if possible, a thematic unity.

Chapter 24, written in the first person, records an experience of Jeremiah in the temple. He saw two baskets, one containing good figs and the other holding bad figs. From this sight Yahweh conveyed to Jeremiah a great truth about the captives in Babylon and those still in their homeland. This chapter is self-contained and has no apparent relationship to the one preceding it or the one following it. But it does serve as a companion to chapter 29.

Chapter 25 dates before the preceding chapter. It goes back to the early years of Jehoiakim's reign, shortly after 605 B.C. In verses 1–7, Jeremiah reminded the people that they had refused for twenty-three years to hear him proclaim God's words and warnings. He then warned, in verses 8–14, that they would suffer a seventy-year captivity. In verses 15–29 the prophet pictured God's wrath poured out, as from a cup. The chapter concludes, in verses 30–38, with a message about God's judgment on all nations of that time.

Chapter 26 also comes from the years of Jehoiakim's reign. It contains a parallel account of the temple sermon found in 7:1–8:3. The earlier record gives a long summary of the sermon but contains no historical narrative. This latter narrative encapsulates the sermon in brief but then follows with an account of the sermon's effect. A concluding section deals with an event in the life of Uriah, another prophet of Jeremiah's time.

Chapters 27 and 28 "hang together," combining to furnish the longest account of any action by Jeremiah found in the book. They reveal Jeremiah's attitude toward Babylon and the prophets who were predicting Babylon's immediate downfall. Chapter 27 refers to the prophets collectively, while chapter 28 records Jeremiah's encounter with an individual representative of the group.

Chapter 29 consists mostly of correspondence between Jerusalem and Babylon. Jeremiah had heard that false prophets in Babylon were telling the exiles they would soon return home. The exiles were making little effort to adjust to their new surroundings and get ready for a long stay. Jeremiah wrote them a letter, exhorting the captives to accept reality, build homes, and plant gardens. He knew they would be in Babylon for many years. The letter also has some words for certain individuals in Babylon who were making misleading statements about the situation of the exiles.

Ⓐ Jeremiah's Vision of Good and Bad Figs (24:1–10)

SUPPORTING IDEA: *God doesn't always do what the unregenerate world thinks he should do.*

24:1–2. Judah is in exile. Now the people of the Southern Kingdom knew at least something of what their fellow Israelites of the north had experienced more than a century before.

Technically speaking, Judah's exile began in 605 B.C. with the first raid by Babylon's new king, Nebuchadnezzar. He took a few captives, including Daniel and his three friends (Dan. 1:3). In 597 B.C., however, the king struck at the heart of the Jewish nation. He took the "flower of the land." The historian says, "As the Lord had declared, Nebuchadnezzar removed all the treasures from the temple of the Lord and from the royal palace, and took away all the gold articles that Solomon king of Israel had made for the temple of the Lord. He carried into exile all Jerusalem: all the officers and fighting men, and all the craftsmen and artisans—a total of ten thousand. Only the poorest people of the land were left" (2 Kgs. 24:13–14).

The evidence indicates that a young man named Ezekiel was included among those taken captive (Ezek. 1:1–2). In many ways this was the most damaging of all three Babylonian invasions. The fatal blow had already been struck. For the death knell to be final, only one more invasion was required. This came in 586 B.C.

The people who remained in Jerusalem and the surrounding area in 597 B.C. felt they were the ones delivered by God's grace. This was because, according to them, they were "special" to him. We do not know how Jeremiah might have felt about this. Perhaps he partially agreed, but a word from God changed his outlook, and he responded accordingly.

As Jeremiah was walking in the temple area, Yahweh led him to a place where baskets of food were placed. He directed the prophet's attention to **two baskets of figs**. One contained **good** edible figs. The other figs were not only inferior but unacceptable: **They could not be eaten.**

24:3–7. Yahweh used the same type of attention-getter he had used twice when he called Jeremiah to the prophetic ministry. The prophet went further this time than in his inaugural vision. He not only replied that he saw **figs**, but he distinguished between the **good ones** and the **bad** ones. This might indicate he was making progress in understanding Yahweh's way of making his point in dialogue.

Why did Yahweh explain this to Jeremiah? A person of his insight should have recognized immediately the "first class" citizens had been taken in the recent incursion of Babylon. Perhaps, as he mused further on the subject, a fresh revelation came to him.

Jeremiah was familiar with the "remnant" concept preached by Isaiah. Who would be in this small group that would continue to exist as Yahweh's "true Israel" in the restoration? The higher class citizens, those already in exile. Why so? Not because God loved the upper scale of society in a favored way. Rather, it was because he realized that they had the resources to return and build the community of believers again. Though the group in Babylon had their shortcomings, the group left in the land were the "culls." God saw no hope of their developing into the type of people needed to serve his redemptive purposes.

What would Yahweh do for his "good figs"? He would protect them and keep them intact so they could perform the service for which he called Abraham and later Israel. They would perpetuate the seed of Isaac and Jacob in whom the call was kept alive during the patriarchal period.

How would Yahweh do this glorious thing? He would change their hearts. Here is grace manifestly exhibited. We have no record of any widespread repentance on a national level. But Yahweh would act independently through his sovereignty to preserve a remnant. This was not a matter of personal salvation for each exile. It was an example of Yahweh acting in history to keep alive the messianic hope. God would bring back a remnant from Babylon so the promise would remain with the seed of Abraham and the descendants of David.

24:8–10. What about the group remaining in the land at that time? God would deal with them as those who were strangers to the covenant of grace. They had no part in Yahweh's plan for the nations. Jeremiah used such words as **abhorrent, offense, reproach, byword, ridicule**, and **cursing** when he spoke of them. God would do with them the same thing we do with food so rotten we cannot eat it. Their uncleanness disqualified them for enjoying the blessings of living on the land he had promised to Moses and Joshua. The expression **live in Egypt** may have referred to those who had already fled to Egypt or those who would go there after the fall of Jerusalem.

B God's Discipline and Wrath (25:1–38)

> **SUPPORTING IDEA:** *Sin eventually brings suffering for all people, no matter who they are or where they are.*

This chapter is one of four inserted between two messages about the exiles by the compiler of Jeremiah's material. It deals with God's plan for disciplining and punishing the nations.

25:1–7. The compiler of Jeremiah's material carefully dated this lengthy oracle. It took place in a significant year, 605 B.C. This was the year when Babylon defeated a coalition of Assyria's remaining forces, including Egypt, after the fall of Nineveh in 612 B.C. The victory of Babylon caused Jehoiakim to change his allegiance from Egypt to the new superior power on the international scene.

Two other important events occurred that year: Nabopolassar died, and Nebuchadnezzar, his son, became the official king of Babylon. Also Jeremiah, at Yahweh's command, dictated a number of prophecies he had proclaimed during the last twenty-three years. He sent them to Jehoiakim, king of Judah, who burned the scroll they were written on. Jeremiah promptly dictated the scroll again and added some other words.

At first reading, verses 3–7 sound as though Jeremiah's ministry thus far had been a failure. Far from it! The canonical prophets always delivered Yahweh's message faithfully. We find no indication of any word of censure for them. The people were without excuse; they deliberately chose to ignore Yahweh's pleadings and even his warnings. A prophet is not a failure if the people refuse to hear him. He is a failure only if he fails to deliver God's message.

25:8–11. In this section Jeremiah left no doubt about the judgment coming on the land: Yahweh would send it. Does this mean God allows an enemy to annihilate people who claim to be his people? It means exactly this and more. He actually *sends* the enemy even though the destroyer is worse than those he destroys.

"Is this fair?" The answer is a resounding "yes!" Those who sin against much light bear more guilt than those who sin against little light. Furthermore, God can use any instrument he chooses to chastise his people. When God finishes the process, he can toss the instrument aside and even destroy it. This he had already done with the Northern Kingdom and Assyria. He would repeat this process with the Southern Kingdom and Babylon. When he did it, the people would be so stripped of their former greatness that the pagan world itself would be disgusted.

25:12–14. Jeremiah went even further in his bold statement to the "bad figs" still in their homeland. Babylon's days were also numbered. Within seventy years this mighty nation, which had become an empire, would suffer the same fate as Assyria. Yahweh would raise up another conqueror that would exterminate this new political power. This coming force that would replace Babylon was Persia, led by Cyrus the Great in 539 B.C.

Scholars differ on how to interpret the **seventy years**. A few interpreters have suggested the expression "seventy years" was a figure of speech for a generation. This harmonizes with the "three score and ten years" the psalmist said God granted to man for an ordinary lifetime (90:10). Others insist on finding a way to fit the dates for the exile into a literal seventy-year period.

One of the favorite ways is to call the first invasion of Jerusalem in 605 B.C. the start and the first return under Zerubbabel the conclusion. Another is to go from the temple's destruction in 586 B.C. to the second temple's dedication in approximately 516 B.C.

In verse 14, Jeremiah gave further details about Babylon's future. The inhabitants, who had been slave owners, would themselves become slaves. This reminds us of Jesus' observation and warning, "All who draw the sword will die by the sword" (Matt. 26:52).

25:15–29. In these verses Yahweh led Jeremiah to the symbol of a **cup** pouring out the **wine** of God's judgment upon other **nations**. The nations listed begin with those immediately surrounding Israel, starting with **Egypt** and moving up the coastal plain to the north. It then crosses over to Israel's neighbors east of the Jordan River and then proceeds downward to the desert people of the northern Arabian peninsula. It also includes nations much farther to the east. Of those against whom Jeremiah uttered oracles recorded in chapters 46–51, only Damascus is omitted here.

The psalmist mentioned the "cup of salvation" (Ps. 116:13), which God's people vowed to bring Yahweh in appreciation for his goodness. In this present context, however, the image is reversed—it is a cup of **wrath**. This teaches us a lesson about interpretation of figurative language. The writers sometimes stood an illustration on its head and made it teach the opposite. For example, Jesus spoke of working while it is still day because the night is coming when we cannot work (John 9:3–4). Paul, however, reversed the image. He spoke of the night being far spent and the day being at hand (Rom. 13:12).

Though this section may seem irrelevant to us moderns, it conveys an important message. The law of sin and judgment applies to all people, whether or not they recognize God's claim on their lives. Sin has its own built-in execution power. We do not break God's laws. We break ourselves on them when we refuse to recognize them as valid.

25:30–38. In these final verses of chapter 25, Yahweh continued the same message, but he led Jeremiah to present it with different figures of speech. The prophet presented, in verses 30–31, the same sentiment as in verses 27–29. The difference is that the former is in prose, while the latter is in poetry. The roaring (v. 30) suggests a lion while juice from the **grapes** hints of the people's blood flowing. Jeremiah then switched to a trial scene (v. 31) as he brought **charges** against the people. He next moved to a worldwide gale (v. 32). The piling of images on images intensifies the coming judgment. Corpses will be so numerous that there will be no place to bury them. Instead, they will be like garbage strewn **everywhere** on the earth (v. 33).

Verse 34 contains Jeremiah's warning to the political **leaders** that their judgment is coming soon. Verses 35–36 contain statements about these men. Verse 37 pictures the land's coming condition, and verse 38 returns to the **lion** image. The prophet attributed all of this to the Lord's wrath against people who had defied his law and defiled his land. Judgment, though long delayed, is on the way.

Second Account of the Temple Sermon (26:1–24)

SUPPORTING IDEA: *Prophets should declare God's message, trust him for safety, and fear nothing.*

Many scholars see the events in this chapter as beginning a section of narrative and biographical material marking a new departure in the book's form. The first unit stretches from chapter 26 through 29 and deals with the general subject of false prophets. After being interrupted by chapters 30–33, it continues through chapter 45. Many scholars speak of these chapters as the "Baruch Narrative" or the "Baruch Biography." This section refers to Jeremiah in the third person and concludes with a personal message to Baruch.

But this designation is not an accurate title because the chronological sequence is violated several times. The truth is that no matter how we attempt to discover a comprehensive plan of the book's arrangement, the effort falls short. The theory of various scrolls placed side by side to form the book remains the best we can do.

Most interpreters contend this account of a temple sermon represents the same occasion as the previous one (7:1–8:3). The fact that these two discourses are substantially separated in the book proves nothing. In the Book of Jeremiah, many examples of nonchronological arrangement exist. The fact that the chapters contain the same location, theme, and content overcome any arguments against these being two accounts of the same event.

26:1–6. Though Jeremiah grew up among proper religious practices, he had come to recognize that spiritual fellowship in worship supersedes any formal approach to God. The former produced an inward motivation that the latter failed to generate in the heart or life of the worshipper.

26:7–11. When a person is speaking to people whose religious concepts have no spiritual base, preaching such as Jeremiah's falls on deaf ears. The prophet's audience, clergy and laymen alike, responded in the only manner of which they were capable: they resorted to force and even physical attack. Jeremiah's salvation lay in the fact that unbiased **officials** of the government, dedicated to peace-keeping, heard the commotion and came to check it out.

26:12–16. Jeremiah's contentions, as his self-appointed defense attorney, satisfied the officials. His calmness under pressure won their respect and convinced their minds. Their verdict must have been unanimous. **This man should not be sentenced to death! He has spoken to us in the name of the** LORD **our God.**

26:17–19. The expression **all the people** is interesting. In verses 7–9 it describes the audience to whom Jeremiah spoke at first. They, including priests and prophets, were offended by the prophet's message and seized him. No doubt the tumult caused officials responsible for keeping the peace to arrive quickly. In verse 11 the prophets and priests called for his death. They spoke to "all the people" and the officials.

After Jeremiah's self-defense speech, "all the people" sided with the officials who said Jeremiah should not be put to death. They respected a prophet who spoke in Yahweh's name. In addition they had a special respect for Jeremiah, who had been preaching for a number of years. Where do **the elders of the land** fit into this scenario? Perhaps the elders' citation of Micah's words had a strong effect on affirming both the officials and "all the people" in their decisions. Many times an explosive issue can be settled by the calm voice of older, wiser people.

A spokesperson for God cannot make the message any clearer, more specific, or sharper than Jeremiah did on this occasion. All those present that day must have realized that his message was relevant for their generation. The only exception might have been the priests and false prophets who saw it as a threat to their income. How tragic when professionals take over the religious functions of a community and subordinate the spiritual to the material. This always happens when spiritual leaders maximize ritual rather than righteousness in order to guarantee the continuation of revenue.

26:20–24. These four verses record how two true prophets of Yahweh responded differently and met different fates when they preached faithfully in the Lord's name. We know nothing of **Uriah** other than what is revealed in these verses: He **fled in fear to Egypt**. Jehoiakim **sent** for him and had him killed.

Jeremiah avoided execution. He stood his ground and fortunately had the support of **Ahikam**. The prophet's befriender was the son of Shaphan, a trusted servant of King Josiah. Ahikam supervised the cleansing of the temple in Josiah's early years. When the law book was discovered in the temple, Hilkiah the priest gave to it to Shaphan. Ahikam his son was one of a group who consulted Huldah the prophetess about its validity (2 Kgs. 22:1–14).

After the fall of Jerusalem, Nebuchadnezzar chose Gedaliah, son of Ahikam, son of Shaphan, to be governor of the land (2 Kgs. 25:22). Jeremiah was fortunate to have the support of this godly and influential family.

Warning About Plotting Against Babylon (27:1–22)

SUPPORTING IDEA: *Be careful about making alliances with people who do not share your spiritual convictions.*

After Babylon defeated Egyptian and Assyrian forces at the battle of Carchemish in 605 B.C., panic seized the nations that were anywhere near the Babylonian Empire. Egypt was Nebuchadnezzar's eventual goal for conquest. In order to subdue it, however, he needed to conquer and control these smaller territories. Conversely, Egypt wanted these smaller nations as allies to serve as a buffer zone against the would-be conqueror.

Some nation, probably Egypt, took initiatives to form an alliance against Babylon. Representatives of the countries met at Jerusalem. This event occurred in the early years of Zedekiah's reign. It is the historical background of chapter 27. We cannot be certain this was the purpose of the meeting. But contemporary events indicate this is probably a correct assumption.

Where was Judah in this scenario? The situation was similar to the days of Isaiah more than a century earlier when the Northern Kingdom allied with Syria. The purpose was to stop Tiglath-Pileser's southwest march through Israel and Judah and eventually to Egypt. They urged Hezekiah, king of Judah, to join them, threatening force unless they agreed. Isaiah urged Hezekiah to make no alliance with either Syria-Israel or Assyria. His advice was, "Trust God and stay neutral" (1 Kgs. 16:1–18; 2 Chr. 28:1–27; Isa. 7:1–15). The material in chapter 27 is divided as follows: (1) a word to the non-Jewish nations, (2) a word to King Zedekiah, and (3) a word to the priests and people.

27:1–11. In most older versions, verse 1 reads "Jehoiakim" instead of Zedekiah. Scholars are in virtual agreement it should read as the NIV and HCSB do. Some students suggest 27:1 is a recopying of 26:1, a logical suggestion. This study will accept the NIV and HCSB translation. Chapter 27 presupposes the exile of 597 B.C. Furthermore, the remainder of this chapter uses "Zedekiah."

Anyone who knew about Jeremiah was familiar with his symbolic actions. Here he used an ox yoke as his instrument. It was a wooden bar or bars tied by leather thongs to the animal's neck. The Hebrew word translated "yoke" is plural, causing some to suggest Jeremiah wore more than one yoke on his neck. This would have symbolized the various kings whom he was advising to surrender. Others suggest he gave each visiting ambassador a yoke to carry home for his king. Another possibility is that it was one yoke made up of more than one yoke bar.

What part did Zedekiah have in this coalition of nations? Some suggest he called the meeting in order to solicit the aid of potential allies against the encroaching enemy. Others feel these other countries came to convince Zedekiah to join their alliance. As far as the record goes, the group took no action. Either they could not agree among themselves, or they felt the risk was too great.

Jeremiah spoke without compromise to these foreign ambassadors, stating Yahweh's sovereignty. He was absolute ruler over all the earth. Since he alone made the earth, it was his to divide any way he chose. In addition, Yahweh was in control of history. All events occurred because of his active or permissive will. This was a bold statement for any prophet to make of his God, cutting across the traditional beliefs of contemporary nations that all gods were relative.

Jeremiah gave Yahweh's decision (vv. 6–7) to divide power and authority at that time. He had chosen Babylon as his servant to execute his will among the nations. This was similar to what he had done more than a century before when he raised up Assyria to execute his wrath on the Northern Kingdom. This did not mean that Yahweh approved of Babylon's lifestyle any more than he had been pleased with that of Assyria. In fact, he would bring on another empire to deal with Babylon in due time. In verse 8 Jeremiah warned the nations as strongly as he warned his own. To ignore God's command would bring disaster.

Jeremiah interrupted his warning to say, in verse 9, a word about those who were counseling the non-Jewish nations. The people of these countries had their own spiritual advisors. They were as erroneous in their judgments and advice as the priests and false prophets of Judah.

Continuing his warning, Yahweh's prophet, in verse 10, gave these mentors of pagan nations the same label as those of his own fellow Israelites. They were liars, and their message, if heeded, would cause their people to be driven from their own **lands**.

Jeremiah offered non-Jewish nations the same option as Judah (v. 11). It was, in essence, "Submit to Babylon's reign and you will be permitted to **remain** in your **own land**." The political reality was that Babylon only wanted control and revenue. If they received it, subject nations could live with reasonable peace and even a measure of security. That's the way large empires were built and held together in those times.

27:12–15. Jeremiah delivered this same message to his own king, Zedekiah. These verses do not say anything the prophet had not already said on several previous occasions. The gist of his message was, "Submit to Babylon. Why will you **die** and take **your people** down with you? Pay no attention to others who are claiming to be declaring Yahweh's will. They are lying. Do as they say, and you, along with your advisors, will die."

27:16–22. These verses contain the same warning as that in the other two main sections of this chapter. Jeremiah decided early in his ministry that some of the nation's problems were caused by their religious leaders. Some of the messages Jeremiah brought as a young preacher contained sharp rebukes of the prophets and priests.

Jeremiah's preaching made both groups uncomfortable. He saw through their sham, hypocrisy, and greed and attacked them openly. Since Jeremiah was from a priestly family, he is an example of a priest who felt the call of God to be a prophet. He could see from both perspectives.

E Jeremiah's Conflict with a False Prophet (28:1–17)

SUPPORTING IDEA: *Prophets of God should be open-minded but not be swayed by anyone who attempts to compromise God's message.*

This chapter is a sequel to the previous chapter. It fits appropriately within the larger collection of six chapters. It begins with a message about the

Jews who had already gone into Babylonian exile (ch. 24) and ends with a letter to them (ch. 29). The final seven verses of chapter 27 contain Jeremiah's rebuke of the false prophets as a class; this chapter records his conflict with an individual false prophet.

28:1–4. Since Hananiah, like Jeremiah, was a Benjamite, and his name meant "Yahweh has been gracious," some contend he was a good but misinformed man. But in my judgment his actions are too arrogant to justify that verdict. His message contradicted everything Jeremiah had been preaching for years. He not only minimized the seriousness of Judah's crisis but went so far as to limit the stay of the group of exiles in Babylon. He claimed that within two years Yahweh would **break the yoke** of Nebuchadnezzar, **bring back . . . the articles** taken away, and restore **Jehoiachin** as king.

28:5–11. Jeremiah wanted to believe Hananiah. No one wants to see his native land spoiled or his fellow citizens taken as captives to a foreign land. His **Amen** had the effect of saying, "Good. Let it come to be. There's nothing I'd like better than seeing what you have said come true." This shows the prophet's honesty and flexibility.

But looking at another person's viewpoint does not mean forsaking your own. Jeremiah still had a word of warning. The few who saw **peace** could only be declared to be true prophets if peace and prosperity came. Jeremiah's words were a challenge to Hananiah, who reasserted his position. He snatched the **yoke** from Jeremiah's shoulders and **broke it**. With a sneer he repeated his optimistic prediction: **Within two years** Yahweh would break **Babylon** and set the captives free. Jeremiah said nothing in reply but walked away.

28:12–17. Verse 12 suggests that Jeremiah spent more time in prayer and self-examination. Perhaps Hananiah spoke so convincingly that he almost persuaded Jeremiah he was correct. The prophet must have said to himself, "Am I wrong, Lord? Did I misunderstand you?" Yahweh gave him the reassurance he needed and in addition put a fresh word in his heart. He told the prophet to intensify the message with an **iron yoke** and even included a word about his sovereignty **over the wild animals**.

Jeremiah wasted no time in returning to Hananiah and his audience. This time he had no doubt or uncertainty. Fearlessly he reaffirmed his previous decree. Rather than returning within two years, Hananiah would die that very same year. The writer of the account added without comment, **In the seventh**

month of that same year, Hananiah the prophet died. This is one of the most amazing fulfillments of a prediction to be found in the Old Testament.

F Jeremiah Advises the Exiles in Babylon (29:1–32)

SUPPORTING IDEA: *When we find ourselves in adverse circumstances over which we have no control, we should wait on the Lord, trust his Word, and be patient.*

29:1–3. These verses give the setting for a lengthy **letter** from Jeremiah to those exiles who had already been taken to Babylon. He sent the letter by two prominent men whose fathers were friendly toward him in earlier years. Many Old Testament students suggest they may have been taking tribute money to **Nebuchadnezzar** from Zedekiah.

29:4–9. Jeremiah offered practical advice to the exiles. The essence of it was threefold. First, carry on a normal life. Do the things you would do if you were back in your own land. Provide a living place, arrange for food, and be satisfied with what you can get. Continue family life in the usual way. Encourage your children to do the same, even beginning their own families. Second, refrain from any rebellion against the government of the land in which you live. Be good citizens. Recognize as it prospers that you will also. Third, refuse to believe the false prophets who, claiming to have a message from Yahweh, are causing you to dream unrealistic dreams.

29:10–14. In these verses Yahweh announced, through Jeremiah, his plan for the people's future. He would **fulfill** them but only after **seventy years** had passed. This was the time he allotted to Babylon before this nation fell to another world power.

Yahweh assured the prophet and the people that he had not forgotten the reason for Israel and Judah's existence. He would provide for their present needs, both temporal and spiritual. At some time in the **future**, they would be ready for deliverance and further blessings. When this occurred, he would be available for them.

Yahweh was not specific on how complete and thorough their national commitment must be before he brought them back to their homeland. They did undergo a transformation during the exile and learned valuable lessons. One of my college professors listed what he called three important results of the exile—(1) a thorough purging of idolatrous rituals in worship and acceptance of monotheism, (2) the rise of synagogues as teaching institutions, and

(3) a deeper longing for their Messiah. This does not mean the Jews were without error after that, but they did learn those valuable lessons.

In verse 14, Yahweh promised to bring back home not only those in Babylon but also those in other places, which he called **all the nations**. Some see this as an unfulfilled prophecy until 1948 when the doors of Palestine were open to Jews from all over the world. Others contend it referred only to the Jews of Jeremiah's day who were dispersed over much of the known world.

29:15–19. Jeremiah anticipated how his words would be received and warned the people about the **prophets** who were preaching a message different from his own. Like the hard-nosed Judaizers of Paul's day, the false prophets continued to press their position. In this case some of them had even infiltrated **Babylon**.

Jeremiah's message to the exiles was the same as that to the people who remained in the homeland. He even used the illustration of "poor figs" to convey his point. The Hebrew word translated **listened** in verse 19 means more than "to hear." It signifies "to hear with obedience." The same horrible things of which the prophet warned those who rejected Yahweh's words would be visited upon those in Babylon who followed their example.

29:20–23. To make his message even more explicit, Jeremiah became specific about two men who were misleading the people in Babylon. We know nothing about these men—**Ahab son of Kolaiah and Zedekiah son of Maaseiah**—except the facts stated here. Jeremiah delivered Yahweh's message to them: **Nebuchadnezzar** would **put them to death** publicly. This would cause a custom to arise among the people. When they wished to bestow a curse on someone, they would say in essence, "May **the LORD treat you like** he treated **Zedekiah and Ahab**."

29:24–28. Jeremiah had a good relationship with many priests who had been left in Jerusalem. He found out that **Shemaiah**, a false prophet in Babylon, had **sent** a letter to Zephaniah, who had been elevated to chief priest. He also sent it to **all the other priests** and to **all the people**. In the letter he had told Zephaniah he should put Jeremiah in **stocks and neck-irons** for acting like a **madman**. He referred to the things Jeremiah had told the exiles in the letter he had written to them (29:5).

29:29–32. **Shemaiah** did not have the clout with **Zephaniah** that he thought he had. The priest showed the letter to Jeremiah. The prophet sought Yahweh's direction and probably received it immediately. The divine mandate was simple and sharp. The words **will have no one left among this people** indicated thorough elimination of the false prophet and his family. The further statement, **nor will he see the good things I will do**, could suggest that he would die soon.

As we conclude the commentary on these six chapters, serious reflection reveals that a twofold thought pervades all of them. First, God has a future for his people. He will not cast them off. The promise to Abraham is still in effect. Second, in the meantime, the people must be patient. God controls his own agenda, and that includes his timetable. Wait on the Lord, trust his word, and be patient.

MAIN IDEA REVIEW: *Regardless of how discouraging a situation becomes, God is with his people. When the outlook gets dark enough, stars will come out.*

III. CONCLUSION

Be Careful Whom You Listen To

When your life is in disruption and disarray, it is always easier to listen to someone who tells you what you want to hear. Such was the situation in Judah with the Babylonian attacks on and conquest of the Davidic kingdom. Two large groups of key leaders, officials, and royalty already had been taken into exile. Questions arose about the exiles' future and how long the current situation would last. Hananiah, a false prophet, told the people that everything would be back to normal in two years. Jeremiah informed the people that the captivity would last seventy years, that those taken into exile were the real future of the nation, and that those exiles should settle down and adapt to their new surroundings.

In the midst of disruption, it is not always easy to discern who is offering the best advice and what one should do about it. Watch out for those who tell you what you want to hear. Sometimes it is in the more difficult counsel that God's will is expressed. And while God's plan for us may not be what we want to hear at the time, we can depend on the Lord's promise that he seeks the best for his people. He offers hope and a future, even when there does not seem to be any future in sight.

PRINCIPLES

- Displaced persons are not always those who have nothing to offer their society. Sometimes they represent the true heart of a nation or culture.

- A nation's current leaders are not always those who represent the future of that nation.

- True prophets must proclaim the word of the Lord faithfully even if those to whom they preach refuse to listen.

- God sometimes uses those who do not acknowledge him to rebuke or punish his people.

- All nations, whether they recognize the Lord or not, will be held accountable to him for their actions.

- Repentance is the proper response to hearing the word of the Lord.

- Not everyone who claims to speak in the name of the Lord has a message from the Lord.

- Exiles, displaced persons, and the uprooted sometimes need to settle down and adapt to a new country and homeland, a new culture and customs, and a new language and lifestyle in order to preserve their heritage and descendants.

APPLICATIONS

- Summarize the issues being debated about refugees and immigrants. State the major positions on these issues. In what ways does God's Word inform this debate?

- Write down some specific ways you and your church could make a positive difference in relating to refugees and immigrants.

- Pray for our nation's leaders. Pray that by the lives they live and the decisions they make they will represent the future of our nation in the best possible way.

- Encourage those who are proclaiming the Word of the Lord faithfully in spite of their hearers' unwillingness to listen.

- Since God sometimes uses those who do not acknowledge him to punish his people, ask yourself, Has anyone called me to account for something I have done that is not consistent with my profession of faith? How did I feel about it? What did I do about it?

IV. LIFE APPLICATION

The Lost Boys of Sudan

Many peoples today have been displaced from their homelands. Sometimes these displacements are the result of natural disasters; other times they have been caused by wars and aggression. Perhaps no group of exiles in recent years has captured the world's attention like the "lost boys of Sudan." The Sudan has experienced one of the most brutal civil wars of the twentieth century. Over two million people were killed or died from famine or diseases in the 1970s and 1980s. Four to five million persons were displaced as the Arab-dominated Islamic government of the north fought against the undeveloped Christian and black African population of the south. Government forces burned hundreds of villages in southern Sudan, stole livestock, and decimated families.

Orphaned and forced from their southern Sudan villages, about thirty thousand Sudanese boys, ages seven to seventeen, banded together and started walking. For two months they walked across the Sudan to Ethiopia. They spent three years in refugee camps in Ethiopia until a change in that government in May 1991 sent Ethiopian tanks and militia to drive them out. Heavy rains had swollen the River Gilo. In seeking to escape, thousands drowned, were shot by the militia, or were eaten by crocodiles.

Mostly Dinka and Nuer youth, the surviving boys found themselves back in the Sudan. They began walking again. They walked for more than a year through the Sudan toward Kenya. Thousands more died along the way. Overcome by dehydration and fatigue, many fell prey to lions and other ferocious beasts. The boys sucked moisture from the mud and ate leaves and wild berries. Only about ten thousand survived the journey.

For nine years the boys subsisted in a Kenyan refugee camp. Then about four thousand of the lost boys were granted permanent resettlement in the United States. Suddenly these Dinka and Nuer cattle herders were living in Seattle, Richmond, Grand Rapids, Boston, Nashville, New Port Richey, and other American cities. They were given three months to support themselves. Most had never seen an electric stove, a microwave, a subway, or snow. They had never cooked meals, applied for jobs, earned an income, or driven a car. Many became discouraged, homesick, and depressed.

Fortunately, people of good will, Christians, and charity organizations stepped in to help. Many of the boys prepared for and passed the GED. Some pursued college degrees. Gradually they became acclimated to American culture. The lost boys of Sudan have adapted to their new cultures, and many of them have prospered.

The lost boys of Sudan are a contemporary example of what Jeremiah centuries before told the Jewish exiles after their trek to Babylon:

> Build houses and settle down; plant gardens and eat what they produce. Marry and have sons and daughters; find wives for your sons and give your daughters in marriage, so that they too may have sons and daughters. Increase in number there; do not decrease. Also, seek the peace and prosperity of the city to which I have carried you into exile. Pray to the LORD for it, because if it prospers, you too will prosper (29:5–7).

Sometimes the Lord uses job loss, plant closings, company transfers, divorce, natural disasters, and other crises that result in a forced relocation to preserve us and to accomplish his plan in our lives. Although all such transitions are difficult and painful, we should seek to reestablish normalcy in our new location as soon as possible. Even if we do not understand why events have happened as they have in our lives, we should place our trust in the Lord's promise, "'I know the plans I have for you,' declares the LORD, 'plans to prosper you and not to harm you, plans to give you hope and a future'" (29:11).

V. PRAYER

Heavenly Father, sometimes our lives get turned upside down. Our carefully laid plans are dashed. Our home and all that is familiar to us are taken away, changed. Disruption, a relocation, a forced move comes into our lives. To us, these experiences often seem like dead ends. We waver in our trust. We become unsettled. Teach us instead to turn to you and seek your wisdom about what you would have us do in each of our life circumstances, situations, and changing locations. Help us to cleave to your promise that you will give us hope and a future. Amen.

VI. DEEPER DISCOVERIES

A. Wooden Yoke and Yoke of Iron (28:13)

Alexander Maclaren, eminent expositor of Scripture, gives provocative insights into this verse. After briefly presenting the background of Jeremiah's conflict with Hananiah, he draws some excellent lessons with a threefold approach.

Though metaphorical, Maclaren suggests a contrast in practical life of the truths represented by "yokes of wood" and "yokes of iron." His basic thesis is that everyone must yield to some kind of control. He expresses it this way: "To throw off legitimate authority is to bind on a worse tyranny. To some kind of yoke all of us must bind our necks, and if we slip them out we do not thereby become independent, but simply bring upon ourselves a heavier pressure of a harder bondage" (p. 323).

Wooden yoke of law and iron yoke of lawlessness. We cannot hold society together without some kind of restrictions on what can and cannot be done. Maclaren explains that cells in a honeycomb are circles squeezed by the pressure of the adjacent cells into the hexagonal shape which admits of contiguity. If they continued to be circles, space and material would be lost, and there would be no complete continuity. So you cannot hold people together without some kind of limitations shaped into a law. We must accept that yoke for the larger good. To refuse that law brings on even more serious consequences.

Wooden yoke of virtue and iron yoke of vice. Every person carries within his nature a law that binds and impresses every fiber of his being. It is greater than any written law. Just as the base of a pyramid is nearest to the ground, so these cravings appeal to the lower parts of our nature. We are bound by the law of our desires, aches, and lusts. If we refuse to accept the law of virtue and discipline, we become bound by the law of vice. We must choose which one we will obey—the law of virtue or the law of vice. Both are yokes. We must choose by which one we will be fettered.

Wooden yoke of Jesus or the iron yoke of godlessness. Do you feel this contrast is too harsh? Put it another way. We have the choice of accepting Jesus as the only full, complete revelation of God or wandering out into the wasteland of uncertainty and relativity. A theism that refuses to accept the historic revelation of God in Jesus Christ as "the master-light of all our seeing" is verbally crippled. It has no message to bring a world now filled with religious diversity. Either Jesus Christ arose from the dead or he did not arise from the dead. It is that simple and yet that profound. In the words of Elijah, "If the LORD is God, follow him; but if Baal is God, follow him" (1 Kgs. 18:21).

You must choose Jesus, who may be compared to the "yoke of wood," or be enslaved by the "yoke of iron." Remember, Jesus said, "Come to me. . . . Take my yoke upon you. . . . My yoke is easy and my burden is light" (Matt. 11:28–30).

B. "You will . . . find me when you seek me with all your heart" (29:13)

In 1940, I (Fred Wood) enrolled as a freshman at Union University and attended my first chapel service. The speaker was Dr. Robert J. Bateman, pastor at that time of the First Baptist Church, Memphis. He said, "Young people, do you know the difference between religion and Christianity? I can tell you in one sentence." He then summarized it this way: "Religion is man seeking a god. Christianity is God seeking a man."

This truth thrills us, but we need to see another side of the picture. Jesus never comes into our heart as an uninvited guest. Another fact needs to receive our attention also. To "seek God with all our heart" means more than a superficial prayer for Jesus merely to "come into my heart." The word translated "heart" means the entire life, every part of our personality. To seek God with all our heart means committing ourselves to the same goals in life for which he lived and died.

Have you sought Jesus with all your heart? You will never be complete in life and happy for eternity until you do.

VII. TEACHING OUTLINE

A. INTRODUCTION

1. Lead Story: Peace in Our Time

2. Context: After two waves of deportations of Judean exiles to Babylon, the Lord revealed to Jeremiah that those who had been dislocated were those through whom the future of their nation would be preserved. He called these exiles the "good figs." Jeremiah wrote to the exiles and told them not to listen to false prophets who told them they would return home soon. The prophet advised them to settle down in their new surroundings and reestablish normalcy in their lives. In the future, after seventy years (25:11–12; 29:10), they and their descendants would return from exile.

3. Transition: No matter what the cause or reason, when people's lives are disrupted and they are forced to relocate, they wonder, *What will happen to us? Will we come back to our city, our town, our home? Will our lives ever be normal again?* These questions were in the minds of the exiles in Babylon about whom Jeremiah prophesied and to whom he wrote a letter.

B. COMMENTARY
1. Jeremiah's Vision of Good and Bad Figs (24:1–10)
2. God's Discipline and Wrath (25:1–38)
3. Second Account of the Temple Sermon (26:1–24)
4. Warning About Plotting Against Babylon (27:1–22)
5. Jeremiah's Conflict with a False Prophet (28:1–17)
6. Jeremiah Advises the Exiles in Babylon (29:1–32)

C. CONCLUSION: BE CAREFUL WHOM YOU LISTEN TO

VIII. ISSUES FOR DISCUSSION

1. How can hearers determine whether someone who claims to have a message from the Lord really does—especially if they are hearing conflicting and competing messages?

2. To what extent should displaced or exiled persons settle down into a new culture and adopt their ways? To what extent should they seek to hold themselves apart from their environment and seek to preserve

their own ways and traditions? What principles might the church glean about its relationship to the world from Jeremiah's letter to the exiles (29:4–7)?

3. How can we determine when God is behind world events and the aggressive actions of nations to accomplish his purposes in the world?

Jeremiah 30:1–33:26

The New Covenant

I. INTRODUCTION
I Have a Dream

II. COMMENTARY
A verse-by-verse explanation of these verses.

III. CONCLUSION
Hope Makes All the Difference

An overview of the principles and applications from these verses.

IV. LIFE APPLICATION
Tornado!

Melding these verses to life.

V. PRAYER
Tying these verses to life with God.

VI. DEEPER DISCOVERIES
Historical, geographical, and grammatical enrichment of the commentary.

VII. TEACHING OUTLINE
Suggested step-by-step group study of these verses.

VIII. ISSUES FOR DISCUSSION
Zeroing these verses in on daily life.

Quote

"It is not that we think we can do anything of lasting value by ourselves. Our only power and success come from God. He is the one who has enabled us to represent his new covenant. This is a covenant, not of written laws, but of the Spirit. The old way ends in death; in the new way, the Holy Spirit gives life."

2 Corinthians 3:5–6 (NLT)

Jeremiah 30:1–33:26

IN A NUTSHELL

Jeremiah 30–33 is known as the "Book of Consolation" or the "Book of Comfort." In these chapters Jeremiah holds out hope, healing, and rehabilitation for both Judah and Israel. He speaks of spiritual renewal of their minds and hearts, of God remembering their sins no more, of a new covenant, and of restoration to their land. The covenant God promises to cleanse them, do good to them, and cause them to prosper. The oracles in chapters 30 and 31 are in poetic form; chapters 32 and 33 are written in prose.

The New Covenant

I. INTRODUCTION

I Have a Dream

The two foundational documents of American democracy—the Declaration of Independence and the Constitution—proclaim equality, the unalienable rights of liberty and justice, and the blessings of liberty to future generations. Yet this covenant was flawed from the start. The declaration's "self-evident truth" that all men are created equal was not self-evident at all. For demographic and representative purposes, the Constitution declared that slaves were counted as only three-fifths of a person. Further, the Constitution permitted the slave trade to continue and authorized an import tax on such persons.

Over 175 years later, in August 1963, more than two hundred thousand persons marched on Washington to claim their unalienable rights. Martin Luther King Jr. declared, "When the architects of our republic wrote the magnificent words of the Constitution and the Declaration of Independence, they were signing a promissory note to which every American was to fall heir. . . . It is obvious today that America has defaulted on this promissory note insofar as her citizens of color are concerned."

Dr. King called for a renewed covenant in America—one that would reflect a new spirit, a renewed spirit of the heart. He dreamed of a day when society would be transformed and people would no longer "be judged by the color of their skin but by the content of their character."

So it was in Jeremiah's day. The nations of Israel and Judah had entered into a covenant with God hundreds of years earlier. But the people had long been unfaithful to the terms, ideals, and conditions of that covenant. As nations and as individuals they had broken the covenant obligations. There was a price to be paid for such failure. The debt had now come due. It was time to pay up.

But there was good news. Jeremiah announced a new covenant—a covenant in which the true spirit of the covenant would be realized, a covenant that would change the hearts and character of the people, a covenant that would make them truly God's people. This announcement is a high point of

Old Testament revelation and one that leads us straight to its New Testament fulfillment.

II. COMMENTARY

The New Covenant

MAIN IDEA: *Above everything else, Yahweh is a God of comfort. He disciplines his people when he must, but he never forsakes them.*

To deal in superlatives is always precarious. But there is no other way to describe chapters 30–33 of Jeremiah. These four chapters contain a collection of the major material that deals with his hope for Israel and Judah's future.

A person who studies this section must recognize its twofold division. Chapters 30–31 contain prophetic discourses, oracles, or sermons. The material is almost entirely in poetical form with only scattered verses of connecting prose. Chapters 32–33 contain historical material in narrative form almost exclusively with only a small number of verses in poetical form. The chapter division is very fortunate in both major sections. A brief overview of the contents should help greatly by forming a background for the ensuing exposition of the material.

Chapter 30 contains material dealing with both Israel and Judah. It opens with a picture of the judgment coming upon them. Beginning with verse 8 and continuing through the rest of the chapter, Jeremiah delivers God's promises for coming days. Yahweh's people will later be delivered from captivity and restored to their own land, and their enemies will be destroyed.

Chapter 31 continues God's assurance of a glorious future for his people. As the chapter progresses, the emphasis moves toward the spiritual blessings awaiting the people. The latter half of the chapter (vv. 27–40) contains the new covenant that Yahweh will make with his people. Many interpreters consider this passage the zenith of Old Testament revelation.

Chapter 32 and the one following it have been called the "prose counterpart" to chapters 30–31. They are narrative in contrast to the two preceding chapters, which are prophetic oracles. The first part of chapter 32 (vv. 1–15) records Jeremiah's purchase of property in Anathoth. The remaining part (vv. 16–44) contains a dialogue between Jeremiah and Yahweh about the reason for and significance of the purchase.

Chapter 33 gives more words of Yahweh to Jeremiah about the nation's future restoration. Although he did not specifically command the prophet to deliver the words to Israel and Judah, the implication is clear that this was his intention.

The Good Things God Will Do for His People (30:1–24)

SUPPORTING IDEA: *Yahweh will not forsake his people permanently. He has chosen them for a mission and will continue to work with them to accomplish the goal he has in mind.*

30:1–3. These verses contain more than an introduction to chapter 30. They form a prologue or foreword to the entire section that extends through chapter 33. Yahweh desired for these chapters to be set apart as a unit of Jeremiah's prophecies.

The declaration **days are coming** was one of Jeremiah's favorite expressions. He used it elsewhere to announce judgment (7:32; 9:25; 19:6; 48:12; 49:2; 51:52). Also, however, it appears as indicating future blessings (16:14; 23:5–7; 31:27,31,38; 33:14). One interpreter contends Jeremiah used it to introduce a major point. The promise to **bring . . . back from captivity** applies to both Israel and Judah.

30:4–7. Even though Jacob (Israel and Judah) **will be saved out of** (v. 7) a time of trouble, the experience will be horrible. Verses 5–7 paint a gruesome picture. Yahweh warns that the **cries** the people are hearing do not represent **peace**, but panic, dismay, and fright. The two rhetorical questions in verse 6 utilize a striking metaphor. Few experiences are as painful as labor pains in childbirth. This is how Jeremiah pictured Israel's and Judah's suffering at the hands of the Assyrian and Babylonian armies.

30:8–11. The next four verses enlarge this promise and go further into the blessings awaiting the people. The expression **break the yoke off their necks** is a figure borrowed from the encounter of Jeremiah with Hananiah in chapter 28. The promise to raise up David their king should not be interpreted to mean a bodily resurrection for the dead king.

God's liberation of his people from their enemies doesn't mean that Israel and Judah would have political dominion over the foes who had exploited them. The supreme purpose was that Israel and Judah would recognize Yahweh as their Lord. In verse 10, Jacob for the first time is called **my servant** and identified with Israel. Students have found some similarities with passages in Isaiah's prophecies (Isa. 41:8–10,13–14; 43:1,5; 44:1–2). We find unmistakably parallel phrases. Verse 11, on the other hand, contain expressions that are found elsewhere in Jeremiah (1:8,19; 4:27; 5:10,18; 10:24; 25:29).

Throughout the Old Testament we find repeated in several places the thought that because Yahweh is with Israel, the people should not fear (Isa. 17:2; Mic. 4:4; Zeph. 3:13; Ezek. 34:28; 39:26; Lev. 26:6; Job 11:19). As God destroys the nations that took Israel and Judah into captivity, he promises not to destroy Israel and Judah but to **discipline** them **with justice**.

30:12–17. Yahweh uses both medical and legal terminology to describe Israel and Judah's condition. They are like an incurable **wound**, an **injury** that won't heal. They are like defendants in court whose attorney has abandoned them. What about friends on whom they could count for assistance? None were to be found. Some versions speak in verse 14 of **allies**. The HCSB, however, translates "lovers," which is the literal meaning of the Hebrew word.

Among the most prominent group would have been Egypt and possibly Edom (Obad. 9–14). Egypt had continually encouraged Judah to rebel against Babylon. This had been characteristic, for a number of years, of that great nation to the south. The suggestion was politically motivated. Judah provided a perfect buffer between Egypt and any invading army from the east such as Assyria or Babylon.

True, Egypt sent an army to help Judah in her resistance to Babylon, as in the days of Isaiah when Sennacherib threatened Jerusalem. But both times they were ineffective. In Isaiah's day Yahweh intervened when Hezekiah fell on his face before God and prayed. But this time Yahweh would allow the enemy to be victorious **because of** Judah's **great guilt and many sins.**

In verse 16 the prophet, speaking for Yahweh, suddenly changed his outlook. He saw the approaching storm, but he also saw beyond it. God's final word to his people through the prophets was not doom. Almost every prophet concluded his recorded messages with a word of hope for the future.

Verses 16–17 not only declare Judah's enemies would **be devoured, go into exile, be plundered** and despoiled, but they also spell out the reason they must suffer.

First, they had done their work in order to hurt God's people. They were not conscious that they were tools in Yahweh's hand, but they were motivated by pride and greed, seeking booty and gain for themselves. These self-seeking people knew nothing about Yahweh's redemptive plan for the world. They had no idea he was using them to discipline his chosen people. But Yahweh would discard them as soon as they finished their task.

Second, they jeered at Jerusalem. They not only plundered but scoffed, taunted, and insulted the people whom God had chosen as his channel through whom the Messiah would come. They also called God's people **an outcast, Zion for whom no one cares**.

The glorious truth of this section is that Yahweh would restore his people to health. He would heal their wounds, which had been called incurable. The Great Physician of the New Testament is prefigured in this prophetic promise. Truly, the new is in the old concealed. The old is in the new revealed. It is the Lord's work—and glorious in his eyes.

30:18–22. The remaining verses in chapter 30 (vv. 18–24) speak with comforting words to Yahweh's people. We find no condemnation or rebuke of Israel and Judah. This section deals with the good things that Yahweh will send them. The last two verses (vv. 23–24) close the poem with a graphic description of the fate awaiting those who pillaged and plundered God's people.

Jeremiah began his beautiful picture of God's gracious restoration with the affirmation of a dwelling place. The first thing people need for happiness is a place to live with their families. Old Testament writers used the word translated **tents** either literally or as a symbolic term for "clans." Both were important to Israel in their nomadic life. (Notice Balaam's words in Num. 24:5–6.)

Following a pattern of thought often used by the prophets, Jeremiah spoke poetically as though each place of dwelling had an independent existence. When Yahweh saw them lying desolate on the hill where they had once sat, he yearned to give them life again. The word translated **ruins** is from an ancient word *tel* which means a mound or heap. It was a place where the ruins of a destroyed or abandoned city were found. This term is applied to areas built up by successive settlement at a single site.

Many scholars suggest the words translated **city** and **palace** refer to Jerusalem and the royal palace. They say this is a strong possibility since Jeremiah later said a "prince" (**leader**) and a **ruler** would **arise** (v. 21).

Having dealt with the structures (v. 18), Jeremiah next (vv. 19–21) gave a glowing picture of the people's renewed lifestyle. Jewish culture, a major part of which came from her religious background, was one of exuberant happiness and spirited praise to Yahweh. The religious observances were, for the most part, called "feasts" or "festivals." When Yahweh restored his people's fortunes, they would burst forth with spontaneous gratitude, praise, and celebration.

To the Jewish mind of that day, one evidence of Yahweh's approval was the sending of children to bless the home. Large families helped cultivate the land, and many sons provided as military assistance in potential conflicts with invaders. One of the rewards awaiting the restored community would be that they would no longer be subject to foreign political domination. Their leader or ruler would be from their own community. He would be chosen by Yahweh.

Some interpreters feel these words speak of a time when the office of king and priest would be combined. If so, that would give this passage messianic overtones. This suggestion is made because of the statement, **I will bring him near and he will come close to me, for who is he who will devote himself to be close to me?**

The rationale for the suggestion is that according to Jewish theology and practice, to enter the divine presence unbidden was to risk death. In this passage, the ruler appeared to be undertaking a priestly function rather than a political role. Who would dare to do such a thing unless he was certain he was approved by Yahweh?

Verse 22 closes this subsection with a summary statement. Because of the facts declared by the prophet, the people can be assured of one truth: In the future they will stand once more in favor with Yahweh as his special people. Then they can get back into the mainstream of living and serving their God.

30:23–24. These two verses repeat a statement Jeremiah had made in one of his previous messages (23:19–20). On the earlier occasion he applied them to the false prophets, but here the prophet directed them to the Gentile enemies. Many interpreters claim that he had in mind especially wicked Babylon. For several centuries this city stood unrivaled. At one time, Alexander the Great had planned to make it his royal city. But it eventually became a heap of ruins. Few words in Jeremiah's recorded messages express as clearly his mind about the doom that comes from human wickedness.

The concluding and summarizing thought is profound. God has a goal in history for which he is working, and he will not be turned from it. He wishes to bring his creation back to himself. The closer we draw to him in fellowship and service, the more we realize its truth. When we adopt his goal as our own, events become not only endurable but enjoyable.

Ⓑ The Covenant That God Will Make with His People (31:1–40)

SUPPORTING IDEA: *God unfolds the ultimate method by which he will reveal himself in redemptive history, the highest point of his revelation preceding the incarnation.*

This chapter is one of the most important in the Bible. It is the climax of all Jeremiah's recorded messages. What chapter 53 is to the Book of Isaiah and chapter 11 to the Book of Hosea, so chapter 31 is to Jeremiah.

This chapter unfolds into two sections. The first division (vv. 1–26) serves as a lengthy prelude to what Old Testament students call the new covenant. Verses 1–22 deal with the Northern Kingdom's restoration while verses 23–26 speak of the Southern Kingdom. According to verse 26, God may have revealed his message to Jeremiah in a dream. In Old Testament days God did sometimes convey his message in dreams. But today he communicates to his people through the Scriptures and the Holy Spirit.

The second division of this chapter (vv. 27–40) is a body of Scripture almost universally recognized as the new covenant. It serves as a complement to the Suffering Servant passage of Isaiah 53 (actually 52:13–53:12). No passage in the Old Testament rises to the heights of spiritual discernment as movingly and with as much heartfelt appeal. Where the Isaiah passage presents the transactional or external side of salvation, this passage from Jeremiah emphasizes the inwardness of the experience. Jeremiah, more than any Old Testament prophet, prefigured the heart of Jesus.

31:1–6. Many Old Testament students contend that verse 1 should be a part of the preceding chapter. The Hebrew text agrees with this interpretation. Actually, no theological point is at issue in this matter, and the verse can effectively serve as the termination of the first message or the start of this chapter.

Although a few interpreters suggest that Jeremiah referred, in verse 2, to the exodus from Egypt, this is not the majority opinion. He meant primarily the inhabitants of the Northern Kingdom who had suffered defeat and deportation by Assyria. In addition, the message applied to the citizens of Judah who would be carried away to Babylon. Each would find mercy. This was done by Yahweh as a sovereign act of his grace.

On the other hand, we should not rule out totally any allusion to the exodus. The Hebrew text of verse 2 contains two analogies. It looks back to the Egyptian exodus, alluding to how God provided for his people's need in the desert. It looks forward to the Babylonian exodus. Some suggest an interesting contrast. The phrase **find favor in the desert** seems to speak of the Egyptian exodus while **survive the sword** seems to look ahead to return from the exile.

Some grammarians add to this thought. The verbs in verses 2 and 3 are in the perfect tense, denoting completed action. They could be either historical past verbs or prophetic perfects, indicating future completed action. Beginning with verse 4, they switch back to the imperfect form, denoting an action not yet completed, usually rendered as future tense in English.

The prophet probably was emphasizing a profound yet simple thought. God was pointing to the Egyptian exodus as a pattern or prototype of what he would do for the people in the Babylonian exodus. He had cared for them in the wilderness under Moses; in the same way he would care for them in their new wilderness experience when they would be delivered from Babylon.

Following this interpretation, the phrase **I have loved you with an everlasting love; I have drawn you with loving-kindness** refers to the Sinai experience. **I will build you up again** refers to the Babylonian exodus.

In verses 4–6, Jeremiah brings a joyful message to Israel. Yahweh will restore the dispersed people to their homeland. The prophet directed his words particularly to the Northern Kingdom. Life will be as it was before the Assyrian invasion. He actually spoke of the kingdom as **Virgin Israel**, a term usually associated with Zion. Jeremiah even promised a day when the Northern Kingdom would return to Jerusalem for worship. The nation would be reunited.

31:7–14. This lengthy section pictures how the returning captives sang with joyful hearts and faces aglow because of Yahweh's goodness. Exuberance characterized the people as they looked forward to being home again. Among the promises God made was a multitude of people with an anticipation of a larger population. He assured them of a safe and peaceful journey.

Social life in the restored nation would be jubilant for young **maidens** and **men** of all ages. Happiness would replace gloom. Freedom from pain and delight would replace grief and misery. Because of material prosperity and renewed religious activity in the land, even the **priests** would share in the **bounty** since the people would be generous. In short, the people would lack no good thing.

31:15–22. This section continues the comforting words of the prophet to the people. Jeremiah began by presenting the trauma of captivity in a foreign land (v. 15). He then delivered Yahweh's word of assurance, urging the people to **restrain** their grief. Yahweh will take note of them and bring them back **from the land** to which they have been taken (vv. 16–17). In verses 18–19, the prophet gives voice to the people's repentance, which he says the Lord has noted. Jeremiah then returns (vv. 20–22) to continue Yahweh's promise to deliver the people because of his love for them.

Jeremiah presents these truths by analogy of **Rachel**, mother of Benjamin and grandmother of both Ephraim and Manasseh. Because of her contact with the Northern and Southern Kingdoms through these three boys, she served as a symbol to both divisions of the nation.

Rachel's lament symbolized a parent watching her rebellious children punished by being carried away captive. She feared they would never again be a nation. The historical Rachel died, having given birth to Benjamin. She named him Ben-Oni or "Son of my trouble" (see Gen. 35:18). Rachel's agony in the birth of Benjamin later became a symbol of Israel's waiting painfully but patiently for the Messiah while in exile in a foreign land.

31:23–26. In these verses, Jeremiah, for the first time in chapter 31, indicated that Judah would have a part in the restoration. The expression **when I bring them back from captivity** in verse 23 indicates that at the time Jeremiah spoke, Judah lay in a state of desolation. Verse 26 serves as a bridge to what is the highest peak of Jeremiah's prophecies. Scholars call the remaining material in this chapter the new covenant.

What about Jeremiah's statement in verse 26 about waking up? Did God reveal verses 1–25 to him in a dream, or was the material revealed to him in the dream contained in verses 27–40, or both—or neither? The fact of revelation and the fact of inspiration are true. The method or methods by which God conveyed his truth are not always disclosed.

31:27–30. The remainder of this chapter (vv. 27–40) deals specifically with the new covenant. The material should be divided into three parts (vv. 27–30,31–34,38–40), with an interlude (vv. 35–37) between the second and third part. In the interlude Jeremiah delivers Yahweh's oath of affirmation and assurance that what he says will be performed.

Each of these main parts begins with the same statement, though for some reason the NIV translators chose to vary the second one slightly. In the Hebrew text, all three are identical. The HCSB renders it the same way each time: "The days are coming."

Jeremiah began the first of Yahweh's three-part covenant with a statement of his intention to repopulate the land with both people and animals. Reflect back to the call experience (1:10). The prophet declared the twofold commission given to him. First, Yahweh had appointed him **to uproot and tear down, overthrow** and **destroy.** Here Jeremiah added **bring disaster,** words which are not recorded in the call experience. This had been accomplished. Yahweh was now ready to fulfill the second half—**to build and to plant.**

Verse 29 contains the heart of this covenant's first part. It deals with personal responsibility. A saying had arisen in Israel about the relationship of parent to child with reference to sin. Before Yahweh could restore the nation, the people must deal with this important issue. Jeremiah faced it squarely as did his contemporary, Ezekiel (Ezek. 18:2). The dilemma arose from the fact that Israel and Judah clung to a proverb the people had developed in their misinterpretation of such passages as Exodus 20:5b: "I, the LORD your God, am a jealous God, punishing the children for the sin of the fathers to the third and fourth generation of those who hate me."

The people were using their interpretation of this verse as an excuse for their sinful lifestyle. Their reasoning was, "Since we are victims of the system, we are not responsible for our sins." Jeremiah rejected this attitude. To us, such an attitude seems ludicrous. But in Jeremiah's day it was common. It stemmed from the idea of corporate responsibility in family life. But Jeremiah insisted that in the coming **days** only the individual who sinned would be punished. No longer would an entire nation be held responsible for the sins of a person within it.

31:31–34. These verses deal with the second of this covenant's three parts. Jeremiah's theme is related to the inwardness of religious faith during the new era of God's revelation of himself. It will differ from the one made at Sinai shortly after the exodus from Egypt. Rather than giving the people laws and ceremonies they must obey, God will work a transformation of the heart of each believer. The parallels to our Christian faith are obvious. Implicit in the prophet's words is the new birth of which Jesus spoke in his interview with Nicodemus (John 3).

The phrase **no longer will a man teach his neighbor . . . because they will all know me** does not suggest that the instructional part of religion is no longer relevant. The word *know* means intimate experience. In the new era every person will be his or her own priest because everyone will have a genuine experience of salvation and assurance of forgiven sin. Peace with God in this area is essential for fellowship with him. To put it in theological language, justification must precede regeneration—or neither is genuine.

31:35–37. In order to emphasize the certainty of Yahweh's love for his people and the certainty of his protective power, Jeremiah interjected words of assurance. The survival of Israel is as certain as the laws of nature that God has ordained. Jeremiah added a second proof of Yahweh's determination to preserve Israel. For him to cast her off was as impossible as a person being able to measure **the heavens** or discover the depth **of the earth**.

The expression **because of all they have done** refers to Israel's evil deeds. In spite of them, God's love is assured. Israel is still his people and always will be. His new creation, "the Israel of God" (Gal. 6:16), brought into existence through his seed, Jesus Christ, remains a testimony of God's unquenchable love.

31:38–40. To the casual or superficial reader, these verses appear to be the most meaningless in the entire chapter. But further investigation and deeper meditation reveal that these are probably the most important in this segment of Jeremiah's prophecies. The text seems clear. God guaranteed Israel's indestructibility! But some students believe there is a different interpretation of this passage.

One school of thought insists on a literal fulfillment of the passage. The return from Babylonian captivity did not satisfy the requirements of verses 38–40. The fulfillment, therefore, rests in the future. Most people who hold this view believe also in an earthly reign of Christ for one thousand years with his throne at Jerusalem. In support of this position is the contention that God made a promise to Israel that has never been completely fulfilled. A further contention of this school is that the promise of God to Abraham was unconditional and has never been canceled. Therefore, a period exists in the future when Israel will once more occupy her land exclusively. This will be accompanied by unprecedented material prosperity and unparalleled fertility. But all interpreters do not agree with those who demand a literal fulfillment of these verses.

◖ Hope in a Hopeless Time (32:1–44)

SUPPORTING IDEA: *Regardless of how dark things look for Israel and Judah at present, God has better days ahead for his people.*

With Jerusalem having been surrounded by the Babylonian army for eighteen months, all hope for deliverance was nearly gone. The stubborn ultranationalistic group held out doggedly, but the masses knew it would soon be over. Judah was as doomed as Israel had been in 722 B.C. Property values plummeted. Everyone wanted to sell, but no one wanted to buy. One of the few persons who had not lost faith was Jeremiah. He was willing to buy a piece of property that any day might become the property of Babylon. That's what this chapter is about.

32:1–15. Jeremiah was confined to the **courtyard of the guard**, under what might today be called "house arrest." This was a place to keep prisoners who were not considered dangerous or had too much status to be confined to a dungeon. The prophet was not unlike Paul "in his own rented house" while awaiting trial in Rome (Acts 28:30). Jeremiah could receive visitors, as evidenced by the presence of Hanamel (v. 8).

When **Zedekiah** visited Jeremiah in the court of the guard, he pleaded with him, but the prophet held his ground. He warned Zedekiah that the city was doomed and the king himself would be taken prisoner.

The Lord spoke to Jeremiah about the coming visit of his cousin **Hanamel** (v. 7). **Then, just as the LORD had said**, Hanamel came to the place where Jeremiah was being held and offered to sell Jeremiah a **field** in their home village of **Anathoth**. Jeremiah recognized in the words of his cousin **that this was the word of the LORD**. Verses 9–15 give the details of the real estate transaction. Notice how carefully the deed to the property was recorded and preserved. This act was one of hope in the darkest of hours. It pointed forward to the time when God's people would be restored to the land and normal economic activity would resume.

32:16–25. Jeremiah responded to Yahweh's words in the form of a prayer. This prayer expressed the aspirations and emotions of the entire nation. It drew attention to the word of hope given to Jeremiah and served to express thanks for that hope.

As Jeremiah recounted the miraculous actions of Yahweh on the nation's behalf, he kept one fact in focus: the victories of Israel were not due to military prowess. They were because of God's sovereign power to work on behalf of his people. He delivered them from **Egypt** so he could bring them back to **this land** he had promised their **forefathers**—Abraham, Isaac, and Jacob. God controls history and works it to his purpose.

Jeremiah then turned to the present. One question puzzled him. He knew God was justified in handing the nation of Judah over to Babylon. God had blessed the people, but they had continued to reject him. But why did he tell Jeremiah to buy property in a land doomed to be conquered by the Babylonians?

32:26–44. These verses contain Yahweh's answer to Jeremiah's query. Yahweh reaffirmed Jeremiah's confession (v. 17) with a rhetorical question (v. 27). The Lord is unlimited and powerful. The people had **provoked** him with their various sins and must be punished. Yet Yahweh had another word. Punishment is not his last message. Because of Yahweh's grace, he will **gather** all his people. This will include not only the ones in Babylon but those from every place where they have been driven. Joy and **prosperity** await these returning exiles. They will eventually live in a land with enlarged borders.

Ⓓ Do Not Fear; God Will Be There (33:1–26)

SUPPORTING IDEA: *God's promise to his people still stands. Though they are temporarily estranged because of their sinfulness, they are still his covenant people, and he will restore them in the future.*

33:1–9. This second message from **the courtyard of the guard** climaxes the four chapters dealing with the dual theme of Israel's impending ruin and future redemption. This material deals with two facts that Jeremiah had emphasized on several occasions. First, the city is doomed. Second, the Lord will bring deliverance and healing to it. In verse 2, Jeremiah used the two words **made** and **formed** to describe Yahweh's work of creation. These same words are found in the Genesis account of creation (Gen. 2:4,7). The Lord who made the world has every right to destroy it.

In verse 3, **call** and **answer** suggest that although God reveals truth, the person receiving it must be in the proper frame of mind. Even God does not generally make his will known to a person who is unwilling to accept it. The word translated **unsearchable** comes from a verb that means "to cut off" or to prune a vine. The passive participle means inaccessible, fortified, strong—

access to it having been cut off. In this context the "idea is not yet revealed" or "the truth is not yet known." This kind of truth comes only to those who seek it in prayer.

In verses 4–5 Yahweh describes the carnage that will come to the city **because of** the people's **wickedness**. But he switches in verses 6–9 and assures the people of a better future. He will bring **healing**, **peace**, and **security**. So great will be Yahweh's blessings on his people that the other **nations** will stand **in awe** and respect.

33:10–13. Jeremiah's picture of **Jerusalem** and Yahweh's vision of the future city and the adjacent lands are contrasted. These verses give a fitting conclusion to this first segment of the larger message. The section deals mainly with the material aspects of the nation's future. Yahweh's final word was not in Jeremiah's message but in Jesus Christ our Savior and Lord.

33:14–26. After beginning in verse 14 with the familiar phrase that speaks of coming events, Jeremiah moved immediately to make a twofold statement about Judah's kingship. Verses 15–16 parallel verses 5–6 of chapter 23, but with a significant difference. In 23:5–6, "The LORD Our Righteousness" is the name of a ruler; in 33:15–16, **The LORD Our Righteousness** is the name given to the city of Jerusalem.

In both passages the Lord promised to restore the monarchy with a **righteous Branch** from **David's line**. In both passages this coming one will act with righteousness and bring justice to the land. Both passages say the same thing about Judah: she will be delivered and live in security. The later passage adds a word about Jerusalem's salvation and safety.

Verses 17–18 add two more promises. In verse 17 the Lord says, **David will never fail to have a man to sit on the throne of the house of Israel.** In verse 18, he adds another thought: **nor will the priests, who are Levites, ever fail to have a man to stand before me continually to offer burnt offerings, to burn grain offerings and to present sacrifices.**

Yahweh used two illustrations (vv. 20–23) from earlier days to reinforce his pledge. First, his promise that David would never fail to have a son reigning on the throne is as secure as God's decree that **night** will follow **day**. Second, God promises that the descendents of David and the Levites will be as numerous as **the stars in the sky** and the grains of **sand on the seashore**.

The chapter closes with another strong affirmation of Yahweh's faithfulness. He begins by urging the people to pay no attention to what some were saying about him. Some were claiming that he had **rejected** his people and perhaps were saying that he planned to cast them off. These may have been the foreign nations or even some people within Israel and Judah—or both! Once more Yahweh pointed to his previous acts of faithfulness to his vows as a guarantee that his promises would be fulfilled.

These promises were fulfilled with the coming of our Savior. He, the son of Abraham and the son of David, is now sitting on the throne of David. His kingdom is not political but spiritual.

> **MAIN IDEA REVIEW:** *Above everything else, Yahweh is a God of comfort. He disciplines his people when he must, but he never forsakes them.*

III. CONCLUSION

Hope Makes All the Difference

On December 17, 1927, an American submarine known as the *S-4* had just completed a run of a measured mile off the coast of Massachusetts. Having checked for surface vessels in the vicinity, the *S-4* housed her periscopes and planed up to the surface. Suddenly, a lookout on the U.S. Coast Guard *Paulding* spotted the *S-4* coming up too close to the destroyer's port bow. An alarm was sounded, all engines were thrown into reverse, and the rudder was thrust hard to port.

But it was too late. The *Paulding* rammed the *S-4* and sent her back to the ocean depths. As water flooded into the dark, cold submarine, crew members sealed off watertight compartments and waited. Rescue efforts were undertaken, but there was no way to lift the stern of the boat. Navy divers discovered six men were still alive in one compartment of the sub. For three days the divers did their best to save the men. As time was running out, the trapped men tapped out the heart-wrenching plea, "Is . . . there . . . no . . . hope?"

Human beings need hope. Hope makes all the difference. Hope overcomes the storms and tempests of life. In the oracles contained in Jeremiah 30–33, Jeremiah offered hope to the people of Israel and Judah. Judgment would come, but after the judgment there was hope—hope of forgiveness and cleansing, hope of restoration to a relationship with God, hope of returning to their land and becoming a nation again, hope of a Davidic king who would rule and reign in righteousness, hope of a heart-changing new covenant with the Lord.

People need hope, and Jeremiah preached hope to them—hope in the Lord. This was true consolation for the hearers, and Jeremiah's messages remain a book of consolation for those who read his words today.

PRINCIPLES

- When the Lord disciplines his people, he does it justly.
- With God there is hope for the future. Even when it seems there is no cure, no remedy, no hope, the Lord is able to heal, to save, and to restore.
- God's desire is for a heart relationship with his people. This desire is so strong that he enters into covenant with them. When his people fail to keep their part of the covenant, God restores and renews his covenant relationship with them.
- When God forgives our sins, he chooses not to remember them any more. Thus he no longer holds our sins against us or remembers the bad we have done when he relates to us.
- People of faith take the long view. They invest in the future even though it may seem foolish to those who are dismayed by present circumstances.
- God delights in doing good for people who love, trust, and honor him.
- God's promises are more sure than the fixed laws of nature. We can count on God to keep his promises more than we can be sure that the sun will rise each day.

APPLICATIONS

- When you were a child, were you ever punished unjustly? Did you ever demand justice from your parents when you felt you were punished unjustly? Do the Lord's words in Jeremiah 30:11 unnerve you, or do they bring you comfort? Why?
- Are you facing something that in your heart you feel even God cannot change, cure, or remedy—perhaps an incurable sickness

or disease, a broken relationship, a rebellious child? Do you feel as if God has said the words in 30:12–15 directly to you? If so, read Jeremiah 32:27. Now turn back to 30:17–19 and read the rest of the Lord's words. How might these verses encourage your heart and bring you hope? Take time right now to pray about your situation again.

- List various types of contracts or covenants that people enter into today. Would you be interested in establishing another contract or covenant with someone who broke a previous contract with you? Then why do you think the Almighty God would restore and renew his covenant with people who failed to keep their part of the covenant?

- Have you ever said, "I forgive that person for what he did, but I cannot forget"? Do you know anyone you have difficulty relating to now because of something that person did to you in the past? How would your life and relationships be transformed if you became more like the Lord in Jeremiah 31:34 and not only forgave people for what they did against you but also chose not to remember it anymore?

- What is the difference in mind-sets, attitudes, and expectations between people who make long-term investments in the stock market and people who make short-term investments? How was Jeremiah like a long-term investor in chapter 32? What lessons could we as people of faith learn from this example?

- Draw a mental picture of God jumping up and down with delight. Have you ever envisioned God as a God who delights in the sound of human joy and happiness, as a God who finds sheer delight in lavishing good on those who honor and reverence him? Read Jeremiah 32:40–41 and 33:6–11 and discuss how this picture of God differs from your usual mental picture of God.

- Do you believe that God's promises are more certain than the fixed laws of nature, that we can count on God to keep his promises more than we can be sure that the sun will rise each day?

Read Jeremiah 31:35–36 and 33:19–26. Praise God for his reliability and steadfastness.

IV. LIFE APPLICATION

Tornado!

On Thursday, April 16, 1998, a severe storm system swept across northeastern Arkansas and western Tennessee, spawning nine or ten tornadoes and killing a number of people. At 3:45 p.m. the system tore through downtown Nashville. I sat in my seventh-floor office where I work and watched the storm approach. The numerous bright flashes of power transformers blowing out caught my eye first. Debris was flying everywhere. Windows blew out of dozens of skyscrapers. Over three hundred buildings, including the state capitol, were damaged or destroyed.

Then the storm leaped over the Cumberland River into east Nashville, into my neighborhood, becoming an F-3 twister. Roofs were ripped off many houses, and hundred-year-old trees were knocked over as if they were matchsticks. Two of my young children had just arrived home from school. They saw the storm coming, ran for the basement, and hid there until the storm passed. When they emerged, their whole world was changed.

Our neighborhood—our home, it seemed—took the brunt of the storm. The police sealed off our area for a week after the storm. Crews worked to clear power lines, cut up trees, and reopen streets. Our neighborhood was declared a disaster area. The city government lowered our property taxes to the lot's salvage value. Land speculators and real estate agents arrived on the scene, offering to take the property "off your hands." Some neighbors were only too glad to get a quick settlement, sell, and move out.

In 587 B.C. Jerusalem and the surrounding area were under attack by the Babylonians. The situation was bleak. This was the final siege of the city. People were desperate and starving. Plague had broken out. When the Babylonian army would finally breach the walls and enter the city, they would burn it to the ground. Humanly speaking, there was no hope. At this time Jeremiah's cousin came to him and offered to sell the prophet a field in Anathoth, just outside Jerusalem. At the Lord's instruction, Jeremiah purchased the field, making sure that all formalities were carefully followed, that witnesses were present, and that the documents were properly recorded and preserved (32:6–12).

Those businessmen and land speculators who came offering to buy out the east Nashville homeowners knew something about the future that those of us in the middle of the crisis were not aware of. They knew there was a tomorrow. They knew the whole area would be rebuilt. They knew that property values would rise dramatically after the recovery. These speculators took the long view of the future, and they were right. Within a couple of years our neighborhood became desirable again.

Jeremiah was not a land speculator. Neither did he take advantage of a bad situation to enrich himself. But he was a prophet, and his actions were symbolic. The Lord told Jeremiah that Judah's present situation would pass— the people would return to the land, houses would be rebuilt, fields and vineyards would be replanted. The Lord also said that there was a time coming in the future when he would do good to the people and cause them and their nation to prosper to such an extent that other nations would be awed by it (32:13–15,36–44; 33:1–13).

Jeremiah obeyed the Lord. In faith he purchased land in his hometown. Jeremiah teaches us that people of faith take the long view as they look to the future. They focus on what God is ultimately doing and make decisions on that basis rather than on what is happening at the moment and on present circumstances.

V. PRAYER

O Lord, God of all mankind, we thank you for offering us hope. We thank you for making possible a new opportunity and a new relationship with you. We thank you that with you all things are possible, that nothing is too hard for you, including the changing of our hearts to know and love your Word. We thank you for being a God who does good to those who love and honor you. So we call upon you, knowing that you will hear us. And we ask that you will show us the great and unsearchable things you have in store for us. Amen.

VI. DEEPER DISCOVERIES

A. Hebrew Poetry

Few of the older Bible translations set Hebrew poetry off as different from prose. This is because the field of scholarship did not begin to recognize the basic structural nature of Hebrew poetry until the eighteenth century. In 1753, Bishop Lowth first presented the concept of parallelism as the primary way of identifying and distinguishing Hebrew poetry from prose. In addition, scholars began to investigate and understand the meter of Hebrew words as an integral mark of this phenomenon. This is still the main characteristic of true poetry in structure while imagery and word pictures supplement these other elements.

B. Placement of the Book of Comfort

Why was the "Book of Comfort" inserted at this place in Jeremiah's material? Leo Green, longtime professor at Southern and Southeastern Baptist Theological Seminaries, suggests that although it seems to interrupt "Baruch's Biography" (chs. 26–45), some links do exist in the context to connect it with the larger division.

In enlarging on and explaining his contention, Green says:

> For one thing chapter 32 is biographical. It recounts the story of a symbolic act, whereby Jeremiah, during his confinement in the court of the guard, gave concrete expression to his unconquerable faith in the future of God's purpose. Some scholars hold that chapters 30–31, originally a separate unit, were placed before 32 to serve as an introduction to chapters 32–33 (Green, 144–45).

Another factor, that of chapter 29, suggests another reason for these chapters being at their existing place. It includes prophecies of salvation and concludes with God's reference to "the good things I will do for my people" (29:32).

Green points out:

> Some think that this explains the position of chapters 30–33. It is possible that the prophecies in chapters 30–33 were incorporated here in conscious contrast to the ethically unconditioned oracles of

the pseudo-prophets mentioned in chapters 27–29. The point is there are biographical and theological ties with the content (Green, 145).

VII. TEACHING OUTLINE

A. INTRODUCTION

1. Lead Story: I Have a Dream
2. Context: A collage of poetic and prose oracles in chapters 30–33 introduces us to a different aspect of Jeremiah's preaching. Beyond God's judgment there is healing and restoration. There are a new relationship and a new covenant with God.
3. Transition: People need to hear a comforting word. They need to be told that judgment is not the only word. There is hope for the future. Life cannot be all negative, or people will slip into utter despair. Jeremiah 30–33 offer a collection of Jeremiah's oracles that have been called the "Book of Consolation." These oracles show us that hope was an integral part of Jeremiah's preaching, just as it needs to be in our lives.

B. COMMENTARY

1. The Good Things God Will Do for His People (30:1–24)
2. The Covenant That God Will Make with His People (31:1–40)
3. Hope in a Hopeless Time (32:1–44)
4. Do Not Fear; God Will Be There (33:1–26)

C. CONCLUSION: HOPE MAKES ALL THE DIFFERENCE

VIII. ISSUES FOR DISCUSSION

1. Jeremiah used several metaphors for God in chapter 31. In verse 9 God is called Israel's father. In verse 10 he is likened to a shepherd watching over his flock. In verses 15–22 motherly imagery is applied to God implicitly. In verse 32 God calls himself a husband to them. Which image of God do you find most meaningful: Father, Shepherd,

Mother, Spouse? What characteristics do you associate with each of these images (protection, provision, comfort, care, compassion, companionship)?

2. In speaking about the future in 30:9, Jeremiah promised that God would raise up David as king for Israel and Judah. But King David lived about four hundred years before Jeremiah's time. What did Jeremiah mean by these words? How do his words of 30:9 relate to the Lord's oracles in 33:14–26? Which descendant of David's fulfills the roles of both king and priest?

3. Jeremiah announced the new covenant in 31:31–34 (see also 32:36–40; 33:6–9). This is the last of a series of Old Testament covenants beginning with Noah (Gen. 9:9–11), continuing with Abraham (Gen. 15:18–21), with Moses and the Israelites (Exod. 19:3–6; 24:3–8), with the Levites (Num. 25:10–13), and concluding with David (2 Sam. 7:11–16; 23:5). How does this new covenant compare with the other biblical covenants? How does the new covenant in Jeremiah 31 relate to Jesus' announcement of the new covenant (Matt. 26:28; Mark 14:24; Luke 22:20; 1 Cor. 11:25)?

Jeremiah 34:1–39:18

Truth That Endures

I. **INTRODUCTION**
Back to the Task

II. **COMMENTARY**
A verse-by-verse explanation of these verses.

III. **CONCLUSION**
Fall of a Nation

An overview of the principles and applications from these verses.

IV. **LIFE APPLICATION**
A Man of Principle

Melding these verses to life.

V. **PRAYER**
Tying these verses to life with God.

VI. **DEEPER DISCOVERIES**
Historical, geographical, and grammatical enrichment of the commentary.

VII. **TEACHING OUTLINE**
Suggested step-by-step group study of these verses.

VIII. **ISSUES FOR DISCUSSION**
Zeroing these verses in on daily life.

"The Bible stands like a rock undaunted 'mid

the raging storms of time;

Its pages burn with the truth eternal, and they glow with

a light sublime.

The Bible stands like a mountain tow'ring far above

the works of men;

Its truth by none ever was refuted, and destroy it

they never can.

The Bible stands tho' the hills may tumble, it will firmly

stand when the earth shall crumble;

I will plant my feet on its firm foundation, for

the Bible stands."

Haldor Lillenas

Jeremiah 34:1–39:18

IN A NUTSHELL

Jeremiah 34–39 bring us to the fall of Jerusalem in 587 B.C. Though not in chronological order, the section begins and ends with Zedekiah, the last king of Judah. Zedekiah's unfaithfulness and capricious behavior in the matter of freeing the slaves and then reneging on the commitment, in chapter 34, is set in contrast to the steady commitment and faithfulness of the Recabites in the time of Jehoiakim in chapter 35. The mention of Jehoiakim brings up the account in chapter 36 of King Jehoiakim's hearing and then burning the scroll on which Jeremiah had written down his messages and prophecies of the first twenty years of his ministry in 605 B.C. Chapters 37–39 bring us back to Judah's final year. Three times King Zedekiah sought counsel from Jeremiah (37:1–16; 37:17–38:13; 38:14–28). Five times Jeremiah was incarcerated during Judah's final days (37:15–16; 37:21; 38:6; 38:13; 39:14). The final siege and the fall of Jerusalem, along with fates of Zedekiah, Jeremiah, and Ebed-Melech, are recounted in chapter 39.

Truth That Endures

I. INTRODUCTION

Back to the Task

$\mathcal{T}$he loss of an author's literary composition is a great tragedy—like the loss of a part of himself. Thomas Carlyle, the famous nineteenth-century Scottish author, experienced such tragedy when the manuscript of his first volume of *The French Revolution* was accidentally burned while in the care of John Stuart Mill. Carlyle had immersed himself in French history. He had labored unremittingly to write the volume. His funds were virtually exhausted. The volume was completed. And then it was gone—destroyed in a fire. One person said, "Rarely has the virtue of 'the hero as man of letters' shone in fairer light than in the manner in which Carlyle received the terrible news, and grimly determined to sit down and rewrite the volume."

Upon hearing the first edition of the scroll of Jeremiah read, which probably contained the first twenty-five chapters of the present Book of Jeremiah, King Jehoiakim cut up and burned the scroll in a fire (36:21–26). The Lord told Jeremiah to rewrite the scroll—to "write on it all the words that were on the first scroll" and to add "many similar words" to it (36:28,32). Jeremiah's latter scroll, our present Book of Jeremiah, became more famous than his lost work—in fact, one of the best known in the Old Testament.

II. COMMENTARY

Truth That Endures

MAIN IDEA: *Constant rejection of God's Word, whether by an individual or a nation, will bring doom.*

The next twelve chapters in the Book of Jeremiah (chs. 34–45) contain material written almost entirely in narrative style. Chapters 34–39 record events up to and during the siege of Jerusalem. The material is not entirely chronological although the chronology can easily be reconciled by a careful examination of the biblical text.

The material in 34:1–7 was delivered while Judah's battle with the Babylonians was in progress. The remainder of the chapter (vv. 8–22) records words that Jeremiah spoke about the people's conduct with reference to their slaves. During a temporary lifting of the siege, citizens of Judah released their slaves, but later they canceled the action and put them back into bondage. In these verses Jeremiah addressed the issue with a special word to the king about his future.

Chapter 35 contains a narrative about the loyalty of the Recabites. They were the descendants of Jonadab and had remained faithful to a vow they had made to their father. Jeremiah praised them for keeping that vow. Chapter 36 records in great detail the preparation, reading, destruction, and rewriting of a scroll containing most, if not all, of Jeremiah's prophecies thus far. This event, to a great extent, indicated the future direction the nation would take.

In the remaining three chapters in this unit of study (chs. 37–39), the events leading to Jerusalem's fall unfold. Chapters 37 and 38 focus mainly on the relationship between Jeremiah and Zedekiah during the prophet's prison life. Chapter 39 tells of Jerusalem's fall to Babylon. A note is added about God's command for Jeremiah to express thanks to Ebed-Melech, who befriended Jeremiah while he was in prison.

What is the unifying theme of these chapters? Chapters 34–39 give events leading up to the city's fall. Chapters 40–46 continue the story until the end of Jeremiah's recorded career.

Ⓐ A Word of Warning to Zedekiah (34:1–22)

> **SUPPORTING IDEA:** Jeremiah spoke plainly to Zedekiah about the city's fate and the king's future. He then uttered a sharp word to him because of his policy toward the slaves.

34:1–7. Jeremiah visited Zedekiah during the siege of Jerusalem shortly after the account in chapter 21. Babylon's army was **fighting against** the Jewish capital, and only two of Judah's fortified cities had not been captured—**Lachish** and **Azekah**. Jeremiah was still at liberty. This utterance must have preceded the temporary lifting of the siege because Jeremiah mentioned the Egyptian army's threatened approach.

The Babylonian army was assisted by fighting men from all her vassal states. According to treaty agreements of that day, Babylon had a right to demand this aid from her conquered slave nations. Babylon's military strategy consisted of a two-pronged attack carried on simultaneously. First, Nebuchadnezzar's forces drove the Judean fighting units into the small walled and fortified towns of the area. Then they conquered the towns one at a time. Second, at the same time, the Babylonian army besieged Jerusalem and held it under a tight blockade.

Verses 2 and 3 record Yahweh's command to Jeremiah at this time. He sent the prophet to **Zedekiah** with a clear message: Jerusalem is a doomed city. No **escape** is possible. The king of Babylon will **burn** the city, and Zedekiah himself will be **captured** and turned over to Nebuchadnezzar. Jeremiah warned Zedekiah that he would personally meet the Babylonian king and they would have a **face to face** meeting. Such meetings normally occurred in situations such as this one at that period of history.

On first reading of verses 4 and 5, one immediately feels Jeremiah was inconsistent. But looking at the fuller picture, we realize this promise was conditional. Refer again to Jeremiah 18:5–10. In my judgment, this is the classical verse on conditional prophecy.

Most promises or pronouncements of judgment have a built-in opportunity for choice. If God declares good for a nation, this nation can negate the promise by sinning. If God declares evil or judgment for a nation, he will change the outcome of that declaration if the people repent. God deals with individuals and groups on the basis of their moral choices.

Verses 4 and 5 are conditional promises. Zedekiah must repent in order to receive the blessings promised. If he heeded the prophet's message, a happy future awaited him. Rather than a horrible death, he would enjoy a peaceful life. The Jews did not practice embalming, but they did burn spices after the death of a king. Description of this practice appears in 2 Chronicles 16:14 and 21:19. Did Zedekiah heed the prophet's call? Obviously he did not. Though his death is not recorded, his capture was certainly traumatic.

Zedekiah was king of the land, and he faced a choice. Would he heed the prophet with a word from Yahweh, or would he ignore him? We do not have any written record of his response to the prophet's message. But we do have a record of what happened. The horrible things the king endured lead us to believe that he chose to reject Jeremiah's passionate plea.

34:8–22. The incident to which Jeremiah referred in this section occurred during the siege of Jerusalem. A report came to the commander in charge of the Babylonian forces about the Egyptian army. They heard that Egypt was on its way to attack the Babylonian army. This caused the Babylonian commander to lift the siege on Jerusalem temporarily.

This action on Babylon's part gave occasion for the wicked and greedy men inside the city to do a terrible thing. On learning the Egyptians were withdrawing, they released the Hebrew **slaves** they held. Why did they perform this "noble action"? Several motives might have moved them.

First, the cost of providing care for their slaves, including food and other necessities, put a huge burden on the slave owners. They wished to be relieved of it. Second, they may have been moved with genuine concern for their welfare. Third, they may have been endeavoring to gain favor with God by this action. Perhaps all three motives were intertwined and motivated the slave owners.

All those who had entered the covenant released their slaves (vv. 8–11). Not expecting their former owners to "go back on their agreement," the newly freed slaves remained in Jerusalem. The biblical account gives no reason why the slaves consented to submit and allow their owners to reenslave them. God was displeased with what the people had done (vv. 12–16). It was a blatant act of selfishness and greed. Just as Jeremiah had condemned sexual sin, so he condemned greed for material things.

Early laws of Israel permitted accepting a person as a slave for payment of loans but prescribed humane treatment of them. Rich people of Jeremiah's day who were powerful enough to get away with it refused to set their slaves free as the law required. Yahweh, through his prophets, sent severe words of condemnation.

Yahweh begins his final pronouncement (vv. 17–22) upon the people with a wordplay on the word **freedom**. What he meant was actually the opposite. Today we might call it a tongue-in-cheek statement. Stated another way, Yahweh said, "You have turned them loose; I will turn punishment loose on you."

In verses 18–20, the prophet illustrated the coming punishment with an ancient custom in making a covenant. Three Old Testament passages (Gen. 15:9–17; Judg. 19:29; 1 Sam. 11:7) help us understand the prophet's statement to his people. As the Israelites **cut** an animal into pieces and engaged in a ritual with it, God would turn his people over to a reprobate people. These **enemies** would show no mercy to the people of Judah, not only killing them but allowing their **bodies** to lie exposed without being buried.

What about the **king**? Although the Babylonian army had temporarily **withdrawn** and lifted the siege, they would return. When it did, Zedekiah and his advisors would meet their doom (vv. 21–22). This closed God's word at that time to Zedekiah.

B Jeremiah's Approval of the Recabites (35:1–19)

SUPPORTING IDEA: *The prophet did not dwell at length on the virtues of their father's requirements but on the Recabites' faithfulness to their promise.*

35:1–19. Why did the compilers of Jeremiah insert this incident from Jehoiakim's reign into prophecies dealing with Jerusalem's final days? Some have contended it was a fragment of a narrative about the prophet that was left over, and it had to be placed somewhere. But it was probably placed here along with chapter 36 of similar date to give an object lesson to the people. Time was running out, and perhaps these two narratives from earlier days would help lead them to repentance.

Who were the Recabites? We first see them in 2 Kings 10:15–17 supporting Jehu when he overthrew the house of Ahab. They were a small community that had developed great consistency displaying integrity and loyalty to their inherited traditions. Their lifestyle maintained the core beliefs of their founder. The Recabites would not live in walled cities, and they would not touch wine. They had promised their father they would never violate these prohibitions. Jeremiah used them for an object lesson or illustration of loyalty to one's vows. He brought them into the chamber of a son of **Jaazaniah** and offered them wine. They refused, citing their vow to one of their forefathers.

Jeremiah pointed this out to the leaders and some of the people. His point was the Recabites were loyal to the teachings of their tradition, but the people of Judah were not loyal to the revelation of God they had received.

C Jeremiah's Scroll Is Destroyed (36:1–32)

SUPPORTING IDEA: *God's word to his people is indestructible whether in written or oral form.*

This chapter records what is probably the most strategic moment in Jeremiah's ministry. For the first time Jeremiah put part of his prophetic messages into written form. The date of this passage is the fourth year of Jehoiakim, which is 605 B.C., the date when Babylon defeated Assyria at Carchemisch.

This enabled Babylon to become the victorious master of the Near East. Judah thus became a vassal of Babylon and retained this position until Jerusalem fell. The rejection of Jeremiah's scroll by Jehoiakim was probably the act that sealed Judah's fate. After this event Jeremiah no longer held out any hope for the nation.

36:1–8. Why did Jeremiah feel God leading him to put his messages in written form? He had been through a crisis in his own life. Earlier he had supported the reforms of Josiah until they became too nationalistic. He learned a great lesson when Josiah was killed at Megiddo and Babylon defeated Assyria at Carchemisch. He saw matters more clearly. Jehoiakim had come to the throne, and this scroll was a warning to the king, who was in the fourth year of his reign.

Jeremiah put either all or a large portion of his previously delivered messages into written form. He hoped that what individually delivered messages had not accomplished, perhaps a cumulative summary in written form would achieve. Jeremiah called on **Baruch**, his personal scribe, to help.

Why, as stated in verse 5, was Jeremiah **restricted** from going into the **temple**? The best explanation is probably because of his clash with Pashhur (20:1–6). In chapter 45 Jeremiah spoke words of comfort and encouragement to Baruch. He seems to have gone through a period of discouragement and depression because of the "fall-out" effect he suffered as a result of this experience.

36:9–26. Why did Baruch wait until **the ninth month of the fifth year** to read the scroll in the temple? Scholars have suggested several reasons.

John Skinner's view of the six months difference between the Hebrew and Babylonian calendars is novel but not really taken seriously by scholars. Others have suggested the battle of Carchemisch had not yet taken place but was only in the making when Jeremiah began dictating the scroll. Others suggest perhaps Baruch waited for a time when the largest possible crowd would be present to hear the messages. Still others claim that preparing the scroll took a number of weeks, perhaps months.

Whatever the reason, Baruch chose a highly appropriate time to read the scroll. The king had called for a day of prayer and fasting. Surely both king and the people would be receptive. The Scripture does not tell us why the special day had been called. Some have suggested the fast was because of a crisis related to lack of rain. But the more likely reason is that the king realized the nation was in danger of invasion from an enemy army. Even the

Recabites had come to the city for protection. The new "foe from the north" was on the way. Surely Judah would hear and heed Jeremiah's warning.

How much of Jeremiah's present canonical book was in this scroll? A strictly literal interpretation of 36:2 would mean that if we could determine what messages in the present book were delivered before the fourth year of Jehoiakim, we could state with finality that they were in the original scroll. But the matter is not that simple.

The Hebrew word translated **all** is a general term rather than a specific term. Jeremiah could have prepared a scroll that contained the totality of his message thus far without including every word of every sermon. The scroll was read three times in one day and seems to have been read straight through without any interruption each time. This suggests that it was not of unusual length. The twenty-third verse speaks of three or four leaves. Thus the reading of the scroll suggests that it may have been a summary of the prophetic messages rather than a reproduction of many large manuscripts.

Another factor that contributes to the difficulty of determining the scroll's contents is Yahweh's commandment to Jeremiah after the first scroll was burned. The final verse of this chapter says, "Baruch wrote on it all the words of the scroll that Jehoiakim king of Judah had burned in the fire" (v. 32). It then adds, "And many similar words were added to them." If this latter statement is taken into consideration, to ascertain the exact contents of either scroll would be an impossible task. Were additions made to each individual message, or were new messages added, or both?

My view is that the large part of the first scroll would consist of chapters 1:1–8:3; 13:1–17; 18:1–23; 19:1–20:18; 22:1–9,13–23; 25:1–38, and also some parts, perhaps, or all of the foreign prophecies. A number of warnings, as well as severe threats of punishments, appear in these sections. They would be sufficient to account for the alarm among the people and princes who heard Baruch read the scroll.

A solemn day for Judah had arrived. The situation was so serious that a fast had been declared. The people were contemplating the peril that might be facing them. Would God protect them if the enemy attempted to invade the city? Already word had spread that Babylon was marching toward Judah.

Baruch chose this as the time to read the words of Jeremiah. He went to the chamber of **Gemariah**, which was near one of the temple gates. At this time, Gemariah had left his son **Micaiah** in charge of affairs. As Baruch read, the words told of Judah's sin and of Yahweh's repeated attempts to bring them back to righteousness. When Baruch closed with the declaration that the nation must repent or face the full force of God's fury, a great silence fell over the people.

Micaiah realized that these statements were right on target and could not be ignored. He dashed to the king's house and went into the chamber of **Elishama**, the scribe. Here Micaiah's father, Gemariah, and all the princes were gathered together. They were probably discussing the possibility of Nebuchadnezzar's following up his victory at Carchemisch with an all-out effort to invade Judah. Micaiah declared what he had heard, quoting from memory as many phrases from Jeremiah's prophecies as he could recall. The group sent **Jehudi** to bring Baruch to their chamber.

At the word of the princes, Baruch **read** the scroll to them. Looking at one another with fear and anxiety, they questioned Baruch about the source of the scroll. They resolved to tell the king immediately, but they first warned Baruch, **You and Jeremiah, go and hide. Don't let anyone know where you are** (v. 19).

The princes went immediately to Jehoiakim the king. But for some reason they did not take Baruch's scroll with them. Perhaps in their haste they forgot the scroll, or more likely they hoped the king would accept their oral report. But Jehoiakim sent **Jehudi** for the scroll. Jehudi then began to read the contents in the hearing of Jehoiakim and the others.

The king was sitting near the **fire**. As Jehudi read three or four columns, the king took his penknife, **cut them off**, and threw them into the fire. As Jehudi read more, the king cut and tossed them into the fire until **the entire scroll** was consumed. Several times some of the princes tried in vain to keep the king from destroying the scroll. As he finished, he turned to his son along with several of his servants and commanded them to **arrest** Jeremiah and Baruch.

The Scripture does not indicate great rage on Jehoiakim's part as he burned the scroll, only a cold and icy defiance toward the prophet's message. The fact that he burned the scroll section by section rather than all at once indicates his deliberate defiance of the word of Yahweh.

36:27–32. The word of the Lord came to Jeremiah the second time. The prophet was told to write in another scroll the same messages that were in the scroll burned by Jehoiakim. The Lord then added an additional note about the king. Jeremiah wrote:

Therefore, this is what the LORD says about Jehoiakim king of Judah: He will have no one to sit on the throne of David; his body will be thrown out and exposed to the heat by day and the frost by night. I will punish him and his children and his attendants for their wickedness; I will bring on them and those living in Jerusalem and the people of Judah every disaster I pronounced against them, because they have not listened (36:30–31).

Some liberal scholars have raised two objections to the pronouncement of Jeremiah. First, they have pointed out that the statement Jehoiakim "will have no one to sit on the throne of David" was not literally fulfilled. Jehoiachin, his son, ruled for three months and ten days. This is another of the many examples of the difficulty we encounter when we demand a literal fulfillment of a spiritual truth. Jeremiah's prophecy was certainly fulfilled in spirit since Jehoiachin reigned only a brief period. He was taken to Babylon, where he remained a prisoner for thirty-seven years.

For those, however, who insist upon a literal fulfillment of every prophecy, we suggest a strictly literal translation of the Hebrew text. It reads, "Therefore Yahweh says this about Jehoiakim, king of Judah: 'There shall not be for him one sitting upon the throne of David.'" The phrase "shall not be" is an imperfect Hebrew verb form, and the force of the imperfect can be repeated or continuous action. This would mean the seed of Jehoiakim would not be able to sit continuously or to remain on the throne of Judah.

This approach seems to reveal exactly the message and meaning of the prophet. The seed of Jehoiakim would not occupy a permanent place on the throne of David. Jeremiah's prophecy was literally fulfilled in this sense. The three months and ten days of Jehoiachin's reign were like an interim kingship. The next king was Zedekiah, another son of Josiah and brother of Jehoiakim. After Zedekiah's reign, the kingdom of Judah ceased to exist and the nation went into captivity. Judah was never ruled again by a king. After the return from Babylon, the nation was guided, both politically and spiritually, by her priests, scribes, and religious leaders.

The other objection that liberal scholars bring against this prophecy revolves around Jehoiakim's burial. The prophet described the treatment that Jehoiakim's body would receive: his body will be thrown out and exposed to the heat by day and the frost by night (36:30). These words should be compared with a similar thought about Jehoiakim, which was undoubtedly written about the same time: "He will have the burial of a donkey—dragged away and thrown outside the gates of Jerusalem" (22:19). These latter words are part of a prophecy about Jehoiakim found in an independent scroll (22:1–23:40) of Jeremiah's messages. The scroll contains a series of prophecies about the kings of Judah (22:1–23:8) and the false prophets (23:9–40).

The question of whether Jehoiakim's death and burial were in accordance with the words of the prophet also arises. The author of Chronicles states nothing about his death or burial, and the author of 2 Kings states only that he "slept with his fathers" (2 Kgs. 24:6 KJV). The significant point is that neither historian gives any details about his burial. This is a strong indication that there was something unusual about his burial when we recall that we have a record of every king's burial except Jehoiakim's.

Ⅾ Jeremiah Is Thrown into Prison (37:1–21)

SUPPORTING IDEA: *When a person's life and testimony for God confront the lifestyle of a wicked person in authority, he can expect opposition.*

The next three chapters of Jeremiah deal with the final days of the prophet and the Jewish community up until the fall of Jerusalem. The prophet faced the most severe opposition and suffering of his ministry. The physical discomfort and pain, intense as it was, was minimal in comparison to the hurt from being accused of being disloyal to his country. In reality, he was the greatest patriot of the city.

37:1–5. These verses serve as an introduction to the remaining material in the concluding narrative section (chs. 37–44). Notice the two men whom Zedekiah sent to request Jeremiah's prayers for the king. The first, **Jehucal**, was no friend of Jeremiah. He later was one of several who demanded the prophet's death (38:4). **Zephaniah** had been part of an earlier mission to the king (21:1).

Some interpreters believe Zedekiah sent these men to the prophet to taunt him because they expected to find security in Egypt's assistance. But this is unlikely. Egypt did give some temporary hope, but no one with good judgment believed this nation would do any more than it had done on previous occasions.

37:6–10. Though a ray of hope for Zedekiah's forces seemed to shine through the darkness, Jeremiah stuck to his message. The true "foe from the north" was now on the scene. Twenty years ago the prophet wasn't sure exactly what nation God had chosen to mete out his punitive instrument. He only knew this enemy was coming. But now he was sure. The temporary respite for Judah would be short-lived.

37:11–15. Jeremiah welcomed the temporary lifting of the siege and took advantage of it to pursue some family business. Intending to exit by the **Benjamin Gate** and go into his native land, Jeremiah received a jolt. **Irijah**, captain of the guard and grandson of Hananiah, the false prophet in chapter 28, detained the prophet and brought him to the authorities.

Knowing of Jeremiah's clash with his grandfather, Irijah used his influence to bring the cruelest and most intense treatment possible to the prophet. One must be fair and admit that Irijah did have a convincing case to present Zedekiah and his officials. Jeremiah had said Zedekiah should surrender, and the situation did seem suspicious. But this was not Irijah's main motive. He opposed all Jeremiah stood for and was determined to destroy him. Hatred and the desire for revenge motivated his actions.

37:16–21. The Hebrew word translated **dungeon** means literally "house of the pits." From verse 20, we can assume this dungeon was a part of Jonathan's house. This location was indeed, as Jeremiah insisted, a place where he was left to **die** had he not been able to appeal to Zedekiah.

The conversation that took place between Zedekiah and Jeremiah shows the king's true character. He was not so much a wicked man as he was a weak person caught in the clutches of a power bloc. The nation had fiercely nationalistic men who were determined to oppose God and his prophet. The king's godly side was shown when he granted the prophet's petition and placed him in the **courtyard of the guard**. The most heartrending cry of this section is, **Where are your prophets who prophesied to you?** They, like all preachers who compromise God's Word, were nowhere to be found when the crisis came.

Ⓔ Jeremiah's Final Crisis Before the End (38:1–28)

SUPPORTING IDEA: *A true prophet of God refuses to compromise his message no matter how great the price he must pay for his faithfulness.*

This chapter continues and concludes the events in Jeremiah's life up to the time when the city of Jerusalem fell. This was the most painful experience of any prophet of whose life we have a record. Only Jesus suffered more.

38:1–5. Jeremiah continued to deliver his same message after he was put in the courtyard of the guard. The quartet who heard him and reported to the king were a motley crew of people who disliked Jeremiah. At least some of them had opposed him on previous occasions. **Gedaliah** should not be confused with the land's future governor. He was probably a son of the man who had Jeremiah put in stocks on a previous occasion (20:1–3). We find no mention of **Shephatiah** anywhere else in the Old Testament. **Jehucal** (37:3) and **Pashhur** (21:1) certainly were not friends of Jeremiah.

Verses 4–5 reveal the helplessness of Zedekiah as king. He was at the mercy of a strong nationalistic group to whom he yielded. How tragic to see a man in a position of leadership who lacks the strength of character to assert himself with authority. The expression **the king can do nothing to oppose you** was Zedekiah's admission of his inability to serve as the nation's leader.

38:6–13. Why did Jeremiah's enemies choose the **cistern** with its filth and misery when they could have killed him outright? They probably wanted to humiliate him as well as add to his agony. By letting him die slowly of starvation, they technically avoided the actual shedding of blood. The intervention of **Ebed-Melech** on Jeremiah's behalf shows God's great mercy and watchful protection of those who obey him.

38:14–23. Zedekiah's secret visit to Jeremiah shows the frustration of this inept king. He wanted to serve the Lord, but he also wanted the plaudits of others. Torn between two conflicting voices, he must have been a pitiful sight as he asked Jeremiah, "Is there a word from the Lord?" Jeremiah refused to budge from the same message he had been proclaiming from the beginning of his preaching ministry.

38:24–28. The final picture of Zedekiah's whimpering reveals his weakness of character once more. The closing scene of Jeremiah and Zedekiah leaves us with a vivid picture of those who try to serve two masters. Jeremiah did protect the frail and fragile king. We should not regard this as a case of lying or even practicing "situation ethics." The prophet did not condemn Zedekiah for his wickedness but only for his weakness. Our final picture of Jeremiah before the city's fall shows us that God stays with his faithful servants.

▛ Third and Final Invasion of Jerusalem (39:1–18)

SUPPORTING IDEA: *Judgment, though long delayed, will come when God's agenda declares the time is right.*

Jerusalem's day of reckoning had arrived. What Jesus said about the city of his day was true of Jeremiah's Jerusalem. Following his blistering words of condemnation to the city's religious leaders, our Master said, "O Jerusalem, Jerusalem, you who kill the prophets and stone those sent to you, how often have I longed to gather your children together, as a hen gathers her chicks under her wings, but you were not willing. Look, your house is left to you desolate" (Matt. 23:37–38).

39:1–10. Jeremiah recorded the facts about the fall of Jerusalem with great detail. After stating the exact day the **wall** was penetrated, he stated exactly where the meeting of Babylonian leaders took place inside the city. He even gave the names of three Babylonian leaders. The details continue as the prophet tells exactly how **Zedekiah** fled Jerusalem. The efficient Babylonian army caught and arrested him near Jericho and transported him to **Riblah**, a town on the Orontes River near the border with Babylonia.

The cruel Babylonian leader first killed Zedekiah's **sons** in the king's presence. Nebuchadnezzar then had the king's **eyes** put out, put him in **shackles**, and transported him to **Babylon**. With the king thoroughly disabled, the throne of Judah was vacant, and the kingdom was no more. We do not know Zedekiah's final fate except that he died in Babylon (52:11). Every day probably seemed like a hundred years to this rebellious young king. What a horrific fate for this man whose chief sin was not his wickedness but his unwillingness to act on the prophet's advice.

Verse 8 reveals the destruction of the buildings in Jerusalem. Jeremiah 52:13 says that the temple was included. The accuracy of this account has been confirmed by archaeologists. They have found amid the ruins on the eastern slope to the south of the present walls sufficient evidence to prove beyond doubt that this account can be accepted as valid.

To complete the job, **Nebuzaradan**, a high official of the Babylonian army, deported the remainder of **the people** except those **who owned nothing**. He gave the land to these, whom he considered "culls," to tend the land. This was Babylon's way of making sure that no one would be left to rebel against them. Though the Scripture does not specifically mention it, Babylon probably stripped the land of its wealth. Judah and all the other regions in the once glorious nation became a vassal territory. Now "Ichabod" was literally true—the glory of God had departed (1 Sam. 4:21; Ezek. 11:22–23). Judah's sin had found her out.

39:11–14. What about **Jeremiah**? He was vindicated. Everything he had said would happen had occurred. But the victory was bittersweet. His triumph brought a heaviness of spirit because the land he loved was demolished. Jeremiah's decision to remain in Judah rather than go to Babylon showed his noble spirit. Few people would have chosen to remain a minister of God with the poor people left in the land. This is another way Jeremiah was probably more like our Savior than any man who ever lived.

39:15–18. The biblical writer, probably Baruch, adds one additional note. It shows the sterling character of the man from Anathoth. While still in the court of the guard after being rescued by **Ebed-Melech**, the kind and gracious prophet sent a word of thanks to Baruch in the form of a word from Yahweh. He promised when the enemy came and devastated the land, no harm would come to this noble "servant of the king." This phrase is the literal meaning of the name Ebed-Melech. This must have brought comfort to the man who risked his life pleading Jeremiah's cause.

In a day when ingratitude is so prevalent, Jeremiah's simple "thank you" to his benefactor is refreshing. Add this to the list of Jeremiah's virtues: He was a man who appreciated his friends and expressed his gratitude freely.

MAIN IDEA REVIEW: *Constant rejection of God's Word, whether by an individual or a nation, will bring doom.*

III. CONCLUSION

Fall of a Nation

What a sad end! The nation has fallen! The Holy City and its temple are destroyed! For forty years God's faithful prophet Jeremiah warned his people of the coming disaster, calling them to repentance and reformation. Yet even as the Babylonian army was ransacking the land and laying siege to the capital, the leaders—both political and religious—and the citizens were still playing games with God, promising one thing and then doing another. God's people were put to shame by the principled actions of a group of people who honored their ancient ancestor's instructions about diet and lifestyle. Yet the people of Judah flaunted their transgressions of divine commandments. In fact, the people's hearts became so calloused toward God's word—whether proclaimed or written—that they tried to destroy both the message and the messenger.

PRINCIPLES

- The Lord's people are to keep their word. The Lord abhors those who make a promise and then go back on their word, those who enter an agreement and then look for loopholes to avoid honoring their agreement.
- The Lord blesses those who keep his commandments, uphold and honor godly traditions, and instruct their descendants to do so as well.
- God's Word is to be treated with respect and reverence; it is to be heard and obeyed. No matter how hard they try, men can never destroy God's Word. How people treat God's Word—both in their response to hearing it and in their handling of it—is a serious matter.
- Sometimes people misunderstand, misinterpret, and misjudge the actions of God's servants.
- The truth is not always pleasant to hear or to speak. It takes great courage to tell someone, especially someone in authority, how things really are.
- When someone asks you to keep a confidence, you should honor that person's request if at all possible.
- The Lord does not forget what we do for him and his servants.

APPLICATIONS

- Recall a time when someone failed to keep their word. How did you feel? Evaluate your own record of keeping your word.
- Make a list of family traditions your parents practiced when you were growing up. Which of these are still important to you? Which should be passed down to your children? What traditions have you added in your own home? Which of these traditions set you apart from other families you know?

- Name several times in history when dictators and tyrants tried to eradicate God's Word. Discuss why they have not been successful. Then consider: Which is worse, to try to destroy God's Word or to ignore it? How do you show your respect for God's written Word?

- Have you ever misjudged someone's actions, acted toward the person on that basis, and complained to your friends about what the person did?

- Have you ever had to confront someone over an unpleasant situation? What guidelines can you share to help others who might have this unpleasant task in the future?

- How important is keeping another person's personal situation and conversation confidential when you are requested to do so? Why is this important for pastors and church leaders who counsel church members? Under what circumstances is it advisable not to keep matters confidential?

- Have you ever done something helpful for one of God's servants or for your church without any thought of compensation or pay back and then been surprised when you were unexpectedly recognized and rewarded for it? How did you feel?

IV. LIFE APPLICATION

A Man of Principle

Eric Liddell was the best sprinter in Scotland. His race was the 100-yard dash. He was also good in the 220-yard dash. At the British Championships and Olympic Trials held in London in July 1923, Eric not only won all his heats and the finals, but he set a new British record of 9.7 seconds for the 100-yard race. In the 220-yard race, Eric clocked his best time ever and was awarded a place on the British Olympic team. He was entered in both the 100-meter and the 200-meter races.

Three months before the Olympic Games in Paris, Eric received a schedule of the events. Eric stared at the list in shock. Next to the qualifying heat for the 100-meter race was the word *Sunday*. Eric had a principle he clung to religiously. He would not run on Sunday. This was God's day and a day of rest. When he refused to participate in these races, the British and Scottish public that had so admired Eric turned on him with a vengeance. Many felt he was unfit to represent Scotland in the games. Some even called him a traitor to his country.

After meeting with the Olympic Committee in Paris and failing to get the races rescheduled, the British Olympic Committee asked Eric to enter two events that were not scheduled on Sunday—the 200-meter and 400-meter races—even though these were not his best events. Eric agreed.

Eric won the bronze medal in the 200-meter final behind two Americans, but no one gave him a chance of winning the 400-meter race that Friday evening in July 1924. It was not his event. He had barely squeaked into the finals during the qualifying heats. Further, he drew the outside lane, the least desirable spot. And worst of all, he was running against two world-record holders. As Eric left the hotel for his race, he reached into his pocket and found a small note that the British team masseur had slipped into his pocket. It read, "In the old book it says, 'He who honors me, I will honor.'"

The rest is history. Eric won the 400-meter race. He set a new world record. He received the gold medal. He was honored as a national hero. By 1925 there was hardly a person in all Scotland who did not know Eric Liddel—and that he was fulfilling his dream of going to China as a missionary. And thanks to the Academy Award-winning movie *Chariots of Fire,* another generation knows the story of the man who stood by his principles.

The Recabites of old knew this truth. According to Jeremiah 35, they refused to yield the principles that governed their lives, even when it was culturally acceptable and would have been politically advantageous for them to do so. Because of that, the Lord honored them (35:18–19).

V. PRAYER

Heavenly Father, help us to be people of our word. Let us not go back on promises we have made or seek ways to wiggle out of what we have promised. Give us the courage to remain true to our principles—principles that honor you and testify to your lordship in our lives—even if people around us are compromising their principles and giving in to the popular culture. And help us, dear Lord, to honor your Word, not only in how we handle it but also in how we allow it to handle us. Amen.

VI. DEEPER DISCOVERIES

A. The Recabites (35:1–19)

These people were the descendants of Jehonadab son of Recab, who supported Jehu when he overthrew the house of Ahab (2 Kgs. 10:15–17). About 599 B.C. the Recabites took refuge from Nebuchadnezzar in Jerusalem (Jer. 35). The Lord commanded Jeremiah to take them to the temple and offer them wine to drink. When he did so, they refused, saying that their father Jonadab (Jehonadab) had commanded them not to drink wine, not to live in houses, and not to engage in agriculture. These regulations may have been intended as a protest against Canaanite religion or settled life in general, but more likely they protected the Recabites' lifestyle and trade secrets as itinerant metalworkers. Jeremiah contrasted their faithfulness to the commandments of their ancestor with the faithlessness of the people of Judah to the Lord.

B. Ebed-Melech (39:16)

Who is this strange man who risked his life for God's prophet? His name indicates his position: he was the personal slave of Zedekiah. Scholars are in basic agreement that Ebed-Melech was a man with black skin.

Three facts argue strongly that he was a highly respected, trustworthy, and courageous man. First, though a slave, he had access to Zedekiah, the king. This suggests he was on a par with such men as Nehemiah, who also seems to have had unlimited access to his king, Artaxerxes. Second, he had the courage to call the king's attention to the cruelty and injustice of powerful men in the government at that time. Third, Zedekiah listened to this man who visited the king and was influenced by him to favor Jeremiah.

This slave was far more deserving of the title "king's servant" than the petty advisors of the king who tried to stir him up against Jeremiah. The only thing they could accuse the prophet of was that he spoke frankly and fearlessly about the spiritual issues of the day.

People like Ebed-Melech exist in our churches today. They are quiet, unassuming people who keep their ears open to need and their eyes observant about how they can help people with problems. The value of such men and women is recognized in many small village and country churches. The "headline crazy" world passes over them, but in God's sight they are the truly great ones. They have one goal in life: they want to help others by alleviating their pain and suffering. These are the truly great people in our world.

VII. TEACHING OUTLINE

A. INTRODUCTION

1. Lead Story: Back to the Task

2. Context: We have come to 587 B.C., the end of the Southern Kingdom of Judah. The focus of chapters 34–39 is on fickle and faithless Zedekiah, the nation's last king, and on persistent and persecuted Jeremiah. Two flashbacks to the reign of Jehoiakim, almost twenty years earlier, introduce us to the honorable Recabites and tell us how King Jehoiakim destroyed the first version of the Book of Jeremiah. Clearly Judah's last kings wanted to put an end to both the message and the messenger of the Lord.

3. Transition: These chapters help us understand that the Lord expects his people to honor both their word and God's Word. The Lord's people are to keep their word; uphold and live by the Lord's commands and all that is consistent with them; and reverently hear, heed, and handle the Holy Scriptures.

B. COMMENTARY

1. A Word of Warning to Zedekiah (34:1–22)

2. Jeremiah's Approval of the Recabites (35:1–19)

3. Jeremiah's Scroll Is Destroyed (36:1–32)

4. Jeremiah Is Thrown into Prison (37:1–21)

5. Jeremiah's Final Crisis Before the End (38:1–28)

6. Third and Final Invasion of Jerusalem (39:1–18)

C. CONCLUSION: FALL OF A NATION

VIII. ISSUES FOR DISCUSSION

1. Discuss the roles of tradition and traditions. When are traditions helpful and good? When are traditions hindrances and detrimental? What is the difference between "tradition" and "traditionalism"?

2. Some people refuse to throw away old, worn-out copies of the Bible. Rather, they choose to burn them reverently. How is this action different from Jehoiakim's when the disposal method and the result are the same? How much respect should we demonstrate toward printed copies of the Bible?

Jeremiah 40:1–45:5

Rebels to the End

I. INTRODUCTION
Et Tu, Brute?

II. COMMENTARY
A verse-by-verse explanation of these verses.

III. CONCLUSION
People Under Pressure

An overview of the principles and applications from these verses.

IV. LIFE APPLICATION
B. C. and Baruch

Melding these verses to life.

V. PRAYER
Tying these verses to life with God.

VI. DEEPER DISCOVERIES
Historical, geographical, and grammatical enrichment of the commentary.

VII. TEACHING OUTLINE
Suggested step-by-step group study of these verses.

VIII. ISSUES FOR DISCUSSION
Zeroing these verses in on daily life.

Quote

"*H*ave you delivered yourself over to exhaustion because of the way you have been serving God? If so, then renew and rekindle your desires and affections. Examine your reasons for service. Is your source based on your own understanding or is it grounded on the redemption of Jesus Christ? Continually look back to the foundation of your love and affection and remember where your Source of power lies. You have no right to complain, 'O Lord, I am so exhausted.' He saved and sanctified you to exhaust you. Be exhausted for God, but remember that He is your supply."

Oswald Chambers

Jeremiah 40:1–45:5

IN A NUTSHELL

*T*he long prophesied end has come. Jerusalem is fallen. Baby-lon is victorious. Chapters 40–44 focus on those who survived the dev-astation and remained in Judah and in the nearby countries. Jeremiah himself was released by the Babylonian officials and was offered the op-tions of going to Babylon or choosing to go anywhere else he pleased. The Babylonians appointed Gedaliah, the grandson of Shaphan, asso-ciate of the royal court in Jerusalem and sympathizer with Jeremiah's message, as governor. With this favorable development, many Jews who had fled to Moab, Ammon, and Edom returned to Judah.

But the king of Ammon plotted with Ishmael, a Jew who was related to the royal family, to murder Gedaliah. Johanan discovered the plot and revealed it to the governor. Gedaliah refused to believe and act on the information. Thus Gedaliah, his staff, a contingent of Babylonian sol-diers, and numerous others were slaughtered. Many, including Jeremi-ah and the daughters of the Jewish king, were taken captive and marched toward Ammon. When Johanan learned the dreadful news, he pursued Ishmael and liberated the captives. Unfortunately, Ishmael and his closest associates escaped.

Fearful of a Babylonian reprisal, the refugees fled toward Egypt. Promising obedience, they asked Jeremiah to inquire of the Lord what they should do and where they should go. The Lord told Jeremiah the remnant should remain in Judah. But the people rejected Jeremiah's revelation, accused him once again of being a traitor, and disobeyed God's word. In spite of Jeremiah's warning, they fled to Egypt, taking the prophet and his scribe with them. This was a fatal mistake (42:20). The section ends with Jeremiah's final warning to the Jews against commit-ting idolatry and apostasy in Egypt (ch. 44). Chapter 45 briefly reverts back to 605 B.C., the fourth year of King Jehoiakim (see ch. 36 for the context), and contains a summary of what Jeremiah told his scribe Baruch in response to his complaint during a period when he was emo-tionally and spiritually worn out.

Rebels to the End

I. INTRODUCTION

Et Tu, Brute?

*I*n Shakespeare's tragedy *Julius Caesar,* he introduces us to Caesar, who is not satisfied with being emperor of Rome but wishes to be king of the Roman state, indeed to be honored and worshipped as a god incarnate. Nevertheless, in spite of Caesar's victory over Pompey, all is not well in 44 B.C. Rome. Powerful forces among the disgruntled aristocracy have plotted against Caesar and intend to assassinate him in the Senate chamber on the ides of March. Caesar is warned by several people of the conspiracy as he makes his way to the Senate. But he dismisses them all. Because of his pride, his doom is assured.

What makes leaders (and others of us who should know better) so naive when it comes to threats against them? Arrogance, pride, and vanity have contributed to the downfall of many. For some, it is a sense of inviolability or that they are impervious to the attacks of others that have been their undoing. Overconfidence has blinded many.

In the case of Gedaliah, the Babylonian-appointed Jewish governor, a naive innocence about the effect of envy and jealousy on human nature seems to have combined with a failure to distinguish his own magnanimous character and attitudes from the true motives of other less-than-honorable individuals. Not all people work for the good. Not all people want peace, cooperation, and success. If they cannot be in charge, some people thrive on creating chaos, dissension, and disorder; and they will take whatever steps are necessary to see failure prevail. What would Gedaliah have accomplished in the rebuilding of Judah if he had not been assassinated? What would the remnant community that fled to Egypt and their descendants have been spared if Gedaliah had been allowed to accomplish his work? Only God knows. But we do know that those who plot a leader's removal also seek to end his work. By not paying attention to credible threats, we not only endanger our own selves but also our part in the work God has called us to do.

II. COMMENTARY

Rebels to the End

> **MAIN IDEA:** *People whose hearts have never been transformed by God's Spirit are still rebels. Nothing but an act of God can change them.*

Chapters 40–45 deal with the final days of Jerusalem after the Babylonians devastated it and took almost all the people into slavery. The few who remained were the "culls" of the land.

Gedaliah Appointed Governor of Judah (40:1–16)

> **SUPPORTING IDEA:** *When one does what he feels is God's will, the Lord will make the results work to the person's good.*

40:1–6. After Neuchadnezzar finished his third invasion of Jerusalem and burned the temple, he left the city and the entire region in shambles. Nobody remained except the poorest of the land, those who had never accomplished much and were limited in education and resources. Such people are easily swayed by any charismatic leader that comes along.

Where was Jeremiah after this third invasion? He seems to have been "lost in the shuffle." Nebuchadnezzar had given **Nebuzaradan** instructions to treat the prophet kindly. The two passages, 39:14–16 and 40:1–6, represent two separate accounts of the same events but with a difference in details. When one reads the two versions superficially, they seem to be contradictory. But a reflective reading of the two reveals that no contradiction exists.

What happened? Probably, when confusion arose, one of two things took place. Perhaps the Babylonian soldiers mistakenly took Jeremiah along with the other captives and brought him to **Ramah**, a small town a few miles outside Jerusalem. The other possibility is that Jeremiah was set free in Jerusalem but decided to go along with the captives and give encouragement to these prisoners of war. Not realizing who Jeremiah was and that he had been freed, someone had him arrested, and he became a prisoner once more. Nebuzaradan **found** him (40:1) and **released** him again. Either explanation accounts for the apparent contradictions.

Consider the options that Nebuzaradan offered and look at Jeremiah's choice. How many modern pastors would stay with a struggling congregation at a small salary if a larger church offered him a well-paying staff position? How many would rationalize and say, "I can be a greater influence for God in the larger church"? Jeremiah could have said that, but he didn't. He chose to remain with his people and be a shepherd of the flock.

Notice several things about the text. First, the expression **the word came** suggests a prophetic utterance to follow. One does not occur, however, until three chapters later (43:9). So we should accept the expression in a wider sense. God's Word includes history as well as spoken words of the prophet. Jews of that day had no problem with such a concept. To them, history was prophecy. This is why they divided their canon into Law, Prophecy, and Writings, including the historical books in the section called "Prophecy."

The speech of Nebuzaradan to Jeremiah has caused some interpreters to claim that an editor reworked this text. They claim a speech like this is out of character for a Babylonian general. But this is a faulty contention. The Babylonians were in the mainstream of life and knew exactly what was going on in the larger world. Though they were devotees of their god, Marduk, they knew the Jews worshipped Yahweh. This Babylonian general wasn't uninformed about other cultures. He knew how to speak to impress and persuade people of other religions.

For instance, during an earlier siege of Jerusalem, the Assyrian king Sennacherib's propaganda agent, Rabshakeh, made a lengthy speech to the leaders of Judah. He outlined why Hezekiah should surrender to their king. Standing on an elevated platform at a strategic place where the people of the land could overhear, he spoke to Hezekiah's special representatives. The Jewish officials pleaded with Rabshkeh to speak in Aramaic rather than Hebrew because they did not want the "grassroots" people to hear the Assyrian arguments about why the city should surrender.

One of Rabshakeh's main contentions was that Judah's God, Yahweh, had sent him to destroy the city (Isa. 36:10). He knew also about the sharp division among the people about the location of worship. Should it be centralized at the temple or should worship at the smaller altars in the towns also be permitted (Isa. 36:7–8)?

Almost everything Nebuzaradan said was in the spirit of Deuteronomy. This is not surprising. The land had been under the influence of this Mosaic book since Hilkiah discovered it in the temple during a remodeling project. It had been the basis for every act of religious zeal during the past thirty years, demanding a renewal of Judaism. When Nebuzaradan gave Jeremiah his options, he must have thought the prophet would join his fellow exiles in Babylon. He must have been greatly puzzled because he did not understand the prophetic heart. Jeremiah felt comfortable with the group in Judah since it was led by **Gedaliah**, a **son of Ahikam**, an old friend. The Babylonian commander showed his good will toward the prophet and his decision by giving him food and another present as a gesture of kindness.

40:7–12. The fact that Nebuchadnezzar appointed Gedaliah, a Jew, to be **governor** of the land after he had conquered it met with favor from most of the remaining Jews. Yet a few militant holdouts refused to give up. Included among them were some of the "top brass" of the nation. We do not know how many men they had with them as followers, but they were all strong-willed men.

The appointment of **Gedaliah** pleased this group, and they approached him at **Mizpah**. A number of towns called by this name are mentioned in the Old Testament. The Mizpah referred to in this context was probably the one located a few miles north of Jerusalem in the territory assigned to Benjamin. Several important events took place at this town, including the choosing of Saul as the first king (1 Sam. 10:17–24).

Nebuchadnezzar chose Mizpah as the seat of government after the destruction of Jerusalem. It had not been ravaged like Jerusalem. In addition, this little town contained many rich religious and political associations for the people. It was an excellent choice, both administratively and psychologically, and the people seemed pleased.

Look at the group of Jewish military leaders who came to Mizpah. They are listed in verse 8. The first two, **Ishmael** and **Johanan**, stand out as the ones who seem to have been most important. The former later killed Gedaliah and a number of his associates (41:1–3). According to 41:1, Ishmael was of royal descent. Perhaps he felt he should have been made governor of the land instead of Gedaliah.

Johanan is a short form of a proper name that meant "Yahweh is merciful." Johanan was probably jealous of Ishmael, which explains his words to Gedaliah about him (vv. 13–14). The others seem to be of lesser importance. A parallel passage (2 Kgs. 25:23) omits Jonathan's name.

Seraiah is mentioned only in this passage and the parallel passage in 2 Kings 25:23. The sons of **Ephai**, like their father, were from Netophah, a small village near Bethlehem. **Jaazaniah** was the son of a man from Maacah, located in the Golan Heights, south of Mount Hermon (Gen. 22:24). The text says these leaders brought their men with them. But nothing is said about how many this included.

Gedaliah, the new governor, realized the men were skeptical and, therefore, hesitant about coming out of their hiding places. He made the first move and assured them they should **not be afraid to serve** Babylon. Nebuchadnezzar had probably given Gedaliah the authority to grant amnesty to any citizens of Judah whom he felt deserved it. The new governor outlined his plan. He would remain in Mizpah and represent the people in their relationship with Babylon. He would be a mediator or advocate, working for their best interests with those who captured them and destroyed their city.

Gedaliah suggested that the people **harvest** the crops and make provision for their **storage**. These crops were the **wine**, **summer fruit**, and olive **oil**. Being already under cultivation, they were not damaged in the siege. Gedaliah's advice was, "Resume normal living. Let me stay here at Mizpah and look out for your interests with Babylon." This seemed to satisfy the people, even Ishmael. When news went out to the Jews in other countries such as Moab, Ammon, and Edom, they also returned to Judah, along with those who had scattered to other regions. Things seemed to be working out.

40:13–16. When a group of strong-willed people with administrative skills get together, a struggle for power soon emerges. In this case it took the form of a conflict between **Ishmael** and **Johanan**. They could have been jealous of each other and the position of leadership. The greater possibility is that Ishmael was envious of the position Nebuchadnezzar had bestowed on Gedaliah. The plan for assassination demonstrates that Ishmael wanted to replace Gedaliah.

Ishmael seemed to be a good man. He did not want the Babylonians to destroy the Jewish faith or bring any harm to Yahweh's people. He was crude and cruel in his methods, but we should give him credit for his motives. He was probably sincere in believing Gedaliah would be tilted too much toward Babylon and would water down the Jewish faith. But he was still motivated by a selfishness that colored every action he initiated.

What about Johanan? Again, we must recognize both sides of this man who supported Gedaliah. He wanted to be the "number two man" in the new organization of the governor. On the other hand, he did speak accurately about Ishmael.

Surely no one can doubt that **Baallis**, king of the Ammonites, entered into a conspiracy with Ishmael to destroy Gedalilah and the remaining vestiges of a Jewish government in Judah. He wanted to take some of the Jewish land and annex it to his own.

Ammon was one of the countries listed in chapter 27 as attending the meeting in Judah to discuss ways of curtailing Babylon's rising power. Jeremiah had opposed this alliance, saying that Yahweh had determined that Babylon would be victorious in the power struggle taking place. No bond of affection existed between Ammon and Jeremiah! Johanan represented the same school of thought as Jeremiah.

Why did Gedaliah refuse to take Johanan's advice? All the evidence indicated he was correct in his prediction and sound in his advice. After considering all the proposed reasons for Gedialiah's reluctance and refusal, we are driven back to one explanation. The governor was one of those men who could not understand evil and malice in anyone and actually refused to believe they existed.

Johanan requested the privilege of taking things into his own hands and assassinating Ishmael before he could do any serious damage. Gedaliah refused to grant him permission to do so. Perhaps he felt Ishmael would not be so foolish as to attempt such an act or perhaps he felt strong enough to deal with such a crisis. Gedaliah's failure to act was his undoing. Like Caesar who refused to believe Brutus and the others were plotting against him, he paid for his naïve attitude by his own death.

Ⓑ Ishmael Murders Gedaliah (41:1–18)

SUPPORTING IDEA: *The path of rebellion against God is a rugged road.*

Things move fast and furiously in this chapter. The writer told of the event that vindicated Johanan. The Jewish military captain spoke accurately to Gedaliah about Ishmael's plot to kill him.

41:1–3. In the ancient Semitic world a visitor in one's home was considered an honored guest. The host considered proper treatment and protection of such a person an inescapable duty. Another custom "written in concrete" was that of sharing a meal with someone. This was the highest type of social fellowship available. To engage in a meal with someone denoted a special bond. To violate this code was considered a flagrant wrongdoing.

Ishmael, however, did this very thing! He and Gedaliah must have been friends, certainly more than mere acquaintances. Furthermore, Ishmael brought **ten men** with him to the "food fellowship." According to verses 1–3, Ishmael and his friends killed Gedaliah and the men with him. The text also mentions **Babylonian soldiers**. We do not know the total number killed or how Ishmael's men could get the job done so quickly.

41:4–10. The scene suddenly changes. **Eighty men** from three different cities arrived in Mizpah. They were bringing **offerings**, probably for the Feast of Tabernacles, and were displaying signs of mourning because the temple had been destroyed. This tragic event had already become a sad situation for the Jews. These men were probably going to worship at the site of the temple, although it lay in ruins.

Acting with hypocrisy, Ishmael went out from Mizpah to meet these pilgrims, feigning signs of grief. Luring these unsuspecting travelers into the city, he and his men **slaughtered** all but ten of them, throwing their bodies into a pit. These fortunate ten escaped because they promised to show Ishmael where they had more food hidden in a field. Obviously, Ishmael needed the food, probably because he planned to go to Ammon as quickly as he could in order to join Baalis.

Ishmael knew the Babylonian king would come against him for attacking his appointee to the governorship of Judah. So he gathered all the people who remained at Mizpah and headed for Ammon. These included the **daughters** of Zedekiah who were still there. They were spared by the Babylonian king when their brothers were killed. Perhaps Nebuchadnezzar spared their lives as a generous act to gain the Jews' good will.

Why did Ishmael take the captives with him instead of killing them to keep word of his action from reaching Nebuchadnezzar? He probably intended to sell these people as slaves or to use them as hostages if the remaining Israelites attacked him. Jeremiah was probably among these captives, since he was probably in Mizpah when the assassination occurred (40:6).

41:11–18. Enter the hero! The question is, Why did Johanan allow Ishmael to go so far without seeking to halt his mad killings? We cannot be certain. Ishmael was already aware of Johanan's suspicions. Perhaps Ishmael waited until Johanan was away from Mizpah to begin his coup. But once Johanan learned of Ishmael's deed, he lost no time going after him.

The spot at which Johanan caught up with Ishmael was a significant one in Old Testament history. It had a bloody image. In the days following Saul's death, a struggle for the throne ensued between the followers of Saul and the followers of David. At **Gibeon**, through trickery, twelve of David's army, led by Joab, killed twelve of Saul's remaining army (2 Sam. 2:12–16).

Recent archaeological findings suggest Gibeon was three miles southwest of Mizpah rather than east in the direction of Ammon as was once thought. Why was Ishmael headed in this direction? Perhaps he circled that way to throw off any pursuers. In terms of distance, he had not traveled very far with his group of captives. Johanan probably inquired of people along the way who had seen Ishmael and his captives and was able to guess Ishmael's strategy.

The captives, on seeing Johanan and his men, escaped from Ishmael and hurried to Johanan. Ishmael and his men, seeing themselves destined for death, decided to flee for Ammon. He and eight of his men succeeded. This is the last we hear of Ishmael. What about Johanan? Should he return to Mizpah? This must have seemed the proper thing to do. Upon reflecting, however, he realized Nebuchadnezzar would hear of this incident. Not knowing all the facts, he would assume Johanan was as much of a rebel against him as Ishmael.

Johanan decided that his hope was **Egypt**, the only nearby country that was free from Babylon's domination. So the Jewish refugees, under Johanan, went southward toward Bethlehem. They stopped at **Geruth Kimham** near the city.

Jeremiah Warns Against Going to Egypt (42:1–22)

SUPPORTING IDEA: *When people come to a crisis, they call on the Lord for guidance.*

42:1–6. These men who approached Jeremiah had already decided they were going to Egypt. In fact, they were on their way to that country when they stopped at Geruth Kimham. As subsequent events demonstrate, they had no intention of changing their plans, regardless of what Jeremiah said.

Jeremiah, for the first time in his life, was being treated with a little respect. This was a new experience for him. For most of his prophetic career, he had been ignored, opposed, and persecuted because of his convictions and advice. After hearing the people's request, Jeremiah assured them he would seek the Lord's will for them. He insisted he would **keep nothing back** when he discerned God's will for them. Replying with pious verbosity, they affirmed, **Pray that the LORD your God will tell us where we should go and what we should do**.

42:7–22. For **ten days**, Jeremiah struggled in prayer for God to reveal his will so he could pass it on to the people. When he felt assured of God's answer, he spoke with confidence. God's message was, "Stay in this land. I share the discomfort you are experiencing because of your sins. I regret your rebellion forced me to bring this disaster on you. Do not be afraid of Nebuchadnezzar. I will be with you and restore you to the land I have promised you."

This plea had a "flip side." If the people refused to heed the prophet's message, a fate similar to that of their fellow Israelites awaited them.

D Another Warning in Egypt (43:1–13)

SUPPORTING IDEA: *When people have made up their mind what they plan to do, spiritual advice falls on deaf ears.*

43:1–7. Old Testament scholars disagree whether **Azariah** in verse 2 is the same as Jezaniah in 42:1 since both are identified as the son of **Hoshaiah**. The majority believe they are the same person, probably because the Septuagint identifies both as Azariah. This man became militant in answering Jeremiah's advice, actually accusing the prophet of lying. He perhaps softened his statement a bit when he attributed Jeremiah's advice to Baruch's influence.

No recorded evidence justifies Azariah's charge against Jeremiah's scribe, **Baruch**. He and the prophet had worked together. They must have shared many viewpoints and discussed Judah's spiritual plight many times. But anyone familiar with Jeremiah's life knows the prophet was not easily swayed from what he believed to be God's will. True, on one other occasion, he did retire for further prayer and consultation with the Lord (28:5–16). This is both good religion and common sense. God does not work in a mental vacuum.

These two occasions, however, seem to show Jeremiah's fairness and objectivity in his pronouncements. He was open-minded to the fact that he might fail to discern the will of God accurately, but this is not a trait of weakness. In fact, the opposite is true. For a person to admit that he could make an error requires strength of character as well as emotional and spiritual security. Jeremiah may have been influenced by Baruch, but he was never "brainwashed" into a wrong decision by him.

Having made their decision, Johanan and his group acted on it. He and his colleagues led the people into Egypt. Included in the group were not only **men, women and children** but the **king's daughters** as well.

The journey must have been difficult. Food and other necessities were probably in short supply. Sickness may have broken out among the people. Many people would have preferred to go back home and trust their fate to the Babylonians. But the stronger voices insisted on continuing their journey. They prevailed, and the first stop was Tahpanes, a frontier town on the eastern border of Egypt.

43:8–13. Tahpanhes transliterates an Egyptian location that means "fortress of Penhase" or "house of the Nubian." Archaeologists say it shows little evidence of heavy occupation before the middle of the seventh century before Christ. The word translated **palace** in verse 9 is actually a house Pharaoh had built for himself. It was not the king's main palace but probably served as a government building and his residence when he visited the city.

The biblical record does not tell whether Jeremiah accompanied the group voluntarily or was forced. My personal judgment is he went because he wished to be with them and provide spiritual guidance. He must have felt led by the Lord in this decision. The prophet continued his message, illustrating it with a symbolic act. He buried the **stones** some distance away from the actual building. No refugee Jew would have been allowed to disturb the actual pavement built by the Egyptians. But the people got the message because the symbolic act was accompanied by the prophet's plain and forceful words.

Nebuchadnezzar did return later to Egypt to complete the job he had left unfinished after the battle of Carchemisch. This time he came not as "crown prince" but as the powerful king of Babylon. The description of Babylon's work in verses 11–13 was typical of how visiting armies plundered nations they conquered. Nebuchadnezzar had no trouble conquering Egypt.

The picture of a **shepherd** wrapping his **garment** around himself illustrated the ease with which Nebuchadnezzar would accomplish his task. The word *wrap* has a double meaning. It can also speak of "removing lice." This translation could suggest the king would strip Egypt of its riches like a shepherd picks lice from his garment. Egypt would not have the power to resist.

Was this prophecy fulfilled? Nebuchadnezzar invaded Egypt in 568 B.C. Complete records are not available, but we have no reason to doubt the outcome was a victory for Babylon. Nebuchadnezzar did, however, allow Amasis, who had become co-king of Egypt, to remain on the throne. In later years Babylon and Egypt established a friendly relationship. The spirit of Jeremiah's prediction was certainly fulfilled.

𝔼 Jeremiah's Final Message to the People of Judah (44:1–30)

SUPPORTING IDEA: *The more people continue to rebel against God, the more they will feel his wrath and punitive hand.*

44:1–14. The Jews who entered Egypt under Johanan's leadership were not the first ones to live in Egypt. Some had been present for many years. Some families probably stayed in Egypt when Moses led the group out. Their descendants may have been present when Johanan and his group arrived.

A man like Jeremiah was too well-known to be limited to a small group such as the Jews who came to Egypt with Johanan. The prophet's reputation preceded him, and soon he was ministering to Jews in a larger area. The words in this chapter were spoken to all the Jews in the area, perhaps to a group of leaders gathered in one central location.

Jeremiah spoke first to the people about the current situation. No one, including those already in Egypt, was ignorant about what had happened when Nebuchadnezzar attacked Jerusalem. Jews knew what was going on among fellow Jews. The prophet reminded the people of how their forefathers had disobeyed God through the centuries. All these words were prelude to his next message.

Speaking directly, Jeremiah told of what God was about to do to the group that had recently come to Egypt. **None** would **escape** or **return** to Judah except a few who were able to run away. Jeremiah held out no hope for the rebellious group under Johanan.

44:15–30. These verses contain charges and counter charges. Both the men and women insisted they would continue their lifestyle. They contended they had been more prosperous when they were engaging in their type of worship than when they were serving Yahweh.

Who was this goddess, the **Queen of Heaven**, to which the people offered **incense** and poured out **drink offerings**? Old Testament scholars and archaeologists are not certain. Part of the rituals included in her worship was **making cakes**, probably in her image, some of which have been found by archaeologists. The devotees offered drink offerings and burned incense to her.

Scholars suggest two pagan deities as the possible major influences of this worship: First, it might have been Ishtar, a Babylonian goddess, whom they called "queen of heaven" and who had been imported to Israel by Manasseh. Second, it could have been Ashtarte, a Canaanite goddess found by Israel when they invaded the land. Archaeologists have found many nude goddesses at Israelite places of worship. They show why the prophet railed against this type of worship.

Jeremiah concluded this message with a sure word by which his message could be validated. God would turn over Egypt's present ruler, **Pharaoh Hophra** (589–570 B.C.), called Aries, to his enemies, not necessarily to Nebuchadnezzar. This Babylonian king was currently seeking Hophra's life because he had tried to help **Zedekiah** in his fight with Babylon.

Was Jeremiah's word fulfilled? The historical facts speak for themselves. Toward the end of Hophra's reign, a rebellion arose against the Egyptian king in some parts of his army. He sent Amasis, one of his generals, to handle the revolt. Amasis had himself proclaimed coruler and reigned alongside Hophra. Within three years Hophra was put to death. Thus, Jeremiah's words were fulfilled.

⬛F⬛ A Message of Encouragement for Baruch (45:1–5)

SUPPORTING IDEA: *For every sacrifice we make to serve God and do his will, he will reward us, although not always in the way we expect.*

45:1–3. Jeremiah's words to **Baruch** in this passage came at the time when he had dictated his scroll in the **fourth year of Jehoiakim**. The prophet then told Baruch to read the scroll in the temple to the people. The result was a hectic day for the faithful secretary (36:1–32). In this passage Baruch, in a depressed state, had complained to Jeremiah. Baruch was like the prophet—a tender soul.

45:4–5. Jeremiah never minimized the difficulties of serving Yahweh. He reminded his scribe of what the Lord had said to him at the beginning of his own prophetic career. Because of the people's sins, he must **overthrow** what he had **built** and **uproot** what he had **planted**. Jeremiah had to have a "tough hide" to serve him as his messenger. Likewise, Baruch had chosen to be Jeremiah's colleague. He must endure the same persecution although not in such intensity as the prophet.

Does verse 5 mean Jeremiah was accusing Baruch of too much personal ambition? Not necessarily. Perhaps he was only immunizing his scribe against expecting a greater reward than a person linked with the Lord should ever envision for himself. Words like those of Jeremiah drive us to examine how "greatness" should be defined for a person who is surrendered to the Lord's will.

> **MAIN IDEA REVIEW:** *People whose hearts have never been transformed by God's Spirit are still rebels. Nothing but an act of God can change them.*

III. CONCLUSION

People Under Pressure

Sometimes what happens in the aftermath of a disaster brings out the best and the worst in people. In Jeremiah 40–45 we have met several individuals who illustrate this truth.

Nebuzaradan, the Babylonian commander of the imperial guard, proved himself to be an honorable and considerate conqueror, not a cruel and sadistic overlord. He released Jeremiah from captivity, acknowledged the truth of Jeremiah's prophecies and the true reason the Lord brought disaster on Judah, offered Jeremiah two attractive options for his future, and then supplied Jeremiah with provisions and gave him gifts.

Gedaliah, the Jewish governor appointed by the Babylonians, rebuilt confidence among his own people and led his nation to set about rebuilding its infrastructure. Yet despite his magnanimous nature he was naive about the evil of human nature and refused to believe the intentions of some of his fellow countrymen were not as charitable as his own.

The Jewish military commander *Johanan* proved himself to be a shrewd judge of character with a reliable informational network in the field. And even though his advice was not accepted, he came to the rescue of many persons in their hour of need. Wisely he sought the Lord's advice through the prophet Jeremiah, but he made a fatal mistake in not listening to the Lord's instructions through Jeremiah when they were not what he wanted to hear.

Ishmael showed himself to be a betrayer, murderer, terrorist, and insurgent. He assassinated Gedaliah the governor, killed all the Jews who were with the governor, and murdered a contingent of Babylonian soldiers. He slaughtered other unsuspecting innocents and took numerous hostages.

Baalis, king of the Ammonites, was more than ready to encourage, support, and protect murderers, terrorists, and insurgents. He sought to bring disruption and chaos to a neighboring country, taking advantage of their weakened condition.

Baruch, Jeremiah's faithful scribe, is brought before us in chapter 45 in a less-than-favorable light during an earlier incident. He had worn himself out in service to the Lord, and in the midst of burnout complained to the Lord. The Lord needed to teach Baruch that he also had great disappointments in his work with people, but at the root of Baruch's complaints was the frustration of his own ambitions. After this, in spite of being falsely accused (43:3,6), Baruch is seen standing firm with Jeremiah as they are taken to Egypt by the refugees.

And finally there is *Jeremiah.* Jeremiah the prophet, who was treated more favorably by the Babylonians than by his own people. Jeremiah the intercessor, whom the refugees still approached to inquire for them of the Lord. Jeremiah the messenger, who after he had inquired on behalf of the remnant, was told by them that he was lying and that the Lord had not spoken to him. Jeremiah the preacher, who at over seventy years old still graphically illustrated his messages with symbolic actions. Jeremiah the faithful witness, who closed out his long life still proclaiming the word of the Lord and preaching against idolatry to those who were blind and deaf to its disastrous consequences in their own history.

Seeing how each of these individuals responded and acted under pressure and when their lives were thrown into chaos should cause each of us to examine our own character. With which of these figures do you most identify? Least identify? Do you see similar tendencies in yourself that might be brought out if the world around you as you know it should fall apart? Let each of us pray that we would be like the best of God's faithful servants.

PRINCIPLES

- Some people cannot accept stability and peacefulness during a time of occupation and nation rebuilding. Instead, through their insurgency they create havoc and bring reprisals upon themselves and their people by the occupying forces.

- Sometimes leaders of surrounding nations seek to bring further instability to their neighbors by supporting, supplying, and providing a safe haven for insurgents during times of nation rebuilding by occupying forces and reasonable nationals.

- Political leaders who are seeking to rebuild their nation cannot afford to be naive about threats made against them. They need to take all threats against themselves and their work seriously. Often the most magnanimous leaders evidence a certain naivete because they attribute the same magnanimity to their opponents as they themselves possess.

- When people ask the Lord for his guidance, they need to obey what he tells them even if it is not what they want to hear.

- Even after experiencing disastrous consequences because of previous habits and choices, it is hard for people to abandon those practices; sometimes they even increase in doing them.

- Those who serve the Lord may experience burnout. Often behind their discouragement and complaints that arise at such times are their own frustrated ambitions.

APPLICATIONS

- Do I thrive on chaos and crisis? Do I enjoy bringing confusion, disorder, and disruption into my environment? If so, I am working for the greatest enemy of all (1 Cor. 14:33).

- Which countries would you name as supporting, equipping, and protecting terrorists and insurgents? Stop and pray that the leaders of these nations will see the error of their ways and abandon such practices.

- All people need to take seriously threats made against them. Have you heard someone make a threat against someone else and you have not reported it? What will you do about it?

- Never promise you will obey what the Lord wants you to do unless you are prepared to do it.

- Without spiritual transformation people will not give up old habits and practices that have brought calamity and misfortune into their lives. Ask yourself, "What sinful habits and practices am I unwilling to give up?" Surrender these to God now.

- List ten personal ambitions you cherish. Now indicate if these are selfish ambitions or sanctified ambitions. Read Jeremiah 45:5 and turn all your ambitions over to the Lord.

IV. LIFE APPLICATION

B. C. and Baruch

Around the world every morning many Christians open and read from a small devotional book that helps set their minds and hearts on God. These Christians are well acquainted with the devotional classic *My Utmost for His Highest*. Indeed, the very mention of the title usually elicits in the same breath the literary identification "by Oswald Chambers." However, few Christians today know much about this beloved writer.

Oswald Chambers, a Scot by birth, was the son of a Baptist pastor. After feeling God's call, Oswald left the University of Edinburgh at twenty-three and began training for Christian ministry. After seven years as a student and tutor, Chambers embarked on an evangelistic tour of Japan and America. Upon returning to London, he continued his evangelistic work throughout the British Isles with the League of Prayer. After several years he accepted the principalship of the nondenominational Bible Training School in London.

With the outbreak of World War I, Oswald and his wife, along with their young daughter, relocated to the Egyptian desert where as a chaplain to British Commonwealth troops they established YMCA camps, prepared meals, and gave comfort, encouragement, and biblical instruction to thousands of British soldiers who passed through the camps. And there in Egypt in 1917

Oswald Chambers died at age forty-three from complications from an emergency appendectomy.

But Oswald Chambers, author of the beloved *My Utmost for His Highest,* didn't write the book—or over thirty other Christian books, thousands of booklets, seed thought calendars, and sermon leaflets that bore his name. Only the most perceptive readers notice the initials "B. C." on Chambers' writings.

Who was B. C.? B. C. was Gertrude Hobbs. At age twenty-four Gertrude was making a trans-Atlantic voyage from Liverpool to New York City to seek secretarial employment. Gertrude's mother, whom Oswald knew from his brother's church, wrote to Chambers when she learned he was sailing on the same ship and asked if he would look after her daughter during the voyage. Chambers felt courtesy required that he accompany the unescorted traveler to meals and that he help her get acclimated to the ship. During these times together Oswald learned more about this young woman and began to develop feelings for her.

Gertrude had not been well as a child. Her illness had interfered with her formal schooling, so she had learned Pitman Shorthand at home and taught herself to type. By the time she was old enough to work full-time, she could take dictation at 250 words a minute. But she was not content merely to function as a machine recording words. She listened for the sense and meaning of the thoughts expressed and recorded them. On their voyage Oswald felt addressing the young woman as Gertrude was too formal. Further, he had a sister by that name. For some unknown reason Oswald decided to call her "Biddy." Within three years Oswald and Biddy were husband and wife.

After Oswald's untimely death, Biddy Chambers returned to England. She purchased a house in Oxford, which she turned into a boarding house for university students. She rose at 6:00 a.m. every day, prepared and served breakfast for the students, and tended to her young daughter. After that she retreated to the basement, which was filled with books and boxes of Oswald's materials. There she transcribed and then typed out her notes of his sermons and lectures dating back to the Bible Training College days.

After her daily trip to the grocer, the butcher, the bakery, and the canned goods store, Biddy returned home to complete the laundry and prepare the evening meal. Then she would return to the basement and the books. It was here that over a three-year period Biddy compiled the collection of 365 daily readings gleaned from her notes and transcripts of hundreds of Oswald's talks that became *My Utmost for His Highest*.

When the devotional classic was published ten years after Oswald's death in 1927, Biddy signed only her initials "B. C." on the foreword. Nowhere in the book did she mention her name. The author was Oswald Chambers. She was only the channel through which the author's words and thoughts were conveyed to those who would read the book. For half a century "B. C." continued her work, calling the Christian world's attention to Oswald Chambers's words and not to herself or her work.

Biddy Chambers and Jeremiah's faithful secretary Baruch are examples of the ministry of the unnoticed. Most Christians, and even many readers of the Book of Jeremiah, have never noticed Baruch's name either—yet he wrote the book. Surely he at least wrote the "Baruch Narrative" in chapters 26–29 and 34–45, where Jeremiah is referred to in the third person. As Jeremiah's scribe, Baruch apparently also wrote down the rest of Jeremiah's messages, recording and preserving them for us.

Even though Baruch's brother Seraiah was a high-ranking officer under King Zedekiah (51:59), Baruch suffered because of his association with Jeremiah. He was with Jeremiah in prison when Jeremiah purchased the field (32:1–16). At Jeremiah's dictation he wrote the first edition of the Book of Jeremiah and read it from the upper courtyard to all who came to the temple to worship. Baruch then boldly read the prophecies again to the king's advisers, after which both he and the prophet had to go into hiding to avoid being arrested (and probably killed) by King Jehoiakim. While they were in hiding, Baruch rewrote Jeremiah's scroll (ch. 36). During this time Baruch was greatly discouraged and needed encouragement from the Lord (ch. 45). Later Baruch faced unfair accusations by the remnant community about his influence on Jeremiah (43:1–3) and, along with Jeremiah, was forcibly taken to Egypt (43:6). Yet Baruch continued his work.

Thank God for secretaries. It takes a person with special skills to do what they do. But even more it takes a special person to let another receive the recognition and credit for what they also have worked so hard to produce. Only those who have discovered the ministry of the unnoticed are content in knowing that they have faithfully done their part, whether anyone notices or not. But isn't that what each of us as believers is called to do (John 3:30; Gal. 2:20; Col. 3:1–3)?

V. PRAYER

O Lord, deliver and protect us from those who love hatred, who seek and bring violence and disruption, from insurgents who kill, murder, and assassinate. Give us, our nation, and the nations of our world peace and security within and between our borders. And cause us to be more concerned with the advancements and setbacks of your kingdom than with our own personal ambitions. Amen.

VI. DEEPER DISCOVERIES

A. Nebuzaradan

This name means "Nebo has given offspring." He was an officer in the Babylonian army during King Nebuchadnezzar's reign. His title is given as "commander of the guard" (Jer. 39:13), a designation which is uncertain. He led his troops in a siege of Jerusalem in 587 B.C. (2 Kgs. 25:8–9), burned the city's buildings, tore down its walls, and carried away the people into exile. Four years later he returned and deported still more citizens (Jer. 52:30).

B. Gedaliah

This name means "Yahweh has done great things." He was the son of Ahikam who was appointed ruler of Judah by Nebuchadnezzar of Babylon in 587 B.C. (2 Kgs. 25:22). Jerusalem had fallen to the Babylonians, and many of the residents of Judah had been deported. Ahikam, the father of Gedaliah, was an ally of the prophet Jeremiah (Jer. 26:24; 39:14), and Gedaliah may have been in sympathy with Jeremiah's political views. That could explain why Nebuchadnezzar selected Gedaliah to be governor. Gedaliah's time in office was brief. After only two months he was murdered by a group of zealous nationalists under the leadership of Ishmael (Jer. 40:1–41:18).

C. Johanan

This is the short form of a personal name—Jehohanan—meaning "Yahweh is merciful." He was a military leader among the Jews who remained in Judah immediately after the exile began in 586 B.C. (2 Kgs. 25:23). He led the effort against Ishmael, who had assassinated Gedaliah, the governor whom Babylon appointed over Judah. Johanan led the people into Egypt to escape

Babylonian retaliation. He forced Jeremiah to go with them, refusing to follow Jeremiah's word from God (Jer. 40–43).

VII. TEACHING OUTLINE

A. INTRODUCTION

1. Lead Story: Et Tu, Brute?

2. Context: After the fall of Jerusalem, the Babylonians appointed a Jewish governor over Judah. When a small group of insurgents assassinated Gedaliah, a remnant of the Jews, fearing Babylonian reprisals, fled to Egypt, taking Jeremiah and his companion Baruch with them. Jeremiah warned them not to do this, but they refused to heed the prophet's message.

3. Transition: Chapters 40–45 tell us what happened to Jeremiah after the fall of Jerusalem and bring us to Jeremiah's final prophecies. From the start of his ministry to the end, Jeremiah's messages, the words of the Lord, were rejected by his hearers. These chapters help us understand that often when people are given the chance of a new start they persist in their old ways, ideas, and habits that brought them into disaster in the first place.

B. COMMENTARY

1. Gedaliah Appointed Governor of Judah (40:1–16)

2. Ishmael Murders Gedaliah (41:1–18)

3. Jeremiah Warns Against Going to Egypt (42:1–22)

4. Another Warning in Egypt (43:1–13)

5. Jeremiah's Final Message to the People of Judah (44:1–30)

6. A Message of Encouragement for Baruch (45:1–5)

C. CONCLUSION: PEOPLE UNDER PRESSURE

VIII. ISSUES FOR DISCUSSION

1. Why do some people prefer insurgency over peaceful, cooperative nation rebuilding? Based on Jeremiah 40:7–41:15, are such people patriots, or do they make matters worse for their own people?

2. After reading Jeremiah 44, why do you think many people persist in practices and habits that have brought disaster into their lives even after they have had a chance to be delivered from them and make a new start?

3. Many people take comfort in the thought that God is watching over them. Compare Jeremiah 24:6 with 44:27. Is there a difference in the way God watches over people? What reasons can you suggest for this difference?

4. Why is burnout a danger for those in full-time ministry? Is there a place for "sanctified ambition" among Christian ministers? Read Jeremiah 45. How do you distinguish between a divinely approved ambition and ambition rooted in one's own hopes and desires?

Jeremiah 46:1–52:34

God and the Nations

I. INTRODUCTION
Nations in the Dock

II. COMMENTARY
A verse-by-verse explanation of these verses.

III. CONCLUSION
Punishment of the Nations

An overview of the principles and applications from these verses.

IV. LIFE APPLICATION
"Recessional"

Melding these verses to life.

V. PRAYER
Tying these verses to life with God.

VI. DEEPER DISCOVERIES
Historical, geographical, and grammatical enrichment of the commentary.

VII. TEACHING OUTLINE
Suggested step-by-step group study of these verses.

VIII. ISSUES FOR DISCUSSION
Zeroing these verses in on daily life.

"*N*ever before in legal history has an effort been made to bring within the scope of a single litigation the developments of a decade, covering a whole continent, and involving a score of nations, countless individuals, and innumerable events. . . . This trial has a scope that is utterly beyond anything that has ever been attempted that I know of in judicial history."

Supreme Court Justice Robert Jackson (American prosecutor at the Nuremberg trials)

Jeremiah 46:1–52:34

IN A NUTSHELL

*J*eremiah 46:1 sums up chapters 46–51. This section contains Jeremiah's judgment oracles against Judah's neighbor nations. Singled out for a special message from the Lord are Egypt (46:2–28), Philistia (47:1–7), Moab (48:1–47), Ammon (49:1–6), Edom (49:7–22), Damascus (49:23–27), Kedar and Hazor (49:28–33), Elam (49:34–39), and Babylon (50:1–51:64). The oracles date from various periods of Jeremiah's ministry. By being grouped together at the end of the book, these oracles serve as a vivid reminder that Jeremiah was also appointed as a prophet to the nations (1:5,10). Chapter 52 is a more detailed account of the fall of Jerusalem in 586 B.C. than that found in 39:1–10. In this closing chapter of the Book of Jeremiah we are left face-to-face with the fulfillment of Jeremiah's constant prophetic warnings—the nation of Judah is no more, the capital city of Jerusalem and its walls are destroyed, the great temple of Solomon has been looted and razed, the kings of Judah have been imprisoned and executed, the chief priests and remaining national leaders have been executed, and the people are scattered in exile in a foreign land.

God and the Nations

I. INTRODUCTION

Nations in the Dock

*N*othing like it had ever happened before. For the first time in history a nation and its leaders were brought before the bar of international justice to render account for their actions during a time of war. The place was Nuremberg, Germany. The time was November 1945 through October 1946. Following the defeat of Nazi Germany, the four Allied Powers—the United States, Great Britain, the Soviet Union, and the Republic of France—established an international court to bring the leaders of the Third Reich to trial.

The International Military Tribunal was not a forum merely to announce summary judgment by the victors on the vanquished. Nor was it designed just to mete out punishment to the principal Nazi leaders for the crimes and atrocities they committed. Rather, the tribunal also sought to establish that a criminal conspiracy, based on the Nazi doctrines of racism and totalitarianism, had been supported by the German people and foisted by them upon their neighbor nations. Germany had waged a war of aggression. They had committed war crimes in violation of the laws of war. And they had perpetrated crimes against humanity—murder, terrorism, deportation, enslavement, genocide, and the destruction of peaceful populations. For this the German nation itself bore guilt and responsibility.

The Nuremberg Trials brought Nazi Germany and its leaders before the bar of human judgment. In Jeremiah 46–51 we see the nations of the world in Jeremiah's day brought before the bar of God's judgment. God is specifically identified as the protagonist behind each of the oracles. The Lord condemned these nations of long ago for waging wars of aggression, invading sovereign neighboring countries, exploitation, wanton destruction and devastation, overweening pride and arrogance, looting, violence, atrocities, deportation of peoples, and defying the Lord.

Jeremiah's oracles may be ancient, but they are not archaic. The present nations of the world need to hear these proclamations from God's bar of judgment and sober up, realizing that all of our nations are in the dock today.

II. COMMENTARY

God and the Nations

MAIN IDEA: *God made the entire world and everything in it. The nations are regarded as dust on the scales. He will write in the register of the peoples, "This one was born in Zion" (Ps. 87:6).*

This final section contains nine messages, ten if we consider the words to Kedar and Hazor separately—to or about non-Israelite nations (Jer. 46–51). Appended to them is a chapter summarizing the major historical events that form the political background to Jeremiah's prophecies during Zedekiah's reign. Though the title does not appear in the Old Testament, scholars are virtually unanimous in calling them the "Foreign Prophecies." Some, however, insist on speaking of them as "Prophecies Against the Nations."

Two questions arise as we study these messages. They are not of crucial importance, but they do enrich our understanding of their content and should be examined briefly. First, were the sermons written only or delivered publicly as well? Further, if the latter, were they spoken only to Hebrew audiences or did Jeremiah actually travel to the various countries? Second, what was the purpose of these messages, and how did they relate to Yahweh's redemptive program for the world?

As to whether the messages were written only or actually spoken, one has great difficulty believing this prophet did not speak them. Though Jeremiah was a poet, he never would have, in my judgment, written messages like these and not preached them.

Where did Jeremiah deliver these messages? Hebrew prophets did travel. God sent Jonah to Nineveh. Amos came from Tekoa in the Southern Kingdom to Bethel in the Northern Kingdom. Elijah and Elisha both went to non-Israelite countries. Yahweh sent Jeremiah to the Euphrates to bury a girdle and then back again to retrieve it, though some interpret this event otherwise. But we don't know whether the prophet traveled to the nations to deliver these messages.

In answer to the second question, several reasons for these prophecies have emerged. First, in speaking these words, Jeremiah made clear to all who heard him that Yahweh was a holy God not only for Israel but for all nations and peoples. A parallel truth is that all the nations are responsible to him for their deeds.

Second, these messages to the foreign nations would serve as a comfort and an assurance to the people of Judah and others who heard them. Most of these nations, at one time or another, had abused Yahweh's people. The prophet's word about the punishment of those harming Judah would inform the latter that Yahweh would punish them for their evil conduct.

Third, Yahweh used these messages to inform the nations that they were included in his redemptive program, which was worldwide in its scope. When God called Abram to a new land, he gave him a sixfold message. He concluded with a promise that through the patriarch all the nations of the world would be blessed. These nations to which Jeremiah wrote were all included in that promise.

Another great prophet said, "It is too small a thing for you to be my servant to restore the tribes of Jacob and bring back those of Israel I have kept. I will also make you a light for the Gentiles, that you may bring my salvation to the ends of the earth" (Isa. 49:6). In a later passage, he said, further, "Nations will come to your light, and kings to the brightness of your dawn" (Isa. 60:3).

In Jesus Christ these promises and predictions found ultimate fulfillment. In Jeremiah's letters to the nations, however, we see God's redemptive program foreshadowed, even if, at some times, only dimly. This truth is the greatest part of the message about the nations.

Two Poems About Egypt (46:1–28)

SUPPORTING IDEA: *Egypt, the braggart nation, can never help those who lean on her. To depend on Egypt is an exercise in futility.*

Egypt's long history challenges even the best historians. An excellent article by Daniel C. Browning Jr. in the *Holman Bible Dictionary* summarizes succinctly yet comprehensively the many centuries of her activities. The two poems by Jeremiah in this chapter grow out of a time when this ancient empire interfered in international politics and paid for it.

46:1. This title verse serves as a preface to the entire group of messages about the Gentile nations. Two other major prophets, Isaiah and Ezekiel, have a grouping of messages addressed similarly although they do not have an introductory verse such as Jeremiah. The Book of Amos also contains a group of messages addressed to other nations, but they are less extensive than the other three prophets.

46:2–12. Jeremiah's first poem (v. 2) was addressed to **Egypt** as she prepared to fight the king who had recently captured Nineveh. Many of his words seem to drip with sarcasm. Speaking for Yahweh, he made light of Egypt's feeble attempt to oppose such a powerful foe as Babylon.

Jeremiah assumes the role of a commanding officer ordering his men to prepare for a critical battle. Verse 3 says, **Prepare your shields, both large and small.** The Hebrew text denotes two different types of shield. The former was small and circular in shape. The latter was long, and it covered the entire body.

The expression **harness the horses** (v. 4) refers to preparing the chariots for use in the coming conflict. The words **mount the steeds** is translated in some versions as "mount ye horsemen," but the NIV translation is preferable. One expositor insists since **helmets** were worn only in battle, the command about them was actually an order to engage.

The word translated **armor** in verse 4 is rendered "brigandines" in the KJV and some other versions. This noun has also been translated "scale-armor" (NASB). The term "brigandines" is connected with "brigade" in the divisions of an army, and the brigadier was the commander of such a division. This armor was probably used by light-armed skirmishers.

A sudden change takes place in verse 5. From a proud and confident army preparing for conflict, Jeremiah portrayed a group of **defeated**, humiliated, and disorganized warriors **retreating** in panic. The prophet did not dignify Egypt's effort at warfare enough to describe the battle. He merely told of the tragic end for the one whom Isaiah called "Rahab the Do-Nothing" (Isa. 30:7). Jeremiah expressed his utter dismay. He simply could not believe such a brilliant host could be so easily and thoroughly defeated, even pillaged and destroyed. The calamity was so sudden and thorough that even the quickest and speediest could not escape to return home (v. 6).

One technical scholar verified the prophet's geographical description. He pointed out that Carchemisch, the city where Assyria and Babylon skirmished, was 36 degrees latitude north as compared with Jerusalem, which was 32 degrees north. The city near which the battle was fought would have been even farther north of Egypt.

We get a hint (v. 7) about the country Jeremiah is talking about. This hint is confirmed in verse 8 when **Egypt** is likened to the **Nile** which rises to flood stage each year and covers the territory around her. Just as the Nile River rises, so Egypt threatened to rise, **cover the earth**, destroying cities. This "gift of the Nile," as Egypt was often called, sought to imitate her benefactor by seeking to cover the entire area but with military power. Her purpose, of course, in contrast with the mighty river, was destructive. Nothing would be better or more productive if her armies succeeded in their mission.

Egypt's staccato commands continue to come to her soldiers. Verse 9 reveals the presence of hired mercenaries from three surrounding countries. The record does not specify whether these non-Egyptian troops represented a second wave of soldiers or a further identification of the primary army.

Verse 10 is a key to our understanding the larger context. Egypt had looked forward to the battle of Carchemisch as the means of moving toward world domination. But the results were different from what Egypt hoped. Carchemisch brought the destruction of all her dreams.

Who won the battle of Carchemisch? Babylon? No, God won it. He was not highly pleased with Nebuchadnezzar. Rather, he was "sick and tired" of Egypt and Assyria. No country ever wins a war. The others merely lose it. Military might and human ingenuity never win victories. God always works events to fulfill his larger purpose and plans.

Jeremiah's description of the day was one of **vengeance** on Yahweh's **foes**. While God is love, he is also holy. We read verse 10 as a vindication of God's holiness. His people and his messengers periodically need a demonstration that they don't labor in vain. Often God lets us see evidences of his sovereignty and justice on earth. This is one of those examples.

Verses 11–12 warn anyone who feels constrained to ignore God. To pursue this path is not only unwise; it is also self-destructive. The title by which Jeremiah addressed Egypt brings to mind when God spoke of Jerusalem as the **Virgin Daughter**. In this context he spoke of Egypt this way for two probable reasons. First, the country had never been ravished in battle. Defeated? Yes, but never completely conquered. Second, a closely related truth was that the Egyptians stayed mainly to themselves as a young girl of that day remained safely with her parents.

The command to go **to Gilead and get balm** reflected a custom of that day. The identity of the plant with healing qualities is not known. But Gilead was famous for some type of medicine that brought relief to sick people. Scholars believe it was an ointment with some medicinal substance, and it was sought after widely. Jeremiah uttered a classic cry earlier when he said to his own countrymen earlier, "Is there no balm in Gilead? Is there no physician there? Why then is there no healing for the wound of my people?" (8:22). The prophet quickly dispelled any hope the Egyptians might have of solving their problems by human effort.

Jeremiah closed this poem with a twofold observation and declaration. First, news of Egypt's humiliation at Carchemisch would become well-known among the nations. Second, confusion would grip Egypt's soldiers. This message closes on a somber and gloomy note. Any reputation Egypt might have had among the nations would be seriously diminished while consternation, bewilderment, and shock seized Egypt.

46:13–26. The second oracle against Egypt comes as a direct sequel. Some interpreters believe it might have been written about the same time. Thoughtful Israelites were aware by now that Jeremiah's original "foe from the north" messages represented the words of a true prophet. Though long delayed, they were finding ultimate fulfillment in Babylon's rise to power, recognized by now as a part of Yahweh's plan to discipline Judah.

Though he had a clear path for further conquest, Nebuchadnezzar faced a temporary delay. The same year he defeated Egypt at Carchemisch, his father Nabopolasar died, making a trip back to Babylon necessary. But after this was over, Nebuchadnezzar was back. Scholars disagree on exact dates since he conquered some of Philistia, especially Ashkelon, before going to Egypt.

The three cities mentioned in verse 14 realized that the conflict would be fought on their territory. Jeremiah warned them to prepare for the struggle. There was no doubt about the outcome. The mercenaries would realize how hopeless the situation was and flee to the safety of their own land. Their cry **he has missed his opportunity** would be an affront to the Egyptian king. No one wants to be on the side of a loser.

To the secularist of that day, the victory might have been the triumph of a superior military machine, but the prophet of God knew better. This was the unfolding of the divine plan announced when God called Jeremiah to the ministry. In verse 18, after stating clearly God's part in the victory, the prophet compared Yahweh to **Tabor** and **Carmel**, two great mountains that towered above everything in sight.

Tabor and Carmel were ideal illustrations of Yahweh's strength and power. The prophet appropriately followed the striking analogy with a warning, in verse 19, to the great city of **Memphis**. Its coming destruction was imminent. The verb translated **lie in ruins** means literally "set on fire."

The metaphor in verse 20 and the simile in verse 21 added to Jeremiah's alarming message. In speaking of Egypt as **beautiful**, the prophet was perhaps referring subtly but sarcastically to Apis, the Egyptian god who was a bull. The Hebrew word translated **gadfly** comes from a verb that means "to nip." These pesky little creatures buzzed loudly and stung a bit but were not life threatening. So with Babylon's attack. Egypt would survive.

The mercenaries in Egypt's army would sense that they were on the wrong side of the conflict and would "bail out." The **fattened calves** description probably referred to their indulgent lifestyle with the money they received from fighting.

Jeremiah used three pictures (vv. 22–23) to intensify his description of the coming calamity. When the enemy came as woodcutters to **chop down** the forest, the **serpent** hid. It then stealthily slipped away. The hissing sound was threatening, but it was actually powerless. Again, the prophet's message confronted the Egyptian religious system. The snake was an important deity to them and appeared often on their royal insignia.

The figurative use of **locusts** added to the vividness of Jeremiah's warning. Locust plagues occurred often in Palestine and the surrounding areas. In one other picture, that of a maiden **put to shame** (v. 24), the prophet used a verb that meant sexual violation.

Jeremiah closed his words to Egypt with a summary statement about Yahweh's judgment (vv. 25–26a). He mentioned especially the **gods** whom the people worshipped and on whom they relied for protection. Though Egypt worshipped many gods, **Amon** held a special place in **Thebes**, capital of upper Egypt. Having dealt with Memphis, the capital of lower Egypt, the prophet turned to its counterpart with a prophetic word. This god worshipped in the temple at Karnak was later merged with Re, the sun god, to become the supreme deity over all Egypt.

Before ending his final message to Egypt, Jeremiah gave a word of hope. The great kingdom would not be destroyed. At a future time, Egypt would once again be **inhabited**. But Jeremiah did not go into detail about Egypt's future. The purpose of his words was to warn the country of their present danger. He then had a final word for Yahweh's people. This follows in the next two verses.

46:27–28. Regardless of how the prophets spoke to the other nations, their major focus was always on God's redemptive purposes. God began with Israel and then extended to the world. How fitting that this oracle against Israel's longtime rival and opponent, Egypt, closes with assurance to those whom God had chosen to implement his agenda.

Verses 27 and 28 contain a beautiful parallelism. But the second verse adds a thought, making it supplementary in nature. Both verses begin with a comforting exhortation, **Do not fear**. This was the most needed word for God's people at this time. Yahweh's promise contained not only a certain word for the remnant who had fled to Egypt but to all Israel wherever they were living as captives.

Ⓑ A Message About the Philistines (47:1–7)

SUPPORTING IDEA: *The Philistines, long-standing enemies of God's people, will be silenced.*

The Philistines never played a major role in world history, but they were a "thorn in the side" of would-be conquerors for several centuries. Their original home was Caphtor, generally regarded by scholars as Crete (Amos 9:7). These "great uncircumcised enemies of Israel" made their first appearance in biblical history during the days of Abraham. They attempted to invade Egypt in 1188 B.C. but were turned back by Ramesses III. They then settled in southwest Canaan. In the early days of Israel's history in Canaan, the Philistines were a formidable enemy. They were finally brought under control by David.

In Jeremiah's day the Philistines were not a dangerous threat. But they were always a potential "blockade" for anyone wishing to go from the north or east to Egypt for military conquest. Philistine life revolved around five major cities—Gaza, Gath, Ashkelon, Ashdod, and Ekron.

47:1. Scholars do not agree with all the dates about Philistia's relationship with Babylon, Egypt, and the other nations. Without investigating all the theories about dates, we can probably limit the background of this sermon from Jeremiah to two dates.

First, Jeremiah may have been referring to an attack that **Pharaoh** might have made after killing Josiah at Megiddo en route to the battle of Carchemisch. This would have been either 608 or 609 B.C. Second, Jeremiah could have referred to a later attack about 601 B.C. This would have followed a time when Egypt met Nebuchadnezzar and defeated him so severely that the Babylonian king retired to his own country and reequiped his army. Flushed with victory, Egypt carried on a raiding expedition against **Gaza**.

Other occasions have been suggested, but in this writer's judgment these are the two most likely. The spiritual truth conveyed by the prophet does not require that we locate with irrefutable accuracy the time of delivery.

47:2–3. Jeremiah spoke in this verse of an assault against all the Philistines by Babylon. This followed an attack against the Philistine city of Gaza, located in the south, by Egypt. The prophet used the same metaphor to describe Babylon's army that Isaiah had used to describe the Assyrians of his day (Isa. 8:7–8). He probably thought also of the Nile River and its annual flooding even as he spoke of Babylon. But there was one distinct difference between the two. The Nile flood brought fresh supplies of silt and water to the land after a long, dry summer. But the Babylonian flood would cause the Philistines to **cry out** with anguish and terror. The army would be so ruthless that parents would forsake their children as they sought safety.

47:4. This verse points out God's purpose in sending the Babylonians and how they fit into Yahweh's redemptive purposes. Jeremiah championed the cause of Babylon not because he favored this nation or approved of their goals in history. Rather, he had become convinced God's will for the present was that Babylon shape the affairs of international history, including Israel's fate. At a later time God would deal with Babylon. For the present this nation was his servant to accomplish his will for his people.

47:5–7. Jeremiah probably chose **Gaza** and **Ashkelon** for special mention as representative of the five-city coalition and thus of the nation. Shaving the head and cutting oneself were symbols of **mourning**, signifying shame and humiliation. The word translated **silenced** could also be rendered "destroyed." Jeremiah pictured Philistia crying out to the Lord and begging him to stop punishing them (v. 6). In the next verse, however, he informed them that this was Yahweh's will.

Sin will receive its proper punishment. The people protested against the **sword of the LORD**. They refused to look within themselves and see their true fault or repent of their unfaithfulness. Rather, they petitioned for the sword of the spirit to be returned to its **scabbard**.

◖ God's Word to Moab (48:1–47)

SUPPORTING IDEA: *Some people can be close to God's revelation yet never seem to understand the true nature of spiritual matters.*

Throughout Israel's history, relations with Moab were sometimes peaceful, but at other times hostility prevailed. During the conspiracy against Babylon, led by Jehoiakim in 600–598 B.C., Moab sided with Babylon. Later Moab did not side with Zedekiah in his final revolt against Babylon that led to Jerusalem's total destruction. In 581 B.C., Moab was conquered by Babylon. A few years later an Arab invasion from the east led to Moab's extinction.

Jeremiah spoke more words to Moab than to any other "foreign nation" except Babylon. This disproportionate amount of attention to Moab indicates that its opposition to Israel was more intense than most scholars have thought.

48:1–10. This section contains Jeremiah's urgent warnings to the various localities of **Moab** as the invader set forth. Lack of space prevents detailed treatment of the various cities. As best expositors can determine, because they have limited knowledge of geography about ancient Moab, the enemy moved from north to south. This forced the Moabites to seek shelter in the desert.

Nebo should not be confused with the mountain of the same name about twelve miles east of the Dead Sea, although it was probably nearby. **Heshbon**, one of Moab's chief cities, lay northeast of the Dead Sea. It marked the northern boundary of Moab and Ammon. Scholars cannot locate with certainty the site of **Madmen** though several suggestions have been offered. A popular view is that it was in the vicinity of a modern village eight miles from the Dead Sea, east of Masada.

One of the greatest tragedies war brings is the suffering of small children. Some translations picture their cries as being heard all the way to Zoar, one of the cities of the plain, probably at the far end of the Dead Sea (vv. 4–5). The site of **Luhith** is unknown, but it was obviously elevated as Jeremiah spoke of the children going down the road to **Horonaim**. The picture is one of grief and suffering.

Having detailed certain cities and given them a special warning, Jeremiah, in verses 6–8, gave a general word of alarm. The figure of speech in verse 6 **become like a bush in the desert** probably meant the people should flee to some isolated place. In verse 7, Jeremiah spoke of the specific reason for

Moab's coming devastation—self-sufficiency and greed. These two sins are like Siamese twins; one feeds on the other.

Jeremiah refused to compromise his stand. He repeated the vision of life that had driven him for years. Sin will bring punishment in the form of destruction. It will result in deportation to another country. The gods made of hands such as Moab's national deity, **Chemosh**, would suffer the same fate as the people, not being able to assist or save them. The chief trait of Moab's god was supposedly his ability to help the people acquire land. Obviously, he would fail to perform that function.

Every part of Moab would experience the coming blight (v. 8). Jeremiah used a familiar figure of that day, scattering **salt** on a city (v. 9). This indicated its total destruction. Nothing would ever grow there again (Judg. 9:45).

Some scholars consider the prophet's comment in verse 10 as an editorial addition, but no evidence exists to confirm this proposal. Jeremiah was accustomed to expressing his personal opinion. Failure to help God's people pursue a great cause is a terrible sin. We call it the sin of doing nothing.

48:11–17. In most of this section the prophet attacked Moab for inactivity and indifference. The **wine** metaphor needs to be interpreted cautiously. Connoisseurs contend wine improves with aging by resting on its dregs or lees. But others tell us that wine, if left too long, becomes too sweet and syrupy to drink. The latter observation is the lesson Jeremiah intended to emphasize. When an individual or a nation becomes too wealthy and prosperous, weakness and decay set in. Complacency leads to disintegration and destruction. This was Moab's great shortcoming.

Following the metaphor, Jeremiah returned in verse 12 to his warning. When the enemy comes, Moab will realize the futility of worshipping her god even as Israel saw the emptiness of trusting in Bethel. Most expositors believe this allusion is to the false worship place that Jereboam erected for the Northern Kingdom. A few claim the reference was to an idol worshipped in Syria.

The remainder of this section intensifies the picture of coming judgment. When the final blow comes, it will happen suddenly. Surrounding nations will be shocked to see the once-glorious Moab become a weak, impotent nation.

48:18–25. Jeremiah addressed **Dibon**, the once gloriously royal city of Mesha, king of the region. The prophet speaks to the city and its people as representative of the entire nation. As children watch a parade today, the prophet drew a picture of Dibon's inhabitants coming down the road as they fled the city. Jeremiah saw no hope. He named a number of cities that would share in the plight of the Moabites.

48:26–30. A new segment begins here. Jeremiah's metaphor—disgusting, repulsive, and sickening as it was—conveyed his point. He used this same figure of speech in 25:15–16 and 27–29 to picture God's wrath. The Moabites were named in the list of those who would be forced to drink the cup of God's fury and anger. The prophet pictured the bewilderment and distraction that Moab would experience when the invader arrived.

Another even more revolting picture was that of Moab wallowing in her own **vomit**. This shows the depth of decadence and degeneracy to which Moab had sunk. Yahweh had ridiculed Israel at a previous time, but as Jeremiah pointed out, Israel had never engaged in such filthy conduct as Moab. The prophet then warned the Moabites to take refuge wherever they could find it. Jeremiah put his finger once more on Moab's major problem—its **pride**, leading to **conceit** and climaxing in **arrogance** (vv. 29–30).

48:31–39. No true prophet of God enjoys condemning people, even if they deserve it. These verses reflect Jeremiah's true spirit as he expresses his profound grief because of Moab's approaching doom. The spirit of our Savior is evident in Jeremiah's words.

48:40–47. This segment concludes Jeremiah's message to Moab. As one reads the chapter, sometimes it seems to be one long discourse. But at other times the feeling is that a number of separate poems have been put together. No matter which is true, this last section is an appropriate close. The prophet painted one final, unforgettable picture of Moab's doom. Any attempt to escape God's judgment would bring an even greater catastrophe.

Jeremiah did not conclude without a message of hope for Moab. Yahweh had a future for Moab. We cannot say with certainty how this was fulfilled. Perhaps the relevant point for our study is found in a comforting thought for Judah. If God was willing to restore Moab at a later date, he certainly would do no less for his own covenant people. The bottom line is that God's kingdom is universal, not national. God can use anyone, anywhere, anytime who is willing to come to him in repentance and commitment.

D A Message of Judgment to Ammon (49:1–6)

SUPPORTING IDEA: *Those who seize what belongs to others should not complain or be surprised when the situation is reversed.*

Like Moab, Ammon traced its origin to Lot (Gen. 19:38). Ammon engaged in warfare with Israel from the days of the judges but could never recapture her land from the Israelites. But when Assyria devastated Israel in 722 B.C., Ammon captured the land occupied by the tribe of Gad. She became a prosperous vassal of Assyria. When Nebuchadnezzar defeated Assyria, she submitted to the victors. She helped Babylon put down Judah's revolt but later became disloyal to Babylon when Judah revolted again. She then became an object of Nebuchadnezzar's vengeance. Later Ammon was devastated by other forces and disappeared as a nation.

49:1–2. These verses condemn Ammon for moving in on territory that the Lord, through Joshua, had granted to the tribe of **Gad**. Jeremiah's message contained two words—rebuke of Ammon and assurance to Israel. He set no timetable for fulfillment, leaving that to Yahweh's discretion.

49:3–6. The **Ai** Jeremiah spoke of was not the one in the Book of Joshua that routed the Israelites after their victory over Jericho. Jeremiah mentioned another Ai, probably near **Heshbon**, perhaps the last line of defense for the greater city.

Rabbah was the capital of Ammon. Jeremiah urged the people of Rabbah to repent and show genuine signs of grief. The alternative was **exile** of the people and their god. In their imagined security, the people of Ammon had become complacent and overconfident. Jeremiah warned them that they would suffer exile. But the last verse of the section promises restoration for the Ammonites at some time in the future.

E Edom's Pride Will Bring Its Downfall (49:7–22)

SUPPORTING IDEA: *An illusion of self-sufficiency will meet with doom.*

The rivalry between Jacob and Esau, sons of Isaac, persisted in history through their descendants. After being tricked out of his birthright and blessing, Esau went to the land south and east of the Dead Sea and founded a country. It became known as Edom. What began as sibling rivalry grew into hatred and centuries of continuous warfare.

49:7–11. The city of **Teman**, which might have also been a district, was named for Esau's grandson. In their early years the Edomites had a reputation for wisdom, but over a period of time that wisdom deteriorated. The three rhetorical questions that Jeremiah posed to **Edom** in verse 7 were actually tongue-in-cheek sarcasm.

The city of **Dedan** was not a part of Edom, but many people from there were living in Edom at the time Jeremiah spoke. The prophet warned them to separate from the Edomites. This would prevent their suffering along with them when judgment came in the form of an invader. He promised the Dedanites their **widows** and **orphans** would be cared for, perhaps referring to the law about gleaning (Lev. 19:9–10; Deut. 24:21).

49:12–18. Jeremiah stated the coming disaster for Edom in emphatic fashion. In verse 16, he put his finger on Edom's problem. Nestled securely in the rocky areas, these people thought they were invincible. But the prophet warned them that no nation is secure when the inhabitants rebel against God's mandates and ignore the laws of decency. Like the cities made famous because of their association with Lot, Edom would live only in infamy and disgrace.

49:19–22. In his closing words to Edom, Jeremiah used several figures of speech. First, the invader of Edom would be like a hungry **lion** emerging from its hidden place in search of food. The prophet asks a question on Yahweh's behalf but does not answer it. The inference is that Babylon is the nation that Yahweh has chosen for the task. Normally, shepherds defended their flocks, but no ruler would be strong enough to provide protection for Edom.

The prophet resumed his metaphor of the devouring lion (v. 20). He offered no hope to Edom. Verse 21 describes the tumultuous effect when destruction comes. Though a small nation, Edom's collapse before the hungry lion would be heard many miles away.

Jeremiah, in verse 22, closed with two new metaphors. He still did not name the aggressor. But the picture of a soaring **eagle**, when compared with 48:40, suggested that Yahweh's instrument of judgment would be Babylon. The prophet closed his message by describing Edom's suffering with one of the sharpest metaphors possible—the pains of a **woman in labor**.

F Coming Judgment on Damascus (49:23–27)

SUPPORTING IDEA: *No city or civilization is so deeply imbedded in history that it can escape God's avenging hand.*

49:23–27. Most historians agree that **Damascus** is the oldest city in the world in the sense that it has been occupied continuously for a longer period than any other city. Damascus, prominent in the Old Testament, was at one time capital of three Syrian states, including **Hamath** and **Arpad**. Damascus fell to Assyria shortly before Assyria devastated the entire Northern Kingdom of Israel. In 605 B.C., Damascus became a vassal of Babylon, following the battle of Carchemisch. Earlier, Syria and Israel fought tenaciously for territory, with neither side winning a decisive victory over the disputed lands.

Jeremiah did not go into detail about the sins of Damascus. A century earlier, Amos spoke of its cruelty (Amos 1:3–5). Jeremiah didn't prophesy the absolute destruction of this great city. But he did warn of approaching suffering. No city or civilization is so deeply imbedded in history that it can ignore the demands of God and the laws of human decency.

G Kedar and Hazor Will Not Escape (49:28–33)

SUPPORTING IDEA: *God's judgment reaches to the most remote places.*

A number of nomadic Arab tribes lived in the Syrian desert region east of Palestine. From time to time, they made raiding expeditions into occupied areas. This was part of the continuous struggle between very different cultures and lifestyles.

49:28–33. The inhabitants of **Kedar** were sheep breeders (Isa. 60:7), traders (Ezek. 27:21), and skilled archers (Isa. 21:16–17). Scholars have had difficulty agreeing on the term **Hazor**. This was not the town north of Galilee, an important location that existed for several centuries. It was a place in the eastern desert. Though probably a specific town, Kedar may denote a collection of unwalled villages.

Jeremiah declared that both Kedar and Hazor would be destroyed. Verse 31 contains a command for Babylon to execute the work. It is followed by a word about the result of the campaign. They refer specifically to Hazor, Kedar having been dealt with in verse 29. The message to these two groups of people is that God has selected Babylon as his agent to bring judgment on them.

⊞ God's Word to Elam (49:34–39)

SUPPORTING IDEA: *God decides when it is time to bring nations or people to an end.*

49:34–39. The history of **Elam** goes back to the days of Noah (Gen. 10:22). The list of Shem's sons places Elam first, probably indicating he was the oldest. This group of people has a long and varied history, appearing sometimes as a strong nation but often as allies to more powerful countries.

Elam was situated on the western edge of ancient Persia, which is modern Iran. At different times Elam touched both Assyria and Babylon in military conflicts. Verse 34 identifies the date when Jeremiah received Yahweh's word about his plan to judge and punish Elam. Verses 35–38 contain the details.

Verse 39 closes the message with a word of hope for Elam's future. This was perhaps fulfilled partially after 539 B.C., when Elam, with Susa as it capital, became the center of Persia's empire. But the greatest fulfillment occurred when a group from Elam, present at Pentecost (Acts 2:7–9), heard the gospel. Some of them probably received Christ as Lord and returned home to establish a Christian community in their region.

⊞ Jeremiah's Message of Doom to Babylon (50:1–51:64)

SUPPORTING IDEA: *Extinction awaits nations that defy God.*

The message of these long chapters about Babylon is simple and direct. This great city and mighty empire will eventually suffer military defeat and be left a desolate ruin. The literary structure and content indicate this material is a collection of various, smaller sermons rather than one long, extended discourse.

50:1–10. This first segment of messages about Babylon consists of two divisions. Verses 1–3 give Yahweh's word to be proclaimed to everyone, everywhere. Babylon will be dealt with in a firm way. The nation will be devastated, suffering humiliation and disgrace. The term **nation from the north** was probably understood by the people in a generic way. The term was a figurative expression, referring to an invader. Military foes always came "from the north." Though other nations assisted, Persia was actually the avenging hand of God against Babylon—his agent of destruction.

Jeremiah prophesies a time when Israel and Judah, in captivity, **will go in tears to seek the LORD their God** (v. 4). Babylon's overthrow would send a message to them: "Get out of the land. The Lord is ready for you to return home." This segment closes with a renewed call for Israel to **leave** their place of captivity. Yahweh is preparing to **stir up** a coalition of nations to destroy those who had enslaved Israel.

50:11–20. These verses give Yahweh's words first to Babylon (vv. 11–13) and then to those whom he has raised up to do his punitive work against her (vv. 14–16). Verse 17 pictures the pitiful position of **Israel**, standing crushed first by **Assyria** and then by **Babylon**. This leads to a gracious promise from Yahweh to his people. He will **forgive** them and restore them to their land.

50:21–32. In these verses Jeremiah prophesied the wrath of God against Babylon. He varies his style, addressing the one he had chosen to do the work and then speaking to Babylon. In verse 21, the localities mentioned, **Merathaim** and **Pekod**, are regions in Babylon. The first was in southern Babylon near the mouth of the Euphrates River. Pekod was more specifically a tribe located in eastern Babylon (Ezek. 23:23).

50:33–40. This segment begins with a picture of Israel's present misery because of Babylon's oppression (v. 33). In verse 34, Jeremiah contrasts Israel's helplessness with Yahweh's strength. The remainder of the section consists of Yahweh's command for the coming conqueror to devastate those who have enslaved Israel. The prophet summarizes and concludes with a graphic comparison. Babylon will be as completely destroyed as **Sodom and Gomorrah** were.

50:41–46. This section shows Jeremiah's flexibility. In verses 41–43, he said to Babylon almost exactly what he had said to Judah earlier (6:22–24). In verses 44–46, he said almost exactly the same thing he said to Edom (49:19–21). Yahweh laid on the prophet's heart the message he had for Babylon just as he did for Judah and the other nations.

51:1–14. This section contains three divisions. First, the Lord speaks to his own people (vv. 1–8). Second, Israel speaks (vv. 9–10). Third, the Lord speaks to those he has commissioned to destroy Babylon (vv. 11–14).

The expression **Leb Kamai** is a code word for Chaldea. Chaldea probably includes a larger group of people than Babylon. God had used Babylon as his instrument of punishment against Judah. But their tenure of service for him had passed. The day of accountability has come. Yahweh was ready to put her on the junk heap as he did Assyria when she had accomplished his will against the Northern Kingdom.

Verses 8 and 9 are a dialogue between Yahweh and Israel. He invites Israel to weep for Babylon's **fall** and to seek healing for her. The righteous people among the Israelite captives had tried to lead Babylon in the right way but found they could not do it. They resolve to go back to their own land and be a witness of God's great grace (v. 10).

In a word to Babylon at the close of the section, Yahweh swore in the strongest way possible. He swore by **himself**. This was because he could find no one greater by whom to vow that his word would be fulfilled.

51:15–19. These verses and 10:12–16 are almost exactly alike. The truth conveyed by this poem was the unique resourcefulness and unlimited ability of Yahweh in contrast to the weakness of idols. Like all the prophets before him, Jeremiah recognized the fundamental belief of the true Israelite. Yahweh is not only the supreme God; he is the *only* God.

51:20–26. This poem is addressed to three different audiences: Cyrus (vv. 20–23), Israel (v. 24), and Babylon (vv. 25–26). Yahweh is opposed to this great empire, described as a **destroying mountain**. When Yahweh's judgment comes, Babylon will be **desolate forever**, a **burned-out mountain**.

51:27–48. To whom is Jeremiah speaking in verses 27–32? No one can be certain. He seems to be sending out a word to everyone affected by Babylon. The great and cruel oppressor's days are numbered. The prophet even mentions specifically the instrument Yahweh will use to destroy this selfish despot. Perhaps at that time Cyrus, the king of the Medes, had not yet added Persia to his list of conquered people.

Verses 33–35 bring together two contrasting perspectives: Yahweh's view and that of Judah. First, Yahweh says that judgment is coming to Babylon. Judah doesn't see this yet. They cry out because Babylon has ravished them unmercifully, closing with a plea that the wicked empire will be held accountable for its misdeeds.

Yahweh assures his people (vv. 36–44) that he will deal appropriately with Babylon. He uses one metaphor after another to reveal how Babylon will be punished and destroyed. He closes with a word about **Bel**, Babylon's chief god. This idol will be disgraced and cease to be worshipped by those in the great empire. Babylon's glory days would come to an end. Yahweh then commands his people to leave Babylon (vv. 45–48). The Jews did not receive permission to leave and return to their homeland until after Cyrus the Great of Persia had conquered Babylon.

51:49–58. These two short oracles about Babylon wrap up all the prophet had said about the wicked empire. In verses 49–53, Yahweh gave a moral justification for the devastation he would send on Babylon. The material consists of a brief dialogue between Yahweh and his people. He states the basic reason Babylon must be punished. The people replied, adding the disgrace that had come when Yahweh's **holy places** were defiled.

The last picture of Babylon's fate appears in verses 54–58. The expression **they will sleep forever and not awake** speaks of finality. Babylon's doom will never be reversed. The glory that once belonged to this proud empire has been buried in the tomb of time.

51:59–64. This prose addendum to Jeremiah's messages tells of a request Jeremiah made to **Seraiah**, brother of Baruch and staff member of **Zedekiah**. The prophet asked him to read **aloud** to the people in Babylon selected passages from his long preaching career. He further requested Seraiah to **tie a stone** to the **scroll** on which the messages were written and throw it into the **Euphrates** River. Jeremiah made one final request. Tell the people that Babylon will **sink** as the scroll sank and never **rise** again. This book ends thus with a solemn warning.

▌A Historical Appendix (52:1–34)

SUPPORTING IDEA: *God brings judgment on Jerusalem.*

52:1–3. Zedekiah followed his brother Jehoiakim's example and sinned against Yahweh. As a result, final judgment came to Jerusalem.

52:4–11. Following Zedekiah's final rebellious act against Babylon, the Babylonian army threw a siege around Jerusalem that lasted approximately eighteen months. When he could hold out no longer, Zedekiah slipped out of the city. Eventually, he was caught and imprisoned until **the day of his death**.

52:12–23. Under the direction of **Nebuzaradan**, Babylon's troops destroyed everything in Jerusalem related to the **temple** and the **royal palace**. The few things worth saving were carried away.

52:24–30. Nebuzaradan took captive the remaining officials and carried them to Nebuchadnezzar, who had taken up residence at **Riblah**. The king ordered them to be assassinated. Nebuchadnezzar carried captives from Jerusalem to Babylon on three occasions. It includes one other deportation that occurred five years after the destruction of Jerusalem.

52:31–34. The Book of Jeremiah closes with a statement about **Jehoiachin**, the young king who surrendered to Nebuchadnezzar in 597 B.C. and was carried to Babylon. Thirty-seven years after his surrender, he was set free by Nebuchadnezzar's successor. In addition, the new king gave Jehoiachin a place of **honor**. He **ate regularly at the king's table** and was given a regular stipend **as long as he lived**.

Why did the compilers of Jeremiah's book include this event, and why did they close the entire record of Jeremiah with it? One commentator offers an interesting opinion. He suggests the last chapter was included to illustrate the two major themes of the prophet's ministry. First, Jeremiah emphasized judgment on the land, and this chapter shows his prophecies were fulfilled. Second, he saw beyond judgment to hope for the future. The freeing of Jehoiachin foreshadowed the coming restoration of the nation.

Whatever the reason, God led the compilers to include this account. The book, so often dark and dreary, ends on a bright note. God chose to move on the heart of a heathen king to free one Israelite. The exiles may have seen in this act the hope that he might lead another king to do even more. This did occur years later when he stirred up Cyrus to issue a decree allowing the nation to return home. Great is our Lord! Great in judgment, he punishes the wicked. Even greater in mercy, he watches over his own. To him be glory forever.

MAIN IDEA REVIEW: *God made the entire world and everything in it. The nations are regarded as dust on the scales. He will write in the register of the peoples, "This one was born in Zion" (Ps. 87:6).*

III. CONCLUSION

Punishment of the Nations

For the second time in human history, from May 1946 to November 1948, a nation and its leaders were brought before the bar of world judgment. Twenty-eight militaristic Japanese leaders who had supported the policy of armed aggression, murder, forced deportation, slave labor, extermination, biological and chemical warfare, wanton destruction, narcotics trafficking, and a reign of terror were brought before the International Tribunal for the Far East, otherwise known as the Tokyo War Crimes Trials.

The judges were drawn from eleven nations representing over three-fourths of the world population. The trial was carefully designed to be an example of law and justice to the world. It was meant to be fair and free of politics and victors' vengeance. Of the twenty-five leaders found guilty, sixteen received life sentences, and seven were sentenced to hang. Later trials would prosecute those who had violated the laws and customs of war and those who carried out the tortures and murders ordered by their superiors.

Just as eleven nations of the world punished Japan and its leaders for their crimes against humanity, so in each of the judgment oracles on the nations in Jeremiah 46–51 the Lord used another nation or nations to punish each wicked nation.

For Egypt it was the gadfly from the north, the Babylonians (46:20,24,26). For Philistia it was again the flood from the north (47:2). For Moab a plot would lead to its downfall to the swooping eagle of Babylon (48:2,40,45). Ammon experienced its terror from those around it, as did Edom (49:14–16). Damascus was first absorbed by Assyria and then became a vassal to Babylon (49:23–27). Kedar and Hazor likewise fell to Babylon (49:28,30). The four winds would come against Elam, and it would be absorbed into the Persian Empire (49:36–37). And even mighty Babylon itself would be destroyed by an alliance of great nations from the north led by the Medes (50:2–3,9,41–42; 51:1–2,11,27–29,48,55–56).

The fact that God uses the nations of the earth to punish the nations of the earth is a truth as old as history, and it is a truth that the nations of the earth need to be reminded of today.

PRINCIPLES

- All nations are accountable to the Lord for how they conduct themselves.
- The Lord is the sovereign Judge of all nations, even of those nations that do not acknowledge his existence or lordship.
- The Lord God Almighty is a God of retribution.
- Exploitation; expansionism; wars of aggression; ventures in world domination; wanton destruction and devastation of other nations; overweening pride, arrogance, and insolence; atrocities against national populations and noncombatants; domestic and

international violence; and defying the Lord and his laws bring about the collapse of nations and empires.

- God sometimes uses the aggressive and exploitive actions of one nation against another nation to accomplish his purposes in the world.

APPLICATIONS

- Evaluate your nation in the light of God's standards.
- Consider one of the nations that is a declared enemy of your nation. How involved is God in the affairs of that enemy nation?
- Has God ever used an enemy to punish your nation? Is it possible that he may do so in the future? Why or why not?
- Describe what your nation would be like if everyone thought and acted as you do. How would God view such a nation?
- Where you see a gap between the practices of your nation and God standards, bring the sins of your nation before God and ask for his mercy on you and your nation.
- Keep God standards before you daily and walk in his ways.
- Pray daily for the leaders of your nation and the other nations of the world.

IV. LIFE APPLICATION

"Recessional"

In 1897 Rudyard Kipling of Great Britain penned his masterful poem "Recessional" in honor of the sixtieth anniversary of Queen Victoria's coronation. In his poem Kipling laid out the temptations of imperial pride and emphasized national responsibility and duty. Kipling believed his nation had become boastful, arrogant, and blasphemous, so he called on God to have mercy on the nation. His poem served as a warning that the British Empire had reached its imperial height and was headed into decline.

Supporting the policies and actions of one's country is patriotic. Citizens should be loyal to their nation and proud of its traditions, customs, and values. But patriots and loyal citizens also need to make realistic assessments of their country's actual role in history. These closing chapters of the Book of Jeremiah show us that God judges nations by his standard of righteousness and justice and that he evaluates how each nation measures up. Thus, it is not sufficient for our nation just to claim to be "under God" or to declare "In God We Trust." Each nation needs to make continuous and intentional efforts to be obedient to God's will.

American Christians claim that the Lord reigns over our nation. This is true, but the Lord reigns over all nations of the earth. And for that reason, the nations should tremble before him. Christians in America should remind their fellow citizens—and the citizens of other nations as well—that being "under God" means being under his judgment.

V. PRAYER

O sovereign Lord and Judge of all nations, we bow before you in humility and confess that our nation—which claims to be "one nation under God"—often has not followed your desires and expectations for the nations of the world. Teach us self-control as a nation. Help us to mend our flaws. And lead us to discover once again that our liberty is in following your law. Amen.

VI. DEEPER DISCOVERIES

A. "You who live in Dedan" (49:8)

Dedan was a caravan center for incense trade (Isa. 21:13). The Dedanites were men of the desert who had become the commercial travelers of their day, traversing the land in long caravans. They were the "middle men" of commerce, producing no products themselves but dealing in the exchange of goods for a profit.

Since God's judgment was about to fall on the land, Jeremiah had a special word for these people. "Stop your caravans. Get away from the path of destruction that is coming. Hide in the caves. Get in some remote place where you will be safe, far away from the march and fury of the conqueror." In modern language, we would say, "Take cover."

B. "Babylon was a gold cup in the LORD's hand" (51:7)

If one city in the world could claim to be entirely independent, it was Babylon. This giant metropolitan center had state-of-the-art equipment, ruled with superlative administrative skills, and boasted the most powerful army of its day. Babylon had its own gods and looked with scorn toward those of other nations, especially the so-called "Yahweh" of Israel. To the mighty Babylonian king, this feeble ruler was too weak to defend his own constituents. Jeremiah described Babylon correctly. She held a golden cup in her hand and served terror to others.

But Jeremiah had another picture of Babylon. The cup of gold in her hand belonged to God. Since he held it, he could "hurl" it as he had "hurled" his prophet against the nations.

C. Tabor and Carmel (46:18)

Mount Tabor stood on the eastern side of the land of Palestine, and Mount Carmel was on the western side. Tabor, about six miles east of Nazareth, stood at the eastern end of the Jezreel valley towering about 1,843 feet above sea level. It served as a boundary line for the tribes of Naphtali, Issachar, and Zebulun (Josh. 19:22). In earlier times these tribes had worshipped there (Deut. 33:18–19). At one time scholars identified it as the Mount of Transfiguration though many today prefer Mount Hermon as the site.

Mount Carmel, where Elijah confronted the prophets of Baal, is a prominent limestone range, about thirty miles long. It is near the Mediterranean coast and ranges in height from 470 feet to 1,742 feet. The Old Testament speaks of it often as a place of great beauty and fertility.

Neither mountain is exceptionally tall, but both appear to be because of their distance from other mountains. Both rise sharply from the surrounding plains.

VII. TEACHING OUTLINE

A. INTRODUCTION

1. Lead Story: Nations in the Dock
2. Context: When God first called and commissioned Jeremiah to the prophetic ministry, he appointed him as a prophet to the nations (1:5,10). Throughout Jeremiah's ministry, beginning with King

Jehoiakim's fourth year in 605 B.C. (46:2) to at least King Zedekiah's fourth year in 594 B.C. (51:59), Jeremiah announced God's messages to nation after nation, whether it was a dominant superpower or a tribal territory. Jeremiah's oracles against the nations that are collected together at the end of his book show us how God rules nations and monitors their actions.

3. Transition: Does God care how nations behave? What does he think about a culture's attitudes and a nation's deportment? And even more important, does God do anything about what nation-states do to their own people and to the peoples of other nations in the world? Jeremiah 46–52 helps us answer these questions.

B. COMMENTARY

1. Two Poems About Egypt (46:1–28)
2. A Message About the Philistines (47:1–7)
3. God's Word to Moab (48:1–47)
4. A Message of Judgment to Ammon (49:1–6)
5. Edom's Pride Will Bring Its Downfall (49:7–22)
6. Coming Judgment on Damascus (49:23–27)
7. Kedar and Hazor Will Not Escape (49:28–33)
8. God's Word to Elam (49:34–39)
9. Jeremiah's Message of Doom to Babylon (50:1–51:64)
10. A Historical Appendix (52:1–34)

C. CONCLUSION: PUNISHMENT OF THE NATIONS

VIII. ISSUES FOR DISCUSSION

1. Other prophets beside Jeremiah also delivered oracles of judgment against the nations. Scan Isaiah 13–23; Ezekiel 25–32; Amos 1–2; and the brief books of Obadiah and Nahum. What does God find commendable in a nation's behavior, and what does he condemn?

2. What is the difference between patriotism, loyalty to one's country, and jingoism (fanatical nationalism)? What are the dangers of accepting the axiom, "My country, right or wrong"?

3. What are some national and theological implications for a nation that claims to be "one nation under God" and professes as its motto, "In God We Trust"?

4. Since God sometimes uses a nation with expansionist goals and an aggressive imperialistic spirit to discipline and punish another nation, how might we be able to determine if or when this is the case in today's world?

5. In 51:56b Jeremiah declared, "The LORD is a God of retribution." Read Jeremiah's "Song of the Sword" in 50:35–38 and his "Song of the War Club" in 51:20–23. How do these verses fit with your understanding and view of God?

Introduction to

Lamentations

The material known as the Book of Lamentations consists of five chapters containing material related to the fall of Jerusalem. Each chapter seems to be an independent poem. The author of these five literary and spiritual master-pieces wrote against the background of the greatest tragedy Jerusalem's inhab-itants had ever experienced. The mighty city lay in ruins, having been ravished by Babylon's mighty war machine. Bible scholars are in virtual una-nimity that Nebuchadnezzar's recent invasions of 597 and 586 B.C. served as the occasion for the destruction.

Although his name does not appear in the text, most Old Testament stu-dents give credit to Jeremiah for the entire book. The graphic and heart-moving descriptions demand a contemporary of that day, a personal witness to the events that took place. Who else could have written so eloquently of the happenings but the prophet from Anathoth? He saw each heartbreaking occurrence with his own eyes and shed bitter tears as each prediction of his long ministry was fulfilled. Even though he warned the people the tragedy was approaching, he suffered intensely when the events actually happened.

TITLE AND PLACE IN THE CANON

In the Hebrew Bible, the Book of Lamentations is called *eka,* which means "How!" It is not the interrogative pronoun but a word of profound exclama-tion. The unusual designation comes from a custom of the Jews. They gave their canonical books titles based on the first word or significant expression in the text. This word *eka* was habitually used to begin a dirge. Later Jewish writers called this book *Qinot* or "dirges." This was based on the Hebrew word that means "dirge or lament."

RELIGIOUS SIGNIFICANCE

Does this book, written centuries ago to people in a far different setting, have a word for our modern world? The answer is a resounding yes. Though external situations and conditions vary, human need remains the same. Some things may be passing, but other things are permanent, never changing. Spiritual values endure, and this book speaks eloquently about issues related to life both temporal and eternal.

Does God punish sin? The Book of Lamentations reinforces what we know from the record of Jeremiah's ministry. Sin may prosper temporarily, but it contains within itself the seed of its own punishment. In addition, God's spokespersons will be vindicated, if not while living, certainly after they are called home to be with him. Jeremiah lived to see his predictions become reality in the life of Judah. All prophets do not realize this earthly reward.

The Book of Lamentations, though unfortunately not one of the most popular or often-read books, conveys one great truth. History belongs to the forces of righteousness, not those of iniquity. Many truths emerge from a serious study of this book. Notice several of them.

A society or nation that "sells out" will deteriorate and eventually perish. The roll call of great people and great civilizations affirms this truth. Popular speakers and writers refer often to Rome, but this great empire was only one of many to flourish and then fizzle. One who reads history sees this recur with regularity.

Another truth assures us that all is not hopeless. Those who anchor themselves by faith to God and his purposes have resources to meet any crisis.

A third message from this great book comes directly from the life of Jeremiah. When the crisis comes, wise people listen to God's messengers. Jerusalem could have escaped the heartbreaking misery she experienced if the king and people had been willing to heed Jeremiah's advice.

A final word should be said about this great canonical book of heartmoving poems. The truly great servants of God—and this includes the prophet Jeremiah—suffer as their people suffer. No person has the right to condemn and warn of impending judgment if he rejoices when the words are fulfilled. Dr. Dale, eminent preacher of Birmingham, England, often said that Dwight L. Moody was the only person he knew who had the right to preach about hell. When someone asked him why, he replied, "Because Moody always preaches about it with tears in his voice."

Jeremiah's ministry began during Josiah's reign. Both were young men and good friends. Josiah was the last godly king in Judah and led the last reform movement in the nation before the exile. It did much good but turned out to be just a "surface movement." He made a bad political decision and was killed in battle at Megiddo trying to oppose Pharaoh Neco of Egypt.

Following Josiah's death, Judah began a downward plunge morally and spiritually from which she never recovered. Jeremiah suffered greatly under the kings who followed Josiah, especially Jehoiakim and Zedekiah. He witnessed the final destruction of Judah and Jerusalem and saw the temple burn. He sat down in the warm ashes with hot tears flowing down his cheeks.

Only one person exceeded Jeremiah in compassion and concern for his people—our Savior and Lord himself. He came to fulfill the prophet's promise of a new covenant and, like his predecessor, wept over his people.

Lamentations 1:1–5:22

From Sin to Suffering

I. **INTRODUCTION**
Mary Widow

II. **COMMENTARY**
A verse-by-verse explanation of these verses.

III. **CONCLUSION**
Restored by the Lord

An overview of the principles and applications from these verses.

IV. **LIFE APPLICATION**
The Army from the Land of the North

Melding these verses to life.

V. **PRAYER**
Tying these verses to life with God.

VI. **DEEPER DISCOVERIES**
Historical, geographical, and grammatical enrichment of the commentary.

VII. **TEACHING OUTLINE**
Suggested step-by-step group study of these verses.

VIII. **ISSUES FOR DISCUSSION**
Zeroing these verses in on daily life.

Quote

"In my End is my Beginning."

M a r y   Q u e e n   o f   S c o t s

Lamentations 1:1–5:22

IN A NUTSHELL

The Book of Lamentations is a series of five dirges or wailings in which the prophet Jeremiah describes and laments the desolation of Judah and the destruction of Jerusalem by the Babylonians in 586 B.C. But the poetic collection is more than a recital of the horrors and atrocities inflicted on the Judeans. It is an acknowledgment that the real cause of the Southern Kingdom's downfall was the nation's apostasy. The five elegies each form one chapter of the book.

The first lament focuses on Jerusalem's plight. The second emphasizes the Lord's anger. The third and longest lament, constructed in triads of verses, is Jeremiah's own. And tucked away at the center of this central poem of the five is the spiritual heart of the Book of Lamentations—hope. The fourth lament describes the horrors the citizens of Jerusalem experienced during the siege. And the last of the five laments is a prayer to the Lord in light of Jerusalem's grave situation. The prayer ends with an affirmation that the Lord reigns forever and that his throne endures and a request that he restore and renew his people to himself.

From Sin to Suffering

I. INTRODUCTION

Mary Widow

*A*s the only child of King James V of Scotland, Mary Stuart became queen of Scotland six days after she was born when her father died suddenly. Through her marriage to Francis II of France, Mary became Dauphiness of France and then Queen of France. Upon the untimely death of her husband, Mary, at the age of eighteen, became queen-dowager of France. Had she played her cards right, Mary could have become queen of England and possibly queen of Spain.

After the death of her French husband, Mary returned to Scotland and, in an attempt to secure her claim to the English throne, married her English cousin Henry Stuart, Lord Darnley. Soon Mary's infatuation with Darnley passed, and she took an Italian musician as her suitor. In a plot driven by jealousy, Darnley and some of his friends murdered the man. Soon Mary fell in love with one of her loyal nobles, the fourth Earl of Bothwell, and became his consort. Within a few months Darnley was found strangled outside his house. Bothwell stood trial for the murder, but Mary saw to it that he was acquitted. Within two weeks after the verdict, Bothwell divorced his wife and quickly married the twice-widowed queen. Aghast at their queen's brazen acts, Mary's Scottish subjects rebelled. She fled to England, where her cousin Queen Elizabeth reigned, and lived there for the next nineteen years.

At first Queen Elizabeth welcomed Mary to England. The British regent not only refused to turn her cousin over to the Scottish government, but she treated Mary as the rightful sovereign of Scotland and her guest. Elizabeth even sought Mary's restoration to the Scottish throne. But over time Mary involved herself in a succession of conspiracies and schemes with Spain and some English nobles against Elizabeth and England. Finally, Elizabeth issued an edict declaring that Mary was to be incarcerated in a place of greater security. But a new opportunity presented itself, and Mary became involved in one last plot to murder Elizabeth and ensure her own succession to the English throne. The plot and Mary's complicity in it were discovered. She stood trial and was found guilty. After months of agonizing, Elizabeth signed Mary's death warrant. Mary Queen of Scots was beheaded on February 8, 1587.

In Jeremiah's first lament in chapter 1 of Lamentations, he compared the city of Jerusalem after the Babylonian siege to a widow—a widow who was once a great queen among the nations. The widow-queen's situation had changed. She who once was the envy of others and the desire of many suitors had been betrayed and reduced to slavery. Others now controlled her fate, and there was none to comfort her in her grief. Her treasures and splendor were a thing of the past. Her enemies and closest allies alike rejoiced over her downfall. What would happen to this widow? What could she do now? Let's turn to the Book of Lamentations and find out.

II. COMMENTARY

From Sin to Suffering

MAIN IDEA: *Continued sin and rebellion against God bring loneliness and disaster, but he is always available for those who seek him.*

A Isolation, Desolation, and Misery (1:1–22)

SUPPORTING IDEA: *Entrenched wickedness leads to agony.*

This first poem may be divided into two main sections. Verses 1–11 lament the sufferings that Jerusalem was undergoing when Jeremiah wrote. Twice in this section (vv. 9,11), the city itself breaks out into a loud weeping or lament that leads to the second section of the chapter (vv. 12–22). In it, the people's suffering is spoken of as the result of sin. This leads to the second poem, where the reason for the disaster is the leading thought.

1:1–11. Have you ever walked through a church building or a town that was once a center of activity but now is almost empty? This is how Jeremiah must have felt when he gazed at the two things dearest to his heart—the temple and the city of Jerusalem.

The word translated **deserted** (v. 1) comes from a Hebrew verb meaning "to be separate, solitary." In this verse it is an adverb meaning "alone." Looking at the barren and forsaken city, Jeremiah saw it as isolated, abandoned, and forgotten. His mind turned to a woman whose husband had died and left her alone in the world. We must be careful to understand the comparison.

His emphasis is on the isolation of Jerusalem from the mainstream of society and exalted status because she had lost her previous companions.

Jeremiah presented his picture and made his point in several graphic contrasts. Jerusalem, who was once a **queen** among the provinces, had **now become a slave**. Once fully populated, the Jewish city had become practically empty. At one time great among political entities, she had lost authority and influence.

In verse 2, Jeremiah pictured the widow weeping **at night**. The time of natural darkness and silence heightened the bitterness of loneliness. The **lovers** of whom the prophet spoke were not the fertility gods of the Canaanites. They were the nations with whom Judah had sought alliance against their two major **enemies**, Assyria and Babylon.

The roads, pictured by Jeremiah as mourning, were once filled with caravans for travel and trading. At the time of the three major religious festivals (Passover, Pentecost, Tabernacles), they were crowded with pilgrims traveling to Jerusalem. All that had changed. No one came to the temple because it had been destroyed.

The **gateways** (v. 4) were the locations at which business was usually conducted. This made it a busy place, teeming with crowds. The **priests** now moaned with distress. They were probably more concerned with the loss of revenue than disturbed about the temple being destroyed, although the two were related. The **maidens** were the young virgins who often took part in religious ceremonies (Exod. 15:20–21; Judg. 21:19–21; Ps. 68:25). This was often the means by which young men chose them to be their wives. This opportunity had been lost.

Verse 5 assesses the situation and places the blame squarely on Judah's **sins**. Often we speak today of sin as enslaving. In the case of Judah in Jeremiah's day, this was literally true. The people had become captives not just of their own lusts but of an enemy nation.

The simile in verse 6 should be interpreted literally. Jerusalem's **princes** were actually weak from lack of food. The city had been under siege for eighteen months. The food ran out. Even when the people were eating regularly, the supply was limited. The princes were weak because they probably had not eaten a good meal for months. They were in no position to flee to safety. No wonder they were easily caught by the enemy.

Verses 8 and 9 contain a double application. The people were **unclean** both ceremonially and morally. At one time other nations had respected Judah, but that was no longer true. To see one's **nakedness** meant to perceive the shame and hypocrisy that lay beneath the pretense. When applied to a woman, it carries the idea of seeing past the adornment of the body that made her attractive. Once that was stripped away and the naked body was revealed, the mystery and allurement were gone.

In verse 10, the word **treasures** refers to the valuables of the temple sanctuary. This included, among many other precious things, the holy and expensive vessels used in worship. No worse humiliation to the nation or blasphemy to God could be imagined than for an outsider to enter the **sanctuary**.

The Hebrew word translated **treasures** in verse 11 is the same as the one in verse 10. But this time another application is made. Since the people were actually starving, they had sold or bartered their precious possessions for a morsel of **food**. One theme runs throughout these eleven verses: We reap what we sow.

1:12–22. In these verses, Jerusalem speaks. This material contains three divisions. In verses 12–17, the city appeals for other groups to have compassion. Several alternate translations have been offered by scholars for verse 12. But in my judgment, only one of them seems to deserve serious consideration.

Many Jewish interpreters render the opening statement in verse 12, "Let it not come to you, all that pass by." This translation has a small amount of support from the Hebrew text and is preferred by some non-Jewish scholars. The words are logical in the mouth of the city. They send a word of warning to any who might be moving in the same direction as that traveled by Judah. The traditional translation is, however, favored by most commentators.

The city pleaded for attention as well as concern and understanding. Those who viewed the plight of the people and ruins of the city treated both with indifference. They neither laughed nor cried but simply ignored the city.

Verse 13 states three successive ways Yahweh had dealt with his rebellious city. The Jewish Midrash interprets the first to mean that Yahweh had set **fire** to the temple so the heathen nations could not boast that they had done it. This figure of speech is used quite differently from another one (Jer. 20:9). In that passage Jeremiah spoke of God's message shut up in him like a "fire in his bones." This prevented him from giving up his ministry.

For the second figure the prophet applied the metaphor of spreading a **net** to Babylon (see Jer. 50:24). In the third picture the idea is that God's people are driven into a corner, the way is blocked, and they are **turned . . . back**.

In verse 14, the prophet pictured the sins of the city knitted together **into a yoke**. They are then placed on the **neck**. This weighs her down, drains her energy, and keeps her from resisting those who attack.

Verse 15 laments the sending of alien soldiers against the citizens of Jerusalem. The Hebrew text interprets **has summoned** as that of a solemn assembly, a tragic inversion of the usual joyful and happy purpose of such occasions. The prophet compared the shedding of blood with the squeezing of juice from grapes. He spoke of Judah as a **Virgin Daughter** because Jerusalem was considered inviolate, having never been ravished. He used the Hebrew word *betulah,* the specific word for virgin, rather than *almah,* the word for a young lady of marriageable age.

Jerusalem's suffering is magnified because there is no one to **comfort** her—**no one to restore** her **spirit** (v. 16). The prophet reiterates what Jerusalem has said (v. 17). In the word about Jerusalem's uncleanness, he used a term that spoke of a woman's monthly period. The KJV reads, "Jerusalem is as a menstruous woman among them."

Verses 18–20 contain the people's confession of sin. They began with a statement of God's character and acknowledged that God's judgment is **righteous**. All sin is first against him because he alone is the standard of righteousness. The word translated **have been most rebellious** means "to resist, contend with, breathe bitterly."

The last two verses present the people's call to Yahweh for vindication. Not only did they have no one on whom they could call for assistance; their **enemies** observed their misery and rejoiced to see them suffer. The people called on God to send a similar fate on those who had been jubilant because of their difficulty.

B The People's Lament and Supplication (2:1–22)

SUPPORTING IDEA: *Continued sin by God's people brings his wrath. This leads to their suffering and hopefully to prayer.*

This poem contains more than just a renewed description of miseries. It views them in the light of a judgment sent from God as the consequence of sin. Verses 1–10 describe in detail the punishment Jerusalem had experienced.

Verses 11–17 give details of how the people suffer together and the cruelty of those who look at her miseries. In verses 18–19, the people urge Jerusalem to pray for the Lord's help in their crisis. Verses 20–22 record the people's cry to him.

2:1–9. The Hebrew text of verse 1 renders the verb in **has covered . . . with the cloud of his anger** as an imperfect. This conveys the meaning of continuous or repeated action. The **splendor of Israel** may be the temple or the city, hurled down like a falling star (Isa. 14:12).

Some interpreters contend that Jeremiah uses the word **footstool** to refer to the temple (Ps. 132:7; Isa. 60:13). Others claim it means the city itself or the ark of the covenant (1 Chr. 28:2). In the following verses Jeremiah uses a number of strong verbs to describe the outpouring of God's wrath: **swallowed up**, **torn down**, **brought . . . down . . . in dishonor**, **cut off every horn**, **withdrawn his right hand**, **burned**, **consumes**.

Throughout these verses Jeremiah repeated a number of times that the suffering was caused by God. He emphasized this so the people would understand that God planned and carried out the city's destruction. The walls had once given Judah a sense of security—but no longer. God refused to protect his people.

The expression **the law is no more** (v. 9) did not mean the people were no longer required to obey it. Rather, the priests were not able to carry out the rituals of the temple because it had been destroyed.

Likewise, the prophets had lost contact with God. These words may have been spoken in sarcasm. Jeremiah was referring to the false prophets. These were the ones who had failed to warn the people, insisting that everything was fine and no punishment was coming.

2:10–17. When Jerusalem was devastated, **the elders**, or leaders of the city, adopted the official stance of a mourner. They had nothing to do and hence nothing to say. The **dust** and **sackcloth** were symbols of their deep grief. The **young women** in verse 10 were the virgins, not just the young women. Jeremiah used the Hebrew word *betulah* rather than *almah*. They were grieved because all hope of an honorable marriage was gone.

Those who call Jeremiah the "weeping prophet" base it on expressions such as the one in verse 11. The sight of his people in misery, especially the children and infants, brought tears to this tender prophet. But we should never forget that he remained an optimist when he focused on the future of God's people.

The inquiry **Where is bread and wine?** was probably a generic term that meant "I am hungry. Where is something to eat?" We can find no sadder picture in the words of Jeremiah than those about the **infants** and **children**. He said they **faint like wounded men in the streets of the city, as their lives ebb away in their mothers' arms** (v. 12).

Jeremiah had almost run out of metaphors to describe the state of the people of Jerusalem (v. 13). Then he found one. Their **wound is as deep as the sea**. For that reason he chose it to precede his rhetorical question that had no answer. In verse 14, Jeremiah returned to one of his favorite themes—the false **prophets**. Jeremiah spoke here of those who were the majority in the land. He pointed back to the past and declared they were "phonies" and their claims of visions from Yahweh were **false**.

Verses 16 and 17 reverse the alphabetic arrangement of the poem. But the thought continues without interruption. The **enemies** of Israel rejoiced because the once beautiful city was in ruins. They took credit for her destruction, boasting of how they fulfilled the plans they had made. But Jeremiah interrupted their boasts (v. 17). He told the people of Judah that the success of their enemy was due not to the heathen's own ability but because Yahweh had **decreed** that it should happen.

2:18–19. The prophet who has wept for the people now calls upon them to shed **tears** of repentance for their sins. The Hebrew Scriptures are filled with statements about the necessity for mourning, turning from wicked ways, and calling on God for pardon. God had promised he would hear if the people would call to him with all their heart.

2:20–22. This poem closes on a note that is less than optimistic. In verses 20–21 the people's complaint is more like a reproach or even an accusation that God is unfair and unreasonable. The last verse of this poem recalled the days when God summoned the people to feast days and prayer. Attendance was not only encouraged; it was mandatory. Jeremiah compared the recent destructive acts of the enemy. They were ordered by God much the same way he ordered his people to attend the feasts. Thus this poem ends on a note of complaint and pathos.

⟨C⟩ Has God Forsaken Judah? (3:1–66)

SUPPORTING IDEA: *Only a conviction that God is with us can lead to peace and serenity in the midst of pain.*

Scholars divide into two camps over this poem. Some say it reveals the prophet's personal experiences. Others suggest it is a personification of Jerusalem and that the prophet speaks for the city. In a sense both are true. Jeremiah's life paralleled in many ways his beloved Jerusalem. Many interpreters see four steps in this literary masterpiece. Jeremiah began with himself, moved to the suffering of Jerusalem, returned to his own pain, and closed by calling on Yahweh to punish the city's enemies.

The alphabetic acrostic continues in this poem but with a slightly varied format. Rather than twenty-two verses, each beginning with a letter of the Hebrew alphabet, we have sixty-six verses. Three continuous verses begin with the same letter, giving a similar literary effect. As in the previous chapter, the sixteenth and seventeenth letters are reversed.

3:1–21. This section deals with the poet's own personal experiences. Jeremiah's ministry is reflected in these verses. The series of calamities reached their climax when Babylon burned the city that Jeremiah loved so dearly. The prophet realized the temple had become a contradiction of all Yahweh intended it to be. But Jeremiah still loved it and was crushed when he saw it destroyed.

Jeremiah spoke in verse 2 of how he had been **driven**, like an animal, **to walk in darkness rather than light**. He was perplexed about why he had been called on to suffer. Like Job he did not claim to be without sin but only that he was suffering disproportionately for his wrongdoings. God had given him a crippling illness of some kind that left him unable to cope. He admitted to some bitterness. The expression **like those long dead** may be an extension of those people already passed away and in Sheol—a place of dark, shadowy existence.

The poetical genius of the prophet manifested itself in the many figures of speech he used to describe his condition: a helpless prisoner (vv. 7–9), an animal whom Yahweh catches and tears to pieces (vv. 10–11), and one through whom an arrow had been driven (vv. 12–13). He had become an object of ridicule among the people.

Jeremiah pictured Yahweh as a deceitful host to a weary traveler. He did give his prophet liquid nourishment, but it was bitterness and wormwood.

The food he offered the prophet was stone and ashes that broke his teeth. He then flung his broken servant into the dirty street! But man's extremity is God's opportunity. In his loneliness Jeremiah reviewed his past experiences. He then began to reevaluate his situation. This brought him a feeling that **hope** might be on the horizon.

3:22–39. At the very moment when Jeremiah was at his lowest, his mind began to clear. God had never failed him. Why should he do so now? A striking miracle took place in his thinking. He ascended from the pit to the pinnacle! The God who had met every need in days past would not leave him now. The prophet gained a new lease on life. He discovered that God's compassions are inexhaustible.

In the Hebrew text, verses 25–27 begin with the word *tov*, which means **good**. The readability is improved and the meaning is enhanced if we read the sentence to reflect this fact. For instance: "Good the Lord to those whose hope"; "Good to wait quietly"; "Good for a man to bear the yoke."

The four occurrences of **Let him** in verses 28–30 are an excellent example of a truly repentant person. Those who come in this attitude can be sure the Lord will hear and restore. Likewise, the trilogy of similar expressions in verses 34–36 indicate an unrepentant person who cannot be heard by Yahweh until these things are changed in one's life.

In verses 37–38, Jeremiah reaffirmed a truth he had emphasized throughout his ministry. No event can occur unless the Lord has **decreed it** beforehand. The typical theological position of that day was that everything came directly from God. Jewish thought had little or no place for secondary causes. Today we can easily attribute good things to the Lord, but Amos said, "When disaster comes to a city, has not the LORD caused it?" (Amos 3:6).

Verse 39 has two interpretations: (1) Why should a person **complain** when his sins are **punished**? He should realize he deserves for this to happen. (2) Since he is still **living**, why should he complain? God has given him more time in this world than he deserves. The first interpretation is more generally accepted.

3:40–51. In these verses Jeremiah called for the people to repent. He made no plea of extenuating circumstances that might lessen their guilt. That God had not **forgiven** should not be taken as an accusation against him. Nor did Jeremiah mean their suffering was disproportionate to their wrongdoing.

This was clearly a cry for pardon because of God's mercy. It is one of the most plaintive cries in the Old Testament.

In verse 51, Jeremiah made a statement about the women of his city that reveals his tender character. This was not just a figure of speech, personifying Jerusalem as the "daughter of Zion," although he did use this figure of speech often. The prophet referred literally to women who were suffering from ravishing by the enemy. This was one of the ways Jeremiah was most like Jesus. Though neither had a wife, both showed a spirit of compassion for the pains women were called on to endure.

3:52–66. In this closing section Jeremiah recalled some personal and merciful interventions of Yahweh in his life. The things he spoke of could be applied figuratively to the nation also. Several incidents in Jeremiah's life fit some of his words in this passage, especially where he spoke of calling from the **pit** (vv. 53,55). The figure of **waters** closing **over** his **head** (v. 54) appears in a number of Old Testament passages, especially in the Psalms.

Beginning with verse 59, Jeremiah showed his true humanity by expressing a bitter spirit toward his enemies. This is a challenge even for good people. Forgiveness of enemies was modeled by Jesus and is commanded of those who follow the Lord.

Ⅾ Deterioration of People Because of Their Sins (4:1–22)

> **SUPPORTING IDEA:** *Regardless of one's status or function, rebelling against God's holy standard will lead to misery and doom.*

One writer has called this poem "Jerusalem in the Past and in the Present." It differs from the previous chapters in two significant ways. First, it states perhaps more explicitly than any of the others that the people's miseries are due to their sins. Second, it emphasizes that three leadership groups—prophets, priests, and princes—were the major cause of the judgment on Jerusalem.

The material divides itself easily and clearly. Verses 1–12 set forth the distress and agony that have come to the people because of the city's prolonged siege. Verses 13–16 point out that the leaders of Judah are responsible for the tragedy that has happened. In verses 17–20, Jeremiah points out the hopelessness of the people. The last two verses (vv. 21–22) tell Edom that its current triumph will be short-lived.

4:1–12. One can feel the prophet's pathos as he recalls the past glory of Jerusalem. He returns to the funeral dirge as he begins. Once valuable in God's service, the people of Judah had become worthless to God. This was tragic because God had formed them for himself (Isa. 43:21).

Verse 3 contains an interesting contrast between the people's former and present states. **Jackals** were considered cruel in the treatment of their young. This Hebrew word is similar to one used for a sea monster or for the wild ass as he sniffed the wind. It also sometimes referred to a serpent or even a crocodile. Jeremiah's point was that even animals of this type cared for their young.

But the people had become like another animal, the ostrich. When an ostrich found her nest had been discovered, she crushed her young and built a nest elsewhere. The female ostrich, at the least alarm, forsook her brood. According to the prophet, Judah's inhabitants had become as pitiless and cruel as the ostrich.

Verses 3–5 present an ascending description of the rejection of Zion's children. Beginning with sucking infants, Jeremiah proceeded to the children and then climaxed with the adults seeking more palatable food. All had been equally deprived, and all faced starvation.

In verses 7–8 the poetical picture of the **princes** ("Nazarites," KJV) before the tragedy in contrast to their present drabness, presented a sad picture. Judah had been greatly shamed. How low she had been brought because of her sin!

To experience death immediately, even if by cruel and painful means, was better than to **waste away** gradually and die from starvation (vv. 8–9). Parents ingesting their own flesh and blood seems almost unbelievable. Many scholars contend that statements such as this should be interpreted figuratively rather than literally. Verse 11 closes and consummates this description. Yahweh had "all he could stand" from the sinful people. And so he **has given full vent to his** anger. No one would have believed this could happen to Jerusalem (v. 12).

4:13–16. Once more Jeremiah named the human cause of Judah's misery—wicked religious leaders. He omitted the politicians at this point, majoring on the **prophets** and **priests**. In these verses he focused on their impure lives. Leaders are called to exemplary living. When people in charge of guiding others make a serious misstep in conduct, they have great difficulty regaining the confidence of their followers. The comparison of a fallen spiritual leader with an **unclean** leper is one of the most appropriate in the Old Testament.

4:17–20. When people face a hopeless situation, they grasp at straws. Judah had only one human hope during the final siege of their city. In desperation the rulers and people turned to Egypt, but they were disappointed. Their last resource was a hope that the Davidic dynasty, in the form of their present king, would be their salvation. Many had looked on Zedekiah as **the LORD's anointed**, their Messiah, but he was not able to save even his own life.

4:21–22. Jeremiah's last word in this poem is about Israel's longtime rival and enemy, **Edom**. The animosity between these two nations dated back to their family founders, Esau and Jacob. Throughout the centuries these two nations had opposed each other, sometimes fiercely. At the time this poem was written, Edom was enjoying a triumph over Israel. The Edomites had stood aside and watched gleefully as Jerusalem fell. Jeremiah warned them that their day of judgment would come—and soon.

ⓔ Final Lament and Concluding Prayer (5:1–22)

SUPPORTING IDEA: *Suffering can lead us to call on the Lord to pardon our sins and give new direction for our lives.*

This poem is a prayer, but the major part is a narration of the sufferings the nation was enduring. It speaks of the wretched conditions of those left in Judah. These were a feeble remnant, deprived of their ancestral possessions, victimized by poverty, forced labor, and oppression. The poem is divided into two disproportionate sections. Verses 1–18 give many details of the destruction. This unit has been divided into two smaller pictures: the people's affliction and suffering (vv. 1–13) and the loss of hope (vv. 14–18). Verses 19–22 contain a passionate prayer for the Lord to restore his favor and bless the people once again.

5:1–13. Jeremiah actually gave little new insight into the people's condition. His succinct, staccato-like way of describing the conditions of Jerusalem amplify what he had said before.

5:14–18. These verses show the result of Judah's humiliation. All hope for the future seems to have been taken away. Every place to which the people had turned disappointed them. The climax was when their king was captured and killed. The expression **The crown has fallen from our head** probably refers to this tragic event. Not so much Zedekiah personally but the entire

Davidic line—in a sense, the expected Messiah—had perished. How could an ideal king rule again when David's line was gone?

5:19–22. This poem ends where it began, with a plea to God. Jeremiah started by voicing a strong affirmation of hope. Yahweh's earthly home, where he sat enthroned among the cherubim, was in ruins. But his true home was permanent and eternal. God's **reign** was **forever**, and the people prayed for his restorative power. This was the poet's way of saying they called to Yahweh in repentance and faith.

This is a marvelous way to present the final recorded material from Jeremiah. These poems began with amazement, signified by "How." They close with an inquiry, "Why?" On both occasions Jeremiah was amazed at God's sovereignty. One can feel the pathos and even desolation of the prophet's dilemma. He pleaded for Yahweh to restore the people unless the most horrible possibility of all was true. Had Yahweh **rejected** them and chosen another instrument?

No answer is given at this point, but we learn a profound truth from later prophets. God will continue to work through Israel even though he must apply severe discipline to purify them. He knows how much purging to do to keep his vessels pure so they can serve him. Once more Israel's valley of Achor will become her door of hope. She must go into the wilderness again, this time to Babylon. But she will come back a purified people, and Jeremiah prays that she will be ready for service.

MAIN IDEA REVIEW: *Continued sin and rebellion against God bring loneliness and disaster, but he is always available for those who seek him.*

III. CONCLUSION

Restored by the Lord

In his first lament Jeremiah used the tragic image of a widow to describe Jerusalem's shame, disgrace, humiliation, and reproach. The widow's situation was hopeless. But God is concerned with the situation of the widow. The widow Jerusalem would rise again and be restored. Her temple would be rebuilt. Her people would be regathered out of their exile. The reproach of her widowhood would pass.

So it is in our relationship with God. When we come to the end of ourselves, hope in the Lord, confess our sins, and cast ourselves upon his great love and compassion, he will restore us to himself and renew our days as of old—and make them even better. Great is his faithfulness!

PRINCIPLES

- That divine justice is a complement to divine righteousness is true not only for the lives of individuals but also for nations.
- When a nation's political and economic distress is rooted in spiritual depravity, comfort and relief will not be found in old or new political alliances.
- In God's economy, national repentance is necessary for national restoration and renewal.
- We can experience hope in God even in the midst of our most devastating crises if we confess our sins and turn to him for forgiveness and renewal.
- The Lord God reigns forever; his throne and his kingdom will endure forever.

APPLICATIONS

- Recall the sources of help you have turned to in times of crisis. Evaluate those sources that have been most helpful in difficult times and those that have been least helpful.
- Consider two people who are disciplined for their sins. One handles the discipline in a mature way and the other person is immature in handling discipline. Describe the differences between how these two persons react to justly deserved discipline.
- Think of a time when you found hope in difficult circumstances. What could you say to someone who was having an experience similar to the one you faced with hope?
- Imagine yourself with only an hour to live. Your family and some friends are with you. What wisdom can you impart to them at this hour of your departure?

IV. LIFE APPLICATION

The Army from the Land of the North

No episode in American history has a greater parallel to the destruction of the Southern Kingdom of Judah and its capital city Jerusalem than Sherman's March to the Sea and the subsequent Carolinas campaign during the Civil War.

On September 2, 1864, after a monthlong siege, Atlanta fell to Sherman's troops. With Atlanta in hand, Sherman proposed to President Lincoln a plan to lead his army through the heart of Georgia to the sea, all the way to Savannah. Sherman's army would destroy everything in its path that could aid the Confederacy. Before Sherman's army reached the sea, his 62,000 soldiers crossed 425 miles of enemy territory, cut a swath of destruction 60 miles wide, and left $100 million worth of damage and a litany of destruction.

But Sherman was not finished yet. Early in February 1865, he crossed the Savannah River and turned his columns northward into the Carolinas. On February 17, Columbia, the very cradle of the secession, fell to Sherman's army. Soon the city was ablaze. Three-fourths of Columbia was destroyed that night—almost fourteen hundred structures. Thousands of families were burned out of their homes. Sherman himself noted in his memoirs that by the time he and his army were finished they had "utterly ruined Columbia."

The destruction wrought by Sherman must have been similar to what Jeremiah saw when he lamented the fate of Jerusalem. In the midst of the destruction of his world, and in spite of the fact that he acknowledged "my soul is downcast within me," Jeremiah declared, "I have hope" (3:20–21). How was this possible? Jeremiah had discovered the Lord's great love, his compassion, his faithfulness, and his essential goodness (3:22–23,25). Jeremiah knew the Lord as his portion and his Savior (3:24,26).

V. PRAYER

Heavenly Father, thank you for being a loving and compassionate God. Thank you for hearing our cries, wailings, and laments. Thank you for lifting our faces out of the dirt and comforting and cleansing us. Thank you for giving us hope even in the midst of disasters we create for ourselves by not following your commands and living according to your ways. Thank you, dear Lord, for being faithful when we have been faithless. Great is your faithfulness. Amen.

VI. DEEPER DISCOVERIES

A. "Jerusalem has sinned greatly" (1:8)

A minister, looking for a sermon idea to use at a youth rally, passed a used clothing store. He noticed among the suits on display a sign that attracted his attention: "Slightly Soiled, Reduced in Value." His creative juices began to flow. "That's it! I need to look no further!" He hurried to his study and began preparing his message.

Jeremiah saw Jerusalem as more than "slightly soiled." She had become contaminated with iniquities and impurities. Those who previously honored her had come to despise her. No one came to comfort her. Her enemy had laid hold of her treasure. Pagans had invaded her worship sanctuary. All her people groaned with hunger. Could anything be worse?

Yes, one thing was even more terrible for this special people. God could no longer use them in his redemptive purposes. Sin had made the people of Jerusalem and Judah too dirty to be used. He must purge them so they could perform the function for which he had called them.

Sin has been given many labels because it affects us in so many ways. It wastes money, wears the body into decay, blights the intellect, withers our moral nature, weakens the will, blunts the conscience, and hardens the heart. Even worse, sin enslaves. It becomes the master of those who indulge in it.

B. "No prayer can get through" (3:44)

An outstanding Christian counselor said, "One problem I must deal with often in sessions is the matter of unanswered prayers." He continued, "This often comes from those who began their Christian experience with much enthusiasm. But somewhere along the way, their prayer life deteriorates. One such person complained, 'God simply isn't answering my prayers the way he did when I first became a Christian.' They frequently cry out, 'Where is God when I pray?'"

Can we not apply this same question to our own lives when we feel God has deserted us? What kind of God do we worship? What kind of book is the Bible? If our sacred book recorded no other experiences with prayer than the enjoyment of successful petitions, it would be inadequate to meet our human needs.

What is prayer? Here is a classic that has survived the centuries: "Prayer is not overcoming God's reluctance. It is laying hold of his highest willingness." These words, if taken seriously and applied sincerely, can revolutionize our concept of the Christian life. God is not a bellboy rushing to answer our ring when we have a minor inconvenience. He is Lord of the universe, Sovereign of his kingdom, Redeemer of those who realize their need of One to set them free from the slavery of sin.

C. "Bear the yoke while he is young" (3:27)

A yoke was a beam of wood put on the neck of oxen by which they drew the cart or the plow. For many years it was a popular symbol for service or even slavery, the submission of one person to another person's will.

Old age binds us with a yoke of limitation. In young adulthood we face the yoke of providing our own living rather than depending on our parents. Middle age usually yokes us with the responsibility of a companion and probably the rearing of children. Jeremiah spoke of the benefit that accrues when we learn the "yoke principle" in the early years of life.

Youth needs to realize that the formative years should be dedicated to preparation for the long haul. This requires the yoke of discipline. One college professor I knew had a favorite expression. He warned, "Every year of preparation you waste in youth will cost you three when you try to catch up later in life."

When we come to the summit of middle age, we often look with regret at our earlier years. People may have robbed us of opportunities for advancement, and disappointments may have crushed our spirits. But nothing can take away the things we learned and the character we earned through bearing the yoke of discipline in our youth.

VII. TEACHING OUTLINE

A. INTRODUCTION

1. Lead Story: Mary Widow
2. Context: The Southern Kingdom and its capital Jerusalem have fallen to the Babylonian army under Nebuchadnezzar. The year is 586 B.C. The city and those left alive are in bad straits. The siege has taken its

toll. The survivors are desperate—for food, for their fortunes, for their futures. No help came from former allies. In fact, former allies had become enemies and turned against Judah in her hour of need. The kingdom and city that was once a queen among the nations is now like a hopeless widow. In this situation the people cry out to God, but they have no one but themselves to blame for their plight.

3. Transition: How do you express your grief at the death of a loved one or in time of great loss? Some attempt to suppress their grief and "keep a stiff upper lip." Others become angry with whatever they perceive to be responsible for the tragedy. They weep and wail and say all manner of invectives against anyone who gets in their face. In ancient Israel, deep-seated grief often was expressed in laments—a stylized form of poetic expression. These laments allowed the mourner to articulate deep anguish and grief and possibly hope. We can learn much about God and ourselves from these five dirges of Jeremiah over the city of Jerusalem.

B. COMMENTARY
1. Isolation, Desolation, and Misery (1:1–22)
2. The People's Lament and Supplication (2:1–22)
3. Has God Forsaken Judah? (3:1–66)
4. Deterioration of People Because of Their Sins (4:1–22)
5. Final Lament and Concluding Prayer (5:1–22)

C. CONCLUSION: RESTORED BY THE LORD

VIII. ISSUES FOR DISCUSSION

1. What value would hearing the constant repetition of the themes found in Lamentations have for modern Christians?
2. How would the acrostic structure of the first four laments in the book of Lamentations aid readers in memorizing the material? Why do you think all five laments do not follow this structure?
3. What evidence can you cite that Lamentations was written by an eyewitness of the events it describes?

Glossary

alien—One who lived in another land as a resident, and, though not a citizen, enjoyed certain limited privileges. Also called a sojourner. Since God owns the whole earth, Scripture writers saw all people on earth as aliens.

almond tree—A large nut-bearing woody plant, the first to bloom in the season, indicating God was still at work in nature after a dreary winter.

autographical—Type of writing that uses first-person pronouns (I, my, me, mine, etc.) rather than third person (he, she, they, etc.)

Baal—Chief deity of the Canaanite religion, worshipped as the one who guaranteed fertility of the crops. The noun comes from a verb that means to marry or rule over. Religious rituals were in the form of sex indulgences.

Balm of Gilead—Fragrant-smelling gum or resin used in Jeremiah's time for cosmetic and medical purposes. Exported from Gilead to other places, especially Egypt and Phoenicia.

battle of Carchemisch—Military conflict in 605 B.C., in which Babylon crushed Assyria and became the powerful leader of international politics.

Book of Deuteronomy—Fifth book in the Old Testament, consisting mainly of speeches made by Moses to the Israelites, shortly before his death. Includes exhortations to faithfulness in the new land and an update of laws given at Sinai.

Chaldeans—People living between lower regions of Tigris and Euphrates Rivers who gradually controlled Babylon, taking over the name Babylonian, with the two often used interchangeably.

chosen one—A person, thing, or movement set aside to be utilized by Yahweh for a specific purpose in accomplishing his will.

cistern—Place where water was stored to supplement the natural supply. Also called *hole, pit,* and often *well.*

courtyard—An open area or enclosure in the Jerusalem palace, which, during the days of Jeremiah, was reserved for detaining or holding prisoners.

covenant—An agreement, pact, or alliance made between two parties, who may be equals or unequals, with each consenting to certain conditions.

Cushite—Citizen or inhabitant of a nation, in Jeremiah's day, south of Egypt, which during different periods of time had varying borders. The nation Cush perhaps contained dark-skinned people and was sometimes translated *Ethiopia*. It was not, however, entirely equivalent with the modern nation by that name.

English text—Copies of the Bible, or any other document, rendered in the English language rather than the one in which it was originally written.

eunuch—A man who was emasculated and who was regarded as especially trustworthy in the Ancient Near East. Often placed in charge of harems.

Euphrates River—Longest, largest, and most important river in western Asia on whose banks are located a number of important cities, including Babylon and Carchemisch.

faithless—Incapable of sustained loyalty or lasting commitment to a person or a cause and applied especially to Judah's relationship to Yahweh.

fallow ground—Land that had either never or not recently been cultivated. Jeremiah used this expression to illustrate a relationship between the people and their God, Yahweh, which was nonexistent or had deteriorated.

fast—To refrain from food for a period of time in order to have a deeper and more meaningful experience with God. It is often associated with grief, repentance, and sorrow for sin.

forefathers—Ancestry, parentage, family who have preceded one's generation.

foreign prophecy—A word from God to a nation or group of people beyond Israel and Judah, either spoken directly or conveyed through other means of communication.

God's redemptive program—The divine plan for rescuing and delivering all the peoples of the world from the captivating and destructive power of sin.

Hebrew poetry—Form of Hebrew writing style that majored on parallelism or repetition of thought rather than rhyming of sounds.

judgment—Specific act or continuous process by which God demonstrates the truth to his creation that obedience or disobedience of his immutable laws produces consequences.

Levites—Descendants of Levi, third son of Jacob, set aside by the Lord for special service in the nation's religious affairs. All priests were Levites, but not all Levites were priests. The nonpriestly Levites served in other capacities related to the nation's worship rituals.

mandate—A command, order, or commission given to a person by one with a higher authority.

mantle—A loose-fitting robe worn as an outer garment by many of the prophets, symbolizing power and personal responsibility.

Marduk—Patron or chief deity of Babylon, also called Bel. Considered the true king of Babylon. Earthly rulers were regarded as the sons of Marduk.

Mosaic covenant—A promise and bond Yahweh made to and with the twelve tribes of Israel at Mount Sinai immediately following the exodus from Egypt. It was conditional in nature, based on the people's obedience.

Mosaic law—Code of conduct given to Israel by Moses and recorded in books of Exodus, Leviticus, Numbers, and Deuteronomy.

nationalistic group—An assembly or party of people who put the interests of their country above that of any other cause that they might also be promoting.

new covenant—A new type of relationship between Yahweh and his people foretold by Jeremiah and fulfilled in Jesus Christ.

Northern Kingdom—Ten tribes of David's united kingdom that, at Solomon's death in 931 B.C., split off from Judah and Benjamin to form a separate nation. Took the name of "Israel" in contrast to the Southern Kingdom, which was called "Judah" (see Southern Kingdom).

parabolic message—A sermon, discourse, or oracle delivered with the accompaniment of a symbol or story. Sometimes called "an earthly story with a heavenly meaning."

pericopes—A term used by biblical scholars to describe small fragments of Scriptures in contrast to larger sections or units.

prophetic call—Occasion when God speaks in a definite way to set aside a person for special service in proclaiming his will to the people.

queen mother—Mother of the reigning monarch who enjoyed special status in the kingdom. Usually served as a trusted counselor for her son.

Queen of Heaven—A goddess worshipped by women in Judah and other cultures to guarantee fertility and material security. Probably developed from Ishtar, feminine deity revered by women in Mesopotamia.

reconcile—To appease and bring back together into one accord, with peaceful relationship and fellowship, parties or individuals who have become estranged.

Sabbath day discourse—Sermon by Jeremiah and recorded in 17:19–27 about need for strict observance of Jewish Sabbath.

scribes—People with writing skills, whose highest duty, among others, was that of copying Scriptures. Later they became a professional class that interpreted and taught the law.

scroll—Sheets of papyrus glued together, with rollers at each end, making a long literary work for public reading.

seer—Name by which most prophets, in the early days of Israel, were called but distinguished from the higher type communicator of God's will. Seers majored on visions and foretelling events, always expecting a fee.

Septuagint—Oldest translation of Hebrew Scriptures into the Greek language. Most New Testament quotations of the Old Testament are from the Septuagint. The name means "seventy," traditional number of scholars involved in the work.

siege works—Landings or scaffolds armies built around and above walls of cities they were besieging, from which they shot arrows and into which they threw missiles.

Southern Kingdom—Two tribes of David's united kingdom that remained loyal to the Davidic line of kings when ten tribes rebelled to form the Northern Kingdom. Consisted of Judah and Benjamin (see Northern Kingdom).

temple—Magnificent worship center, constructed during Solomon's reign, destroyed by Nebuchadnezzar, and used for religious activities, including especially sacrifices. Rebuilt on a lesser scale after nation returned from Babylonian captivity but enlarged magnificently by Herod the Great.

theocracy—Government of a territory by leader or group of officials perceived by the constituents as being divinely guided and possessing a mandate to rule totally.

unclean—Person or thing considered as impure, dirty, filthy, either physically, morally, or ritually and, therefore, unfit to be a part of Yahweh worship.

visions of your prophets—Messages received directly from God in personal experience. Considered as special revelations to be delivered as mandates for the people's conduct.

word of the Lord—A single statement from Yahweh, one specific work attributed to him, or his entire expressed will, either written or oral.

Bibliography

Ball, C. J., general editor. *The Expositor's Bible*. Grand Rapids: Wm. B Eerdmans Publishing Company, 1956.

Baughman, Harry. F. *Jeremiah for Today*. Philadelphia: Muhlenberg Press, 1947.

Birmingham, George A. *Jeremiah the Prophet*. New York: Harper & Brothers, 1939.

Bright, John. *Jeremiah*. The Anchor Bible. Garden City, N.Y.: Doubleday & Company, 1985.

Butler, Trent, general editor. *Holman Bible Dictionary*. Nashville: Holman Bible Publishers, 1991.

Case, Harold C. *The Prophet Jeremiah*. Cincinnati: Woman's Division of Christian Service, Board of Missions, Methodist Church, 1953.

Cunliffe-Jones, H. *The Book of Jeremiah*. Torch Bible Commentaries. New York: The Macmillan Company, 1961.

Davidson, A. B. *Old Testament Prophecy*. Edinburgh, Scotland: T. & T. Clark, 1903.

Davidson, Robert. *Jeremiah*. 2 vols. The Daily Study Bible, Old Testament Series, ed. John C. L. Gibson. Philadelphia: Westminster Press, 1983.

Elliott-Binns, L. E. *Jeremiah, a Prophet for a Time of War*. London: Student Christian Movement Press, 1941.

Erdman, Charles R. *The Book of Jeremiah*. Westwood, N.J.: Fleming H. Revell, 1955.

Francisco, Clyde. *Studies in Jeremiah*. Nashville: Convention Press, 1961.

Freedman, H. *Jeremiah*. Soncino Books of the Bible. A. Cohen, general editor. London: Soncino Press, 1949.

Green, J. Leo. "Jeremiah" Vol. 6. The Broadman Commentary. Nashville: Broadman Press, 1971.

Hastings, James. *The Book of Jeremiah*. The Speaker's Bible. Edinburgh and London: Morrison and Gibb, 1944.

Bibliography

Honeycutt, Roy. *Jeremiah: Witness Under Pressure*. Nashville: Convention Press, 1981.

Huey, F. B., Jr. *Jeremiah*. The New American Commentary. Vol. 16. Nashville: Broadman Press, 1993.

Ironside, H. A. *Lamentations and Jeremiah*. New York: Loizeaux, 1906.

Jellie, W. H. *A Homiletic Commentary on the Book of Jeremiah*. New York: Lon, Funk and Wagnalls, n.d.

Johnson, Talmage C. *The Crucifiers—Then and Now*. Nashville: Broadman Press, 1942.

Keil, C. F. *Prophecies of Jeremiah*. 2 vols. Biblical Commentary of the Old Testament. Grand Rapids: Wm. B. Eerdmans Publishing Company, 1950.

Kelly, W. *The Tender-Hearted Prophet of the Nations*. London: C. A. Hammond, 1938.

Laetsch, Theo. *Jeremiah*. Bible Commentary. St. Louis, Mo.: Concordia Publishing House, 1952.

Leslie, Elmer A. *Jeremiah*. New York and Nashville: Abingdon Press, 1954.

Maclaren, Alexander. *Isaiah and Jeremiah*. Expositions of Holy Scripture. Vol. 5. Grand Rapids: Wm. B. Eerdmans Publishing Company, 1944.

McCall, Duke K. *God's Hurry*. Nashville: Broadman Press, 1949.

McGee, J. Vernon. *Jeremiah and Lamentations*. Nashville: Thomas Nelson Publishers, 1991.

Merrill, William Pierson. "The Book of Lamentations: Exposition." In vol. 6 of The Interpreter's Bible. New York and Nashville: Abingdon Press, 1956.

Ottley, R. L. *The Hebrew Prophets*. London: Rivingtons, 1923.

Peake, A. S. *Jeremiah and Lamentations*. The Century Bible. Vol. 1. Walter F. Adeney, general editor. Edinburgh: T. C. & E. C. Jack, 1906.

Peake, A. S. *Jeremiah and Lamentations*. The Century Bible. Vol. 2. Edinburgh: T. C. & E. C. Jack, 1911.

Reid, John Calvin. *We Spoke for God*. Grand Rapids: Wm. B. Eerdmans Publishing Company, 1967.

Self, Rose E. *The Work of the Prophets*. London, New York and Bombay: Longmans, Green, and Co., 1904.

Skinner, John. *Prophecy and Religion*. Cambridge and London: Cambridge University Press, 1922.

Smith, George Adam. *The Historical Geography of the Holy Land.* Fourth edtion. London: Hodder and Stoughton, 1896.

——. *Jeremiah.* The Baird Lecture for 1922. Fourth edition. Revised and enlarged. New York and London: Harper & Brothers, 1929.

Streane, A. W. *The Cambridge Bible for Schools.* J. J. S. Perowne, general editor. London: Cambridge at the University Press, 1882.

Thompson, J. A. *The Book of Jeremiah.* The New International Commentary on the Old Testament. Edward J. Young, general editor. Grand Rapids: Wm. B. Eerdmans Publishing Company, 1980.

Welch. A. C. *Jeremiah, His Time and His Work.* Oxford: Basil Blackwell, 1951.

White, K. Owen. *The Book of Jeremiah.* Shield Bible Study Series. Grand Rapids: Baker Book House, 1961.

Wood, Fred M. "A Chronological Reconstruction of the Life and Prophecies of Jeremiah." Unpublished Thesis, Southern Baptist Theological Seminary, Louisville, Kentucky, 1948.

——. *Fire in My Bones.* Nashville: Broadman Press, 1958.